YESTERDAY, TODAY, AND FOREVER

Books by Jeane Dixon

MY LIFE AND PROPHECIES
(as told to Rene Noorbergen)
REINCARNATION and Prayers To Live By
THE CALL TO GLORY: Jeane Dixon Speaks of Jesus and Prophecy
YESTERDAY, TODAY, AND FOREVER

YESTERDAY, TODAY, AND FOREVER

by Jeane Dixon

William Morrow and Company, Inc.
New York 1976

Inquiries should be addressed to William Morrow and Company, Inc., 105 Madison Ave., New York, N.Y. 10016.

Printed in the United States of America.

4 5 80 79 78 77 76

Library of Congress Cataloging in Publication Data

Dixon, Jeane.
Yesterday, today, and forever.

1. Astrology. 2. Apostles-Miscellanea. I. Title.
BF1708.1.D58 1976 133.5 75-29145
ISBN 0-688-02984-1

BOOK DESIGN HELEN E. ROBERTS

This book
is dedicated to
man, believing and unbelieving,
in the surety that perhaps someday it will help to remember these things.
And to
Evelyn "Pinky" Brier, my aviatrix sister of the skies,
Erny Pinckert, my all-American brother,
And most of all to
Jimmy D., a precious part of my yesterday, today, and forever,
Believers all, and all beloved!

Jeane Dixon

In Appreciation
Reverend Stephen Breen, Ph.D.
Paul Bannister

CONTENTS

YESTERDAY, TODAY, AND FOREVER

Somewhere in the velvet vacuum of interstellar space, at some uncertain future time, mankind will discover as fact what today we can only accept on faith.

Some event, some object, some measurement or discovery will prove to us what we have always known in our hearts: that in all that happens in the cosmos, whether in the smallest bit of matter or in the life of the greatest king, there is a logic, a reason, determined by a Supreme Intelligence and Power, which continues to shape our lives. Skeptics will no longer claim that God is only an inner need of maladjusted human minds. On the contrary, His presence will be more and more universally recognized as the Ultimate Reality.

That new knowledge, that confirmation of man's ancient faith in a divine order, will lead us forward to a true understanding of our own worth and the value of every other person.

I believe I have been allowed a precious glimpse at that future discovery. The series of visions which inspired me to write this book has comprised, in my judgment, the most significant prophetic experiences I have ever had.

Its most startling moment came unexpectedly one day while I was kneeling in meditation at St. Matthew's Cathedral on Rhode Island Avenue, only a few blocks from my office in Washington, D.C. That grand old church became known to the entire country in 1963 when our slain President was brought there for a solemn, heart-rending funeral service. It remains as it was then, a hallowed and peaceful place of marble, majesty, and memories.

In the beautiful Cathedral, there are quiet recesses, intimate corners for private prayer. Kneeling before a side altar, I began to experience that familiar sense of alertness and exhilaration that have always heralded my visions. I swallowed hard, knowing I was on the verge of a tremendous experience, and focused my eyes, blinking hard as I did so.

Abruptly, as if an actor had just stepped on stage with a flourish, a pair of red, thigh-length riding boots—the elegant type I have seen in old paintings—strode across the altar in a determined, purposeful manner, not actually touching the altar but remaining several feet above its surface.

I gasped and shook my head in disbelief as I watched the boots actually march right across the altar. They moved with a man's stride, forceful, even prideful, as if their wearer were arrogantly proclaiming, "Here I am."

Then, as suddenly as they had appeared, the boots began to disintegrate, fading from sight like the gradually dissolving trail of a high-flying jet. Before my astonished eyes, their remnants formed clear and distinct words—"and the Devil wore red boots." This very graphic manifestation convinced me that I had not imagined the curious spectacle. I knew I had actually glimpsed one of the major forces which shape this world, and I knew with equal certainty that it was not one of goodwill.

Needless to say, that was a most disconcerting vision! But a few weeks later, again in St. Matthew's Cathedral, I was to be reassured, comforted, and overjoyed by another experience, which I can only describe as mystical. And it was the complete opposite of my brief but vivid view of red boots. But I am getting ahead of myself! In my eagerness to share with you what may have been the most important moments of my life, I have neglected to tell you what led up to my encounter with those red boots. Only after I have explained that will you be able to see, as I did, the meaning of my subsequent and most majestic vision.

For those who are not familiar with my previous writings, I should explain that, since childhood, I have had numerous visions. They are by now a familiar occurrence with me and come at any hour of the day or night, at varied times and places.

I never have any previous intimation of what I am about to see. Always the vision begins in the same way. I glimpse something in my mind's eye. I feel a watchfulness like the anticipation one senses between a flash of lightning and the resultant thunder. As the vision clears, it often resembles a television picture coming into focus and gradually assumes a distinct form. Sometimes, what I see is symbolic, with its message wrapped in obscure references. At other times, it is truly specific, revealing faces already familiar to me, making them easily recognizable within a dreamlike setting.

In my life, I have been privileged to be the confidante of countless people, including many eminent and powerful persons. Through divine intervention, I have occasionally glimpsed certain future events. I take no credit for this perception. On the contrary, I hope I have been, and may continue to be, as long as I am permitted, foremost a servant of the Lord.

I am thankful my work has given me such a rewarding life. I look back at its highlights with appreciative awe. And because we are told by Scripture to extend to others the good things we have been given, I want to make real and vivid, for all my readers, the greatest vision with which I have been blessed.

That revelation, which has led me to write this book, was an accumulation of many things, a veritable jigsaw puzzle placed together slowly over a period of twenty years. And then, within the space of a few weeks, it finally fell into place, taking on a definite meaning.

It was as if the design, the tapestry of our lives was being revealed to me one small stage at a time, one color, one weave, one tiny square by one, until the whole meaning was laid out before me. Then I could finally see what before had been only an element of my own faith: that there is indeed an overall plan for the evolving cosmos and all that it embraces, involving all human life.

Let me tell you how that gradual accumulation of knowledge was at last shown to me as one coherent whole.

For almost two decades, I had been experiencing partial glimpses of things I did not understand. It was like a scene viewed through heavy mist, a tantalizing uncertainty. I could only guess at the details. At first, this incomplete vision preoccupied me with wonder. After considerable thought, I knew I need not seek its meaning. That would all come to me in time—that is, in God's time, not my own.

Sure enough, in a matter of weeks or months thereafter, I would behold again almost the same vision in splendidly bright colors. Once more I would meditate for hours, wondering whether this was the last piece of knowledge I would receive in this strange way, meditating until the press of daily business drew away my attention.

For several years, the recurring vision would enter my consciousness and then depart before I could wholly comprehend it. Time and again, I would reassure myself that whenever I was meant to know its message, I would be told. That calmed my mind, and again I was able to see the vision and remember in an orderly way what it had revealed to me. My faith was steadfast that, one day, I would understand all I had seen. I am amazed now in retrospect that the entire revelation took twenty years to reach completion!

In the meantime, my life continued as always, busy with travel and speaking engagements, with work for my children's charities, and with my visions, some happy, others tragic. Among the latter were the somber revelations and predictions concerning the imminent deaths of the talented Kennedy brothers and, later, the national trauma of Watergate.

At long last, in the autumn of 1974, a period filled with Watergate tension and the high drama of official Washington's rendezvous with destiny, I finally received the full vision which I had awaited for two decades. It occurred several weeks after the frightening appearance of those malevolent red boots. It was as good and joyous as those boots had been evil. It was a thrilling revelation of God's unchanging care for mankind, and it convinced me that I need never again fear the power of the wearer of red boots.

I was again in the Cathedral, kneeling in silent prayer. I became aware of what seemed like a rainbow of colors, forming directly over the main altar of the Cathedral.

As I beheld this marvel of lights and hues, the scene underwent a gradual change, becoming a circle of beautiful, brilliant intensity. There seemed to radiate from within it a great sense of calm, of tranquillity, as if I could rest my whole soul within its depths and allow the peace it generated to permeate my mind and body.

Again the scene changed. The center of the circle began to form distinct and definite shapes. It divided into twelve segments, each containing the figure of an Apostle and a sign of the Zodiac.

I became oblivious to everything around me. Absorbed in the overwhelming sights before me, I reached for my purse, took out the small notebook and pencil I always carry, and wrote down in it the names of the Apostles and the Zodiac sign which was visible next to each of them. By the time I had hurriedly jotted down that information, the vision was fading. Within seconds, it was gone. I waited there intently for another three hours, missing appointments and, as

I later found out, causing much consternation in my office by my absence. But the vision was over—at least for that day.

As I left the church, I felt spiritually and physically renewed. I was exhilarated and joyful. I knew I was approaching the end of my many years of vigil, that I would soon understand the purpose of this, and of so many other extraordinary visions. No wonder I walked briskly along the street, stepping fast and lively, returning to my business with an inward elation that is hard to describe, even now.

Back at my office, I immediately had my notes typed. They composed a simple list of the Apostles' names and the corresponding signs of the Zodiac:

Peter—Aries
Simon—Taurus
James (the Less)—Gemini
Andrew—Cancer
John—Leo
Philip—Virgo
Bartholomew—Libra
Thomas—Scorpio
James (the Greater)—Sagittarius
Matthew—Capricorn
Jude (Thaddaeus)—Aquarius
Judas Iscariot and Matthias—Pisces

Looking at that list now, I must admit that although I knew the signs of the Zodiac by heart because I write about them every day for newspaper readers across the country, I had to be sure about the Apostles as well. So, I checked to see if all the Apostles were included. Was Thaddaeus among them? Bartholomew? Yes, they were listed in the tenth chapter of St. Matthew's Gospel. I learned later that Bartholomew was sometimes called Nathanael and that Jude (Thaddaeus) was also named Lebbaeus in some ancient texts.

That evening, I showed the unusual roster to my husband, Jimmy. He studied the names for a moment. "Was Peter an Arien?" he inquired.

"I'm sure he was," I replied, certain that this was in fact the key to interpreting what I had witnessed in the Cathedral.

Jimmy's question about the relationship of the Apostles and the respective signs of the Zodiac was challenging. Perhaps the Holy Spirit guided his thinking at that moment, as we can all be guided whenever we open our minds to Divine counsel. I know that the

Spirit's guidance is available to every one of us for the asking, for we are not here alone on this "spaceship earth." We are not carelessly set adrift at birth, nor do we vanish into nothingness at our death. We are, each of us, tiny individual elements and powers in God's universal mosaic. Our lives are programmed at conception and are endowed with purpose and meaning. That was the message given to me in my many visions.

The message is startlingly simple: life develops in a set pattern, as each different kind of seed must invariably grow into the specific kind of plant it was meant to be. Recognize your own place in God's plan for you, and your life will be more meaningful, fruitful, and better disposed to be elevated and transformed by faith in the redeeming life of Our Lord.

Astrological influences can prepare us for future events. Those influences cannot give the abundant life, which comes only from God, through Christ. If followed in their positive aspects, they can help bring us to the door of the Kingdom; but only Christ gives us entrance.

In this book, I limit myself to the relationship of the signs of the Zodiac to human life, to that expression of order and harmony in the universe as it disposes mankind for participation in the still higher designs which God has already revealed in His Son. All things, great and small, work toward the fulfillment of one's intentions and the realization of one's ambitions. In one's daily affairs, the marvelous will become commonplace as one enters the company of history's great women and men, who, throughout the ages, have seen themselves as instruments of their Creator.

While I contemplated what had been revealed to me, I studied the names of the Apostles with their corresponding Zodiac signs. Looking again in my Bible for the names of Christ's closest followers, as recorded by Matthew, I glanced across the page to another passage (Matthew 10:26), whose message seemed to leap up at me. Christ said, "Nothing is concealed that will not be revealed, and nothing hidden that will not become known."

Within days, I knew more.

I write a daily horoscope column for many newspaper readers in the United States and abroad. Some of my friends consider this a strange practice for a Roman Catholic. As I understand it, however, the Catholic Church—and many other religious bodies as well—has never condemned the study of astrology. Indeed, many religions accept the idea that the motions of the heavenly bodies exert an influence upon our lives. The Catholic Church has, of course, quite rightly opposed turning astrology into a religion in itself, as did some peoples of old. The ancient Egyptians, for example, after seeking personal insight and wisdom, fell into following weird systems of magic and superstition. The Babylonians of ancient Mesopotamia actually considered the various planets to be living creatures, minor gods who personally controlled men's lives from on high. Even today, some people try to distort astrology into a substitute for religion. Disenchanted with the faiths in which they were reared, they seek a sense of mystery and power in the study of the Zodiac. I appreciate their sincerity and sympathize with their search for a supernatural order in life, but I must respectfully remind them that although astrology is a tremendous source of wisdom, it can never, by itself, take the place of our faith in our Creator. Astrology must never be made an object of adoration, as it was in ancient Egypt and Babylonia. God alone is to be worshiped. All else is folly.

I like to draw a parallel between astrology and the physical sciences. Today's powerful religions do not condemn biology, chemistry, or physics, or any of the sciences, as they once did; but they remind us that those sciences are systems of useful learning, provided by God for the service of man. They must never take the place of our faith. Similarly, when astrology is assigned its proper role as an aid to our self-understanding and to a better appreciation of God's will for us, then it will complement our religion and not contradict it.

I have never experienced any conflict between my faith and the guidance I receive from my church on the one hand and the knowledge I find in the stars on the other. What happens to my life depends upon whether I react positively or negatively to the Lord's will for me. Actually, much of what I know about astrology I learned from a Jesuit priest, who was one of the best-informed scholars I have ever met.

Although astrology was used as a religion by many pagan cultists of ancient lands, it is not, never has been, and never will be a religion. True students of astrology claim only that people having similar astrological aspects and signs tend to share certain common traits in terms of character, personality, temperament, and life patterns.

Given certain astronomical information, a knowledgeable astrologer can calculate a program of personal guidance that can be useful to people in daily life. Here is an illustration we all understand. I frequently compare astrology to weather forecasting. The weather forecaster uses a set of known facts, based on accumulated data and experience, to predict the weather, without guaranteeing that it will occur.

We all know that nothing can be guaranteed absolutely. Astrology can provide a good road map to our futures, while we retain the option to choose our exact routes. Remember that we human beings have free will, and so we can change even the most likely patterns of events. The great William Shakespeare used various astrological references throughout his writings. In a famous instance, he nicely balanced the forces of free will and destiny in his play *Julius Caesar* by having Cassius remind Brutus:

> "Men at some time are masters of their fates:
> The fault, dear Brutus, is not in our stars,
> But in ourselves, that we are underlings."
> (Act I, scene II)

Thus the world's greatest dramatist reconciled man's responsibility for his own conduct with the planets' influences over our lives. The renowned Dr. Samuel Waksman, developer of streptomycin, testified, "The cures to all of man's illnesses are under our feet. God put them there. It is up to science to identify and apply them." Abraham Lincoln, whose whole life was a march toward destiny, once said, "I claim not to have controlled events but confess plainly that events have controlled me." Perhaps former President Nixon feels the same way.

Astrology was very much involved in the events surrounding the birth of Christ. The Three Wise Men, whom Christians honor on January 6, feast of the Epiphany, were astrologers. As such, they knew the meaning of the beautiful strange star that hovered over the sleepy little town of Bethlehem. They came from those Oriental lands which had been the birthplace of astrology. That system of learning originated among the Chaldeans in what is now Iraq and Kuwait. It had already spread over much of the ancient world, thousands of years before the first Christmas. The patriarch Abraham, forefather of the Hebrew people, was originally from the Chaldean city of Ur (Genesis 11:28–31). When he obeyed God's command to migrate with his family to the land of Canaan, he must have taken along with him the Chaldean understanding of the heavens.

History tells us that centuries later, Babylonians introduced the science of astrology into Egypt. There was a period in the history of the Nile kingdom when astrologers virtually ruled the land of the Pyramids through their advice to the pharaohs. Their counsel governed every matter: decisions of state, the best times for war or travel, even when and how to build the massive tombs that still endure and attract visitors to the land of Nefertiti and Tutankhamen.

The Jews of the time of Christ were familiar with the import of astrology. Indeed, the Old Testament sometimes refers to any wise man as a Chaldean, so renowned was their wisdom of the skies. Eventually, the Greeks and Romans learned the secrets of the stars from the peoples of the Middle East, while the sea-roving Phoenicians carried astrology with them to every shore they visited, perhaps even to South America, where they may have ventured as early as 500 B.C.

After the decline of the Roman Empire and the fall of its pantheon of gods, the astrological heritage of antiquity survived quite well alongside Christianity. Pious kings had not only a personal chaplain but also a personal astrologer, just as the King Arthur of legend had the seer Merlin, who knew the meanings of heavenly events. There was no conflict between a monarch's spiritual adviser and his astrological counselor. Indeed, many Pontiffs were interested in the science of the stars, and I suspect that there is no better collection of ancient writings on the subject than the holdings of the Vatican Library.

In more recent times, Winston Churchill, as Britain's Prime Minister during World War II, employed an astrologer to inform him of what Hitler's astrologer was telling the Fuehrer, thereby accumulating strategy to help him win the war. Today a great many individuals, famous and obscure, leaders and followers alike, are coming to a renewed appreciation of very old wisdom. We seem to be returning to the ancient idea that science cannot, by itself, answer all our questions about life or solve all our problems. We have at last learned enough to know that, after all, we know very little.

That was just how I felt on the momentous day after I had received the vision of the Apostles in St. Matthew's Cathedral. I tried to assemble all the facts like the scattered pieces of a puzzle. Perhaps by fitting them together, I could understand why my vision had combined Christ's closest followers and the Zodiac.

What had been the personal backgrounds of those first disciples of the Galilean? Did they have social influence or political friends?

Not at all. They were, by and large, as seemingly inconsequential as their Master. Most of them were fishermen, Matthew was a minor official. Only Judas seemed somewhat different from the rest. Yet they all rose to incredible heights of inspiration. They became preachers and evangelists, movers of mankind. Though most of them had never been far away from the villages of their birth, they eventually traveled as far as Rome, Spain, Ethiopia, and India to preach the Gospel. They became the bearers of a message to all mankind; and through that power, they set the world spinning in new directions.

Where was the pattern for the greatness they achieved? Was it known to Jesus when He called them to His Father's service? Popular legend holds that after Christ began His public ministry, He simply took a walk and invited twelve strangers to join Him. But that was not the case. Most of the Apostles were hardly strangers to one another. Four of the Twelve were two pairs of brothers. Two Apostles were cousins of their Teacher; and several had been disciples of John the Baptist, another of Jesus' cousins.

It occurred to me that Jesus knew those twelve men better than they realized, even though their backgrounds had nothing special to recommend them. To me, it seems they were chosen to be leaders on the basis of the varied astrological compositions of their lives. They had been preordained to become Apostles at the moment of their conception. Here was the pattern I had been seeking, the explanation of my vision. Here was the answer which could pull together the facts of Scripture and the data of astrology. This natural phenomenon in no way impugns or lessens the Divine power inherent in the call to discipleship of Christ.

Now I understood why, in my vision, each Apostle was associated with a different Zodiac sign; for each was being revealed to me as the archetype of that sign. Each embodied all the mental and emotional characteristics of his own segment of the Zodiac. And so, each of them can show us, through his personality, what are our own best and worst natural traits, our own strengths and weaknesses.

That simple yet profound truth was the message I received both through my meditations and in subsequent visions during the following weeks. Through the gradual growth of that realization, I was being told, "These twelve men show mankind the patterns of human life. These are people to whom all men and women can relate. Learn about them and you will know about yourself as well."

It is a wonder of God's providence that although He reveals Himself in countless ways, each way leads eventually to Him. So the numerical correspondence between the Twelve Apostles and the twelve signs of the Zodiac is no coincidence. It is a demonstration that every aspect of human behavior, every trait of human character, can somehow be turned to the Lord's service. He selected those twelve followers because each had a different set of talents and abilities—yes, and faults and weaknesses, too—which could serve Him in fulfilling His Father's plan for mankind.

In this way, the astrological signs of the Twelve Apostles are reminders that each of us—from Aries to Pisces—is disposed to be called to the Father, just as Jesus invited twelve different men of the people to follow Him. By accepting his invitation, they discovered life in His higher life. By retracing their steps, we can be open to what in the life of Jesus is for each and every one of us.

He invited. He did not command. Like all of us, no matter what Zodiac sign we call our own, the Apostles retained their free will and could have refused to accept their preordained destiny. That was, in fact, the negative response of the rich young man who asked Christ for counsel. He was told to give his possessions to the poor. The young aristocrat could not bear to abandon his affluence and declined the advice.

Whether to accept the call to glory is a decision each of us must make for himself, and it necessarily involves every part of our being. It involves our intellect and personality and character, and even that bodily frame of ours which will inevitably perish.

It involves our soul, for the response we make to Christ's invitation determines the soul's eternal destiny. Because our soul is the interpreter of the Holy Spirit, it enables us first to understand the Creator's will for us as individuals. All the world's wisdom, including the lessons we learn from astrology and the lives of the Apostles, exists only to assist us to comprehend God's design for our lives.

Thus, every aspect of human life is involved in our acceptance or rejection of our part in the Divine Plan. During the jubilant days and sleeplessly happy nights after my vision, I came to know that God's plan is directed toward the spiritual unity of all mankind.

Each of us on earth must contribute in some small way to the goal of unity in Christ, which is our salvation. If we do not cooperate, at worst we can only slow down the progress of the Creator's plan for peace; but no one will ever prevent its accomplishment. This plan is written in the heavens. It is immutable. It is a plan for *yesterday, today, and forever.*

ARIES—PETER *(March 21–April 19)*

In the astrological division of the heavens, Aries is the first sign of the Zodiac, just as Peter was Christ's first Apostle. We might also consider Aries as the first of twelve different paths leading to the Lord of Creation. So it is that all of us, regardless of our individual places within the Zodiac, must be concerned with all segments of it, so that we can become aware of the many disparate ways man can reach his Maker. There is surely something in Peter's horoscope, as in each Apostle's, which will illuminate the path of each of us.

And why is that information so important? Because, sooner or later, no matter which road to eternity we are following, we will find in our dusty path the unmistakable imprints of those red boots. We will have to overcome the snares they set, the lures they plant, the false signs they leave for us, in order to reach the common destination to which we are all moving.

Life is always a risky road, no matter which of the twelve approaches we are assigned through the time of our birth. But the surest guarantee that our journey will be safe is the reliability of our Guide, Who once declared Himself to be "the Way, the Truth, and the Life."

That is the splendid assurance we find in the life of Jesus. It is the same assurance the Apostles received from knowing and working with Him for three years. Let us, then, examine the paths each of them took, through their respective astrological influences, to reach union with their Teacher. And in the process, let us remember that everyone must follow one or another of those paths; for the only alternative is to fall by the roadside, waiting there until our final confrontation with those trampling red boots.

With that in mind, we can survey the astrological character of Peter, who was in many ways the most endearing of the Master's followers. Headstrong, impulsive, outspoken, he was a diamond in the rough. In all these respects, he was a perfect reflection of his astrological sign: Aries, the Ram.

Although his aggressiveness made him at times a bull in a china shop, it also enabled him to become a dynamic leader. He knew his duties, accepted his responsibilities, and was firmly single-minded. Capable of great deeds, he achieved them. All those admirable traits are embodied in Ariens throughout the world.

If your sign is Aries, you have tremendous potential for success. In fact, that success may come easily to you because, to reach it, you need only become more sensitive to God's will and rightly interpret His plan for your life.

Although Ariens are battering rams, they don't bruise easily. They learn quickly and are not too proud to admit their mistakes. Peter was once rebuked by Christ for his bluntness and replied, "Depart from me, Lord, for I am a sinful man." His "sin" was merely the Arien trait of being eager—perhaps overly eager—to get things moving. He wanted to pick up the ball and run with it. And that is a common Arien fault.

Ariens often forget that not everyone becomes as enthusiastic as they over a new idea or project, and in their headlong rush to move events along, they often find themselves so far ahead of their fellows that the cooperation they need is not forthcoming. More so than most others, Ariens have to learn that a good leader is also a good administrator and is able to delegate responsibility. Too often an Arien wants to do everything himself—or herself, because Arien women, although usually excellent managers of their homes and careers, frequently perform chores which others could easily handle. Their attitude asserts, "Only I can do it right."

This results in an Arien tendency to spread their talents too thinly and, consequently, devoting insufficient time to really important matters. Remember that we all have certain talents and abilities according to God's overall plan. He has even given us, through the stars, the means to understand His scheme of things. We can learn our strengths and weaknesses and thereafter can choose to go whichever way our talents are best directed. Thus, within our own limitations, we can improve the world instead of merely complaining about everything that is wrong. Even Peter had to learn this.

Peter's real name was Simon Bar-Jona, meaning Simon, son of John. In the early Latin versions of the Bible, the authors used the word "*petrus*"—rock—in the phrase used by Christ: "Thou art Peter, and upon this rock I shall build my church . . ." We are told it was a pun on the words "Peter" and "*petrus*," but the message was clear. Peter could become a man of rock if he fulfilled his Arien potential for spiritual greatness, and he would thereby be the enduring cornerstone of Christ's new church.

This is as true for Ariens today as it was two thousand years ago. Their path to greatness has to be one of self-discovery and self-realization. Their personal fulfillment requires both a realistic view of themselves and undaunted creativity. Inside every Arien is an even better person than he or she realizes. Their spiritual growth depends on their willingness to recognize and foster their innate, but often undeveloped, qualities.

As natural leaders, most Ariens can perceive leadership ability in others and respect it. Peter, who with his brother Andrew was engaged in a successful business as a fisherman, gave up his commercial life because he was so impressed by the leadership, the authority, the presence of Christ. He sensed that by following the charismatic Nazarene, he could develop himself more fully. I feel certain that Peter was not consciously aware of his own inner strengths at that time; but he did have the redeeming feature, possessed by many Ariens, of recognizing the opportunity for growth that was being offered to him.

Over the years, I have spoken to dozens of older Ariens; and as soon as I know their birth sign, I usually ask them about someone who has influenced them greatly and perhaps changed the pattern of their lives by a single decision. The great majority of them respond with astonishment, telling me of someone—a teacher, a counselor, employer, or older friend—who one day indicated, in one way or another, "No, not that way. Go this way." And their lives were radically changed.

This is true for any Arien who may be reading these words. If it hasn't already happened, one day you will meet the person you sense is the right teacher for you to heed; and your life will be changed. The pattern is as immutable as the order of the stars. Yet you will retain your free will. You need not respond to the challenge of change. You may recognize your opportunity but reject it. Most of your fellow Ariens, however, will accept the choice offered them; and their spiritual development will thereby be advanced.

A dominant personal characteristic of Ariens is tenacity, which can be a two-edged sword, working for either good or bad. Tenacity should be motivated by love. Use it, Ariens, only to do your work well and to enjoy your rest fully. Avoid turning it to personal gain.

Your capacity for leadership also must be used prudently. In the short run, it is all very well to be headstrong and forceful. But if you move into a supervisory position (and many Ariens gravitate there naturally), you will one day realize that these traits, while bringing short-term success, don't create stability, security, or trust. Imitate Peter. Be patient, thoughtful, and kind. Explain your decisions and plans to your staff. Invite their opinions. Then you will find yourself surrounded by happy, enthusiastic workers who are as willing as you to strive for the common goal.

These points apply equally well to Arien housewives. Because mothers usually spend more time in the home than any other member of the household, they have a correspondingly greater influence on their families. Arien homemakers can be the happiest women in the world. They have immense skills for organization, for establishing a well-run and comfortable home, and their relish for activity gives them the stamina for the many tasks this entails.

Arien women have another vital organizing talent, if they learn to allow it free rein: they can easily encourage their children and husbands to participate in domestic decisions. Let the children clean their rooms and help choose decorations for festive occasions. Urge your husband to select menus, to buy furnishings, and so forth. Not only will your loved ones enjoy their active roles in the family, but you yourself will also be best fulfilled when you are guiding others in the expansion of their talents and interests.

Many famous Ariens have fulfilled their own creativity by helping others. The poetry of William Wordsworth (April 7), for example, taught millions to love the beauties of nature, as did the lyrics of Robert Frost (March 26). The collective literature of all mankind has been enriched by the fairy tales of Hans Christian Andersen (April 2) and the stories of Washington Irving (April 3).

In politics, the Arien zeal of Thomas Jefferson (April 13) helped create the first nation on earth which fostered freedom and equality. Our third President shared the sign of the Ram with Henry Clay

(April 12), Senator Edmund Muskie (March 28), and his former colleague, Senator Eugene McCarthy (March 29).

The history of motion pictures would be less brilliant without the talents of numerous Ariens, topped off by the great clown himself, Charlie Chaplin (April 16). In his company are Mary Pickford (April 9), Bette Davis (April 5), Doris Day (April 3), Debbie Reynolds (April 1), Ali MacGraw (April 1), and Steve McQueen (March 24).

The world of music has been expanded by the diversity of Arien talent, from Johann Sebastian Bach (March 21) to Arturo Toscanini (March 25). Nor should we overlook the many vocalists who have brought to their songs that special exuberance of the children of the Ram. Prominent examples are Pearl Bailey (March 29), Diana Ross (March 26), and Elton John (March 25).

A different kind of performing art, but one which is ever more vital to our daily lives, is represented by the special gifts of Howard Cosell (March 25) and Harry Reasoner (April 17), whose broadcasting skills are as similar as their personalities are contrary.

Many women of the sign of Aries show a remarkable forcefulness and capability. Dorothea Dix (April 4), the nineteenth-century reformer, was as much a path maker and pioneer in women's rights as was Clare Boothe Luce (April 10) more recently. The famed aviatrix Evelyn Pinckert Brier (April 12) showed the same Arien trait of determination and sense of purpose as did an earlier Arien, St. Theresa of Avila (March 28).

Two of the world's greatest artists—Raphael (March 28) and Leonardo da Vinci (April 15)—were Ariens. The magnificent Leonardo still inspires humanity with his declaration, "Come, men, to see the wonders which may be discovered in nature by such studies." That sums up the creed of the children of the Ram: "Let me show you." And in most cases, they can show us all quite a bit.

Those are general traits noticeable, to one extent or another, in the character of all Ariens. To apply them to an individual, however, we must examine the specific influences which constitute each astrological division within the sign of Aries.

Somewhere in the next twelve chapters, you will find yourself. You will also find your relatives and friends. And you will discover characteristics which each of you shares with the Apostle who shares your Zodiac sign. In this way, you can become more sensitive and responsive to the mission which the Father has assigned to you in His plan for the world.

Each sign of the Zodiac is comprised of nine divisions, and you can determine your division by adding up the numbers of your birth-date. For example, if you were born on the 15th of the month, the 1 and the 5 add up to 6, putting you in the Sixth Division of your sign and making you a Six person. If the total is 10 or if you were born on the 10th, 20th, or 30th of the month, drop the zero and the remaining number is your division. If you were born on the 29th, the 2 and the 9 add up to 11, but this is regarded as 1 plus 1, or 2, making you a Two person.

Under your sign, you will first find my general impressions about you and your Apostle. In your division, you will find specifics about yourself and your future, plus indications which have been given to me regarding your finances and your health. You will also find my recommendations for the right colors for you to use in your clothes and your décor. Using the right colors can be like having a spotlight on you, enhancing your personal magnetism, your luck, and your influences on others.

Help yourself to your stars.

ARIES—FIRST DIVISION *(March 28, April 1, 10, 19)*

As an Arien of the First Division, whom we will here refer to as an Aries One, you are an extremely fortunate person. Probably no other division in the entire Zodiac offers such a potential for leadership. You are:

- ambitious
- unorthodox
- talented at handling people
- happy to be in the limelight
- affectionate
- active

Your ambition is a driving factor in your makeup, and the powerful planetary combination under which you were born affords you every opportunity to achieve whatever you wish. If you are not already a decision maker at your work, you have the potential to be one; and you should work toward that goal because you are a natural organizer, manager, supervisor, and director.

At home, you are the head of the family. There is no doubt about that! An Arien husband doesn't hand over his paycheck; he attends to the family budget. An Arien wife soon teaches her mate that the best way to keep a happy home is to include her in the decision making. Is it any wonder that Peter, the Arien archetype, was selected to lead the early Christian community? Who else would have been so well suited to protect the faithful, guide the erring, and oversee the growth of an international church?

If you were born an Aries One, you like people and enjoy having them around, but not if they are hangers-on or yes-men. Being direct yourself, you cannot tolerate evasion or flattery. You respect people most when they are frank and forthright.

Owing to the ruling influence of Mars in your astrological chart, you are aggressive and tend toward both a quick temper and outspokenness. You must train yourself to think before you act or speak. Otherwise your sometimes too hasty responses will provoke opposition and resistance to your ideas. Know yourself: although you are the kind of person who can take instructions and advice from those you admire and respect, you often speak too soon. Your independence of thought makes you unorthodox. You always want to handle things *your* way and seldom consider someone else's way better than yours. Despite the difficulties this can create, your natural abilities usually carry you through them.

You are good at handling people. In fact, most Ariens make good military officers or politicians. Women Ariens usually become presidents or chairpersons of the social and civic clubs they join. Their talent for human relations lets them balance several projects at one time with great success.

Most Arien people—and especially those in the First Division—are happiest when at the center of things, are courageous under pressure, and in fact tend to prefer constant activity to anything else. Beneath their busy exteriors, however, Aries Ones are romantic. Although subject to occasional depression when you feel you aren't sufficiently appreciated, you are able to swing very quickly to the opposite side, like a pendulum, and to display your affection for others in positive ways.

This conflict of emotions is the result of a crosscurrent between the planetary influences of Venus and Mars, the forces of love and war. Aries Ones have a strong Venusian streak and face the dilemma of reconciling their Martian side (which says, "People must love me, or else!") with their Venusian side (which proclaims to the world, "I want to love people"). You must therefore train yourself to steer a middle course when your emotions of anger or love are energized. Otherwise, you will be hurt. Aries Ones can secure their lasting happiness by learning to live with the world as it is.

The influence of Mars also gives an Aries One a need to be active. You love sports and would much rather participate in them than watch. Venus brings you a keen sense of beauty. You enjoy nature, and you appreciate it best when you are out on a camping trip.

You have, as well, an appreciation for literature and the arts, and are sometimes inclined (at least as a sideline) to try to make a living from writing or painting. Try it. You could succeed at either.

HEALTH: You tend toward a robust, vigorous constitution and lead a charmed life in avoiding accidents, but you should be extremely careful in the use of firearms and explosives. Your health index indicates, however, that you may occasionally suffer acute indigestion and stomach trouble, caused mainly by your busy schedule. After middle age, you are susceptible to heart trouble and to excess weight. But those problems can be avoided by careful diet, by not smoking, and by drinking only moderately. If you guard your health, you will be long-lived.

MONEY: Early in your career, you may not make the money you would like, especially if you enter a profession or the arts; but as you mature, money matters improve, and you are more likely than most to acquire considerable wealth. You must beware of risky, impulsive investments. Over the long run, they could prove extremely costly.

COLORS: There is nothing pale about the colors that suit your temperament. You favor all shades of blue and crimson, rose and red, as well as the more demure violet and mauve. You are, in a way, the hardy purple crocus that pushes bravely up through the snow. You are the scarlet rambling rose that boldly flourishes along an untended roadway. Their colors harmonize with your spirit and complement your appearance.

RELATIONSHIPS: You are apt to experience an ambiguity,

an uncertainty in your relationships with loved ones. You must reconcile your need to be loved, obviously and directly, with your need for solitude. It isn't always easy for others to understand these opposite poles of your emotional makeup. You should not feel hurt too easily, for people are often fond of you but, for one reason or another, they don't show their feelings as openly as you would like.

Especially in romantic affairs, it is important for you to learn to interpret subtle signs of affection. It would be foolish for you to neglect your most enriching relationships just because others are not as effusive as you are in expressing their love.

ARIES–SECOND DIVISION *(March 29, April 2, 11)*

An Arien of the Second Division is gifted with excess energy, which presents both an opportunity for significant achievement and a risk of serious problems. If you are an Aries Two, the attributes of both Mars and Venus are active within you, as they obviously were within Peter. They can interact in such a way as to cause repeated romantic difficulties. Of course, that need not happen, especially if you use astrological foresight to anticipate and avert them. Like Peter, you have unlimited potential and tend to be unorthodox and rambunctious. Your chief qualities, then, are:

- boldness
- directness
- forcefulness
- creativity
- imagination
- enthusiasm
- romance

You are a dynamo! You may have already discovered that parties are enlivened by your presence, committees are directed by your suggestions, and community projects depend upon your zestful participation. On the other hand, possible problems can stem from the first three qualities listed above. They can be admirable characteristics; but when they are unleashed and ungoverned, the result can be chaos. An Aries Two who has not developed self-control soon becomes aware that he or she doesn't keep friends for long. Their marriage is liable to failure, and they always seem to be job-hopping.

Yet there is much good in such a person. He or she is creative, imaginative, and enthusiastic. They work hard and can make their exuberance contagious, but they never seem to know when enough is enough.

I once had a secretary who was an Aries Two. I liked her and appreciated her loyalty and her ability to handle many details independently when our work piled up. But I quickly discovered that being around her was like walking into a hurricane. She never slowed down and could not stand being idle. I had to take on extra work just to keep her busy. I couldn't dismiss her, for she certainly gave me no cause to do so. But I did wonder how long I could survive her hectic assistance. Fortunately, she soon married and left her position.

She was a good example of an Aries Two. Those of you who share her segment of this Zodiac sign may not realize your effect on others. If you fail to harness your energies and restrain your zeal, you can actually hinder more than you help. Then if you are rebuffed or rejected, your spirits collapse. You become morose and an even bigger problem for those who love you and are trying to understand you. The result is that you feel misunderstood and are apt to be bitter about it.

In personal relationships as in business, your virtue of enthusiasm can become a vice. It can make marriage a risk for you. Your eagerness for having many things happening around you carries over to your love life, and so you may minimize the importance of fidelity to one person. If left unchecked, this attitude can rob you of happiness and security. You should develop self-control in this and in other aspects of your life. Remember, there is a great difference between a tendency and a habit. The difference is whether we allow ourselves to be dominated by impulses or whether we master them through our free will.

You can succeed at most kinds of work, once you decide to settle down to them. You have original ideas and can express them clearly. How fortunate you are as a public speaker and an effective communicator! You inspire others to follow you, as long as they can maintain your speed. In order to make the fullest use of your charismatic abilities, learn to pace yourself and to help others keep up, both in your work and in your life.

A woman who is an Aries Two faces the challenge of balancing her life both inside and outside the home. Her temptation is toward the bustle of the exterior world. There is certainly nothing wrong with that, for she will have great contributions to make. But she should be careful to reserve a sheltered place in her life for her home and family, or she will risk losing them altogether.

Persons who are within the Second Division of Aries can do great good for the world because of their dynamism and wide range of talents. You are simply too important to the general welfare of your fellow man to keep your talents hidden. So whenever you are inclined to act impulsively, recall that your presence on earth is part of an overall plan and that you must act for the benefit of all rather than for your own welfare. You will find your greatest contentment in work that involves improving life for others.

HEALTH: Your external appearance of hardiness and good health is often just a reflection of the nervous energy you burn so prodigiously as you rush about in your perpetual hurry. It is difficult for you to take time out for regular dental and medical checks; and because of the way you pressure yourself, with irregular hours and meals, you are subject to fevers and blood disorders. Of course, proper health habits can prevent those ailments. In middle age, you may require intestinal surgery. But no matter what your age, today is not too early to start taking better care of yourself, especially in tending to what you might regard as minor infections of ear, nose, and throat.

MONEY: Because you insist on working so hard, you shouldn't suffer money problems except when your forceful disposition leads, in one way or another, to periods of unemployment. Your temperament makes you unsuited to a partnership, so try to work either in your own business or in a job where you are accountable to only one person. Financial security will come to you after you acquire the self-control which is necessary to obtain it.

COLORS: Perhaps because you are frequently caught up in strong gusts of emotion, like the wind-swept boughs of sturdy trees, shades of green flatter your appearance. For your moments of quiet, you are comfortable with grays and the muted tones of wine and rose. Beneath it all, however, you are like a single crimson blossom which, by its very brashness, dominates an entire garden of subtler blooms. No wonder you favor an occasional touch of shocking red in your furnishings and apparel.

RELATIONSHIPS: By nature, you are a loner. That is natural for a hard-driving person who is often impatient with others who may be less direct and less forceful. Nonetheless, like all of us, you do have an inner need to be really loved, not just admired. To meet that need, try to inspire true devotion in others. You can do this not by proving how good you are at what you do but by revealing to them the sincere and concerned person you really are beneath your external façade of authority.

This is most important in your romantic relationships. Marital happiness will not come automatically to you, but it is within your grasp if you are as determined to have it as you are to assert your leadership. Remember that it is usually wiser to sacrifice success in business than to forfeit your lasting happiness in love.

ARIES—THIRD DIVISION *(March 21, 30, April 3, 12)*

An Aries Three shares some of the problems associated with Aries Twos, but to a lesser extent. Being more introspective, persons in the Third Division of Aries are therefore more aware of the contradictions within them. Consequently, they can better control conflicts which arise from their internal tensions. If you were born under this division of Aries, you may have already learned from experience that although you live under a fiery sign, you can achieve great things as long as you keep calm. Your main characteristics, in addition to those common to an Aries Two, are:

- ambition, but with success coming in a surprising way
- temper
- mental agility
- good parental abilities

Although you are extremely eager to get ahead, your eventual success will not come directly through your own efforts. Just as Peter didn't become an Apostle through his own initiative, so it will be with you. To your surprise, you will be appointed to a position of authority in your chosen field. I would expect to find you in a working situation that involves frequent changes in methods of operation because of technical advances. So always remain a student, alert for improvements and shortcuts, and keep up with professional publications which concern you; you will need their information when your important appointment comes along.

Mars' influence on your life gives you a short temper, yet this is not entirely bad. You frequently argue with people because of their ideas, not because of personalities. Better ideas make better friends. With effort, you can learn to moderate your emotions while standing steadfastly by your beliefs.

You do have one habit which annoys your friends. As an exercise in mental gymnastics, you enjoy taking any unpopular view in a discussion. You defend it not from conviction but because of the intellectual stimulation it affords. You usually have the good grace to clear the air with a joke at the end of the conversation; nevertheless, what is fun for you isn't always enjoyable for your friends. Many are irritated by your habit, and some think you childish because of it. Perhaps there would be fewer hurt feelings all around if you would speak a little less and listen a bit more.

With their balance of exuberance and self-control, Ariens of the Third Division make good parents and run a calm home, although they are inclined to be a little too strict with their children. Remember that children are well behaved not when they fear their parents but when they know their parents love them.

HEALTH: Your Arien superabundance of mental and physical health can often cause you to overwork. This naturally leads to periods of exhaustion, when you feel too tired even to move. You need a hobby or community activity to take your mind from your job. Do take care with your diet. Keep it simple. Avoid sauces, cream, rich gravies, and fried foods, or you will have stomach and heart problems. No project, no matter how noble or profitable, is worth the sacrifice of your health.

MONEY: You are cautious and prudent in small things and can easily gain a reputation for being tightfisted with money. Housewives who are Ariens of the Third Division often skimp unnecessarily on household spending. That's because all Aries Threes are inclined to be overly anxious about the future. Don't worry so much, but do provide prudently for your later years. Aries Three men should retire early to ensure that they get more pleasure out of life than just labor and thrift. That way they will also have more to give to others.

COLORS: Your magnetic vibrations are attuned to the fiery impulses of gold and orange and bronzy brown. Your colors are those changing shades of flames and sparks, shifting momentarily from yellows to reds. Like any burning thing, you sometimes show a streak of blue, a symbol of the interior calm that is within your reach.

RELATIONSHIPS: It is advisable to restrain your mischievous impulses. Do not be so readily proud to demonstrate your superior mental abilities. You are, in fact, highly likable to your friends and would be even more so if you would stop trying to score points. Ease off. Your merits stand on their own. You needn't impress others.

Beware the habit of setting your own personal value exclusively in terms of your intelligence. The standards of the heart are quite different from those of the mind. When you find yourself romantically involved, don't allow differences in I.Q. to disrupt a relationship that could bring you more enduring happiness than all your mental accomplishments.

ARIES—FOURTH DIVISION *(March 22, 31, April 4, 13)*

If you are an Aries Four, you live under a strong sign with a peculiar planetary combination. It creates strange contradictions. Although you have everything going for you, sometimes nothing seems to go right. Your personality is balanced between great strengths and serious weaknesses. If you neglect to develop the former and correct the latter, the result will be alternating periods of success and failure. Your setbacks will invariably surprise you. They will never seem your fault. Unexpected events will keep forcing changes in your plans. Perhaps people will disappoint you. Just when everything seems ready to go, some element will fail and you will be left to take sole responsibility.

In your disappointments, as in everything else, there is a pattern discernible to those who look closely. Aries Fours are perfectly suited to be life's teachers. Their reward lies in helping others by sharing the benefit of their own hard-won experience. Admittedly, there can be a certain painfulness in seeing one's pupils surpass their teacher, but you must overcome that feeling as you accept the vital role you have to play. Among your mixed personality traits, the following are most prominent:

- talent in technical fields

- ability to be content while playing second fiddle
- a gift for mathematics
- liability to marital problems

Aries Four men are technically competent and perform well in matters involving electronics or mechanics. They are inventive, always seeking ways to improve working methods both at home and on their jobs. But they shouldn't expect to be given credit for their improvements unless they take the initiative to secure it. Automatic recognition just is not in their stars.

Yet Aries Four men can be, and usually are, quite happy to take a back seat. Every army needs privates as well as generals. Although they possess sufficient talent to rise higher than they usually do, they are fulfilled by unselfishly putting forth their best efforts to secure the success of a project rather than by making similar efforts to advance themselves. Aries Four women are usually apt mathematicians and are well equipped for business, for they not only make admirable aides and secretaries, with a gift for unselfish industry, but also bring to higher positions a rare dedication to their work.

In domestic life, the pressures an Aries Four feels from marriage can often be too much to withstand. If this applies to you, then you probably will not have an easy marriage unless you find a mate who isn't worried about such things as "keeping up with the Joneses."

HEALTH: You have great vitality and a splendid constitution, although, like most Ariens, you may endanger your fitness by stress and overwork. Take active steps to protect your health. Make recreation a part of your day in order to take your mind off business problems and home conflicts. Gardening is a good Arien hobby, satisfying simultaneously both the yearning to be productive and the need for relaxation. Because of your inner tensions, you are prone to problems of blood pressure and heart disease after middle age. So train yourself early in life to get away from it all.

MONEY: You will experience ups and downs in money matters, but you will always be able to earn a living. Aries Four men are less likely than others to work for a company that provides a pension plan. So it would be a good idea for them, while they are young, to consult an expert about setting up a small annuity to supplement whatever retirement benefits may come to them.

Women in the Fourth Division of Aries are usually too active to remain at home once their children are in school, and they often return to their former jobs. It is obviously a good idea for them to maintain their working skills in order to cope with a job later in life.

COLORS: For you as an Aries Four, the best colors are like those for an Aries Three; shades of yellow, gold, or orange; variants of red and crimson. In fact, all light and bright colors match the sparkle of your enthusiastic personality.

RELATIONSHIPS: When you do find yourself in one of those occasional periods of depression, remember that you Ariens of the Fourth Division are more popular than those in any other division of that Zodiac sign. There is a reason for the esteem you enjoy: you have a wonderful depth of character and can be one of the world's greats. All that can hold you back is the bitterness you may understandably feel at seeing others, who are less talented but more fortunate than you, advance beyond you. Before wasting your time and spirit on ill feelings, remember you already have more good and true friends than most people do. Aren't they worth more than enough to compensate for your disappointments?

You probably have already discovered that a happy relationship with one special person outweighs all of life's little failures. If you haven't yet been so fortunate, remember that your best romantic prospects will be with someone who doesn't demand constant financial success and doesn't put professional accomplishments above loyalty and kindness.

ARIES—FIFTH DIVISION *(March 23, April 5, 14)*

Aries Five people are perfect examples of what we might call the "wild cards" in the plan set out in the stars. They have totally free will to choose radically different courses. They can be wonderful individuals or a complete loss to those around them. It is their choice and their responsibility.

If you are an Aries Five, you possess a versatile, clever mind. Your intelligence and glib tongue enable you to exert great influence on those around you. But I warn—those very traits, allied with the influence of Mars on your astrological chart, could lead to the abuse of your gifts. Let me be frank about this: your talents can either bring you great happiness and achievement in the service of others or can lead you to reckless self-indulgence. Remember that you have been given the strength and courage necessary to make the right decision. Your main traits are:

- a strong mind
- love of a challenge
- liberal views
- a good memory
- clouded prospects for marital success

With your active mind and masterful control of the language, you find it easy to sway others. Whether or not you have developed your gift, you are a born orator. Capable of leading others in noble causes, you could also become like a spoiled child, able to obtain your every whim by wheedling or screaming. I don't wish to sound critical, but I want you to realize the power for both good and evil that is in your hands.

Your influence over others can go astray. Because you love a challenge, and especially the risks of gambling, you are sometimes tempted to go off on a spree. In extreme cases, an Arien of the Fifth Division can drink to excess and become sexually irresponsible. Even though each of us is susceptible to irresponsible behavior, we all share the obligation to direct our lives in constructive channels. But you Aries Fives have a special obligation because your popularity and charisma make it easy for you to persuade others to either follow your good example or imitate your escapades.

Although you are eloquent in public discussion, an Aries Five is nevertheless guarded in expressing personal feelings and rather cool in matters of affection. This doesn't mean you disdain strong emotional attachments but only that you are reluctant to express them in vivid words and open deeds. If you persist in your refusal to open your heart to others, you will cause more sadness than you realize. Perhaps you don't understand how deeply others value your regard for them.

You probably have liberal, sometimes radical views on public issues and can be violently aggressive against rock-bound conservatives with equally fixed ideas. However, this needn't be a disruptive trait. You can make it a positive force through political and social action to improve the lives of the poor and mistreated. Like all Aries Fives, you have a remarkable memory for facts and dates, which is probably an offshoot of your fondness for reading history.

I must point out that you may have poor luck with marriage.

You might marry more than once, and each time you will face the same problems caused by your yearning to indulge yourself as freely as you speak. But a yearning is not an action. Your willpower is sufficient to prevent potentially harmful misconduct. With a little practice, you can control that biting sarcasm with which you could easily hurt those you most love. Your determination to harness your wayward urges, together with your amazing ability for interpersonal communication, enables you to achieve great things. Yes, you do have to keep your contrary impulses in check; but by doing so, you can reach heights that most of us cannot attain.

HEALTH: You are sensitive and high-strung, thanks to the intensity of your excellent mental powers. You could easily develop facial twitches, symptoms of overtaxed mental faculties. You must therefore practice proper control of your nerves by deliberately calming yourself. Meditation is an excellent way to do this. Consider, for example, the relaxing powers of yoga. Study the path to inner peace achieved by the great mystics of East and West alike. If you neglect your need for occasional quiet, you may also have stomach or intestinal troubles. So be prepared to coddle yourself a little in order to reduce the tensions that surround you.

MONEY: Again, everything is up to you. As long as you keep your higher nature in charge, you will always be solvent. You have the strength to cure yourself of any fascination with gambling, and by doing so, you can only improve your bank balance. You will tend to hold reasonably well-paid, though taxing, jobs.

COLORS: Your vibrance demands that you wear light colors as much as possible, with just a hint of red, crimson, or rose. Bright colors are best for you, and provide the cheery atmosphere to assist you in struggling with those tendencies you wish to subdue.

RELATIONSHIPS: With your reservoir of charm, everything in life should go well for you, especially in your dealings with other people. But beware of superficial friends. Many weak people will be attracted to you by the very strength of your personality. Consider carefully who your faithful friends are before you abandon them for associates whose loyalty will prove dubious.

This goes double in your romantic relationships. You don't need a mate who will be impressed with your charm and intimidated by your leadership. You need a partner, not a follower; a calming friend, not a fellow racer at life's track. I suspect you may have already met the right individual, but may consider him or her too bland for your exciting life. Eventually, you will learn that you need someone to balance your energy, not to intensify it.

ARIES–SIXTH DIVISION *(March 24, April 6, 15)*

The Sixth Division of Aries combines such favorable planetary influences that if you were born within this segment of the Zodiac, you could probably be a successful gambler. Throughout all your days, you will enjoy good luck. Use it wisely.

Your astrological combination also indicates that you have a genial, generous nature, strongly influenced by the energy and enthusiasm of the planet Mars. This means you are socially popular, making friends wherever you go, and are charitably inclined. Your open, sympathetic nature responds readily to appeals for assistance. In addition, an Aries Six is apt to be:

- home-loving
- hospitable
- artistic
- fond of travel

Most Sixth Division Ariens enjoy their homes. Although they are inclined to spend too much to make them comfortable, they are extremely hospitable to friends, whom they love to entertain. Be careful not to impoverish yourself with excessive spending. Your friends and relatives appreciate you for what you are; you needn't impress them with material things. It is interesting to note that archaeologists have recently uncovered the ruins of what may have been Peter's house at Capernaum and report that it was evidently a home of some size and comfort. This may explain in a way the grandeur of St. Peter's Church in Rome, which is actually a massive memorial to him covering his grave site. Of course, its magnificence exists to honor Peter's Master rather than to celebrate the Apostle's own glory. With Peter's example before you, let your home's comfort serve your guests rather than your own reputation for gracious living.

It is possible you will marry early, acting on impulse rather than from mature love. Regrettably, early marriage is not beneficial for any Ariens. A later marriage or, more commonly, a second marriage later in life is much more favorable for their domestic contentment.

Those born within the Sixth Division are artistic but usually lack the discipline for the lonely, hard work which is necessary to succeed in painting, music, or sculpture. Poetry or literature are possible outlets for their creativity, but my own vibrations and the ordained patterns of astrology tell me that most Aries Sixes are happier working for a company or a shop related to the marketing of artistic materials.

Aries Sixes are intensely fond of travel, and their imagination is frequently captured by the customs and habits of other peoples. They are well advised to put aside some of the money they would otherwise spend in entertaining and to use it for their own contentment through study and visits to distant lands.

HEALTH: As an Aries Six, you have a good constitution and are quick to recover from illness. You are prone to afflictions of the head, involving the throat, nose, and ears. Sometimes you suffer bad headaches or migraines. Pacing yourself properly in your everyday routine will help prevent these ailments.

MONEY: Especially during the early years of your life, you will be very lucky in money matters; but, because of your own openhandedness, your extravagance, and your failure to provide for the future, you may face grave financial difficulties later in life. This need not happen if you plan ahead. For you, savings accounts, bank stocks, and U.S. bonds are the best investments. And do break your habit of grabbing the check every time you are socializing with friends.

COLORS: You should wear all shades of blue, from the light color of a robin's egg to the darkest hue of a moonlit sea. Don't forget the complementary shades of purple, violet, and mauve. You will also look and feel at your best when you wear red, crimson, and rose. In fact, when you entertain people, a passion with you, those shades help to express your warmest greetings to your guests.

RELATIONSHIPS: Consider your loved ones before you consider your friends. Because you are naturally gregarious and sympathetic, you are too openhanded for your own good. Remember, "Charity begins at home." You naturally have plenty of friends, but it is your responsibility to see that your loved ones are not neglected because you place too much emphasis upon less important ties.

A well-suited life-mate for you should be concerned about the home you will share together. But try not to set up artificial standards for that lucky person. Even if the one you most cherish dislikes travel and cares little for art, your willingness to compromise your own life-style can result in a happy and stable home life.

ARIES—SEVENTH DIVISION *(March 25, April 7, 16)*

As an Aries Seven, you were born under a strange combination of planetary influences which have given you a complicated personality structure. Your characteristics are likely to result in an unusual, even eccentric life.

You feel a deep interest in the occult, the mystical, the psychic; and if you aren't already involved in those areas, you will become so eventually. Despite adverse opinions, I encourage you to pursue your studies in those matters, and I believe you will! We humans are more than flesh and blood. We are spirit, too. The more we can discover about the human spirit, the better we can fulfill our part in the cosmic pattern of life. Your major traits, then, are:

- interest in the occult
- restlessness
- musical ability
- desire to belong

I feel obliged to add a frank word of warning about your interest in the occult. Many people still regard the investigation of psychic phenomena as a weird practice and consider those interested in it to be equally odd. Be prepared for criticism and ridicule. An Aries Seven who wishes to develop innate spiritual gifts will be wise to limit discussion of that endeavor to sympathetic friends. Don't try to convert anyone to your interest in the supernatural.

A prominent trait of Ariens of the Seventh Division is a certain restlessness, a constant search for fresh ideas, new horizons, for change in their surroundings. You find it hard to settle down in a conventional job or routine. My suggestion for solving that problem is to find a position which allows you to travel, affording a degree of innovation. Otherwise, you will frequently change employment, homes, areas, simply to satisfy your inner longing for something different.

That means, unhappily, that you will probably have few lasting friendships; but one consolation is the likelihood that you will make several very close friends who will stay with you spiritually through life, even though you are physically far apart. You could be a bad marital risk because of your zest for moving around, and you would be wise to face that possibility now. But never despair; your future remains in your own hands, although it is essential that you use your own free will to shape it.

Because you have an innate musical talent, you should develop some skill with a musical instrument. This will help you find fulfillment and will also open doors for another aspect of your personality—the part of you that needs to belong. Because Aries Sevens are great joiners, you are apt to be a valued member of civic, social, political, and religious organizations. You enjoy belonging to such groups and relish the team feeling of working with them. Perhaps you could combine your musical talent with this emotional need by joining a choir or orchestra. This will not only help you enrich yourself culturally but also bring much pleasure to others.

HEALTH: You are subject to rapid and sometimes drastic changes in your condition, and your health is apt to be influenced greatly by your surroundings. You will frequently suffer colds, chills, fevers, influenza, and the like unless you avoid taking foolish risks. Any unusual strain on your system can easily cause you to become run-down. You can indirectly strengthen your health if you stop daydreaming. Don't waste your time on romantic fantasies which lead only to frustration.

MONEY: Because you change your living arrangements so frequently, you rarely stay on one job long enough to earn a significant promotion or a major raise. The large sums of money that do occasionally come your way result from your inventive ideas. It is vital that you avoid all speculation or any kind of gambling. To invest your earnings, stay with safe, proven channels of profit, like government bonds.

COLORS: The best colors to complement the aura of your personality are greens, creams, and white, as well as tempered tones of dove gray. These can be especially effective in expressing your intimate spirit when accented by the standard Arien colors of red, crimson, and rose. The combination of sedate hues with bold ones will not only reveal something about yourself to others but also reassure you when, during your traveling, you yearn for a touch of the familiar in your surroundings.

RELATIONSHIPS: Because of the strange juxtaposition of planetary influences, your personality is an odd amalgam. You respond to different people in so many different ways that some will think you mercurial or fickle. Essentially, you tend to maintain only a few close friendships, although you make determined efforts to relate well to people. Don't be discouraged. You have a high worth and are well regarded by a large circle, even though you may be surprised to be told of their esteem for you.

It is possible that the ultimate antidote for your incessant restlessness will be your discovery, sooner or later, of someone who will become such a treasured part of your life that you will abandon the lure of change and travel to settle where you are most loved. Be sure that you recognize a good thing when it comes your way!

ARIES—EIGHTH DIVISION *(March 26, April 8, 17)*

The most trying period for an Aries Eight is young adulthood. The astrological combination for this division requires those born within it to display prudence and self-control, to hold their ambitions in check, even to set aside their own development in favor of the needs of those who depend on them. They will thereby delay, but make more certain, their own eventual success.

As an Aries Eight, you will find yourself responsible for the support of several people, whether or not they are close family members. This will mean less time and money for your own interests. Understandably, you will resist this situation; but there will be little you can do about it. Despite your disappointment, it will be a blessing in disguise. Your astrological signs show that most projects or relationships initiated during your young adulthood could be neither happy nor successful. This includes both business partnerships and marriage. You would be wise to postpone such major decisions and all fundamental choices concerning your life-style until later in life. You can be described as:

- ambitious
- determined
- outwardly tightfisted
- reserved with others

Your ambition, a common Arien trait, will let you move ahead rapidly once you are free of those early impediments to your plans. Other traits—determination and perseverance—will be invaluable to you in making a successful career, although you should be wary of riding roughshod over others in pursuing your goals too keenly.

You must make it plain to people that your consistency and steadfastness are not stubbornness or an inability to compromise. Aries Eight women are often considered bossy by their friends when, in fact, they only wish to get on with the task at hand. Though your intentions are good, you must remember that efficiency doesn't outweigh politeness. It is better to delay a project than to slight others by hurrying it through by yourself.

Another misunderstood facet of the Aries Eight character is its attitude toward money. You will carry with you the memories of your early years, when money was tight, and so you will always have a fear of poverty. People who don't understand this could consider you mean or miserly, and their resentment could be a burden to you. Indeed, our country needs much more of your type of frugality! I will only suggest that you might let those who are close understand the reason for your caution.

You tend to be acquisitive, hoarding things in closets and trunks, even though you realize you may never use them. The habit of carefulness can be an asset, especially in business, for your planetary influences indicate strong abilities in starting new commercial enterprises. Because of the failure of others to properly understand, you are reserved with them and don't trust people easily, especially when they are strangers to you.

Your intelligence leads you to keep a card up your sleeve, although not, of course, literally. An Aries Eight born on April 8 or April 17 is disposed to making an outstanding career in medicine or science.

HEALTH: You are likely to have the extraordinary experience of an incorrect diagnosis by your doctor and the prescription of the wrong medicine. Avoid this hazard by choosing your personal physician carefully and by staying with a reliable one who will know you well. You should shun drugs and alcohol, and must watch your diet closely because of a tendency to suffer digestive complaints and maladies of the blood. Without the proper precaution, you may at some time in your life undergo surgery involving your jaw, either for your teeth or following an accident to your head.

MONEY: Your frugality has already been mentioned. In business dealings, you will have difficulty finding a suitable partner. You are well advised to try—and probably to succeed—alone. Your chances of becoming wealthy are excellent.

COLORS: Your color vibrations suit all shades of gold, yellow, orange, brown, and bronze. Shades of blue, especially a sapphire tone, are good for you and make charming contrasts with the more dazzling sun colors. Of course, Arien hues of red, crimson, and rose are as natural to your self-expression as they are to all those born under the sign of the Ram.

RELATIONSHIPS: Your habitual reserve is apt to prohibit casual friendships, but you will always enjoy a close relationship with members of your immediate family and will draw great support and satisfaction from that. They know that your apparent obstinacy is really dedication. And others who manage to break through the outer armor of your emotions will also value your hidden qualities.

Imagine, for example, how one very special person, who may at first be disappointed by your thriftiness, would respond when he or she learns that your penny-pinching is actually a precaution for the security of your life together. As for your reserve, your love has only to discover that, especially in your case, the old maxim is true: still water does run deep.

ARIES—NINTH DIVISION *(March 27, April 9, 18)*

If you are an Aries Nine, you are Peter at his most blunt and forceful. Like him, you would even cut off someone's ear to defend a friend. You would criticize your boss with well-meaning independence and shout someone down when you disagreed with him. You are autonomous in thought and action and strongly dislike restrictions of any kind. You really live up to your symbol: the battering ram. Your chief qualities are:

- aggressiveness
- dynamism
- tactlessness
- social-mindedness
- good marriage prospects
- fearlessness

Because most persons with whom you deal realize that you mean well, your aggressive qualities are tolerated by them, especially by those who take the trouble to understand your better side. Indeed, there is a better side, and a powerful one! You battle not for profit but for ideals. You shout not from arrogance but from total commitment to your principles.

You should organize yourself more efficiently, for you tend to waste too much time on minor details. You possess all the qualities necessary for success—except diplomacy. As a typical Arien, you speak first, think later. And because you are not only dynamic but also tactless, there is little likelihood that you will work your way up in any organization. You refuse to play politics, and you don't have enough patience to wait out an awkward situation. So, as soon as you can, try to branch out into a field in which you can be your own boss. It would be a loss to your entire community if you allowed your talents to be stifled by your less adventuresome supervisors.

An Aries Nine is a social being. You love parties and give them frequently. But you may be inclined to feel that social acceptance must be measured by the extent of your sexual involvement, and so you may be tempted to have affairs, less out of passion than from sheer recklessness. This tendency, if freely indulged, is sure to bring much misery both to you and to those you love. It should reassure you that your dynamism can easily be turned into an insuperable commitment to one person. This makes your chances for a good marriage excellent! That is, once you find someone who can bear to live with a tornado.

Be careful about your social drinking. Anyone with your personality makeup could, under great pressure, use alcohol as a crutch, which would cause you to drive ahead when actually you should slow down and rest. This could lead to a dependence on drinking, which would be especially foolish in your case, for you have within you all of the psychological resources you need to face any problem.

HEALTH: With your splendid vitality, you will recover quickly from illnesses, but still must guard against accidents. You are prone to mishaps. This is partly due to your fearlessness. Whether working with tools around the house, driving your car, or participating in the sports events you enjoy so much, you run a greater risk than most other people. This is no reason to limit your physical exertion, only to exercise due caution, both for your sake and for the sake of your loved ones. Concentrate on what you are doing!

The tempo of your life indicates that you are liable to develop high blood pressure, even heart trouble. If you are determined to preserve your health, you will find short rest periods, even a midday nap, most useful in keeping fit.

MONEY: You have a great ability to make money in industry, business, or investments, and could easily become a major speculator. You invariably find your way out of difficulties and are self-reliant, confident in whatever course of action you have decided upon. In fact, you are a bit too headstrong. In general, however, your good luck will compensate for all but the most serious financial errors.

COLORS: Your color vibrations are the greatest! Most of the color spectrum is conducive to your personality, from palest yellow to golden brown, from lightest pink to deepest cerise. Even some shades of blue are good for you. The magnetism of your stellar influences is like the gay jumble of a child's set of water paints. Even when the colors clash, the overall effect is one of good-natured satisfaction. More than most people, you benefit from the colors you wear if you suit your appearance to your moods by wearing bright shades when things aren't going well and darker ones when you don't need that extra lift.

RELATIONSHIPS: Despite your lack of tact and your excessive exuberance, you will always enjoy solid friendships with a large circle of people. They see clearly how well meaning you are, and many of them receive a boost to their spirits simply from being near your vibrant energy.

The person who chooses you as a marriage partner will be either extremely blessed or woefully disappointed. It is up to you. If you fail to use the personality gifts your Creator has given you, then your home life will be unpleasant for you and for your family. But if you develop your many strong points, there will never be a more devoted partner or more loving parent. Take heart! For the pattern of your stars indicates that your chances are weighted toward marital success. All you need do is cooperate with your more generous and selfless instincts.

TAURUS—SIMON *(April 20–May 20)*

Taurus is the second sign of the Zodiac. Its symbol is a bull: strong, courageous, enduring.

Before we continue our study of this and all the subsequent divisions of the Zodiac, however, it is vital that we understand our purpose in doing so. Astrological knowledge is not a magical code to give us power over other people. Nor is it a system of charms and hexes to be used for our own advantage. On the contrary, it is self-knowledge, a deeper understanding of the uniqueness in each of us. It doesn't make us slaves to the stars. Rather, it frees us to recognize and develop our own individual potential for good. By learning about our own segment of the Zodiac, we can come to appreciate more fully the special gifts and talents God has given us. By studying the other segments, we can better comprehend and respect our fellow pilgrims, no matter what sign they call their own.

That understanding of ourselves and of our neighbors can help us greatly each day of our lives. In moments of jubilation and triumph, it can remind us that credit for success is not ours alone. In times of sorrow and defeat, it can assure us of our worth and remind us of the Creator's eternal consolation. Most of all, the wisdom of astrological study can help us through those times in our lives when we come face to face with the power of evil, when, in one way or another, we confront the master of the red boots.

I don't mean to suggest that all of us will see visions. I do mean that the malign force, symbolized by those arrogant red boots which

I saw marching in air, somehow challenges each of us. Whenever we are tempted to harm another for our own profit, whenever we observe one human being doing wrong to another, whenever any child of Adam and Eve abuses one of his brothers or sisters in our somewhat polluted Garden of Eden, then if we listen with our hearts, we can hear the tramping of those red boots. Like an aggressive army on the march, they press forward whenever we yield to evil.

We can resist their ruthless steps by knowing what we are, what we can do, and what we can become. Fortified by astrological assurance, we needn't fear the power of that supernatural being who, after all, was once expelled from Paradise. With that understood, let us see what we can learn from the sign of Taurus.

In my first vision in St. Matthew's Cathedral, I saw the sign of Taurus along with an Apostle whose name, I confess, was unknown to me. Later, in the third or fourth successive vision, which helped me to understand the entire meaning of what I had first seen, I noted again the same symbol and discovered that the man to whom it applied was Simon, known in Scripture as the Zealot.

Everything we know about Simon substantiates his Zodiac sign. He had been a member of a political faction, the Cananeans, which sought to overthrow the Roman occupation of Palestine by violence. Before accepting Christ's invitation to follow Him, Simon was the stereotype of an Angry Young Man, uncompromising and fanatical. Like many young people in recent times, he began his career with a belief in force and later learned better ways to change society by changing his own life.

Yet there was a place for Simon's zeal in the Divine scheme of things. Christ turned his fanaticism to more worthy matters and made him a man of peace and love. All you who are Taureans, who are spiritual kin to Simon, are like him in this most fundamental way. You are bulls, with the hearts of lambs.

As we have already seen, everything has its place in the Creator's overall plan for humanity. Every piece of the cosmic jigsaw puzzle fits neatly into its appropriate position. A Taurean who takes the time and effort to understand the role assigned to him has a huge advantage, for Taureans have more to do in life than most of us and also possess more ability to perform their tasks and accomplish their goals. They are good examples of the maxim that Joseph and Rose Kennedy taught their children: "Much is expected from those to whom much is given."

Taureans are blessed with tremendous determination and endurance, both physically and mentally; and as a consequence, they feel that they must always be busy at something. They respond readily to any call to a worthy cause. Proud of their ideals, as a fighting bull seems proud of his stamina, they will work hard to defend and to vindicate them. This commitment can be a most effective weapon in the armory of righteousness when it is needed. And even a pair of red boots cannot lightly defy it.

Taureans foster confidence in the people they meet, for others quickly perceive how selflessly dedicated a Taurean becomes to the projects he supports. In fact, Taureans often act as a binding force in a political or civic campaign. Their enthusiasm and enterprise can keep a plan rolling when, without their involvement, it would slow down or grind to a halt.

Like Simon, you Taureans are patriotic. You could succeed in politics as a candidate, but usually prefer to be down in the "engine room," serving in a less glamorous but very important role where you will be effective. That fact, more than credit or fame, makes you most happy.

That is the general pattern of life which the interaction of the heavenly bodies has determined for Taureans. After all my years of study in astrology, I still marvel to see how often people find their places in their astrological pattern. Sometimes, when I answer my door to a canvasser or to someone collecting donations to a charity, I ask his or her birth sign and am not at all surprised to be told that it is Taurus. How well we discover, often unknowingly, the best activities for our special makeup! A Taurean's sense of service and loyalty often leads to efforts to assist others. Moreover, Taureans are not easily discouraged, even when their aid is not appreciated, and tend to stay with whatever they start, no matter how difficult the path.

Centuries of careful astrological observation have proved that Taureans are usually strong, steady, systematic, and kindly people. But as always in human affairs, these admirable qualities have a less pleasant aspect. That's the bull in you! It can make you stubborn and difficult. You hate to change your plans once you have made them; and on those occasions when you must rearrange things, you let everyone know your objections, loud and clear.

In your heart, you never enjoy making such a fuss, and unfailingly you regret your outbursts later. Even so, your regret will not prevent still another repetition of your forceful expression of opinion. Unfortunately, when you have regained your composure, you do not always realize the hurt feelings you have unintentionally caused.

You have an alternative open to you, one which will not only spare the feelings of others but also save you later remorse. It is simple enough. Stop and think before you bellow. With a little love and understanding, you can be a lamb.

It is part of the design of the universe that you have the conflicting extremes of bull and lamb embodied within you. One counteracts the other, making a balanced pattern of force and counterforce —what in Oriental philosophy is called Yin and Yang. Just be sure you know your strengths and weaknesses, and make the right choices in the light of your self-understanding.

Taureans certainly know about the right choices in good living. You know fine wines and good food. You love to entertain and like to serve the best of everything to your guests, not to impress them but to treat them well. Occasionally your hospitality can be overwhelming, because you take your friends beyond their depth. They worry that they cannot reciprocate in the way you would like them to, and so they feel alienated from you. You may lose their friendship, killing it with too much kindness. The solution to that problem is simple. Remember that people visit you for your company, not primarily for your menu.

Let me explain this by adding a personal note. I have a Taurean friend in Washington who let me know that she was aware of her possible weakness in this regard. She is a gourmet cook, and her dinners are a delight, even for connoisseurs of haute cuisine. But when my husband, Jimmy, and I wish to repay her hospitality, we play safe by taking her and her husband to a fine restaurant. For though I enjoy cooking, I am unable to spend the time necessary to prepare a meal as painstakingly as you Taureans would wish.

As we continued to entertain each other in this way, it began to seem as if the basis for our friendship was only the excellent food we were eating. That hadn't been true at the beginning; we'd always had extensive interests in common, and we still enjoyed chatting about a wide range of subjects. But I sensed that our restrictive pattern of socializing was limiting a rewarding friendship. And—bless her for it—my friend realized it too. One day when I telephoned to make a date, I was just about to suggest a restaurant when she said, "Jeane, the weather is so marvelous. Why don't you just get some hot dogs and we'll have a cookout in your garden?"

We did, and it was great fun. It also meant a new beginning for our friendship, as a certain sense of competition and strain was banished. This was a perfect example of a Taurean recognizing her inborn traits and being sufficiently astute and gracious to offer a way out of the social dilemma both of us had helped to create.

All you Taureans can be tough competitors. Again, it is the bull in you. You want to win, but not from selfish motives. Your major concern is for the victory of your principles and beliefs. Like Simon, you are a zealot. Properly directed, that emotional inclination can make you a good friend, a dependable co-worker, and an inspiring organizer.

Moreover, because you care so much, you can make others care. That is the secret of your strength and the reason you can sometimes accomplish so much, uniting others to your own resolve. If you are puzzled as to why your ability to move others is only occasional, remember that you can succeed in that effort only when you allow your finer instincts to shape your relationships with those around you. You can be bullishly successful when you apply your drive to your many interests; but in personal matters, you triumph only when you expose the lamb side of your personality to the world.

Profit from the lessons painfully learned by your Apostle, Simon. As a young man, he was ready to die to take a few Romans to the grave with him. He was out for blood, as long as it was that of his enemies, as if the suffering caused by violence could ever be confined to a few. How often we have had to learn the folly of that dangerous assumption! For Simon, the initial attractiveness of Christ was that He seemed to be the leader who could unite the Jews as a political force. Once Christ became King, Simon thought, the Romans would be driven out of a resurgent Palestine.

It took three years of almost daily contact with Jesus for hotheaded Simon to comprehend his Master's teachings. Finally, he realized that the plan ordained by God did not divide people into nationalities, races, or classes determined by accidents of birth. Simon got the message, which even today many are not willing to accept: all mankind is one family. That was when Simon became a lamb. He no longer went among his countrymen preaching war against the Romans. Instead, he taught them love among all people. And that is the plan for us all.

Taurus, then, is the Zodiac sign of the practical person: the builder, the producer, the one who takes care of business, who gets the job done. Taureans are the kind of people we need today to share the world of tomorrow.

As your neighbors on this small planet, we need you Taureans far more than you need the rest of us. Luckily, it is one of those wonderful subtleties in the overall pattern of things that you are happiest when working for the good of others. In fact, all those traits which are yours by nature are the very ones most vital to the service of humanity.

Taureans are versatile, free spirits, kind and forgiving, responsible and strong, in will as well as in mind. You are:

- too loyal to be self-seeking
- too artistic to be an opportunist
- too tenacious to risk your ultimate goals to achieve short-term and temporary success
- too idealistic to sell out your principles for financial reward alone

Only a few Taureans will find themselves wealthy in a financial sense—as opposed to being rich in spiritual satisfaction—because the majority of those born under the sign of the Bull do not regard money as a primary aim in life.

For this reason, most Taureans make excellent teachers. Without thought of recompense, they are willing and able to guide and advise others, especially the young. By sharing their learning freely, they fortify an inner strength that enables them to reach spiritual heights to which others, not armed with their determination, will never ascend.

For you Taureans, the secret of a happy life is obvious: remain unselfish and stay true to your ideals.

The roster of prominent Taureans justifies that advice. Presidents Harry Truman (May 8), Ulysses Grant (April 27), James Monroe (April 28), and James Buchanan (April 23) were all children of the astral Bull. So, too, were Empress Catherine the Great of Russia (May 2), whose personal discipline enabled her to direct her millions of subjects, and Queen Isabella of Spain (April 22), whose beneficence toward Columbus aided in the discovery of America.

In literature, the contributions of William Shakespeare (April 23) have never been surpassed; and Taurean talent has marked the printed page from Anthony Trollope (April 24) and Honoré de

Balzac (May 20) to Vladimir Nabokov (April 22) and Rod McKuen (April 29).

In art, Taurean masters have included Salvador Dali (May 11); Thomas Gainsborough (May 14); and John James Audubon (April 26), the world's greatest painter of birds.

Music and the theater have been enriched by the fantastically diverse gifts of Tchaikovsky (May 7) and Liberace (May 16); of Irving Berlin (May 11) and Franz Lehár (April 30), the operetta king. Fred Astaire (May 10) and Audrey Hepburn (May 4) are Taurean performers, as are Orson Welles (May 6) and Bing Crosby (May 2).

The surging energy of Taureans is evident in the number of them who have achieved fame in athletics, including the world's best-loved boxer, Joe Louis (May 13); tennis great Pancho Gonzales (May 9); Erny Pinckert (May 1), famous football star of a few years ago; and Willie Mays (May 6), everybody's favorite baseball player.

Yours is a wide world, and you will realize your fullest potential as a participant in it and as a contributor to it if you combine bullish courage with the self-effacing tenderness of the lamb. Make that your blueprint for life, and you will achieve far more than you ever dreamed possible.

For a more detailed analysis of your own particular place in the eternal pattern of the heavens, we will review the distinctive characteristics of the various divisions within the sign of Taurus.

TAURUS—FIRST DIVISION *(April 28, May 1, 10, 19)*

As a Taurus One, you live under a very powerful planetary combination, which, with the exercise of foresight and self-control, should bring you great success. But it is crucial that the two halves of your nature work together to enable you to derive the full benefits which each can provide.

The usual Taurean quality of self-reliance is practically overdone in Simon's brethren of the First Division. You are utterly autonomous. By that, I mean your self-confidence makes you a one-man committee, a single voice with the force of a crowd. This can annoy some people; but, in general, it keeps you interested in life and others interested in you.

Yet there are dangers built into those admirable qualities. You have a tendency to overextend yourself, both in your work and in your personal relationships. That means you dilute your best efforts and fail to accomplish the deep potential of your many talents because no single one of them gets a fair chance to be shown off at its best.

The remedy is not to let short-range problems deter you from your long-range goals. Set goals for yourself that you can reach realistically and avoid taking on too much at one time. Remember that energy alone won't solve every problem. The bravest bull wears himself down charging about in the arena, and it is then that he becomes vulnerable to the matador. In addition to your self-confidence, as a Taurus One you also possess:

- excess generosity
- patience
- concern for others
- great powers of observation and deduction
- and above all, drive

Your natural openhandedness is not confined to your money and worldly goods. You are also generous, sometimes to a fault, with your time and talents. Don't you spend many hours on volunteer work and nonprofit projects? Because many people sense this habit of yours, you are often surrounded by a crowd of freeloaders and brain-pickers. People without the initiative or ability to think or act for themselves will unashamedly steal your ideas, and you are all too willing to allow them to do so.

This willingness stems from your desire to be helpful. You think you are teaching people to solve their problems by giving them sound advice and the benefit of your experience. But the effect of your generosity is that you frequently end up with their problems on your broad shoulders. That's when you overextend yourself, with ill effects to all. Altruism and selflessness are commendable, but there are limits.

So discriminate a little. Continue being helpful. Carry on your practice of helping other people help themselves. But then leave their problems right there! They *can* help themselves; you needn't do everything for them. In fact, it will be more beneficial to them if they have to face their own responsibilities without you. Remember that no one ever learned to walk by relying on a crutch. This might seem a hard thing for you to do because you are by nature gentle and concerned. It is those inherent qualities which suit your personality to a teaching role.

Like your Apostle, Simon, you, too, can be goaded to strong action, even to violence, by injustice or dishonesty. These evils are always a part of life; and you must realize that this world's wrongs won't be changed by adding to them, but only by exercising patience and its accompanying blessings of peace and brotherhood.

As a Taurus One, you have a natural concern for others. That is a part of your makeup as a teacher. It also means there are pitfalls waiting for you if you allow your own interests to be sidetracked for the schemes of others.

You should therefore make some definite decisions early in life. Probably the most important one is your choice of career. You are so gifted that it would be unwise for me to suggest only a few prospects for you. You have almost endless choices of occupations to follow. Whichever you do select, make that decision early and determine to stay with it, regardless of the detours you are tempted to make for the sake of others. Those disruptions and postponements will force you to take much longer than necessary to achieve your goals, unless you know what you want and keep working toward it.

Although I will not specify one career for you, do consider that most Taureans, and especially those of the First Division, have exceptional problem-solving abilities. They untangle knotty questions on a simple basis of observation, knowledge, and deduction, along with a healthy measure of intuition. So if you are thinking about a career as a medical diagnostician, a lawyer, or a skilled auto mechanic, you are already considering strong areas for Taurean talent. Taurean women often find fulfillment as teachers of scientific subjects or as supervisors in businesses that handle cost estimates.

Whatever your eventual profession, your colleagues will sense your drive, your almost animal determination to forge ahead and do a superb job. This tremendous asset characterizes you more than those born under any other Zodiac sign.

COLORS: Your colors reflect the successful side of your long life. Your emotive vibrations react best to gold, orange, or golden bronze, as if those shades subconsciously remind you, and those around you, of the darkly gleaming sands of the arena in which a charging bull delights the viewers with his prowess. Green is another color of success, and so it naturally shows strongly in your spectrum. Complementary hues are blue, white, and cream; and by combining their mild reassurance with flashes of golden assertiveness, you can let the world know that beneath your external vigor is a mild lamb, perhaps a cream-colored one with a light blue ribbon around its neck.

Do not be embarrassed by that comparison. If it describes you, be proud of it!

HEALTH: The powerful restlessness of Taurus can keep you overly active, to the detriment of your health. You must be sure to get enough rest and relaxation. Although you do have a strong constitution and tremendous vitality, even the most powerful engines need maintenance or they will break down. And that is the risk you face from your ceaseless activity.

With huge expenditures of energy, you do need adequate rest and sensible food, or you will wear out long before your time. Be systematic about recreation and sleep, or you will fail to get enough of both. With your heavy schedule, you must plan for them. When you chart your week ahead, see to it that you reserve sufficient time to do nothing but loaf. And because you are the type who plans to accomplish too much even during a vacation, you should spend your free time away from business or household duties in long weekends at a resort or secluded retreat rather than trying to sight-see your way through Europe in two weeks.

MONEY: As a Taurus One, you will be luckier than most Taureans in money matters, but you still have a financial blind spot. Your generosity is your basic flaw here. Resist that impulse to grab the check. Turn your back on the expensive present you were considering for a friend. Although your blind faith that "something will turn up" has usually proved correct, stop living beyond your means. That's the only way you will ever avoid all those first-of-the-month worries when your bills come in.

Avoid the get-rich-quick schemes that just "can't fail." You already know they can collapse and usually do. It is only your urgent need for action which tempts you into them. In money matters, use the same rules of moderation and forward planning that you should apply to your health regimen. The results will be not only a long life but also a comfortable one.

RELATIONSHIPS: Because of your outgoing, self-sacrificing nature, people invariably relate well to you. But beware of those who are friendly for the wrong reasons. A few wish only to exploit you. With your analytical mind, you should have no trouble deciding which friends are for real.

You have few problems other than that. Your true friends tend to be fiercely loyal to you, for they recognize that you would, and sometimes do, give anything for them. But remember that you don't have to keep giving all the time.

How does all this apply to that one person who is closest to you, who holds a place in your life approached by no one else? Consider for a moment what you have already learned about yourself. What have you to offer? The answer should be clear: everything he or she needs! If there is presently trouble between you—occasional misunderstandings, sharp words, lingering doubts—you needn't do more, but less. Stop trying to be what you are not, or to say what you do not mean, or to act like someone else. The Taurean path to happiness, in love as in all else, is to let your tender actions reveal what you may be unable to put into words.

TAURUS–SECOND DIVISION *(April 20, 29, May 2, 11, 20)*

As a Taurus Two, you are among the most unworldly of the Taureans. Religion is probably the most important factor in your life; and you are interested in mystical studies, spiritualism, and the occult.

Just as the teachings of Christ became the motivating force in Simon's life during his middle years, so do Taureans of the Second Division, already inclined toward spiritual matters, become still more involved in religious activity as they grow older.

They also have a lively interest in the human psyche. Like Taurean Sigmund Freud, who forever altered the field of psychological research, they are fascinated by the interface between the soul and the mind, that overlapping area between the spirit and human intelligence. This interest could be an indication of the role which you have been assigned in God's overall plan for the world. For men do not have to be of one mind in order to be of one brotherhood, and the mind is as good a route to the fellowship of souls as any other.

When you Taureans of the Second Division perceive this special interest of yours early in life, you often seek a career in religion or in the mental sciences, or even in both. When you make the same discovery about yourselves later in life, you take up similar studies as a hobby rather than as a profession, and are likely to become expert in them.

It is significant and revealing that Pierre Teilhard de Chardin, the Jesuit paleontologist who spent his lifetime reconciling religion and science, was a Taurean born on May 1, a few hours too soon to join you Taureans in the Second Division, but nonetheless sharing the same planetary influences that you experience.

In addition to your fascination with the human mind's participation in religious experiences, you have other qualities which reinforce that interest. You are:

- imaginative
- responsive to beauty
- restless
- romantic

Your imagination leads to artistic expression, whether in writing or art, in music or acting. And you always have the potential to excel because you apply spiritual values to your efforts.

Your creative sensitivities are reflected in your personal life. You respond enthusiastically to beautiful things and surround yourself with them. Look at your home, your place of business, your choice of clothes, your car, even your choice of friends. All of these reflect your superior taste. They may not be the most expensive in the world, but they tend to have a certain charm, to display an enduring style. You are never attracted by the garish or the extreme.

But notice how even an asset can become a weakness. Because you have many friends, you are typically Taurean in allowing them too much of your time, thereby interfering with your personal growth in important matters. Try to limit your closest friends to those who share your active interests. That way, you will be better able to realize your potential for creative expression.

There is a certain restlessness in you. It results from your constant searching for the secrets of your own mind, your attempts to define the relationship between your soul and the external world. This vague uneasiness may cause you to change your residence many times during your life. When you are young, this could lead you to travel; but as you mature and better understand yourself, this potentially disruptive trait will decline and you will be increasingly content with the life you lead.

Your strong romantic impulses could become another weakness for you. You regard too highly new relationships with members of the opposite sex. To safeguard your real happiness in matters of the heart, you will have to learn, perhaps the hard way, that men and women can have valuable friendships without the intrusion of romance, emotional dependence, or marriage.

You could learn this lesson too late. Early in life, you might rush into what could become an unfortunate marriage, and later the same unrestrained romanticism could jeopardize a subsequent union.

Know this weakness for what it is. Interpersonal relations are seldom like the fairy-tale versions about Prince Charming and the beautiful damsel. Your affections need not always become sexual affairs. Often, the most enriching ties are those between platonic friends, who are free to fill one another's lives with their own good qualities without demanding any commitments or restrictions in return.

COLORS: Your magnetic vibrations sometimes need a boost to keep you stepping lively. By wearing light blues and greens, you can draw yourself out of too much contemplation while expressing the association you feel with the clear sky and the fertile earth. Isn't that the universal relationship you feel during your moments of mystical introspection? Then don't be shy about it! And when your spirit soars, as if you want to hug all of humanity, level off your enthusiasm by favoring creams and pale grays. Remember that even the bright blue vault of heaven must sometimes be wrapped in cloudy whites.

MONEY: Face up to it now: money will be a problem all your life. At least you can understand why. Your restlessness is one reason. You will not want to stay with any one organization long enough to move up within it. You will also change jobs, even at a lower salary, just because the new one can offer the chance to work more closely with your special interests. That is fine and admirable, as long as your dependents are not deprived of their needs as a sacrifice to your ideals.

Better news awaits you in the future, when your finances will take an upturn, but even that will not make you rich. It is possible that you will be hired by a research company or similar organization for which you had earlier worked as a volunteer. If so, you will be more than happy.

HEALTH: Be especially wary of chills, influenza, and colds that linger more than a few days in the lungs or throat. Sinus trouble is apt to prove a nuisance as you grow older, and you will probably have an allergy or two.

For some reason, there is a widespread belief that Taureans must be especially careful of their hearing and of infections in the nose, ears, and mastoid area. It will not hurt to have a specialist examine you occasionally and to have tests made if you suspect an oncoming illness.

RELATIONSHIPS: Although you gravitate toward people with artistic tendencies, you easily form friendships with all kinds of individuals. Be more selective about those persons to whom you give large amounts of your time, or your career and talents can suffer from dilution of effort. Because you tend to be a poor marriage prospect, due to your unrestrained romantic tendencies, you could have an early, and unhappy, marriage. Notice that I said "could have." You can't blame the stars for every disappointment. Your marriage partner will deserve your best efforts. You *can* be happily wed if you have the honesty and courage to recognize your wandering tendencies and to restrain them.

TAURUS–THIRD DIVISION *(April 21, 30, May 3, 12)*

As a Taurus Three, you have so many assets that you would really have to make an effort to avoid success. You have the world in your pocket, guaranteeing every good fortune you could wish. You even possess that rare commodity in our modern world: common sense.

There is one booby trap in your life, but even that can be avoided if you use your native wit. At the risk of inflating your ego, I have to admit that you are:

- hard-working
- infuriated by injustice, as a righter of wrongs
- personally charming and talented
- ever ready for new challenges

In short, you are the Taurean most likely to succeed. You work hard even at play. Personal achievement means everything to you, and you will not tolerate halfway measures. This rigor can turn you into a loner, but that touch of isolation suits you. You probably prefer casual relationships anyway, because you know that extensive personal involvement can slow you down and hold you back from your goals.

You expect much from life, and not only in the material sense. It has always been important to you to feel of value, to your friends and to society at large. In fact, you are of value. Like Simon, you are angered by injustice and inequity. You are more than a well-wisher and sincere talker. You not only fight the perpetrators of evil but also help their victims. In this regard, you remind me of the Chinese saying: "If you give a man a fish, you give him a meal. But teach him how to fish and you feed him forever." That could be the motto of a Taurus Three.

With all your strengths, you can succeed at whatever you attempt. In fact, your very charm and wide range of talents can create, let us say, a desirable dilemma. For you will receive so many career opportunities that you will have difficulty deciding which one to take. Let your Taurean intuition be your guide. Equally important, never hesitate to admit it when you realize you have made a false start.

Face it, you *are* inclined to be impulsive, getting too enthusiastic about people and projects, many of which will disappoint you. Don't fret over them. Your invariable stamina may be too much for those around you to take. You will often leave other people behind when they cannot stand the kitchen heat in which you thrive.

For you, every day is a fresh challenge. Once you have gained a victory, you want to move on. You feel compelled to hurry on to the next adventure life has to offer. This characteristic often makes you lonely, even though you are not necessarily alone. It provokes frequent changes in your social environment. But that is the price of success.

Now we come to examine the booby trap I mentioned earlier. You might fall into it several times, so the sooner you get to know it the better off you will be. I am referring to your love life.

Because of your impulsiveness, your habit of making snap judgments, and your rampant enthusiasm, you are predisposed to mistakes in love. An early marriage is not usually good for you, as you may have already discovered.

The reason for your likelihood of romantic disappointment is that you will continue to grow as an individual throughout your life. If you marry early, you will not know whether, with the passage of time, your new partner will want to settle down, take root, and watch the world pass by. Needless to say, that life-style would be the opposite of yours. With an unresolved conflict like that, intimate communication and genial sharing stop, and eventually there are two married strangers living under the same roof, alone in everything but their names.

There is great pain in a faulty marriage, and the best way for a

Taurus Three to avoid it is to mistrust impulsive romantic reactions until you are out of your twenties. You will then have a clearer idea of the social and intellectual fields for which you are headed. By charting your own spiritual location for the future, you will know where your best marriage will be made.

Taureans of the Third Division tend to rise to the highest economic and social strata because that is where they belong! Material possessions will not mean much to you in themselves, only as symbols of your successful circumstances.

Your heart will always be with the underdog, and in your later years, you will probably make substantial donations to charities and become active in philanthropic organizations. Your guiding theme throughout life will be to serve others rather than yourself.

COLORS: So vital to others, color differences are not important to you. Your intuition usually guides you correctly, telling you what shades you should wear and when. Of course, the standard Taurean palette of blue, cream, and white, when used to decorate your living quarters, ensures a psychologically comfortable environment for your spirit. It is not surprising that purple and mauve are added to your favored colors. After all, for the most successful of the Taureans, a touch of royal purple is only appropriate.

MONEY: Money will never be a serious problem for you, but will seem to be drawn your way. In fact, your major economic difficulty will be deciding which opportunity is the best. Avoid rash decisions, not merely to protect your finances but also to prevent wear on yourself.

HEALTH: The same rule must be repeated: save wear on yourself. The greatest demands on you will come during the early years of your professional or childbearing life. Although you have tremendous reserves of energy, you must not waste them. There is a long life ahead of you, but only if you budget your resources properly.

RELATIONSHIPS: You are a charmer. There is nothing you cannot do, no heart you cannot win. Along with that power comes equally great responsibility. Make sure your motives are sincere. Otherwise, despite your passing triumphs, you could be the loser in the long run. In love, as in all else, suppress those impulses to brash action which constitute your fundamental weakness. To guarantee your own contentment, marry later in life, and be prepared for a partner whose intellectual capabilities demand a degree of individuality and free expression.

TAURUS–FOURTH DIVISION *(April 22, May 4, 13)*

Resign yourself to the fact that a Taurus in the Fourth Division does not have an easy life but does have a good one. You were born under a planetary combination that promises rewards and distinction, but you must work hard for them and face occasional setbacks on the road to happiness.

You have the advantage of knowing that, like Simon, you are likely to discover a way of life that is far from dull or ordinary. At least one major career change awaits you. It will be suddenly and unexpectedly before you. At first, you may not even recognize the offer or may decline to act on it. But when you do see it for what it is, you will be wise to go ahead despite its uncertainties. For it will be the outstanding chance of your lifetime.

That eventual good fortune will result from your contact with some already successful, perhaps famous, person. Here again, you are so much like Simon, whose life was radically changed when he met Christ. As in his case, your destiny will involve travel, some hardship, and much personal satisfaction. In terms of psychological characteristics, you are:

- possessed of a good sense of humor, which will come in handy
- curious
- individualistic
- intuitive and impractical

You often need your strain of good humor because, from time to time, you think everything in the world just isn't up to your standards. That mood develops when you have so many irons in the fire that you cannot tend them all at once. Consequently, some of your dealings develop too quickly, and you fear losing control of things. For this reason, you must constantly return to matters that were left incomplete, require your attention, or need to be patched up. This is true whether it involves a business project or a personal relationship. All that innate humor in you serves to release your frustration and prevent your quitting before the work is all over. In fact, as a Taurean, you are not likely to quit as long as you can still breathe. In such ways, God gives us the strengths we need for our own tasks in life.

Another controlling trait is your curiosity. For you, happiness means diversity. Wandering from the beaten path of custom and tradition, you will discover new things in life. Your curiosity is not easily satisfied and can lead you into endless experiments. By following through with one or two of your innovative ideas, you could become wealthy.

Your marriage may experience problems originating in your fascination with diversity. Your deeply individualistic spirit tends to cause trouble for you in any liaison or partnership, and marriage is no exception to this pattern. You find it difficult, often impossible, to adapt to beliefs you do not share, or even to tolerate them. This doesn't mean that marriage isn't a viable alternative for you. It only means that you should choose your mate very carefully indeed, and that you should utilize that bullish determination of yours not to get your own way but to make your marriage work.

You tend to be intuitive rather than logical. Possessing a strong psychic streak, you could come to depend on it in all your dealings. This will make you creative rather than practical. But that needn't be a handicap. Indeed, it can often be quite the opposite!

You are a free spirit who shuns crowds. These are your instincts at work, protecting you because, whether you know it or not, only in solitude can you elaborate your best ideas and develop your inspirations free from disturbing pressures. However, being a lone wolf does not mean you should become a hermit. Stay out in the world. It needs your unique contributions.

COLORS: The shades of your magnetic aura range as widely as your talents. To enhance the vibrations of your personality, wear golds and yellows and browns. Electric tones of blue can convey to others your essentially optimistic sense of humor, finding some benefit even in disappointments. When you feel you should slow down and restrain your zealous impulses, especially when you are trying to become more tolerant of others, a touch of gray can help to calm you. It can also help you to appreciate that everything is not definite in this world, not entirely black or white. Remember that your colors are an opportunity for self-expression, not a set of restrictions. So use them freely and, most of all, enjoy them.

MONEY: You will not make your fortune in ordinary ways.

A nine-to-five routine is not for you. Find a basic occupation that can pay your bills and then branch out in your spare time into pursuits that fulfill your talents. Here is an example from my own knowledge. A Taurus Four friend of mine in Chicago continued to work as a secretary after she married. But now that she had a home to run, she became interested in interior decorating. She developed her interests along that line, and now has a secretary of her own in her successful business in home furnishings. She demonstrates a trait common to Fourth Division Taureans. You take your hobbies seriously, and could turn them into profitable occupations which would eventually supersede your job.

HEALTH: During adulthood, your good health depends upon keeping yourself free from worry and stress. You may suffer ailments difficult to diagnose: headaches and stomach cramps, back pains and general depression. These vague ills are often attributable to overexertion. Chills, colds, influenza, and lung inflammations are common among Taureans of the Fourth Division. Their remedy is to eat lightly and often. Do not fear to try unconventional foods, but never bring your problems to the dinner table with you. Discover for yourself that life is a joy, not a job. Once you make yourself live life fully, you will never look back on past patterns of worry.

RELATIONSHIPS: Close personal ties are not always easy for you to sustain because you have a highly individual spirit. You do not suffer fools lightly. Without beating around the bush, you speak your mind bluntly, and in the process, you are not always as tolerant as you should be. So choose your friends with care; choose your mate with even more deliberation. Trust your intuition, but only after your contemplation and self-examination assure you that you are not merely acting on impulse. A fulfilling love life, stable and enduring, is indeed possible for you. But it will not happen by accident. You must build for it and preserve it with effort and concern.

TAURUS—FIFTH DIVISION *(April 23, May 5, 14)*

What a bright person you are! As a Taurus Five, you have been gifted with exceptionally fine mental abilities. All those born under the planetary combination of the Fifth Division have unusual keenness, originality, and alertness of mind. Those qualities are complemented by good reasoning powers, fine observation, and an analytical bent.

Yet there is a hidden snag among all those blessings. Your personality leads you to go along with life for the ride, so to speak. Of all the Taureans, you are least aggressive, perhaps because you realize the futility of it. You are most like the lamb and least like the bull. Appealing as that might sound at first, it actually means that you are subduing one vital side of your personality and therefore losing the independence of spirit which you deserve as a birthright. You allow yourself to be too easily led and thereby neglect your own potential for leadership. Stop waiting around to be asked or ordered. Get on with your life! And trust in your intelligence to discover what is right.

The very fact that you were born at all means you have a part to play in the cosmic plan of mankind's development and happiness. We each have our own orbit to follow; and, like planets circulating through the depths of space, we affect others as we pass by them. For the good of all, you must hold to your orbit.

Taureans of the Fifth Division tend to be pulled from their own proper paths and to be drawn into those of other planets. Don't let this happen! Refuse to be swayed or dominated. Like Simon, you can have an effective life if you just get involved with matters important to you and take over the responsibility for them. Be positive.

Remember that although Simon changed from being a political activist to being an Apostle, he did not change completely from bull to lamb. He carried his new beliefs forward and even died for them.

The qualities most prominent in your personality—brilliance, detachment, a lack of demonstrative action—usually affect you in these ways:

• Your brilliance enables you to solve the everyday problems of life. But you are inclined to do what you are told, even when you know your own judgment might be different and better. Despite your good intentions, that is not an honest habit, because it doesn't give your own capabilities a fair chance.

• Your detachment from ordinary life means you don't like to settle on one fixed career. Your wide range of interests makes it hard for you to decide on one job or profession. Despite the excellence of your work, you will not always receive rightful recognition for it. So meditate long and well on what may be your best course of action, and prepare to commit yourself to it.

• Your inherent reserve, your distaste for demonstrating the way you feel, means you hold something of yourself back from others. People are understandably cautious about you. They sense you are not sharing yourself with them, and they wonder why. If you want to alter that situation, the remedy is easy: try to be more outgoing and extroverted.

COLORS: Do you want to start reaching out to others? You can do it! Think yourself into it. Wear bright colors. Turquoise is especially good. Its vibrance reminds us of the brilliant sun and gleaming minerals of the southwestern desert from which it comes. How appropriate it would be when you want encouragement in becoming more open and exuberant!

Similarly, gold, yellow, and light brown—all of which are suited to Taurean vibrations—will help you come out of your shell. Lavish a buttercup outfit on yourself or buy a canary tie. You will be surprised at their effect on the way you react to those around you.

MONEY: You will probably be fortunate in money matters. Both your astrological combination of planets and your inborn intelligence dictate that. You (and your friends as well) will be amazed at the ease with which you make money. The best bets for your spirit of enterprise are real estate and securities. Use your capital to buy into a company where your diverse talents will have free rein to explore and innovate.

HEALTH: You have a tendency toward nervous disorders. More than anything else, being more outgoing with others will help you combat that disposition. You are apt to require major surgery more than once, and are inclined to suffer from inflammation and circulatory diseases, especially of the abdomen.

RELATIONSHIPS: Your reserve with people means that those who love you have doubts about your ability to love them in return. Can you blame them when you hold back from expressing your affection? This inadequacy accounts for the brevity of your romances and for the poor prospects you face in matrimony.

It need not be that way. You can try to confide in more people, especially those dear to you. Realize that it is not undignified or shameful to do so. People will love and respect you more for it.

After all, intelligence cannot substitute for that closeness of body and soul which enables lovers to face all things with contentment and joy.

TAURUS–SIXTH DIVISION *(April 24, May 6, 15)*

Above all other Taureans, you of the Sixth Division have the greatest chance for happiness. You have an immense capacity to love, and you are happiest when giving your affection to others. Of course, that means you receive a lot of love in return. How rich that makes you, no matter what your bank balance may be! You also have a strong love of God, and will accomplish great things for Him. You are:

- most rewarded when doing good for others
- a joiner of groups
- skilled in administration
- frequently religious

Your rewards in this life will not be measured in material terms. They will be more personal to you: a constant, warm glow from the knowledge of the good you have done. But remember, there are drawbacks in being a do-gooder.

Many people don't want to be helped, by you or anyone else. They don't want to have to thank others or feel obligated to them. Of course, your need to assist others doesn't require their gratitude; but unless you understand the perversities of human nature, specifically the kind of person who cannot stand to be in your debt, you will be hurt and bewildered, time and again, by their ingratitude.

Although you are a great joiner of organizations and clubs, you are not trying to fulfill a hidden need to belong. Quite the contrary. You possess inner strengths which make you independent. The reason you join is that you believe you can best help others through your group activities and interests. As a consequence, much of your time will go to civic, ecclesiastical, and youth groups. Less of your effort will be directed toward professional organizations, while a great deal of it will serve coordinated activities for social improvement.

That is all fine, but do not neglect your loved ones. I know of women who get up at dawn to put flowers on the church altar while their children go to school without breakfast. The same is true for civic-minded men who spend several days each month at community meetings and never play with or counsel their own children. You idealistic Taurus Six parents can be a source of pride and inspiration to your offspring, but make sure you set aside ample time for their needs.

You have the skills necessary to be an administrator, and are consequently much in demand among the groups you belong to. You should do all you can to develop these abilities, and might consider such jobs as hospital administrator, social worker, or field representative for a philanthropic organization.

You also have a strong religious strain in you. You seek your rewards in helping people in need. It is as if God Himself had personally revealed to you His plan for the world, and you become impatient to carry out His mission. And that, Taurus Sixes, is exactly what you were meant to do and are doing!

Because you do not put labels on different kinds of love, you are often astonished when the platonic love you show for a member of the opposite sex is interpreted wrongly. Without proper self-control, you face many brief and meaningless love affairs with people who have no true love in them at all. At such times, you must remember that your greatest love is what you share with God. Acting with that realization in mind, you will definitely experience all the love that is promised in your stars.

COLORS: Your warmheartedness and ample affection are reflected in your magnetic color spectrum. It is nearly all-encompassing! You have no unsympathetic colors. But your best shades are those with which the Creator filled most of His world: blue and green. White and cream, mauve and purple are also beneficial. Because of your concern for others, you will find it useful to wear and to live among colors that will make people around you feel at ease. As for yourself, because your spirit seeks the good in everyone, you will also appreciate beauty in every hue on earth. It is no exaggeration to say that your soul is filled with rainbows, and at their end is no pot of gold but the love you dispense so freely.

MONEY: Because you care little about money, you will always seem to have more than you need. The truth is that you are giving away so much of yourself that the Lord is providing for you.

Don't bother with investments, for you will be too busy to look after them. Save a little money each week. It will help you meet emergencies later in life. But monetary success is not in your stars.

HEALTH: From a good start in life, blessed with an excellent constitution and good looks and a fine physique, you could begin to dig your grave with your own teeth by overeating. If you indulge yourself in that manner, you will become less active physically. That can be a fatal combination. So be especially careful about your diet and begin a gentle program of easy exercises. Your service to your fellows is far too precious to be cut short by foolish neglect of your health.

RELATIONSHIPS: As I said earlier, you must beware of shallow, superficial affairs with members of the opposite sex. They will always be attracted to your warm and loving personality. It is your responsibility, however, to make sure they are attracted for the right reasons. If you fail to do so, you will surely be hurt. Your marriage partner will deserve more attention than you are apt to provide. So reduce your worthy extracurricular activities and spend more time with your spouse. Charity is always good, but it is best brought to your home.

TAURUS–SEVENTH DIVISION *(April 25, May 7, 16)*

The number seven is of great significance in astrology and carries with it all kinds of connotations. Because of their special planetary influences, Taurus Sevens find that their lives center around two seemingly disparate subjects.

You Taurus Sevens usually have two major passions in life: a fascination with the mysterious and occult and an interest in history. You frequently visit museums, read history, and feel an affinity for the past and its personalities. Meanwhile, your curiosity about the occult leads you to study it in your own way, perhaps informally by random reading. Only after some time has passed in these pursuits will you sense that they may be related, that there is an essential connection between the world of the past and the realm of the supernatural. Whether you discover that connection, and profit spiritually from it, is entirely up to you.

Psychic gifts are not exclusively within the domain of any one

Zodiac sign or division within it. We are each a part of eternity and have in us a latent awareness of our eternal origin and destination. But Taureans of the Seventh Division are more likely than most of us to experience remarkable presentiments and dreams and yet still be sufficiently practical and skeptical to feel uneasy when they come true. It is as if you do not want to recognize the facts, the truly startling facts, about yourself.

You have probably had the disconcerting experience of meeting total strangers and knowing that something has recently happened to them, or is about to. You occasionally see mental images of an event you know nothing about and later read about in a newspaper.

There is nothing wrong with you. Believe me, I should know! Make a detailed study of these experiences and of all psychic matters in your life so that you can be aware of what is happening to you. I might add that if you do possess special psychic powers, then they are a gift to you, and you have an obligation to develop them so that you may use them for the good of all.

Apart from your psychic abilities, you have several other positive qualities. You are:

- inventive
- gregarious and extroverted
- kindhearted
- charitable

Although you are inventive, you don't usually follow through on your innovations. By a curious lapse of Taurean character, you seem satisfied with just proving to yourself that your mechanical skills are above average. And so you stop right there, with your ideas vindicated but not applied to the problems they could solve for others.

You like to give large parties. In fact, you enjoy being involved in any activity that includes a large number of people. You are not only a good conversationalist but also an adept public speaker, if you seek out opportunities to develop your ability. Because of your sociability and eloquence, politics could provide a bright future; but you tend to be more content with industrial or labor concerns. In any case, your activities certainly are not limited to any one field of endeavor.

Because you are gregarious, you don't usually adjust well to the narrow horizons of marriage. That is why, like most Taureans, you are well advised to marry later in life.

Despite possible marital difficulties, you are kindhearted, open-handed, and have depths of patience with your own problems and the troubles of other people. You are also exceptional in that you make regular and handsome donations to charity. For all that, you are still independent of mind and don't like to have others suggest how you should spend your money. Although you are benevolent with your prosperity, your quite understandable attitude declares, "It's mine. I'll spend it the way I please."

COLORS: In order to project your dynamic nature, your best colors are green, gray, cream, and white. Not at all by accident, these are the shades of the past. They recall the delicate marble of old sculpture, the faded pages of dusty volumes of forgotten lore, the mossy blankets that cover ancient burial sites. All varieties of blue also suit your magnetic aura. Certain jewels are lucky too, as well as the colors named for them: emerald, pearl, and turquoise. Balance your interest in history with flashes of blue that will remind you of this day's business and tomorrow's inevitable dawn.

MONEY: In your younger years, your business and personal life will most likely be plagued by financial troubles. Take heart, for there is every indication that matters will steadily improve. You will master them through your own efforts and abilities, without any dependence on lucky breaks. You will make it alone, and can deservedly take satisfaction in the good things that come your way.

HEALTH: In general, you will not be too robust and will tire easily. That isn't due to any inherent weakness but to your persistent attempts to accomplish too much too soon. You are liable to suffer an intestinal ailment, so be careful what you eat and drink at those big parties you enjoy so much. Your physical stamina is not equal to the demands which your nervous energy places upon it. This could cause occasional spells of mental depression, though that isn't inevitable. To avoid such depression, all you need is regular rest and distraction from your hurried concerns.

RELATIONSHIPS: Because of your sociable nature and relish for crowds, you will always form friendships easily, and they will tend to last longer than those of most other people. Your self-effacing attitude toward your talents will endear you to some acquaintances, who appreciate your modesty and are reassured by it.

Be cautious about straining your relationships with loved ones. Don't automatically assume that they, like you, are not particularly proud of their accomplishments. Most people need compliments and enjoy being praised for their success.

With your uncanny ability to see things others do not notice and to feel the future before it occurs, you have reason to be confident of discovering, sooner or later, that special individual with whom you can combine the past and the present in joyful expectations of tomorrow.

TAURUS–EIGHTH DIVISION *(April 26, May 8, 17)*

Yours, Taurus Eight, is a life of contradictions. For every period of good fortune, there will be a subsequent reversal of luck. For every positive or negative situation you encounter, you will later meet with its opposite. And through it all, you will be more the creature of circumstances than of your own decisions.

The extent to which you learn to cope with those ups and downs will be the major factor in shaping yourself and your future. With the personal assets you have been given, however, there is every reason to expect that you can meet both good times and bad head on. You're a solid package with these attributes:

- a deep, thoughtful nature
- a craving for affection
- reserve in your dealings with others
- the ability to work hard

Intellectually well equipped, you possess an inborn intelligence of which you can be proud. You are both thoughtful and sober. Consequently, you are cautious and reserved with other people. In matters affecting your career or life-style, you are deliberate and slow to act, but once you are committed to a decision, determined to carry it through.

Like Simon, you are adamant once you are devoted to a cause, but you are slow to be convinced and wary of being misled.

You crave affection and relish the outward signs of others' love for you. But, paradoxically, while you want displays of their regard, you are so reserved that you decline to show similar, reciprocal affection for them. This reaction on your part could make people think you dislike all such demonstrations of affection. You seem to be cool and distant, while only you know the truth about your hungering for their esteem. You fail to communicate your feelings to those who need to know them. That is why, at times, you feel isolated and unwanted. You are the kind of person who declares that you don't want any birthday presents and then are hurt because you don't receive any.

Because you are industrious and will succeed on your own, others who are not so fortunate will want to share your success, even though they don't deserve it. To turn around the words of an old song, your silver clouds may have a darker lining. Relatives will depend on you and, deliberately or not, will impose on you. You should prepare for the headaches caused by their exploitation of your sympathy. It is no pleasure to be known as an easy touch.

Your best chances for happiness will come from your work and your ability, if you do develop it, to roll with the punches of life. This should not sound pessimistic. Your future is by no means gloomy, not when you have so many enviable qualities. Moreover, your chief fault, your exaggerated reserve, can easily be overcome, although it will take time for you to climb out of your shell.

COLORS: To break your undesirable pattern of emotional restraint, to teach yourself to be more freely expressive with your feelings, use color to increase the intensity of your magnetic vibrations. Yellow, orange, and golden browns are best; but greens and blues can be effective too. Some jewelry is lucky for you, especially amber, green jade, and pearls. Remember, when someone compliments you on your golden tie, your sunshine-bright hat, or your green and blue jacket, express your delight at the compliment and return it with interest. That's the first step in securing the affection you need and shedding the reserve you don't need.

MONEY: Like the tortoise of the fable, you will reach your goal in the end. Because of your natural caution, your economic fortunes will only rise slowly throughout your life. There will be no dramatic successes in the stock market, no fabulous profits from risky investments.

Your major financial setbacks will be in the nature of bad loans to relatives. Long-term investments suit your personality and are recommended by the pattern of your stars. Consider real estate as an avenue for your surplus capital, especially land development deals. Chancy as they are, your habit of prolonged deliberation before acting will usually keep you on the safe side.

HEALTH: Your solid, somewhat phlegmatic constitution is robust. But without sufficient care, you will experience gastric problems and rheumatism. If possible, you should live in a high, dry climate. The American Southwest, with its perfectly suited environment and potential for land sales, could be ideal for you, both physically and economically.

RELATIONSHIPS: Here, too, you avoid extremes and are not given to great passions. You are predictable and sometimes considered dull, though dependable. Learn to shake up old relationships now and then with an unexpected action that will lift you out of the ruts of life. From time to time, make people remember that you are an individual. They too often think of you as old faithful, always there, never changing.

Of course, that image of you can be comfortable, both to them and to you. But if you want to enjoy livelier relationships with those close to you, whether your friends or romantic partners, then it is important that you initiate a fresh and exciting atmosphere by becoming less constrained and more demonstrative of your affections. Then, when the time comes, as it surely will, when you desperately want to express your love for one irreplaceable individual, you will be prepared to abandon your reserve forever. The rewards will be too great to refuse.

TAURUS–NINTH DIVISION *(April 27, May 9, 18)*

Unlike your close Taurean kin in the Eighth Division, whose planetary combinations you may have missed by only a few hours, you Taurus Nines were born under a powerful arrangement of heavenly bodies which ensures for you a life that is eventful, tumultuous, and sometimes mercurial.

Your life will contain danger and upheaval, conflict and zest. But you have been given the courage and willpower to come out triumphant after all. You belong at the top of the ladder and usually get there after considerable battling. En route, however, you collect more than your share of enemies; for you are often:

- blunt and outspoken

- undiplomatic
- hard-working and hard-playing
- strong-willed

You are already convinced, and rightly so, that you were destined for success; and so you are determined to obtain it. In short, your makeup reflects more of Simon the Zealot than of Simon the Apostle.

Your life-style has a fury about it that others will attribute to frustration. But that is not the cause. Rather, it is bullish willfulness. Seeing your goal, you go right for it. And in the going, you will trample the few people who are in the way rather than stop or make a detour. Having marked your objective, you will reach it at whatever cost.

Your direct approach to life makes your blunt outspokenness the major weapon in your psychological armory. Although you possess great talent, especially for organizing, you provoke opposition and resentment by your very drive and take-charge attitude.

Your desire for grandly ambitious schemes arouses jealousy and creates enmity which you can ill afford. You can, and often do, garner wealth and power, but only at great cost. You invariably have heavy expenses and sometimes are forced into long, expensive legal actions. These occasionally require you to pay substantial damages; and as a result, you may even receive threats against your person.

The stellar patterns for your life predict that you will suffer injuries and be involved in serious accidents, usually because of your tanklike attack on life. The common remedy for all these ills should be obvious: slow down and learn the art of diplomacy.

As a Ninth Division Taurus, you not only work hard, you also play the same way. You are inclined to overdo all your activities. When business or your job goes badly, you plunge headlong into relaxations that are hardly restful. You drink too much, gamble recklessly, and excessively indulge your sexual appetite. Even so, your bullish stamina provides tremendous powers of recovery. Once you regain your fascination with your work, you hurry back to the grindstone with as much enthusiasm as you left it for rigorous amusements.

Needless to say, your will is powerful, perhaps too strong; and you will accomplish your ambitions if you persist in the same one long enough. You will attain the heights, all right, but scarred and worn by battle.

COLORS: You hardly need colors to enhance your vibrations, but rather to tone them down! To do that, cream, white, and pale yellow will work wonders. The calming effect of pastel shades can reduce your abrasiveness and reassure people you meet that you are not entirely force and passion. Among darker shades, subdued browns and greens are best for you, probably because they bring to your hectic affairs a reminder of cool forests and stable growing things.

MONEY: You will make money, a lot of money, despite the great amounts you will lose on lawsuits. You could have a calmer and better life if you had more patience and less drive. You would also cause less worry and sorrow among those who love you. Whereas some Taureans have too much lamb in them for their own good, you Taurean Nines are the ones with too much of the bull.

HEALTH: You have a magnificent, animal-like vitality. Your constitution seems able to take all the strains that alcohol and high living can put upon it. You may even be able to shrug off ailments as inconsequential because they would otherwise interfere with your plans. Envying your hardiness, I can only advise that you take things a little easier. This is especially important if you hope to avoid accidents and their resulting injuries.

RELATIONSHIPS: To be frank, you have few good relationships. You seem not to care about people unless they can help you. Take time out to consider the implications of that emotional habit. Granted, your place in the Creator's overall plan is as a doer. But to be effective in Taurean energy, even the most zealous activist must temper his drive and control his impulses.

Try this psychological exercise. Look hard at how your loved ones regard you. Is their affection limited? Is their devotion stifled by your lack of response to it? Once you realize how you treat them, you will turn your inexhaustible energy to the improvement of your relationships with them. Take my word for it: you will be able to do so with wonderful results that will mean more to you than all your worldly accomplishments.

GEMINI—JAMES (THE LESS)

(May 21–June 20)

Gemini, the third sign of the Zodiac, is symbolized by twins. In my vision in St. Matthew's Cathedral, the Apostle identified with Gemini was James the Less, who was, in some ways, a twin himself. His mother, Mary of Cleophas, was the sister of the Virgin Mary and, therefore, Christ's aunt. Thus James was the cousin of Jesus and, in the ancient Hebrew custom, is referred to as "the brother of the Lord" in Scripture.

Gemini is dominated by the influence of the planet Mercury, and this creates a certain tension or contradiction—duality is the best way to describe it—in the lives of those born under this sign. Indeed, it was because of this influence that the word "mercurial" came into the English language to mean changeable or fickle. Among the hundreds of millions who use that word, few realize its astrological origin, but it explains why Gemini individuals can be the most difficult persons in all the Zodiac to understand.

It is difficult to make predictions about them. Indeed, it is a real problem even to understand them! Paradoxically, they should be relatively easy to know and analyze, for they are all great talkers. They love to communicate their ideas and express their opinions, usually with convincing eagerness.

If you are a Gemini, consider whether this pattern applies to you. You seem to lead two lives, one public and another private. People think they know you well and then are surprised to discover abruptly a hidden personality within you. I am not suggesting any psychological malady, but rather the habit you have of shielding the most essential aspects of your being from the world's glare.

There is certainly nothing wrong with this. Indeed, it can be a double blessing to have, so to speak, two lives, two different realms of service and fulfillment.

The duality of Gemini characterized the Apostle James, who, by the way, was called "the Less" because his short stature distinguished him from another Apostle with the same name. Like Simon Peter, he had been a Zealot in his youth; and as a member of that group, he may even have taken part in guerrilla raids against Roman military establishments. Later, another aspect of his character became dominant, and he became a man of peace. This is one example of the preordained program that typifies Geminis. It constitutes a complete about-face during life.

The astrological pattern for each Gemini offers a guaranteed opportunity for a personal turning point, an individual chance to readjust their lives in new directions. For all of us, our own about-face will occur some fateful day when we confront the power of those red boots and tell their wearer to go his way while we go ours. For we will realize that, in the current jargon, those stomping boots are on a bad trip and we want no part of their dead-end journey.

James's own about-face happened even before he met Christ. He had left his political associates for the life of an Essene monk and dedicated his life to prayer, meditation, and the study of those scriptures now known as the Dead Sea Scrolls. James again changed his direction when he met Christ. He left his austere monastery and went back to his family home to await the call from the remarkable Man Who was stirring the villagers with His words.

Such changes are common to Geminis. Because you are prepared by nature for them, you are adaptable and versatile, intelligent and witty, busy and talkative. You take pride in being modern in outlook and up-to-date in your appearance. Those traits are all to your credit; but to most assets, there are corresponding liabilities. On the opposite side of your balance sheet, when you do not use your gifts properly, they can make you changeable, restless, inquisitive, inconsistent, gossipy, and nervy.

Your enthusiasm shifts rapidly, as you turn your attention to whatever happens to be momentarily urgent. You transfer your loyalties to whatever cause is at hand, be it a football team, a loved one, a hobby or career. It is not that you are insensitive or shallow; it is just the way your personality was programmed from your birth.

When you appear, in the eyes of others, to be flighty or unreliable, it is just a symptom of your mercurial horoscope. It indicates that one part of your twin personality is asserting itself over the other, and you are allowing it to happen despite your better judgment. Time and again, I have seen this pattern and the way it disrupts relationships. And yet, it is difficult for anyone to really resent Geminis for their lack of reliability. After all, those born under the sign of the Twins are given enormous charm as their birthright.

You can charm the birds out of the trees. You have probably already discovered this talent of yours, and I hope you are using it for worthy purposes. It's no wonder you can play one role at one moment and another the next. For words come to your lips easily, and your smile is as brightly engaging as your humor. It is fortunate that you need people to like you, for indeed they do!

But what about more meaningful relationships? What do you do when someone offers you more binding affection and less casual esteem? How do you respond when someone's love threatens to tie you down and end your freedom? You want to run from them, even when you suspect that by doing so you will be fleeing your best chance for happiness. Let me repeat that: you *want* to run. That doesn't mean you must do so. Your Gemini impulse can be restrained, and you can remain master of your own life. The stars only determine the tools you have to work with. The way you use them to build your future is your own responsibility.

Anyone who falls in love with an unrestrained Gemini is in for a rude shock. Because you demand change and variety, you may see no wrong in "little infidelities." Perhaps you will tell yourself that your transgressions are inconsequential because you intend to go back to your partner later. It doesn't matter if your infatuations are fleeting matters; they can still be as damaging as any actions that betray the human heart. Needless to say, an experience with your fickleness is not easy for those whom you hurt, but that old Gemini charm can usually woo back an offended fiancé or a justifiably angry spouse.

The most serious effects of your changeability occur outside the limits of romance. They pertain to your career, and they touch your family and friendships. Because you do not attach much importance to letting people down, you fail to comprehend how badly others are hurt. Consequently, you feel no sense of disloyalty to them, and you may even wonder why they resent the cavalier way you have treated your commitments to persons and projects. Whether you see their point or not, you will find, if you have not already, that their resentment can cripple your potential for success.

Although your subtle and versatile mind makes you a problem solver, there are times when you abdicate your responsibilities, walking out on a joint effort just as it is about to succeed. If its completion really means nothing to you, and if its collapse hurts no one but you, then your abrupt decision cannot be faulted. But too often your sudden departure pulls the props out from the work of others and is fatal to it. Because you play with fire, so to speak, others get their fingers burned; and they will not forget the reason for it.

It is essential, therefore, that you be more consistent and reliable, especially in your career. Curb your mercurial instincts. Your prospects for success are virtually guaranteed if you will just see things through to their arduous end. If you continue to change jobs frequently, you will leave your positions just when you are about to win the promotion that would put you at the top. Ever alert for a challenge, Geminis may even change their professions after years of study and labor invested in one career. Although this drastic shift can bring initial emotional satisfaction, it also threatens the greater disappointment of never fulfilling yourself. You may have to learn the hard way that although the grass looks greener elsewhere, it is seldom any better than in your own yard.

Because Geminis are usually as high-strung and tightly wound as the strings of a fine violin, there is no calm spot, no middle way for them. Life is all highs and lows. The taste for excitement generates their love of travel and yen for the exotic. No wonder they enjoy the zest of creative writing. In fact, the best professions for Geminis concern literature and the rousing clash of ideas. They excel as journalists, lecturers, teachers, scriptwriters, and authors. In those fields, their ability to communicate and to entertain are major assets. Thus, their negative trait of restlessness can be transformed into an asset for a varied career.

Remember that the Apostle James had to cope with the same stellar influences that affect every Gemini today. He turned them to his own advantage and became a responsible servant of mankind, so much so that even his religious opponents in Jerusalem called him James the Just.

In fact, the sign of Gemini seems to foster more than its share of religious leaders and spiritual thinkers, including the philosopher Ralph Waldo Emerson (May 25); the Mormon pioneer Brigham Young (June 1); the present Dalai Lama (June 6), an exile from his beloved Tibet; and Father Stephen Hartdegen (June 16), editor in chief of the New American Bible.

Geminis who have led in the field of government include Marshal Tito of Yugoslavia (May 25); Jefferson Davis (June 3), President of the Confederacy; and former Prime Minister Anthony Eden (June 12) of Great Britain.

Many Geminis have achieved fame after resolving crises in their lives, probably provoked by the same duality that characterized James. The list is as powerful as it is long, beginning with Judy Garland (June 10), Bob Hope (May 29), John Wayne (May 26), Cole Porter (June 9), Joe Namath (May 31), and Richard Thomas (June 13), young star of "The Waltons."

The roster of prominent Geminis would not be complete without mention of one of the nation's capital's most colorful men about town. Lawyer and sportsman, civic leader and canny politician, businessman and humanitarian, Edward Bennett Williams (May 31) sums up the diversity of the Gemini spirit.

It is important for Geminis of today to reflect that James did not seek change for its own sake. Whether he realized it at the time or not, each departure he made, each alteration in his goals, each about-face of his spirit was to further God's will for him. So, too, are our own life programs directed, and our opportunities for change are only crossroads along the path to our eternal destiny.

When we come to one of those crossroads and are puzzled as to our proper direction, when we wonder which road is rutted with the tracks of red boots, let us remember what another Gemini said. In his Inaugural Address, President Kennedy, whose birthday was May 29, declared, ". . . on earth, God's work must truly be our own."

Remember, brilliant Geminis, if you make your life stable and steadfast, you are superbly equipped to accomplish that work.

GEMINI—FIRST DIVISION *(May 28, June 1, 10, 19)*

As a Gemini One, you were born under a planetary combination which allows the gentler aspects of your twin personality to dominate your life. You already know you have a quick temper and, being aware of it, can take measures to control it. By taming that emotional tiger before someone is mauled by it, you will avoid hurt to yourself as well as to others.

Because gentleness dominates your character, you are exceptionally kindhearted and sympathetic. But in this and in every instance, there is bound to be a corresponding weakness to balance every strength. And so you are easily swayed by praise or sympathy and must beware of flatterers, who play upon your emotions like a musical instrument. A healthy dose of self-composure will fortify you against their insincere blandishments. Someone with your noble qualities needs no false esteem from opportunists. For, in addition to your mildness, you are:

- active
- logical
- a splendid parent
- dedicated to your home life

Like the Apostle in whose way you are following, you are restlessly energetic. James was for a time a political extremist, fanatic in the service of his single-minded cause: the anti-Roman Zealots. I don't mean to disparage those early nationalists, who, after all, wanted only the freedom of their people. But James found that there was a greater freedom to win and a much larger nation to serve in the family of man. The same discovery awaits every Gemini and can become the greatest moment of your life.

As a Gemini One who shares James's qualities, you probably have two occupations. You may teach and write novels on the side. You may run a home and do part-time office work for pin money. Or, after a day on the job, you may pursue a hobby or avocation in your spare time so persistently that it becomes virtually an unsalaried profession. Additional income is not the prime motive in your extra activity. Your subconscious motivation is your innate duality, your constant yearning for something different. That is why Gemini teen-agers start fretting about their summer jobs around Christmas and plan their college courses long before they graduate from high school. If they do not carry this tendency to extremes, it can be the foundation for a lifetime of accomplishment.

In the home, Geminis work hard to make a good life for their families. It comes as no surprise to find in Scripture much evidence of the close ties between James and kin. Indeed, it was his own mother who accompanied Mary at the Crucifixion. Success in your own efforts to maintain a happy home will be won, as in all human affairs, by bringing together in mutual understanding those who need reconciliation.

Because your mental abilities include excellent logical faculties, your talents will serve you best in legal matters, scientific research, or any kind of investigative work. You retain what you read and make an excellent student, able to rise to the highest levels in education if you pursue your studies diligently. In the search for wisdom, Gemini's fickleness is not allowed!

You are equipped to be a fine parent because your wide-ranging tastes and your passion for ideas will stimulate the developing mind of a child. Similarly, your devotion to home life makes youngsters dear to you. Even when they are not your own—if you work in a school, for example, or as a youth counselor, or hospital aide—children are doubly interesting to you because of the rapid changes they experience during their early years. In that sense, they are all little Geminis, revealing in the fancies of childhood the same love of the new which you have carried over into your adult life.

COLORS: Because of your mercurial influences, you change the colors of your clothing as often as you change moods. The patterns and shades of your life shift as rapidly and as wondrously as the visions in a child's magically mirrored toy kaleidoscope. Of course you are color-conscious! You may already have discovered that golden yellows and gay oranges express the sunny enthusiasm you bring to your home and family, while muted grays reinforce your scholarly bent. After all, in Greek mythology, the goddess Athena, patroness of learning, was unique among the immortals, for her eyes were gray! After you learn to employ the power of colors as adjuncts to your personality, try experimenting with the textures of your clothes. By complementing your fanciful attitudes, silks and lightweight fabrics will cheer you. Do not neglect the lift they can give your spirits in times of trouble.

MONEY: Your segment of the Zodiac is favorable for money matters, though you will get no thrill from investing through a stockbroker, even if his use of your money brings you ample returns. Consider starting, or at least financing in part, a small business in which you can personally become involved. It might not be wise for you to assume direct supervision of it, as you possess that Gemini tendency to lose interest in your projects. You should surely retain a voting interest in your corporation. It will profit from your participation in it, and your hunger for activity will be satisfied by this business responsibility.

HEALTH: Like most Geminis, you are quick-moving, more likely to be wiry than thickset, more likely to be underweight than corpulent. You will sometimes try to live on your nervous energy alone, and will run down like a battery in need of recharging. None of us, not even Geminis, are made to function that way. So you will need rest and plenty of sleep to sustain your busy ways. You are blessed in being free from any strong orientation toward specific diseases. Your major health nemesis is likely to be acute attacks of indigestion, caused by overloading your mental and emotional circuits. By taking as good care of yourself as you would of any irreplaceable machine, you will not only calm your mind but also settle your stomach.

RELATIONSHIPS: Your talent for expressing yourself eloquently will bring spice to your love life, while your duality will sometimes make you feel the need for dual relationships, perhaps an extramarital affair. But there is a much happier solution to your problems. Whenever your home life seems stale and tired, it is then that you should unleash your liveliness to transform your really enduring relationships into exciting ones as well. There need not be any contradiction between fidelity and enthusiasm, between constancy and romantic adventure. You don't have to suppress your mercurial forces altogether; just direct them toward the renewal and creative rearrangement of your bonds to the ones you love.

GEMINI—SECOND DIVISION *(May 29, June 2, 11, 20)*

Among all the Geminis, you are the peacemaker. That is your allotted role in life, your part in the universal jigsaw puzzle that forms the Creator's cosmos. Apart from the general attributes of all Geminis, your total commitment to conciliation is your only distinctive trait.

Christ once said, "Blessed are the peacemakers, for they shall be called children of God." No wonder your astrological character is limited. Those who can perform the most essential tasks are given only those to do, for their gifts are too precious to be squandered in other activities. That is why your personality's assets have been narrowed somewhat. By being so acutely focused on man's search for peace, your talents, like sunlight pointed through a magnifying glass, are made all the more effective.

Gemini Twos have an aversion to discord of any kind. You are always attempting to bring opposing factions together. You could have a noble career in diplomacy—in fact, in any job that requires the solving of problems through compromise and negotiation. Prepared from birth for your life's mission as a peacemaker, you possess tact, a readiness to listen, an attractive and sympathetic personality, and great depths of patience. This last asset is an unexpected gift among Geminis, and it surely is part of the Divine Plan that it has been given to you; for you will need it in your work as a conciliator.

You are well equipped as a mediator; but there is a danger inherent in that job, whether it is a formal position or an informal role you assume among friends. Remember that the facts of any situation have a way of becoming jumbled as they are carried back and forth between opposing factions. Sooner or later, one side or the other in a dispute will feel you are not impartial. If you are not ready for that outcome, your feelings will be hurt and your dedication threatened. But if you foresee the possibility of this trouble, you will be able to either avoid it or deal with it when it confronts you. As a safety measure, when you do act as a go-between, ensure that both sides are represented in all your dealings. Be frank with everyone so your fairness cannot be questioned. This rule applies as well to a family quarrel or a community disagreement. As you become more experienced in your role, you will realize that the art of bringing two hostile sides face to face is the first necessary step on the road to their reconciliation.

Gemini Twos are warm people with broad views and a perceptive mind. You are neither aggressive nor competitive. This is not of itself either good or bad, but depends upon the nature of your work and associates. You are best advised to stay away from the world of business and industry. Its demands will hardly match your skills and tastes. Of course, a position as an arbitrator between labor and management or as liaison with government regulatory agencies would be a different matter. These opportunities for bringing cooperation out of stalemate would perfectly suit you. Your most natural place, however, is in the academic world, in either the arts or sciences. Your love of the written word qualifies you for publishing and allied fields as well.

COLORS: The low-keyed magnetism of your personality demands colors which will reflect your noncompetitive attributes. Perhaps you feel garish or brash when you wear exotic shades. Try muted tones of pearl and dove gray, of cream and tasteful greens. When you surround yourself with those sedate hues, you are the very picture of quiet elegance. Your appearance reassures those with whom you must deal. Of course, when you are trying to bring some cheer and optimism to your peacemaking efforts, you may find it necessary to use brightly shimmering colors, electric with zest and sparkle, to lift the spirits of all concerned.

MONEY: As a member of that lovable class of people more concerned with dreams than with hard cash, you will never care deeply about money. You have the resourcefulness to see that your immediate needs are met, and you are justified in doing so. Especially for your family's sake, make several alternate long-term financial plans and take out prudent insurance policies. Those precautions will be the extent of your desire to be involved with monetary transactions.

HEALTH: Although your stellar combination does not promise great stamina or a robust constitution, you can nevertheless enjoy good health if you take commonsense steps to care for it. Your upper stomach could be delicate, and this demands a prudent diet. Obey the basic rules about rest and exercise, and you should not encounter any major problems. When you are tempted to tire yourself, remember that your service as a peacemaker is far too valuable to be endangered by illness. By caring for yourself, you will be caring as well for your divinely appointed mission.

RELATIONSHIPS: Dreamer that you are, you will be forgiven any lapses in your treatment of friends and loved ones. They always make excuses for you when your dedication to work leads to neglect of your personal responsibilities. Your natural desire to avoid conflict and foster harmony will preserve your friendships and make them multiply. You will always enjoy loving relationships with tolerant friends.

Make sure that the one individual to whom you commit your

life shares your dedication to peace and decency. A money-hungry spouse will make you both miserable. On the other hand, a mate who shares your feelings about the world will guarantee you a singularly happy home.

GEMINI–THIRD DIVISION *(May 21, 30, June 3, 12)*

Ambition is the hallmark of Gemini Threes. Just like the Apostle James, whose spiritual kin you are, great things have been assigned to you; and you are eager to tackle them.

Direct your ambition toward positive ends. All your life, you will feel that success, of itself, is not enough to satisfy you. It is the challenge of accomplishment which you need more than anything else. Make sure your causes are worthy before committing your phenomenal energy to them. You can become a great achiever as long as you develop your potential for good.

All the positive aspects of a Gemini personality are yours just for the effort of striving for them. You are:

- versatile
- witty
- diplomatic
- spontaneous
- intellectual

You love change for the challenges it brings, and your versatility lets you readily adapt to them. Your wit and diplomacy enable you to rally supporters for your various projects without effort; and although your biting witticisms can sometimes wound people, usually without your knowledge, your generous and thoughtful nature usually brings them back to you.

Your spontaneity and intellectual verve make you exciting company. No wonder people are attracted to you. Many instinctively sense your forward movement to the top and would like to go along with you. Once you have defined your goals in life, you are better able than most Geminis to gain them. Indeed, your driving ambition can not only fulfill your own objectives but also bring success to those associated with you.

You should, I think, consider arranging a comfortable life-style that will allow you to travel. In that way, your restlessness can be satisfied without disrupting your professional commitments. Gemini men can be happy as traveling representatives for large companies. Gemini women can be most effective as inspectors for public or private concerns. Even the housewife who is tied to her home by the care of small children can find suitable outlets for her need for change, and not only by rearranging the furniture every week. She can try innovative recipes, exotic menus, challenging civic projects, unfamiliar subjects in special educational courses. The important point is that you must recognize your favorable qualities. Then you can plan to strengthen them. You will be fulfilled only when you do.

COLORS: Color is important to Gemini Threes, and your best shades are those most appropriate to an ambitious individual on the pathway to success. Violets, mauves, and purples, in fact, all rich and slightly exotic colors, can enhance your vibrations. You are no shrinking wallflower and should not try to appear as one. Only when you feel overly restless, when your zeal for work gets out of hand, should you use restful and calming shades of green, together with light cream and white, to harness your emotional resources.

MONEY: Your money problems will always be directly linked to your stability. By staying with one job with a developing company, you will help it grow and could become moderately well to do by joining your ambition to the needs of a forward-looking business. But you Gemini Threes are so curious and challenge-seeking that your eyes will always be on the next pasture, where the grass looks greener and opportunities seem greater. Risking your security, as you are often tempted to do, will also mean limiting your personal hopes for riches. So learn to balance your adventuresome spirit with prudent financial goals.

HEALTH: You are prone to physical breakdown in your middle life, and the root cause will be easy to see even when you are young, for you always want to overwork. Be consoled: you will always recover quickly. Of course, a better approach to the problem is to avoid it altogether by pacing yourself and thereby preserving yourself. Other ailments likely to afflict the overly ambitious Gemini are headaches, lung troubles, and neuritis. Take good care of your eyes; and if you wear eyeglasses, have periodic checkups to ensure that your vision is under no unnecessary strain.

RELATIONSHIPS: Your Gemini restlessness threatens to bother you with the same old marriage problems; on the other hand, it can be an asset if your partner does not mind your being away from home in frequent traveling. Because your very unpredictability will keep a sparkle in your marriage, all you need is a carefully chosen mate to guarantee you both a happy marriage. You will never lack for friends all the way through your Gemini-charmed life. It is important for all ambitious people, be they Geminis or not, to recognize that their old friendships must not be sacrificed to secure social or financial profit. When you do reach the heights of success, be sure that you haven't abandoned those who helped you when you were struggling to make a start.

GEMINI—FOURTH DIVISION *(May 22, 31, June 4, 13)*

For Geminis of the Fourth Division, the Apostle James can serve as both an appropriate model and a strong influence. Like him, you will have a turbulent and eccentric life. You will always attract —and be attracted to—the odd and the extraordinary. In short, you have a most unusual life program. Like James, you will always want the real thing, the ultimate truth, the final purpose. No halfway measures will ever satisfy you. Your chief attributes are:

- individuality
- clear-mindedness
- intuition
- interest in the psychic

Though you are ever an individualist, some people might call you stubborn, but what they misinterpret is just your own strong-willed determination to do your own things in your own ways.

From your birth, your combined planetary influences have determined the outline of your unusual life. You are the material of which heretics, naysayers, and discoverers are made. You see your course and go directly for the goal. You will not be diverted from your objectives. Your unshaken faith in yourself is justified, for your clear thinking and objectivity eliminate any pretense or superstition that could interfere with your true purposes.

It is an interesting sidelight to your stars that you relate to the air. By that, I mean that your spirit is at home in matters dealing with the atmosphere. Gemini men, particularly, are interested in all aspects of air travel and would like to learn to fly. They are apt to take up such sports as sky-diving, gliding, or even springboard diving.

A female Gemini Four friend of mine is the only woman among all the vice-presidents of one of the world's biggest airplane manufacturing companies, and she handles the extremely demanding job of negotiating government contracts. Her stars have equipped her perfectly for the challenge, and she is more than a match for it.

Like any environment, the atmosphere will not always be a friendly place for Gemini Fours. You are likely to experience danger from airplanes, from tornadoes and lightning and other threats associated with the air. So be cautious, especially in your relish for the wind. Your intuition should guide you when danger is near, for you have finely tuned intuitive faculties and often know things in advance, without being aware of why. My advice is to keep your mind open to these vibrations. They are a gift of God, and you would not be given these special insights unless He wanted you to make use of them.

From your initial, halting appreciation of your intuitive power, you will be led, quite naturally, to investigate other areas of extrasensory perception and mysticism. You should pursue these interests, especially through clubs, associations, and professional groups. Just be sure that those whom you join are sincere in their pursuits and that their organizations treat psychic powers as the gifts of God rather than as a source of gratification or an object of magic. In the honest and respectful study of psychology, you will find so much new learning and old wisdom that you will be dazzled in wonderment that you had never been exposed to it before.

Your friends may consider many of your ideas offbeat, but carry on with them. James's fellow villagers may have considered him a bit peculiar too, but he refused to abandon his beliefs. Whether your views are directed toward one radical extreme or the other, from liberal to conservative, the pattern will always be the same. You will reject the traditional and seek the novel and untried.

Marriage is a good idea for you Gemini Fours only when you are lucky enough to find someone whose eccentric ideas are similar to your own. Otherwise, you are asking for trouble by either limiting your own horizons or inflicting your peculiarities upon an unwarned and very unhappy spouse.

Yet another offbeat facet of your personality is your strong sense of being a citizen of the world rather than a member of only one nation. You are inspired to break down barriers of mistrust between nations and to overcome historical enmities. Be prepared for those ideals to provoke harassment against you because you will be ahead of your time in your generous sentiments.

COLORS: Color channels are not too important for you because you obtain your extra charge of psychic energy from different sources. But magnetically you react best to electric colors. This is probably due to your affinity with the air, which, permeated by electricity, from time to time breaks forth as lightning. Moreover, as if to emphasize your atmospheric ties, you feel comfortable with most shades of gray, from somber charcoal to delicate dove. Your inclination to these colors may be strongest when you are preparing to take a plane flight, and after you have landed, you may be impelled to carry around with you the heavens' electric fields by displaying a tie or hat or shirt of the boldest green or blue.

MONEY: Economically, the overall pattern of your life is like a child's drawing of a mountain range, a zigzag of ups and downs, with more downs than ups, I regret to say. You will make money in fits and starts, but your inclinations make you unlikely to keep what you do make.

Your ideas are too advanced for the generation in which you live, and so you will often find it difficult to secure proper backing for them. You will lose money by supporting the underdog, which is certainly no reason to stop. To harmonize your finances with your personality, your best investments will be in electronics and, as part of your own program of personal development, in the air travel and air transport industry.

HEALTH: You live under uncertain planetary indications, which show that you have a tendency toward little-known ailments. Your sensitivity to drugs makes you difficult to prescribe medication for, and you will have little faith in the authority or wisdom of doctors. Because of your interest in the mystic arts, you may experiment with faith healing and mental cures of your illnesses. To the surprise of those who think otherwise, you will have a very long life, depending, of course, upon the precautions you take to avoid dangers in the air.

RELATIONSHIPS: Within your closely knit family circle, you will enjoy warm and rewarding relationships. Your children will be especially dear to you, and you to them. Outside the home, among your broad range of acquaintances, you will find only a few intimate friends. Many people will be attracted to you by your value as an oddity, by a fascination to know you better because you seem so different from others. Be careful of such curious and flighty people; they could do you harm through their insipid probing and unfeeling inquiries.

Especially in your most intimate relationships, it is important that those dear to you be sympathetic, or at least not hostile, toward your psychic interests. If they will only grant you an opportunity to discover your full self, they will be amply rewarded by sharing their lives with you.

GEMINI—FIFTH DIVISION *(May 23, June 5, 14)*

The life of a Gemini Five reflects those traits of the Apostle James which led him to a life of forceful preaching: a relish for travel and a need for vigorous action. The pattern of your life has been preordained to change frequently. You are:

- brilliant
- temperamental
- changeable
- agitated

Your unusually sharp mind is always seeking stimulation. You resent monotonous work, not because you disdain hard labor but because your alert faculties cannot stand routine and repetition. Consequently, you may have difficulty finding partners or colleagues with whom you can work easily unless you are frank with them about your need for constant challenges.

You are scheduled to make many detours and shifts in your progress through life. Superficially, these changes will make it seem as though you are shallow and inconsistent. That will not be the case. In truth, you are only seeking new worlds to conquer, like a gifted child who loses interest in the too slow pace of his everyday classmates. This is not snobbery or elitism. The stimulus of intellectual challenge is vital for all minds, especially those of your brilliance.

When you lack a fresh and demanding project in your everyday life, you are apt to become temperamental, feeling that your talent is being wasted because of the inferiority of those around you. So stamp your foot—metaphorically—to stir up some action. Be positive! Then the very people whose shortcomings have held you back will become involved in your new endeavors. Instead of waiting with them, you can hurry them along with you. You will not only enjoy the leadership you exert but will also be doing them a favor.

Gemini Fives are focal points of change. You need action, fast travel—in fact, speed in everything in your life. Because you get bored with the familiar, you will never fall into a rut; for you refuse to follow the same pattern long enough to wear a regular pathway! You live, as it were, with your bags packed, ready for the next move; and so you change residences more often than most of us could bear to do.

Your personality is well adapted to your nomadic impulses, for you are skilled at meeting people in new and strange places. Indeed, you are the sort who, put down in the center of an unfamiliar city at midday, would be dining with new friends at their home that very evening. Utilize those skills in all aspects of life. They will allow you to excel in public relations, in sales, or in advertising.

As a born migrant, you feel a natural agitation, a restlessness, which may make you incapable of deep and lasting relationships. Here is an instance in which the ancient wisdom of astrology is supported by the contemporary findings of sociological and psychological research. Social scientists tell us that highly mobile individuals, like those who dash about the country in pursuit of more rewarding jobs, usually maintain few enduring friendships. So it is in your case. Friends who are out of sight are also out of mind. Acquaintances who discover that you are flighty in this way will leave you to seek more stable companionship. Their defection will not bother you a bit, for your Gemini duality lets you turn off that side of your personality until the sense of loss has faded.

All this means that marriage is a bad risk for you, especially in your younger years. Remember that Benjamin Franklin once observed that an often moved family is like an often transplanted shrub; it does not thrive! His sage advice is still pertinent for anyone who loves to be on the go all the time. Although divorce has become commonplace in our society, it is nonetheless painful to all concerned. And, for all your temperament, you Gemini Fives hate to cause anyone pain.

COLORS: It should be obvious that through your personality alone, your character is colorful enough without being boosted through external adornment. The best shades for your magnetic aura are delicate and subdued pastels, especially airy yellow and shimmering green. They convey to others the alertness of your mind and the lightness of your spirit. They are fleeting colors, as transient as sunlight, and so they perfectly match your facile mind and mobile life-style.

MONEY: As a born gambler, you love any sort of get-rich-quick scheme. The law of averages should forewarn you that only a few of these projects will work out. So try to put money aside for shelter against ruined plans and miscarried proposals. When you do have money, you want to spend it like sand; and when you have little, you will live happily enough at a subsistence level and welcome the change for the challenge it affords. Hold your impulses in check to prepare for the biggest successes. By and large, they will be undramatic and routine investments, which pay off gradually. Force yourself to consider prudent offers rather than flashy promises of instant wealth.

HEALTH: You are your own worst enemy in health matters. Your excellent constitution is endangered only by your vitality. You strain your reserves. You reject sensible, staid, boring rules for good health and must pay the price. If you continue along that line, you will have nervous complaints in middle age, such as facial twitches, a speech defect, skin complaints, or blood disorders. Consider well whether the accomplishments of your present agitation are worth those ailments later. Remember the maxim of the philosophers of old: "*mens sana in corpore sano,*" that is, a sound mind in a sound body. To get the most from your brilliant intellect, cherish the health of your too often neglected body.

RELATIONSHIPS: Only a few close friends, who understand that at heart you are not fickle, will stay with you all your life. Despite this dearth of intimates, you will never lack a wide circle of acquaintances and party-going associates. After all, many lesser minds will seek to reflect the light of your thought and the sparkle of your intellect.

Your family will always be dear to you, but your male children could easily grow away from you if your genius becomes overbearing and dominating. To maintain close ties with them, learn to allow your offspring a measure of independence and self-expression. There is no reason for you to always have all the answers to their every problem. Your partner, long-suffering and patient if you remain married, will probably never really understand you, but will stay devoted to you anyway. Recognize this as a tremendous blessing, which has marked you as among the most fortunate of people. Work at your marriage, using your nervous temperament to make life exciting, rather than disruptive, for your beloved.

GEMINI–SIXTH DIVISION *(May 24, June 6, 15)*

Robert Burton, the English scholar and astrologer who died in 1640, once said that our astrological patterns "incline but do not compel." By that, he meant that we have a choice: we can either be masters of our fate by understanding our astrological character and learning to develop its virtues or we can aimlessly follow the pulls of our planetary influences and become the slaves of fate.

Geminis of the Sixth Division are poised on the razor's edge of those alternatives. Not only do they have the usual potential to know their star programs and act in harmony or opposition to them, but they also have the added option of being emphatically dual personalities. This further complicates their decisions.

Thus the situation for Gemini Sixes is intricate: their star combination is so finely balanced that they are subject to equal countervailing forces in both aspects of their personalities. They therefore enjoy a huge degree of freedom. Perhaps James was a Sixth Division Gemini. He certainly demonstrated remarkable free will in choosing to join Christ; and for the rest of his life, he was respected, both among Christians and among their adversaries, as a trusted decision maker. St. Paul, for example, sought his opinion in disputed matters (Galatians 2:2,9). It was as if those who knew him could perceive that he had made himself the complete arbiter of honesty and truth.

These are your foremost qualities, from which you can chart the way your life will go. You are:

- charming and intelligent
- liable to depression
- able to inspire others
- personally magnetic

Like all Geminis, you have most things going for you. Personally charming, you are also intelligent and an excellent conversationalist. In serious pursuits, you are as determined as a bulldog. Taken together, those traits let you achieve most of your ambitions with minimal effort. You can charm your way through life to reach your goals as a matter of course.

Your wide range of interests encompasses music, art, and literature. You would be adept in lecturing on them or in preaching about spiritual matters. Somewhat limiting all your powers, however, is the fact that you are prone to periods of depression. During these periods, you are inclined to abandon your struggle for fulfillment and achievement. When this happens, you are, in effect, surrendering your free will to your astrological environment and thereby neglecting your share of responsibility for the completion of God's eternal plan for us all.

Don't do it. Fight off depression. Reason with yourself, asking, "What have I got to be down about?" List your blessings, then compare them with the items that depress you. The balance sheet will certainly show a heavy surplus on the favorable side.

Learn to inspire yourself, just as you frequently inspire others. You can foster in others a zealous devotion to whatever you yourself believe in. James did just that. He probably led his own mother to become a follower of Christ. As she stood with Christ's mother at the foot of the Cross, she doubtless knew that her son had already secured for her more happiness than the kings of Judea could have purchased for their families. Similarly, your own example can change the lives of others.

While your magnetism gives you the ability to inspire others, it also opens the pitfall of surprising them, and perhaps disillusioning them, with sudden revelations of your hidden side. Especially in romantic matters, it is essential that you give your partner plenty of time to get to know you. It would be folly to rush someone into a marriage without any foreknowledge of your complex unpredictability. Whether in business or personal relationships, it is best for Geminis to proceed on sure grounds. Know your associates and let them know you. A miscalculation about you on their part could be just as damaging to your prospects as your own mistakes would be. Remember that others will usually underestimate your intricate nature, so help them avoid rash and simplistic judgments about you.

COLORS: Your magnetism is already so strong, even without accentuation, that the aura of your personality almost needs to be played down by the colors you wear. The entire range of blues, from the pale tint of birds' eggs to the richness of navy and royal blues, is ideal for this purpose. Recall how often you have seen a splendid piece of jewelry set off against a blue velvet display case. That same contrast applies as well to the use of blues, whether cool or warm tones, to display your mind and emotions, which are, after all, as brilliant and multifaceted as a superb jewel.

MONEY: Your intuitive good judgment means you will never have serious money problems. Because of your many friendships, you will find yourself the recipient of legacies and valuable presents after your thirtieth birthday. Remember that no matter how favorable your stars are in money matters, a reckless lack of regard for normal precautions will thwart the beneficial influences of your astrological chart. Especially in times of psychological depression, be wary of snap judgments that could undo years of labor and careful investment.

HEALTH: Ailments of the lungs and chest are most likely to afflict you. You are an apt candidate for asthma, hay fever, and bronchial infections, all brought on or worsened by overwork. Like your periods of depression, these troubles stem largely from negative traits within you; and by training yourself to relax and enjoy life, you can maintain unimpaired both your mental and bodily strength.

RELATIONSHIPS: In dealing with others, you win the gold medal! Your obvious sincerity, a result of Mercury's influence over you, endears you to many people; your intellect recommends you to others, and your vivacity attracts still more.

Your family will be devotedly loyal to you. You must try to be as loyal to them. Relationships must be two-sided, you know, even for a complex Gemini. When you find it difficult to put your personal responsibilities above sudden whims and dramatic adventures, consider that those who love you are sacrificing their wants and impulses daily. You owe them no less. By keeping your best qualities to the fore, you can inspire them to reach new heights in their lives. A better gift for your family members is hard to imagine.

GEMINI–SEVENTH DIVISION *(May 25, June 7, 16)*

Geminis of the Seventh Division are, in terms of emotional makeup, the softies of this Zodiac sign. They are born under planetary circumstances which make them shy, sensitive, and withdrawn.

Many of you to whom this applies have misread your personalities and are steering your life off its destined course. You think your tender feelings are a sign of weakness, and so you may try to bluff your way out of a mild-mannered reputation by acting at the other extreme. You become abrupt, brusque, almost dictatorial, as if to compensate for the gentle creature that is the real you. The grave mistake you may already be making is to try to eradicate those very qualities which lead others to cherish you. You have:

- humility
- sensitivity
- psychic abilities
- little aggressiveness

At heart, you are gifted with unusual idealism and refinement of thought. You have a poetic imagination and could develop it into a vibrant artistic ability. But you are so humble that you think nothing of these talents. You shrug them all aside and, in so doing, neglect the enrichment of your own life and the contributions you could make to the lives of others. In the jargon of popular psychology, you have an inferiority complex.

Are you not an acutely sensitive person, with a deep spirituality? Don't you often pray silently? And aren't you reluctant, indeed, somehow ashamed, to let others know just how you feel? Too self-effacingly, you believe that in this materialistic era of the twentieth century, you are out of step with the spiritless world. I won't mince words with you. Those attitudes are all wrong! If anything, you are actually avant-garde, far ahead of your time. The world is gradually returning to the faith it abandoned in the arrogant aftermath of the Renaissance. You are not a throwback, but a pioneer in the immaterial! Be more open about your spiritual life, and you will be able to help others develop theirs. For you are a Columbus or Magellan of the spirit, a Neil Armstrong or Jonas Salk of the soul. Your discoveries are too precious for man's future to remain hidden.

You have another set of abilities about which you seldom speak. You are quite psychic. You may sometimes feel that you are deluding yourself, that you are not really gifted in this way by the Holy Spirit. Break out of that inferiority complex! Recognize your blessings for what they are. Consider how often you know someone is coming to visit before he or she arrives on your doorstep; how often you know what is in the mail before you receive it; how often you are sure what a stranger is going to say to you.

Develop these gifts as best you can. Your humility can be an asset, for you will not be trying to impress anyone or secure fame for yourself. That will make it easier for you to open your mind to whatever vibrations await it. Seek others with knowledge; share your psychic experiences with those whom you fully trust; and as your self-confidence increases, it will allow you to reveal your true self to the world.

Your lack of aggression, though commendable, can frustrate your talents. You are humble enough to think of yourself only after others. You are the kind of uncomplaining employee who rarely asks for a raise or promotion but who is grateful when either comes your way. Then you work even harder to show your gratitude. That is splendid, except that you should not allow your employer or colleagues to slight your abilities or take your industry for granted.

Another facet of your preordained life-style is a taste for travel. You strongly desire to take long journeys, without realizing why, especially if the trip is by water. You delight in living or vacationing by the sea, or near a river or lake. Water claims you, and you are wise to seek it out, especially in times of crisis and stress.

Your chances of finding a suitable mate could be risky if you limit your search to normal social means. You are not gregarious and tend to mix with few people, even at large parties. If you fail to explore the whole range of human character and to meet many disparate individuals, you chance a failed marriage with an inappropriate partner. Singles bars are definitely not your environment. Better play safe and examine groups, like church clubs or parapsychology organizations, conducive to your finely tuned vibrations. Seek out someone in whom you can see an image of yourself, and a long lifetime together will be at your command.

COLORS: Physical surroundings are not usually a great help in bringing you out of yourself; you are more interested in reading the responses of others than in sending out your own messages. Do remember that despite what you may fear, acquaintances are as interested in knowing you as you are in fathoming them. In some situations, the softening tones of creamy colors will help you become more assured and expressive. All vibrant shades of green will assist you in relaxing your guard. And if the combination of cream and green suggests a dove with an olive branch or the gentle contrast of a lily of the valley in bloom, those are perfect portrayals of the real you. Once you realize that, what a delightful addition you will be to any social gathering!

MONEY: A Gemini softy makes a soft touch. Some people will try to take advantage of your openhandedness. Remember Shakespeare's caution: "A loan oft loses both itself and friend." If you can't afford to lose money, don't lend it. There is a difference between generosity and foolhardiness. Keep on helping people, as you love to do, but don't let them take advantage of your benevolence.

You are likely to have a long life. So, early in your productive years, you should save as much money as you can, either in bonds which will not be affected by stock market fluctuations or in shares of a growing business. That way you will be spared worry about self-support when you are older.

HEALTH: I have just let slip the prediction that you are likely to be long-lived. This is true despite your inclination to colds, lung congestion, and poor circulation. The only real threats to your physical well-being will occur during your spells of depression, when you fail to attend to your needs. That danger is easily averted by common sense and vigilance.

RELATIONSHIPS: You will always enjoy the quiet, unspoken affection of your family, and that is the kind of relationship you hold dearest. You face marital problems if you fail to exercise considerable care in your choice of a mate. If, on the other hand, you marry with prudent insight, your home life will be a model of wedded happiness. Seek a spouse whose eyes reflect your unspoken ideas rather than someone whose lips echo facile phrases. You will be able to tell the difference as soon as you become more accustomed to the give-and-take of social conversation.

GEMINI—EIGHTH DIVISION *(May 26, June 8, 17)*

If you are a Gemini Eight, I don't know if reading what I have to say here will do you any good. Your rock-hard convictions make you a strong-minded individual, adamant and unyielding. Only you can convince yourself of anything. Others can argue, cajole, explain, and insist, but you alone make decisions for your life.

Even though you demand absolute control over your own mind,

I will assume that you are going to read on. Your intentions are invariably good. The trouble with them comes when your uncompromising beliefs put you at odds with the very people who should be closest to you. Even they do not understand—although you erroneously suppose that they must—that your stubbornness is really faithfulness to your principles.

In this regard, you are like James during the time immediately after he left the Zealots. I am sure he carried his aggressiveness with him into the monastic community of the Essenes, and I expect that his fellow monks were quite tried by it. You, too, are always searching for truth, but usually certain that you are closer to it than anyone else. Properly directed, that can be a tremendous asset. If you don't become complacent or superior, your assuredness can surcharge your will with righteousness. Here are your other qualities. You are:

- charming
- bold
- able to go it alone
- an inspiration to loyalty in others

You possess all the best Gemini virtues. You are a real charmer: adaptable, versatile, lively, and talkative. Your winning ways attract friends by the flock, until they enter a conversation with you that turns into an argument. Then, in their eyes, you become intractable, stubborn, and unyielding. Rest assured that you can strike a balance, although it will require patience and effort, like any self-improvement.

Back off a little from your hectic search for immediate and all-encompassing truth. There is no need for frenzy. Wisdom is best acquired slowly, just as a venerable redwood tree reaches its majestic heights, inch by inch, over centuries. When you must listen to contrary views, learn to analyze them rather than argue with them. Discuss rather than debate. Ask rather than tell.

In your professional life, your gifts will make you a success at any profession that attracts you. You are bold enough to take a daring chance with your career now and then, as a Gemini Eight friend of mine did. She was unhappy at her job as a teacher in New Jersey. So she put her life savings into a dress shop and gambled her hard-earned security on the new venture. But it paid off! She is happier than she ever was in a classroom, and her expanding business is thriving. She was able to "go it alone," as are most Gemini Eights. Indeed, you must be able to do so; for you often feel, rightly or wrongly, that you lack friends on whom you can depend in a crisis. I hate to say it, but you are probably correct; and it is no one's fault but your own.

What is the reason for your occasional isolation? Your independent spirit keeps most people at arm's length, and those who remain close to you do so despite your frequently aggressive attitudes. Many others would like to become closer friends with you but are unsure about your interest in them because of your apparent aloofness. If they surmount that initial barrier, they react strongly to your virtues, with the loyalty you so easily inspire. Consequently, you never face an emergency alone unless you choose to do so.

Another aspect of your individuality is your dislike of being pushed around. You are ready to take on anybody, in or out of court. This is one characteristic you absolutely must control. Litigation is always expensive, both in terms of time and money; and it devours your creativity. You must become more philosophical about difficulties and learn that if your goal is blocked one way, there is usually another route to it.

My vibrations indicate that as long as you don't hurt yourself by rushing too rapidly up the ladder of success, you will do well. Here, too, so much depends upon your willingness to restrain your boldness for the sake of solid, if routine, progress.

COLORS: The proper use of color can bring out your creativity and simultaneously subdue the too aggressive aspect of your duality. Avoid those dark and heavy colors you fancy. They do nothing to reassure your acquaintances. Stay with milky cream, turquoise, and elegant blues, even pert and friendly pinks. These are colors of exuberance and vivacity, yet they neither affront nor boast. It is likely that their tasteful use will strike the emotional balance you need between forcefulness and tolerance.

MONEY: Security in money matters will come to you, but usually later in life. Be prepared for some of your early investment plans and business efforts to go wrong. Don't be daunted by your losses. If you keep trying, you will eventually accumulate a comfortable amount. But that success takes years, even decades. Invest in yourself above all, broadening your tastes and expanding your intellectual horizons.

HEALTH: Like most Geminis, you will find your major physical complaints center around nervous conditions. You will be easily annoyed, too introspective, and overly anxious. All those emotional habits will cause headaches during your youth. After the ailments pass away with maturity, they are apt to return in greater intensity during middle age. Then, if you haven't yet learned to control your temper and tame your moodiness, you will pay for your neglect with discomfort and possible disability.

It is never too late to take your health into your own hands. The best cure for headaches and related disorders is preventive medicine —that is, the development of inner tranquillity. Add to your new-found serenity a simple diet, with ample fibrous vegetables and plenty of water. Under such a regimen, even a lifetime of nervous headaches can be ended and a new life of calm and contentment begun.

RELATIONSHIPS: You are often brusque and uncompromising, and yet a small circle of friends think you are wonderful. Why? Because they know what you are like when you are relaxed and off guard. Then you become a different, and much more enjoyable, person. Let your defenses down more frequently and to more people. You will be surprised to see how well they react to your softer side. Moreover, your previously dogmatic views will be listened to more respectfully and accepted more often. That matters greatly to you.

Who can tell? If you Gemini Eights have read this far, you may be susceptible to these suggestions after all! I hope so. They chart your path to personal happiness and social achievement.

GEMINI–NINTH DIVISION *(May 27, June 9, 18)*

As a Gemini Nine, you live under a combination of planets that will make you more like James the Zealot than James the Apostle. As a consequence, more than any other Geminis, you need to develop self-control if you are to reach your goals in life.

You have a keen intellect, and it commands respect. But you are inclined to spoil your authority by being argumentative. You declare instead of suggesting. There is no insincerity or posturing in you. You believe in what you say, and you expect everyone else to follow suit. You are:

- frank
- humorous

- inventive
- a lover of detail

While forthrightness is a virtue, your frankness can be too much of a good thing. Outspokenness has its limits, and they begin at the point where other people's feelings are needlessly hurt. You may have the facts on your side, but there is no reason to hurl them at others. If you shoot from the hip, so to speak, with your barbed observations, you will needlessly alienate the very people whom you hope to convince. Indeed, they may be forced to admit the truth of what you proclaim, but they cannot be forced into giving you the assistance you need to put your opinions into practical effect.

Your wit is as sharp as your intellect, and it, too, can be a two-edged sword. In the service of a good cause, your sarcasm carries all before it. But how many are needlessly hurt by it? You would never exploit them or rob them or assault them, and yet you think nothing of turning your bitter humor against the innocent, not from malice surely, but from a failure to think things through. Others will be happier if you train your wit to run in less hostile channels. More important, you yourself will be the major beneficiary of that change, for you will thereafter be spared those twinges of remorse you now feel when you realize your sarcasm has injured the guiltless and offended persons of good taste.

Your inventive curiosity is sustained by a broad streak of mechanical genius. You are well suited for the technical sciences because of your fascination with detail. Painstaking in all your efforts, you especially relish the collecting and analysis of statistics. For example, you are the typical person who reads every small "filler" paragraph in the newspaper about the number of cars that cross the Golden Gate Bridge on a given day. You can spot an error in a mass of detail in a few seconds, and it is no wonder that you are the kind of employee most valued by the Internal Revenue Service.

The many small problems that will crop up in your life should be dismissed with tact and diplomacy. That is, of course, more easily said than done. The first step is always the hardest; but you will find that one kind word leads to another, until they become habitual. You are well equipped for settling disputes, if—and it is a mighty "if"—you mold your humor into an instrument of conciliation. Remember that the opposite side of sarcasm is an engaging self-deprecation. Your wit can bring opponents together in good spirits, but first you must trim its claws.

COLORS: Your best colors are all shades of red, from vivid scarlets to pale rose. It is not surprising that with your bull-like attributes, your Gemini impulses should be akin to the spectrum of Taurus. When you feel that the red-flag part of your dual personality is carrying away your better judgment, use the language of color to get back on the right track. Substitute pink for the flaming red you would prefer. Remember that your sympathetic shades are not just the colors of fire trucks and emergency lights. They are also the hues of Valentine cards and the shy cardinal of aged claret wine and the healthy blush on a baby's cheek. So, too, even the most forceful of your attributes can be turned toward peace and beauty.

HEALTH: You are more prone to accidents than to sickness. Electricity and motors of all kinds can be the causes of injury for you. I sense that your most vulnerable areas are your hips, shoulders, hands, and arms. The solution is simply to be more careful. We have no such magic as that which made the legendary Greek hero Achilles safe from all harm except for his fatal heel. Your health is your own responsibility, and your concern for detail can preserve your safety if you don't take things for granted.

MONEY: Because of your impulsiveness, you are inclined to rush into projects without completely examining all that they involve. You will thereby score some outstanding losses until you learn better procedures. Of course, there is the consolation that in some risky ventures, you will be lucky. The clever and original ideas which come naturally to you make it unlikely that the lack of money will be a real problem for you.

RELATIONSHIPS: It is probable that casual acquaintances, like business colleagues and those in the outer circle of your social life, respect your abilities but deplore your aggressiveness. They are rightly afraid of your biting wit.

Your family, on the other hand, should be a great comfort to you, just as James's clansmen stood by him in times of trouble. You are inclined to have difficulties with your siblings; but, like James during his monastic period, you can reconcile yourself with those close to you and transform taut lines of communication into mellow relationships.

In marriage, you will be happier as your spouse grows to understand you better. From time to time, you must deal with your beloved in total honesty, without your protective façade of sophisticated wit. Like the only man I know who has made a living from sarcasm, Don Rickles, you must show that it is really only an act. (If it were not, there would be nothing funny about it; it would be only pathetic.) Your marital happiness depends upon your willingness to abandon occasionally your sharp humor for sweet sincerity. Your children's respect for you requires that you never apply to them the stinging jests which even adults find hard to take. In dealing with your youngsters, lead with your heart rather than your lip.

CANCER—ANDREW

(June 21–July 22)

Cancerians are children of water, and of the moon as well, for that small planet controls the ocean tides. From time immemorial, thoughtful men and women have believed that the moon exercises great influence upon the human mind and body. After all, our bodies are almost entirely composed of water, and that fact reveals our kinship to the sea and our susceptibility to lunar impulses. More than most of us on earth, Cancerians are tied psychologically to this planet's water in all its forms. In fact, they owe their name to the Latin word for crab, which is, of course, their Zodiac symbol.

In the several visions which impelled me to write this book, the Apostle identified with Cancer's segment of the Zodiac was Andrew, the older brother of Simon Peter. Andrew's qualities complemented those of his hotheaded Arien brother so neatly that when I recognized the astrological link between Andrew and Cancer, I said aloud, "Of course!"

Andrew is the veritable blueprint for Cancerians; and like him, they are sensitive, protective, shrewd, and cautious. They are people who make, and rigidly abide by, quick decisions. To their credit, they are usually the right decisions. Andrew's career as an Apostle demonstrated that.

Before he met Christ, Andrew was already a disciple of John the Baptist. He probably spent much of his time along the banks of the River Jordan, baptizing others and preaching that the Messiah was soon to come. That explains why, when John acclaimed Christ as the Messiah, Andrew lost no time in making a decision. He immediately believed without hesitation and became one of Christ's followers, at least in spirit, for Jesus was not yet ready to begin His ministry. Like his brother Peter, Andrew returned to his everyday work on the Sea of Galilee as a fisherman, until his Master's call came and took command of his life. Even before that moment, however, he had already made up his mind to go with the Carpenter from Nazareth. Like Cancerians the world over, he persisted in his choice.

This doggedness of spirit is an inborn trait that sometimes makes Cancerians hard to bear; but it also makes them faithful friends, especially to anyone in need of help. If you were born under the sign of Cancer, you may rightly feel you are more sensitive than most people, more attuned to the emotional needs of those around you. That characteristic helps you to be an excellent companion, for you are well equipped to understand another's viewpoint and usually take the trouble to do so.

Within this combination of virtues, however, there is a hazard. Often I hear from Cancerians who write me to confess, "I wake up at night with an unaccountable feeling of loneliness. My loved ones are with me, asleep under the same roof. They are safe, for I walk around the house to check. I have many good friends, only a telephone call away. My relatives are wonderful to me. My life is secure and fulfilled, or so I think until I wake to these dreadful hours of longing and loneliness. What causes it?"

I will tell you the answer bluntly and hope you will receive it in the same spirit of concerned fellowship in which it is given.

Your problem is that your natural sensitivity, which sometimes manifests itself as psychic ability and intuition, makes you especially receptive to feelings that are part of us all. You are lonely for the comfort of religion, for something more enduring than material benefits. Your unspoken need is for the meaning and direction which result from personal contact with Christ.

That unheard noise which keeps you awake is the steady, silent tread of red boots down the sleep-filled corridors of your mind. You are aware of the presence of evil in the world and don't know how to combat it and shield your loved ones from it. Even though things are going well for you, you fear that sooner or later, when you turn a corner in the maze of life, there ahead of you in the darkened hallways will stand the personified power of malice. And that fear is a waking nightmare. How fortunate we are in knowing that if we dare to defy its power, that hideous dream cannot touch us! For there is no difference between the corridor of the red boots and that "valley of the shadow of death" mentioned by King David in his Psalms. In both cases, we are reassured by Scripture that "I will fear no evil: for Thou art with me; Thy rod and Thy staff they comfort me."

Perhaps Andrew, well versed in the Hebrew writings, found comfort in the same Psalm whenever he experienced that longing you feel for an indefinable something. Perhaps he recognized that the guidance it promises had been at last made real in his Teacher. He thereafter gave his life joyfully to the cause of serving others through his new faith, until his death in the Greek city of Patras at the hands of hostile rulers.

Of course, Andrew's total commitment to a life of service is not the answer for every Cancerian. But if you do occasionally sense that something is missing from your life, consider whether you can adapt Andrew's answer to suit your own life-style. You might find that weekly charity work through your church or social club, or even simply reserving fifteen minutes of each day for prayer and meditation, will enrich your life beyond belief.

Quiet contemplation is especially vital for you Cancerians, for your role in God's plan for humanity is a special one. With your added powers of imagination and insight, you Cancerians are ordained to be the planners of our society. You do sometimes have wild and harebrained schemes; but they are the random sparks, the unpredictable catalysts which encourage mankind to move forward in its journey toward union with its Maker. Use your powers, develop your potential, and you will not only fulfill yourself but will also achieve the purpose for which you have been placed on earth. Whether your role in the cosmic mosaic is small or mighty, there would be something missing in the Creator's pattern without that one piece which only you can contribute.

So your decision—and it must be yours alone—is to choose how your gifts can be developed, even though you will sometimes feel that you don't want to bother with that challenge. It is tempting to remain comfortably in your rut. Some Zodiac signs allow us that indulgence, but not Cancer! It will not let you rest easy in spiritual stagnation. Your astrological personality dictates your restless creativity. You will always be a rolling stone, at least intellectually, and your restlessness will spur others to greater heights. That is your role among your fellow humans; and by accepting it, you will unleash powers you may not yet realize you possess.

One of those Cancerian powers is a self-sacrificing humility. This was one of Andrew's lovable traits. Like him, you seek neither applause nor gratitude. Your concern is to get on with the job at hand. Consider Andrew's example. He could have presented a strong case to be considered the chief among the Apostles. He had been first to accept Christ as the Messiah, the first to follow Him, the first to convert someone—actually his own younger brother, Peter. And yet, Christ selected Peter as His deputy. Nowhere have I ever seen, in any ranking of the Apostles, any indication that Andrew was higher than fourth in eminence. Despite all that, in my meditations on this humble saint, I have never sensed vibrations of resentment over the fact that he had been passed over for positions of leadership. He was content to be near Christ as one of the Twelve.

His example is a lesson for us all, not only for those who share with him the sign of the Crab. Few among us are destined to achieve public prominence. For most people, life is circumscribed within the limits of friends, relatives, and jobs. We seem to be crossing the sea of life without leaving a ripple on its surface. As the immortal poet Keats said of himself in his own self-effacing epitaph, "Here lies one whose name was writ in water." But we are nonetheless as important to God as those who move nations and create empires. Our very existence is the surest proof that we have been given specific tasks to perform for Him.

As Christ did when He taught, we might use a parable from nature to illustrate this. We can all learn a lesson from the intricate society of the beehive. We may be the human counterparts of those nameless worker bees who go about their business every day, stinging no one and laboring for the good of all. Without those workers, there would be no honey in the hive. Remember that when you examine your own importance to the world.

Cancerians usually sense the value of their own modest work, especially those who make an effort to develop their spiritual sensitivity. They are therefore content to be the anonymous powers behind the throne, knowing that their quiet efforts are essential for the good of all. Their reward is an inner satisfaction that makes them serene through life's storms. We all have heard about the miracle of the loaves and fishes, when Christ fed five thousand persons, both the faithful and the curious, though He had only a few small loaves of bread and a handful of fish. How many of us realize that it was Andrew who knew that those people were hungry? He located a small boy with some scanty food and, hoping his Master would do something with it, brought the lad to Christ. That was a fine example of the way Cancerians will quietly serve others without seeking credit or praise.

Needless to say, not all Cancerians are modest or lowly. Many have used their gifts to reach fame and worldly power. Some of history's greatest figures were Cancerians who understood their own minds and emotions and thereby fulfilled their total potential. National leaders among them included American Presidents John Quincy Adams (July 11) and Calvin Coolidge (July 4); Italy's patriot and national unifier, Garibaldi (July 4); and Julius Caesar, who laid the foundations for imperial Rome (July 12).

In music, George M. Cohan and Stephen Foster were also Cancerians (both July 4). Richard Rodgers (June 28) and Oscar Hammerstein II (July 12) combined their Cancerian talents to create the greatest Broadway musicals of our time.

Cancerian artists include Rubens (June 29), Degas (July 19), Rembrandt (July 15), and Whistler (July 10). Their counterparts in literature include Ernest Hemingway (July 21), Marcel Proust (July 10), William Thackeray (July 18), and Henry David Thoreau (July 12).

The inclination toward leading and helpfulness among Cancerian women is obvious in the lives of Pearl Buck (June 26), Ann Landers (July 4), playwright Jean Kerr (July 10), and Mary Baker Eddy (July 16), the founder of Christian Science. Another religious leader, Mother Frances Xavier Cabrini (July 15), was a guardian angel to thousands of immigrants to America. A dear Cancerian friend of mine, Amalya Reifsneider, is one of the most learned ladies in Washington, D.C.; and her friends are almost as numerous as the thousands of books in her beloved library.

Among Cancerian philanthropists have been the explorer Cecil Rhodes (July 5), whose famous scholarships bear his name, and John D. Rockefeller (July 8), the founder of the great philanthropic institutions that have benefited millions.

Obviously, there is a wide diversity of opportunities open to you Cancerians. You must discover yours for yourself. Once you do that and decide to turn your talents to your Creator's purposes, then, in both good times and bad, your sleep will not be broken by nameless fears. Your nights will not be disturbed by the echoes of scarlet boots in shadowy passageways. And each day will be a fresh invitation to wisdom, peace, and joy.

CANCER—FIRST DIVISION *(June 28, July 1, 10, 19)*

Cancerians of the First Division tend to be quiet and reserved by nature, and only occasionally reveal their sensitive dispositions and deep emotional resources to others. You are probably liked by everyone. You know what it is to attract strangers at parties without trying. This is because they see the way you unconsciously down-play your own personality. They bask in the sympathy of your generous feelings.

You Cancer Ones are destined to enjoy personal success in life, love, and business because of your unintentionally charming ways. There is a strong streak of loyalty in you, a two-way fidelity that allows others to respond to you as strongly as you react to them. You stand by your relatives during their ordeals. Your associates know they can rely on you, and employers never question your dependability in your work.

In every group, there is someone, probably a Cancerian, to whom people look for reassurance, certain that he or she will cope with problems on behalf of them all. You might not be the group's spokesman, but you are the one who organizes their efforts, quietly and efficiently. Small wonder that you are the confidant of so many, for they are always certain of receiving a sympathetic hearing. This can be a burden to you when they ask your advice. You shouldn't always feel compelled to give it. Help them reach their own conclusions, as, most of the time, they need only a good listener. When they find one in you, encourage them to handle their own problems with their own strengths. Stop short of attempting to advise them too extensively, because there is a danger being drawn into personality conflicts. This is especially true in dealing with those outside your own family circle. Use your reputation for fairness to mediate disputes and resolve differences, but don't risk personal involvement by taking sides. That can only worsen situations you wish to remedy and destroy your effectiveness as a force for peace.

Your overall competence equips you for success in whatever work interests you. The vibrations of your Crab sign indicate that you Cancerian men of the First Division will make at least one major change in your career before settling down to your life's work. That shift will probably involve travel over a considerable distance, perhaps to another country. Women in the First Division, though they are excellent homemakers, also take an active interest in their husband's work as well, sometimes by extensively entertaining his associates, but more often by helping him with paperwork and organizational details.

Cancerian men and women both share an innate sensitivity leading to profound spirituality, and they tend to be religious without flaunting it. Because you are quiet about your own personal commitment, those who admire your virtues may, nonetheless, be at a loss to understand your character. They fail to comprehend your motives. They question whatever isn't directed toward profit. Because of your interest in immaterial rewards, some will suspect that you lack drive. Such people measure all payment in coin. But you weigh your wages in your heart rather than in your wallet. This is the kinship with Andrew in you. You feel it unnecessary to be boss, either in your labor, your home, or your community. You work hard to support what you believe in, and it is more important to you to have things go well than to have them go your way.

COLORS: So much of the world is open to you—your wide choice of careers, your ample range of talents—and that universality of your spirit is reflected in the broad spectrum of colors which enhance your magnetic vibrations. So many hues suit you well, but shades of gold and yellow are most appropriate. Because you treasure natural things and because your friends cherish you as a wonderfully natural person, you may prefer the color of corn in a country field at harvest time or the tone of vivid old brass, polished and cared for over the years.

Electric shades of blue, as gay and sparkling as a tropical lagoon, will not only match your vibrance but also reflect your astrological ties to the water. Green, cream, and white will also enhance your personality. As a lunar child, you will find a special psychological affinity to the color of the moon when it is overcast with the water vapor of clouds, the delicate blue-gray tint of a wood pigeon's breast.

MONEY: Be comforted to know that you should never have major money problems. Your wants are simple. Because you don't lust after material possessions and refuse to keep up with the Joneses, you will avoid financial headaches. I do see a definite financial improvement for those of you Cancer Ones who seize opportunities to change the style of your life. But the monetary benefits will not be the reason you do so. Rather, you will take a business or professional risk because it offers an added challenge, not for the financial gain it could bring.

HEALTH: You possess great physical vitality, although your outward appearance leads others to think you are not strong. Diet, rather than exercise, will be your best strategy for avoiding digestive complaints; and through sensible eating habits, you will enjoy a long and energetic life.

RELATIONSHIPS: Because of your kindly, sympathetic nature, your parental instincts are strong; and so you could smother your children with too much indulgence of their wishes. Remember that they will respect you as much for the discipline and guidance you give them as for your generosity. Beware of a tendency to be too clinging with your children. In all likelihood, they will learn your own habits of thoughtfulness and loyalty by example; and so, when the times comes, they will be well prepared to shape their own lives with honor and concern for others.

Outside your family, you will always be sought after as a friend and confidant. Here, too, you must avoid being too protective of your acquaintances. Although it pains you to see them making mistakes that will bring grief to their lives, you simply can't assume full responsibility for their happiness.

In romantic matters, the only thing you need to remember is to be yourself. It would be foolish for you to mask your spirituality with a false display of worldly sophistication, and it would be tragic if you hid your real merits from those to whom you are attracted. Let that special person get to know your tenderness and modest charm. Your chances for happiness together are too great to miss the opportunity.

CANCER—SECOND DIVISION *(June 29, July 2, 11, 20)*

The planetary combination which influences Cancerians of the Second Division makes you even more restless than those born under other divisions of the sign of the Crab. By itself, that characteristic is neither good nor bad; and if it is constructively used, it can become a great force for good.

Your intellect craves stimulation. Your emotions constantly

search for new and exciting relationships. Even in the simplest physical terms, you enjoy the sensation of movement and hate to sit still. You twitch, cough, and fidget. It would seem to a casual observer that you are bored, while, in fact, you are an internal dynamo, as uncomfortable with restraint as a penned stallion. Harness that surging energy, and in all aspects of life, it will carry you wherever you want to go. Your other major traits are:

- diverse interests
- powerful imagination
- protectiveness
- untidiness

Your hyperactive mind is responsible for your diversity of interests. There seems no end to your hobbies and studies and projects, because each new subject demands your attention and excites your curiosity. This inclination is relatively easy to handle for Cancer Two men, for they can often incorporate into their workaday lives the change of pace and variety of activity they crave. On the other hand, the home-loving natures of Cancer Two women incline them to be housewives rather than career persons. This creates an awkward contradiction and a difficult challenge for them. They usually have their housework finished bright and early each day. Then what can they do? They are as eager for new horizons as they are attached to their homes. The answer is that they can do almost anything they set their minds to. With your zest for new ideas and fresh experiences, you Cancer Two women can discover new worlds in painting, needlepoint, and ceramics. Your handiwork will not only afford you creative satisfaction; it will also provide pleasure to those who receive it as a gift.

Your intellect demands that you give yourself ample scope to explore your talents, whether through your own investigations of knowledge or through formal education. Your powerful imagination operates in tandem with an excellent memory. But although your imaginative faculties are a blessing, they can pose a hazard as well. You tend to worry needlessly by imagining every worse possibility. Use your sense of humor to counterbalance this habit, allowing your imagination its full rein as a release from tension, not as a troubling force which increases the stress you feel.

Because you are protective of those dear to you, you can be an excellent parent. In fact, Cancer has traditionally been considered the astrological sign of motherhood. While you take justifiable pride in your fondness for children and your skill in guiding them, be careful that your love doesn't turn into the smothering affection that harms the little ones you want to help. It is quite possible that Cancerian parents will be reluctant to see their children grow up. Guard against that tendency through the awareness that maturity can be even more a blessing to young people than the innocence of youth. If, by coincidence, you should have Cancerian children, they are best disciplined by appeals to their finer sensibilities. A parent can usually correct them best by saying, "It makes me sad to see you do that," rather than by scolding or smacking them; those measures will only make the small Cancerian more determined.

A primary source of disagreements between Cancerians and other people is the Cancerian habit of being notoriously untidy. Concentrating on more important matters, they just don't consider neatness and order of great concern. When your nonchalance verges on sloppiness and offends those around you, direct your Cancerian imagination to novel ways to expedite your business and put order into your affairs. Placating your fastidious friends and colleagues in this way will be worth the effort.

The major pitfall you face is one created by your restlessness. There is a chance that you won't settle into one career or even a single marriage. Individuals of a constant and routine mind won't understand your eagerness for new challenges. You can avoid their perhaps unkind misjudgments of you by finding a career that allows you diversity and travel. Guard your marriage by establishing numerous and varied friendships beyond your family limits, and be open about those relationships with your partner. The friendships you make should, of course, be platonic, so that your ties of interest don't become affairs of passion. Remember that your purpose is not to wreck your marriage but to improve its stability. So make your spouse an integral part of these friendships, which will strengthen your home life by expanding your joint horizons.

COLORS: Color is not as important to you as it is to many people, perhaps because your constantly changing intellectual pursuits fill your mind with the colors of ideas. Nonetheless, springlike shades of green, cream, and yellow, reminiscent of sunshine on budded boughs, can work wonders for your morale when it needs a boost. Light up your favorite room with those colors and retire to it when you feel the need for a lift. In fact, if you learn to use color to create excitement and express your appreciation for diversity, you will be less inclined to yield to aimless restlessness.

MONEY: The constant search for challenge will probably lead you to exchange one job for another in your early years. Avoid major purchases or financial speculation until your middle years, when a new project may call for all the money you can raise to invest in it. The right business interests for you would involve transportation and shipping, especially import and export dealings, which relate to your Cancerian kinship to water. Later in life, you may find yourself dealing with governmental offices in matters relating to licensing and tariffs.

HEALTH: Cancer Twos are especially sensitive to their surroundings. Your health is related to the way things are going for you in business or personal relationships. When all is well, financially or romantically, your health reflects it and you glow. For you, it is all a question of mind over matter. Once you recognize that good news will cure you faster than anything else, you learn to look on the brighter side of life and thereby preserve your health. The standard rules for physical fitness apply to you: exercise moderately, eat simply, and drink plenty of pure water. This last item is vital for someone with your Cancerian affinity to the oceans and rivers.

RELATIONSHIPS: Among the members of your family, you will enjoy close and long-lasting ties, as long as you don't strain them with too much kindness. Avoid the admirable but troublesome impulse to be too protective of others at your own expense. All children must totter and fall in trying to walk; otherwise, they would never learn. The same holds true for adults, although we might have to think awhile before we see all its implications.

While you are very affectionate and well loved for it, you are simultaneously practical and independent. In short, you want your own way. If you realize that other people have minds of their own, your friendships will be more secure and more rewarding.

Although we tend to think that romance is affected only by heroic deeds or great betrayals, a little fault like your disregard for neatness can grate on your beloved so cruelly that over a period of time, a marriage can be ruined. Does that sound impossible? Remember that through constant friction a grain of sand can destroy a huge machine. So attend to whatever areas of your conduct need improvement, even if they seem inconsequential to you.

CANCER—THIRD DIVISION *(June 21, 30, July 3, 12, 21)*

The planetary combination governing the Third Division is probably the most favorable one within the sign of Cancer. For those of you born under it, your personal and professional lives should be a steady upward progress toward happiness and success.

The reason for your good chances of success is the strong array of personality traits you have been given. You take nothing for granted. Diligent and persistent, you will be rewarded appropriately for your hard work. The list of your attributes is a roster of powerful assets:

- ambition
- independence
- creative ability
- leadership

Sparked by a desire to do things well, you have high ambitions. You are neither overpowering nor overly aggressive. That is why, as time and again you succeed in your ventures, people nod approvingly. They take your accomplishments for granted and are accustomed to your triumphs. Most important, they don't resent your progress, for you haven't antagonized them en route to the top, just as you don't look down on anyone after you have reached it. That is why your ambition is constructive and laudable, unlike the eagerness to get ahead which leads some people to exploit others and distort themselves.

Like the crab which is your astrological symbol, you have a tough exterior. Your personal independence may make you seem unconcerned over affection and good fellowship. Moreover, you can frequently be forceful in expressing your views, so much so that some who disagree with you may be reluctant to express their dissent. They fear that your rebuttal of their argument may be as snappy and painful as a crab's claws! But they misjudge you. Your closer associates, who have had time to know you fully, realize that your rigorous speech and commanding opinions are only the hard shell that covers a soft heart. If you learn to tone down the emphasis with which you address issues under discussion, more people will discover your natural sympathy for their problems and their views.

Another of your major assets is a natural creative ability, which you instinctively use to its fullest. You don't limit your spontaneous ideas to your work or to the arts, but also apply them to your everyday dealings with others. You have already learned that the greatest creativity lies not in painting or sculpture or music but in the harmonies of the human spirit, in seeing grounds of cooperation where others find only obstacles. You are in the habit of coming up with effective improvements which make others ask themselves, "Why didn't I think of that?" With all those strong points, you shouldn't be surprised to be told that your career opportunities are endless, once you learn to combine your creativity and leadership toward the same end.

For many Third Division Cancerians, a change of life-style is due in your middle thirties. Let me reassure you that despite your doubts, it will be for the better. Significant improvements in your career will combine with a good home life and happy marriage to keep you more than satisfied. But you do have one strong trait that can inhibit you from reaching the heights of professional success. Just as Andrew, the first Apostle to heed the call, stepped aside for his brother Peter to become the leader, so you are quite happy to relinquish the foremost positions of leadership to others, even though you yourself may be better equipped to fill those roles.

I became interested in astrology when I was still a teen-ager, and I noticed that my school friends who were natural leaders—the class presidents and officers of student clubs—were very frequently Cancerians, and often of the Third Division. They were eager workers, adept organizers, and respected advisers; but they would invariably step aside for someone else to take over if they thought he or she could do a better job. My advice in dealing with this trait of yours is to step aside if you think relinquishing your leadership would further your goals and accomplish your purposes. By all means, don't force yourself to carry burdens that others are eager to share. But never hesitate to voice your opinions, for your contributions to a joint effort are too valuable to be suppressed by modesty. Any group of which you are a part will need your guidance, whether as its chief or as counselor.

COLORS: Just as your personality is bold, your colors should also be forceful. In fact, your magnetic vibrations are best enhanced by the traditional shades of kingship: purples and violets as rich and varied as the fading African sunset. There is a special kinship between your commanding character and the exotic fire of an emerald, so use that luxuriant green to announce your presence to the world.

MONEY: I foresee no problems for you. An unusually high percentage of Cancer Threes have been raised in prosperous households, and those who didn't grow up in comfortable surroundings will very likely achieve economic independence early in their careers. Whether you become really wealthy will depend upon how soon, if ever, you make one important decision: not to step aside so readily but to advance to still higher levels of leadership. That is the important step which can put you on the escalator to fortune.

HEALTH: Your sound constitution and optimistic outlook on life free you from major illnesses. The same talents for organization which you bring to your work will also ensure that you eat properly, and your relish for activity in the outdoors will guarantee you proper exercise. The only threat to your well-being stems from your readiness to take on too much. Guard your own health by insisting that others do their fair share of the work.

RELATIONSHIPS: You will always have friends to rely on and a loyal family to stand by you. You have probably come to take those blessings for granted. And why not? Your personality, cheerful and commanding at the same time, has won them for you and always will. The only disappointments you may face in personal relationships will be due to someone's jealousy over your success. That need not bother you, for envy is only the problem of those whom it possesses. But do avoid criticism from your professional colleagues. If they warn you against overextending yourself, heed their caution: don't bite off more than you can chew. You will not only do better work but also have more time for your family.

You will make some lucky person a splendid mate, as long as you give the one you love sufficient time to get to know you. Sudden exposure to your powerful personality can mislead others into thinking you are insensitive. Turn your creativity toward finding ways to surprise and delight the one who means most to you.

CANCER—FOURTH DIVISION *(June 22, July 4, 13, 22)*

Cancerians of the Fourth Division are endowed with an unusual and vibrant personality by the combined planetary influences on their birth. Your personality is marked by an originality of thought, which is not only a great blessing but also a source of problems.

Quite often, Cancer Fours are not easy to get along with because they don't tolerate fools lightly. You expect everyone to either match your rapid pace or stand aside while you take care of business. All aspects of your life will be influenced by your quick intellect and your equally quick temper, unless you take steps to liberate the first while harnessing the second. By doing that, you will eliminate the disruptive force of anger from your life and will also keep unimpaired your positive qualities:

- confidence
- mental ability
- sensitivity
- concentration of your energies

The worst that can be said of you Cancer Fours is that you can be intolerant of anyone less gifted than you. Usually, this attitude is directed against pretentious people who falsify their credentials and boast of imaginary accomplishments. With sincere people, no matter what their shortcomings, you are all charm and kindness. If someone honestly admits his inabilities and humbly asks you to wait for him to catch up, you will tactfully offer your aid and encouragement. But Heaven help those who fail to live up to their promises to you! Then your intolerance is at its worst, and your scathing tongue will reduce them to emotional rubble. Whether or not they deserve that damage, you must realize that it also harms you. Your temper demeans you unnecessarily. It spoils your day and weakens your health. For everyone's sake, including your own, accept the fact that few people can always live up to your own exalted ideals.

With that one warning given, everything else in your forecast is good. The gift of an agile mind incites you to seek new challenges and allows you to retain a childlike wonder at the marvels of God's universe. Your sensitivity, especially to the needs of others who put themselves at your mercy, indicates a high degree of intuition; and you are likely to have experiences that border on the psychic. You are especially predisposed toward precognitive dreams, in which you will be given glimpses of future events. When they occur, and when your hunches prove correct, you treat the incidents as routine workings of the mind. I suggest you pay more attention to them. By developing your psychic faculties, you will see trouble when it lies ahead and be able to avoid it.

Another powerful weapon in your intellectual armory is an incredible ability to concentrate all your energies, mental and physical, on the project at hand. Your mind focuses like the beam of a laser, compressing tremendous force into a single point of burning power. By concentrating on one problem, you sear your way through to a solution while others are still debating the ground rules. This skill lets you accomplish difficult feats. It is a key to success. For mothers who are Cancer Fours, it ensures that their children will grow into fine adults, because their energetic maternal devotion builds character and integrity better than a whole committee of child-care experts.

I often think that Andrew, the Cancerian Apostle, must have had a personal tie to the Fourth Division, because he was so single-minded in his devotion to his Teacher and so successful in his evangelistic career. It is recorded in an old legend about Andrew that as he was dying on the X-shaped cross that is still called St. Andrew's Cross (and is part of the British flag), he continued to preach his message of love to those nearby. What a total concentration of effort! And how typical it is of Cancer Fours!

COLORS: Your intense magnetic vibrations need no more power but, rather, the cooling influence of blue. Until you actually experience the way properly used colors can tone down your emotions, especially that temper of yours, you may be skeptical of their efficacy. So try it! If you have a meeting scheduled with someone who habitually gets on your nerves, dress in any shade of blue from the pale glint at the heart of an ice crystal to the unequivocal blue of a cloudless Florida sky. If you are dealing with someone whose shyness and insecurity need reassurance, a splash of gold or yellow on your part can do wonders, whether it is a tie, a scarf, a blouse, or a sunny flower in your lapel.

MONEY: Money tends to slip through your hands like grain pouring into a silo. You are casual about it because you know you can always find more of it. As long as you are working on a payroll, you will live comfortably and make ends meet. But your real financial opportunities will come in your middle years, when you strike out alone. Your vibrations are akin to those of a counselor, and you might find yourself doing well as a consultant. Needless to say, your inventive mind makes you perfectly suited to that role.

HEALTH: Because you are vocal about your ailments, some

people will consider you a hypochondriac, though you are not. Don't be dissuaded from seeing a doctor when you want medical attention, but try not to change physicians, as you are inclined to do, whenever their advice doesn't suit you. You are predisposed to an allergy to foods rich in protein, especially seafood. That means that even though you are under the sign of the Crab, you may have to forgo this and other ocean delicacies.

RELATIONSHIPS: As a son or daughter, you are faithful to your parents even after you have reached maturity. As a husband or wife, you are devoted to your mate. But the same energies that make you an extrovert can also lead you to seek exciting companionship outside your marriage. You can avoid the potentially disastrous impact of this tendency by focusing that tremendous concentration of yours on the home and family you treasure.

Though you usually have only a small circle of friends, each of them would do anything for you if you asked it. Your more casual acquaintances are more numerous, which is just what a gregarious person like you requires.

The one rule to apply to all categories of relationships—with a lover, a friend, your family, your associates—is this: unleash your sensitivity and curb your temper.

CANCER—FIFTH DIVISION *(June 23, July 5, 14)*

The planetary combination governing the lives of Cancerians of the Fifth Division makes them highly impressionable individuals. You are easily influenced by other people or by your surroundings.

In equal measure, you respond to thoughtfulness displayed toward you, react with renewed effort to praise and encouragement, and dig in your heels in resistance when others try to force compliance with their will. In each case, you return kindness for benevolence and defiance for threats. In addition, your astrological character indicates that you are:

- organized to an extreme
- often intractable
- and, paradoxically, too easily led
- hospitable

Your mind is as systematic as a computer. It collects data, stores it away, and organizes your activities in detail. Your personal habits reflect this love of order. Even before you are out of bed in the morning, your day is planned and your work scheduled. That's a fine practice and can be of great value to you in advancing your career and furthering your studies. It can also be a way to reassure yourself against unforeseen intrusions. Your programmed life-style doesn't allow for changes in your plans.

This can lead to too much rigidity in your affairs. Other people make plans that will not always coincide with yours. When your business and theirs overlap, there will inevitably be irritation and frustration. If you honestly examine your attitudes, you will see that your penchant for organization often becomes sheer intractability, that is, a love of determination for its own sake. You are reluctant to budge from a comfortable rut and prefer that others change their expectations rather than interfere with your settled ways.

This is an inconsistency in your character, for you are normally gracious and thoughtful. Perhaps the reason you staunchly defend your control over that one small corner of your life is that in most other aspects, you allow others to call the shots for you. That statement requires some explanation. While you carry your fondness for order and pattern to an extreme, you are seemingly defenseless in the face of clever manipulation. You can easily be led by praise and accolades that are really flattery. We all love to win approval, but not at the price of renouncing our own ideas for those of someone else.

Be more confident of your work and values. You are more often right than wrong, so why should you allow another to do your thinking? In fact, once you appreciate your talents regardless of outside opinion, you may find less need for rigid organization in your life. Content with your abilities and achievements, you will be able to loosen up and enjoy things.

Your hospitality is your hallmark. Like Andrew, who must have frequently entertained Christ in the house he and Peter and their family shared at Capernaum, you delight in pleasing your guests. Like him, you would be concerned about feeding the multitude and would fret about their welfare. You use your organizational skill to plan and program for their benefit, and many individuals love you for it. You are the perfect host, and your dinners and parties are so well prepared—naturally!—that you can spend most of your time entertaining your guests.

COLORS: Especially in your entertaining, colors are an important channel of expression. Your magnetic vibrations are in harmony with light shades, especially pastels of blue, green, and yellow. It is no accident that you are partial to pale blue; for you do love to sit your friends down to dinner, and psychological tests have revealed that most people enjoy their meals best in a calm blue environment.

Let me make a helpful suggestion. When you want to assert your own mind and go your own way, assert your budding spirit by using the shade of green that bejewels the first spring grass or the faint lemon glow of sunlight after a shower.

MONEY: Once you choose a career and begin to apply your talents to it, you won't have money problems. If, at first, you are discouraged by the slowness of your progress, learn to take an overview of your life. You will then see that your work is part of a larger enterprise marked out for you and that its rewards will come in due time. Because of your managerial ability, both in your own affairs and those of your business, it would be wise to try your hand at keeping accounts.

HEALTH: Your chief physical asset is your power of recovery. No matter how serious the ailment, you will bounce back from it in double time, sometimes to the consternation of your doctor. Find ways to get away from your work occasionally, for you are one of those people who overburden themselves with responsibility. Prevent sickness before it approaches by relaxation and amusements.

RELATIONSHIPS: Your innate hospitality will win you numerous friends, but beware of opportunists and spongers. Learn to read hearts rather than lips, and you will soon be able to discern your true friends from casual good-timers.

There is a strong chance of serious disagreement between you and your parents during your late teen-age years, but then you will enjoy close ties to them on a basis of mutual understanding and respect. In marital matters, your prospects are excellent. If you want to guarantee a happy marriage, turn your attention to your own abilities. Many potential partners will appreciate your talent for organization, especially if they themselves need a helping hand in that regard. You will naturally win the affection of a great many guests, whose initial pleasure at your hospitality may grow into a more profound delight with their host's personality and thoughtfulness. In this way, entertainments can generate enduring romance as well as passing amusement.

CANCER—SIXTH DIVISION *(June 24, July 6, 15)*

Good things come easily to Cancerians of the Sixth Division, for the planets which influence the patterns of their lives have preordained, by an especially interesting juxtaposition of heavenly bodies, a noble personality for them. If you are included in their number, you are:

- generous
- kindly
- peaceable
- optimistic
- devoted to your parents

Andrew, the Cancerian Apostle, enjoyed the ability to bring people together in brotherhood, just as you do, because all his virtues were right there on the surface of his life, for all to see.

Your innate goodness shines through. It can't be hidden. Some people may regard you as open to exploitation, and others may mistake your kindliness for weakness; but everyone recognizes that there isn't an ounce of harm in you. To sum this up in a metaphor: the Devil's red boots, and all the negative forces they represent, have left no imprint in the path you are following. Your generosity is renowned. Without seeking publicity, you are openhanded to a fault. Indeed, your friends must sometimes step in to make sure you aren't deceived by false claims of poverty and want. Heed their warnings, for you have no obligations to tricksters and the indolent.

Your penchant for charity is even exceeded by your devotion to peace. You realize that respect and cooperation are necessary for any project to succeed, and you apply that maxim to your own work. Your colleagues note that you are dedicated and industrious but that you lack what is popularly called "the killer instinct," which many businessmen need to survive. You are reluctant to press debtors or stall creditors; and rather than exploit the mistakes of your competitors, you are more likely to offer them helpful advice. As a result, you will probably remain lower down on the totem pole than your talents indicate. But when rising to the top requires walking over others, the trip isn't for you. Even when things don't go your way—when someone else gets the promotion you expected or a rival wins the affections of your favorite date—you sense that things will turn out for the best. Usually your optimism is justified.

Your chief strength is as a middleman, the go-between. You can arrange differences between opposing factions when others have abandoned hope of compromise. Just as Andrew was sought out by Philip when he was asked to arrange a meeting with Christ for some Greeks visiting in Palestine, so you are the one to whom people turn as a mediator or arbiter.

Your devotion to your parents borders on reverence. A Cancer Six will put his family above all else and so make a wonderful parent in his or her own adulthood. You will forgive and forget any injury for the sake of your clan. Your tenacious defense of your home and respect for its elderly members are much needed strengths in contemporary society. You can serve, deliberately or not, as an example to those whose family ties have been strained or broken by rancor and misunderstanding.

Of course, by putting your family's good above your own, you make yourself vulnerable to impositions by relatives, although you never seem to mind. You regard yourself as being on earth to serve others, and your greatest reward for doing so is the loyalty you find among those who have been blessed by your assistance.

COLORS: The colors which best reflect and magnify the aura of your personality are blues and greens, especially the richer, vibrant hues, such as the beauty of aquamarines or turquoises, the sparkle of plainly set emeralds, or the mixed shades of a tropical sea in sunlight.

While you remain devoted to the welfare of others, the flattering use of color is something easy for you to indulge in. Especially in decorating your own home, strong colors will declare your welcome to one and all.

MONEY: Your luck in money matters is oriented toward steady, long-term gains rather than quick and speculative profits. Your personality is best suited to dealings in residential real estate; for matching a proper family to the proper home would be, for you, not only gainful employment but also a rewarding public service. Although these matters cannot be predicted with absolute certainty, you are likely to marry into money or to inherit a large sum without seeking it.

RELATIONSHIPS: As I have already said, you will always be close to your parents and family members. As with most Cancerians, your own marriage will be solid and loving, blessed by your own devotion to your children and the external support of a wide circle of friends. To make sure that you will be prepared to enjoy all those good things, select your mate with care, avoiding anyone whose principles and practices you wouldn't gladly call your own. Your marital prospects are too bright to be clouded by an uninformed or impulsive selection of a wife or husband.

CANCER—SEVENTH DIVISION *(June 25, July 7, 16)*

Highly intellectual and artistic, Cancerians of the Seventh Division are sensitive to beauty and, whether or not they understand their own instincts, are driven to create expressions of man's best hopes. Their medium may be visual, through ink or oils or wood or stone, or the written word. It may be music or the abstract beauty of philosophy or the very concrete beauty of a garden. However you express yourself, you Cancer Sevens must develop your gifts if you are ever to feel fulfilled.

Let me illustrate the way in which your lives have been patterned by your planetary influences.

I once received a letter from a Cancer Seven, a high school student, who wrote, "I feel a desire to become a writer, but I can't explain it to myself. There are no writers in my family. I've never even met a writer and I don't know anybody else who wants to become a writer. Am I just daydreaming?"

I assured him that he was not. We don't inherit our talents, and we don't acquire them by association with others. God alone gives us our innate abilities, and they are in tune with our astrological role in His cosmic symphony. There is no way we can renounce them, although we are free to neglect or abuse them. Even so, each of us is constantly made aware of our divinely given potential by longings and apparently odd whims. They may lead us to want to attempt something completely foreign to our regular routine.

As I told the searching student, if his longings were in accord with God's will for him, he would be able to fulfill them, even against great obstacles. I urged him to enroll in a writing course, to read books by great authors, and above all to write and rewrite his own thoughts. That was much the same routine followed by the young Ben Franklin two centuries ago as he struggled to improve upon the classics. I look forward to receiving someday a copy of that high school lad's first book; for I know, as he must now know, that it will arrive in due time.

All Cancerians must guard against the tendency to discard apparent whims that are really indications of their purpose in life. Within reason, anything that appeals to your creative instincts is within your reach. There is only one condition to consider, even though a significant one. You must be prepared to accept initial hardships and sacrifice material satisfactions for the sake of your artistic commitment. It won't be easy for you to watch your classmates prosper in their careers while you struggle with your writing or painting, your acting or dancing. You may have to work for years to achieve the perfection, not to mention the income, you want. It will require all your determination, and a healthy dose of good cheer, to turn your daydreams into reality.

You do have a powerful asset on your side. You care little for material things; and so a lack of riches, at least in your youth, won't depress you or stifle your spirits. But that doesn't mean you can automatically cope with deprivation, especially if you marry early. Be warned now: you can concentrate on either your marriage or your career in the arts. Both are so demanding that a rare maturity and saintly self-sacrifice are necessary to sustain them at the same time. By postponing a romantic commitment until you are established in your creative field, you will be able to have the best of both a happy home life and a distinguished artistic career.

COLORS: Color should be important to you. Indeed, it is essential to most forms of creative expression. The life of the mind demands a certain calm if ideas are to flourish. No one ever wrote a sonata while a brass band was playing, and no one ever originated great thoughts that would benefit mankind in the midst of a turbulent and troubled spirit. Reduce your tensions and tame your sporadic magnetism with pastels. Let delicate flower tints soothe you as they invite your companions to join in your mental ease. This is especially important if your artistic work is dark and heavy, either physically, as in the case of sculpture, or figuratively, as in the case of a somber novel or tragic play. At those moments in your work, splash on sunlight colors of pale greens and yellows.

MONEY: Needless to say, you will not be wealthy in monetary terms. Even when you have become successful in your work, you will remain uncertain of your financial security. If you are wise, you will invest your major earnings when your fame brings you sudden prosperity. Be careful with those few windfalls, and remember that a rainy day inevitably comes along, even to those who have made a name for themselves in the theater or the academic community. In the meantime, don't regret your lack of riches. You will enjoy life more than many wealthy individuals who lack your appreciation of the beauty that surrounds us all.

HEALTH: Though you don't appear to be physically robust, you are like a creaking gate that just keeps hanging on. You will outlast everyone. Especially when your work is going well, you possess tremendous endurance. It is as if your body's energy is recharged from the fulfillment you find in your labor and in all aspects of life. That promises a long life, free from major ailments.

RELATIONSHIPS: During your most creative years, you will meet many supposed sponsors, who express interest in furthering your artistic talents. You will usually find that their true intention is to exploit you, either financially or sexually or psychologically. Steer clear of them. Rely on your own talents, and you won't need the self-serving intervention of opportunists.

Your relatives will be your best sources of friendship and support. They will always admire you for what you do, even if it doesn't bring you wealth. You may be working in a factory or library or restaurant or operating room, able to pursue your creative interests only in your spare time. Then you will recognize your best friends, for they will do all they can to keep your commitment strong and assist the realization of your dreams.

Before you enter a marriage, make sure your intended understands the vitality of your intellectual concerns. A spouse who expects and demands riches will make you miserable, but a mate who shares your certainty that beauty makes the world go around will live happily ever after with you.

CANCER—EIGHTH DIVISION *(June 26, July 8, 17)*

If I had to sum up all my advice in a few words for a Cancer Eight, I would say, "Stick with it." For you will need to utilize every bit of your considerable determination, patience, and persistence to succeed. But once you make that total commitment, then, as if by clockwork, you will progress directly to your goals. You are:

- tough-minded
- selfless
- a leader
- an organizer

And you will need every one of those qualities to fulfill your purpose in life. By one of those quirks of Nature, determined by the endless motions of the stars, you Cancer Eights are usually the ones who are burdened with responsibilities that threaten to divert you from your mission on earth. For instance, you may find yourself running a small business that once belonged to your parents. You would not be particularly interested in its operations but feel that someone must take charge and it may as well be you. You would be too tough-minded to grieve over those circumstances or consider yourself a martyr. It would never occur to you to complain to anyone about your lot in life. You would selflessly continue to meet your duties, even though, from time to time, you felt that life was slipping past you.

In fact, it may not be a domestic situation that is holding you back. It could be an investment you made or an undertaking you began many years ago without realizing that it would tie you up and demand your attention for so long. Perhaps you have settled in an area for personal or professional reasons but now feel an inexplicable desire to be living somewhere else. It may be that you have entered the wrong career but are reluctant to change course now that you are established. This would usually be true for a Cancer Eight whose work is in education, the church, or farming. Despite your vague anxiety concerning your profession, you plod ahead as if nothing can be done to improve your situation. Most of all, you don't want to be considered a quitter or a failure. Whatever the reason, your star-set pattern of life shows a period of frustration for your real ambitions before you begin to work toward their fulfillment.

It is an apt blessing that you are a natural leader and organizer, because you will need those gifts to achieve what you want, especially since you will probably start to pursue your true ambitions a little later than most people. Your future will be brighter if you understand that there are cycles in life, some as long as seventeen years, when we are either the victims or the masters of our circumstances. As a dominant character and commander of others, you must wait for a favorable cycle which will allow you to quickly make up for your late start. You need only marshal the determination that typifies Cancerians. Recall the fable of the tortoise and the hare. It doesn't matter if we are behind at the start of the race; all that matters is the finish line.

As you forge ahead, remember that your selflessness is an asset, even when it leads you to postpone your own accomplishments. It ennobles your character and will bring you hidden satisfactions. Try to retain that trait as you strike out toward your own goals.

COLORS: Your magnetism needs to be stirred with the effective use of colors, especially green in all its shades. Sage green, the color of desert plants after a rare day of rainfall, suits you perfectly. It may represent the new lease on life awaiting Cancerians of the Eighth Division in the star-planned pattern of their lives. Silver or platinum ornaments on your clothing are excellent morale boosters. Perhaps they emphasize your leadership role, like insignia of rank; you are, after all, a figure of authority to many.

MONEY: You are probably already off to a good start with your savings, and should accumulate money you will not have opportunities to spend in your early life. By the time you move out on your own, you will have a comfortable nest egg in reserve. Plan ahead how you will use it. It can provide either a brief, expensive fling or solid investments and long-range income which will guarantee your personal independence.

Avoid speculation. Financial risks are not your strong point. The only impulsive investments you should make are in yourself, by developing your own talents. That way, you will face no money problems in your later years but will have the personal abilities to work your way out of any pinch.

HEALTH: As is the case with most Cancerians, your health is directly related to your emotions. During your youthful years of frustration and consequent depression, you are inclined to intestinal troubles brought on by emotional upset. As you grow older and are more fulfilled in your work, however, your health will improve. When you enjoy your labor, even when arduous, it will boost your spirits and fortify your body.

RELATIONSHIPS: No great drama characterizes your relationships. You rarely care for exuberant expressions of emotion and stormy personal ties. Both in youth and in maturity, you will probably have few close friends, because you prefer solid bonds to flimsy ones. Your family regards you as dependable, and indeed you are. They know the sacrifices you make of yourself, even if they don't vocalize their appreciation.

The trouble spot in your relationships will come in your mid-thirties. As your life suddenly broadens and new horizons appear, as your long-postponed plans are put into operation and you take the initiative to realize your dreams, you could be tempted to throw over old ties as outmoded parts of your previous life-style. That would be a tragic mistake.

This is doubly true with regard to your sexual relationships. As your star ascends to a commanding position, casual romances will become as easy as they are disruptive of your true happiness. Guard against that danger by discounting flatterers and by remembering the faithfulness of those who have stood by you in hard times.

CANCER–NINTH DIVISION *(June 27, July 9, 18)*

The future of Ninth Division Cancerians is entirely in their own hands. Their positive characteristics assure them success in a variety of fields, but their progress hinges upon how well they co-operate with other people. If this is your division, you are:

- headstrong
- forceful
- fearless
- accident-prone

All of those qualities, save for the last, are fine, if you live on a desert island. But Robinson Crusoes are rare these days, and you must make your way in school, in business and industry, and in social and civic affairs, not in the wilds. It is necessary, therefore, that you carefully direct your personality characteristics into fields and activities in which they will actually be beneficial.

Your traits can be negative if uncontrolled. If they are allowed to dominate your thinking and emotions, they will hurry you along into paths well worn by the Devil's red boots. Like any powers for good, yours will harm you if employed recklessly. Think of your abilities as strong medicines which, cautiously administered, can mend and heal but which, when abused, create misery.

Andrew makes a fine example of prudent leadership. He made

speedy decisions and was willing to accept all their consequences, but he was not headstrong, in marked contrast to his brother Peter. His forcefulness was quiet and controlled. Imitate him in this, for he is a model of the way Cancer Nines can adapt their personality patterns to most rewarding purposes.

Cancer Nines are masters of the frontal attack, not realizing that, on many occasions, the best way to reach a goal is not necessarily the most direct one. You may be building up resistance to your ideas simply from the way you move to take charge of circumstances. Learn that in most aspects of life, we have to deal with others even when they are shortsighted, hesitant, and indecisive. The very qualities that would make you a superb boss on a cattle drive can cause you trouble at work or in your home. There is no question that you are fearless, but you can also be blind to danger. For the sake of those who depend upon you, temper boldness with caution. And make no mistake about it: people *do* depend on you, recognizing your prospects for success and profiting from your willingness to take command.

Your personal advancement means much to you, and there is surely nothing wrong with that, as long as it doesn't demand the sacrifice of your principles. By easing off a little, however, you will find that you can have both success and friendships if you take time to enjoy the good life you have earned.

As a predictable sidelight on your high-speed approach to living, you are prone to accidents. You practically overpower life and are careless around machinery and vehicles. Time after time, you hurt yourself in ways that a more deliberate, slower individual would have avoided. It may not do any good for me to tell you to slow down, since you already know that your speed and frenzy are counterproductive. But they are habits by now, and so they will require time to break.

COLORS: Your magnetic vibrations spark out from you like an electrical storm. You can soothe yourself and reassure those with whom you deal by wearing cream, white, and rose. Especially in combination with one another, those shades express a warmth and concern which you do, in fact, feel, even though you may not be adept at putting your tender feelings into words. Until you try it, you will never know how a white suit makes even the boldest leader seem gentle and approachable.

MONEY: Money matters are usually all-or-nothing situations for you. Because you are intelligent and keep informed of current trends, many of your odd schemes will work out and thereby encourage you to your next venture. But your luck will not be constant, and what you make on one windfall will be lost in a subsequent fiasco.

Make provisions for your old age early. Examine your business ventures more carefully. The months of April, July, October, and December are notably bad times for financial deals in which you are involved. As a general rule, remember that the same headstrong rush which makes you susceptible to physical accidents also leaves you vulnerable to economic disasters. Both can be avoided by a deliberate regimen of prudence and reflection.

HEALTH: You are a firecracker whose vitality shrugs off ailments rapidly. But the damage done by accidents cannot so easily be dismissed. For your own sake, and for the well-being of your family, slow down to live longer.

RELATIONSHIPS: Your dynamism both attracts and repels people, depending upon their own personality makeup. With proper tact, there are few individuals who can't be swayed by your bearing. Some will follow your authority. Others need to be handled with care, conciliated and soothed. Even the suggestion of your raw energy will stir antagonism in them. Cloak your forcefulness in diplomacy, even if your urge to speak out and act directly seems to choke your efforts. You can make it; and in the process, you will find new ways to exert your leadership for its fullest accomplishment.

The same holds true in romantic affairs. Explain your feelings and intentions, even if the words come awkwardly to you. Otherwise, those you most cherish may be at a loss to understand you. Commander that you are, don't try to run your home with the same authority you exert elsewhere. There above all, your leadership must involve listening and learning.

LEO—JOHN *(July 23–August 22)*

Leo is the fifth segment of the Zodiac, the sign of the Lion. And I confess that it caused me some initial bafflement when, in my vision, I saw that it was identified with the Apostle John. For this was the youngest of the Apostles, sometimes called John the Beloved, the faithful youth whom Leonardo da Vinci portrayed in his masterpiece, "The Last Supper," leaning close to Christ like a lamb seeking security and protection.

Was this a Leonine character? I didn't think so. Without really having any evidence, I had always assumed that John was timid and gentle, a kid brother, so to speak, to the other Apostles. A little research, however, soon showed me the error of my assumptions. Christ had once referred to John and his older brother, James the Greater, as the "Sons of Thunder." The Greek word used in Scripture is *Boanerges,* derived from the original Hebrew phrase, and it indicates a boisterous zeal in expressing opinions and in condemning opponents. In fact, there was a time when Christ and the Apostles were entering an unfriendly town and the Sons of Thunder asked Him if they should call down the fires of destruction upon the place! Their Teacher told them they should not; and they surely must have learned from His patience the error of their roaring ardor, just as we should learn that righteousness without kindness is intolerance.

In so many ways, then, John was a lion indeed, especially when he and his fellows set out to evangelize the world with the good news their Master had given them. John preached through much of Asia Minor, tirelessly and incessantly; and, despite the infirmities of old age, was writing and teaching until his death, probably in the year A.D. 101. No wonder he has often been represented in painting and sculpture by an eagle. And as the spirit of his Gospel soars, we can hear its message delivered with the unequivocal forcefulness of a Leonine heart.

Those of you who share the sign of the Lion with John also share his characteristics. But before we see how this affects your daily life and determines your role in the universal plan for mankind, I want to remind you—not just you Leos, but all my readers—that it is not sufficient wisdom just to learn about ourselves. To appreciate the diversity of God's handiwork and to understand the worth of each individual on this earth, we must also learn about our fellow pilgrims on the road to Paradise. So as you now read about your own sign of the Zodiac, be sure that, afterward, you turn to those preceding and following this one. Remember that a single note of the musical scale, no matter how lovely, requires all the rest in order to become music. So, too, you Leos need to perceive your relationships with Ariens and Cancerians, with Capricorns and Libras, in order to play your part in the divine symphony.

And what a part it is! Like the Sons of Thunder, you have a quick temper, but it is directed through your strong personality toward tenacity and determination. Warm and generous by nature, above all magnanimous, you know you are a leader, even when you do not formally assume that role.

Leos are probably the most forgiving people in the world. They bear injuries without revenge and seldom retaliate for personal offenses. But they can be provoked by lassitude or indifference, just as John was when townsmen ignored the message of Christ. Because you get so much out of life, you are shocked by people who sit on the sidelines, watching the world go by. Though you are gentle with foes and considerate with boors, you may be angered by someone who wants others to do everything for him.

Your tolerance is grounded in your habit of taking an overview of things, looking for good even in a bad situation, anticipating some benefit from every setback and misfortune. You are especially attracted by other strong personalities which are not swamped by your own vigorous spirit, and you may overlook any faults they may have out of admiration for their individualism and sense of purpose.

You share that trait with your Apostle. Not only was John closest to Christ, but after the Crucifixion, he became the Apostle closest to Peter. Those were the two who went into Jerusalem to prepare the Passover meal that became the Last Supper. Those two ran to the tomb owned by Joseph of Arimathea to find out for themselves the facts of the Resurrection. It is an interesting sidelight on Leonine character that John, younger and faster, reached the tomb first but showed his respect for Peter by waiting outside until the older and more senior Apostle arrived. No wonder, then, that Peter and John went together through Asia Minor when the time came to carry their message to the Gentiles.

It must be noted, however, that the Leonine personality—creative, powerful, and impressive—can generate its mirror image, so to speak, of negative traits. When I saw those red boots stride arrogantly across the altar of the Cathedral, I realized that in this world at least, for every force there is a counterforce, for every merit there is a potential fault, and for every virtue a possible vice. Properly applied, Leo's qualities are great powers for good. Misused, they are equally potent sources of sorrow. Indeed, it is a little disconcerting to observe that Lucifer himself seems to have possessed Leonine traits, albeit distorted ones. No, I am not saying that the fallen Prince of Angels was subject to the influences of the Zodiac; but I am reminding Leos, and all of us, that his red boots come in all sizes to fit the misguided feet of anyone who cares to put them on.

Leos are tremendously loyal and, in their role as leaders, demand corresponding loyalty from others. Usually you will receive it; but on those occasions when your faith is betrayed by insincerity or guile, you are vulnerable to be deeply hurt. When someone close to you falls short of your expectations, you are more than disappointed; you are disillusioned and apt to demand an explanation. As I have already said, you are normally reasonable and long-suffering; but discover that a confidence has been broken or a trust betrayed, and you become Leo the Lion, with a terrible temper and violent words.

You have probably already realized that you are a compulsive worker. Others notice that you always put forth your best effort, but you know of no other way to do a job and are mystified when your colleagues try to get by with slipshod work. Your self-respect is so tied to your labor that any chore, even a menial one, becomes an exercise in perfection. This means that as your responsibilities build and the action centers around you, you are well equipped to take charge of the situation and sustain the demands of leadership.

That doesn't indicate that you are egotistical, but rather theatrical. Leo is the sign of the actor, and you are always conscious of your audience, even if it is only a mirror. For you are your most demanding critic. Leos usually display their theatrical flair in the way they dress, in the way they organize events or projects on a grand scale, and in their habit of tipping generously and expecting the best of everything when they seek leisure and entertainment.

Another major asset on the Leonine balance sheet is an alert mind. This enables you to move in many career directions, generally doing well. You are apt to change your profession several times in your early life until you find that special niche that suits your temperament, either in a supervisory position or in a less ordinary role as a professional athlete, dancer, or actor.

Your open heart keeps your family dear to you and gives you excellent prospects of a happy home life and sound marriage. The only problem you will face in this regard is your tendency to demand that those closest to you toe the line and at least equal your virtues. While it is commendable for you to want to raise your children to develop their fullest potential, sooner or later you will have to realize that they cannot be carbon copies of their gifted parent. Instead of expecting them to possess your own good qualities, learn to see in them their own unique talents. Perhaps they have strengths and powers you yourself are lacking.

One sure step toward a happy family situation is to turn your temper away from your loved ones. When you need to blow off steam, go for a walk. That's even better than a drive, for too many angry drivers end up as statistics in traffic accidents. Learn to dispel your occasional aggressiveness with a brisk ramble through the glories of nature, even if it is winter and you must bundle up against the cold. In a way, that is how those Sons of Thunder learned to turn their Leonine aggression to worthy purposes, only their walks through the countryside were taken in the company of an unexcelled Teacher. Nonetheless, John and his brother faced the same challenge as Leos today: to harness all that lionlike strength and so to draw the world a little closer to its eventual reunion with its Creator. What they did, you can do too.

In the roll of history's famous Leos, the best known is probably Napoleon Bonaparte, who was born on August 15. As a lionhearted leader, he was gifted with immeasurable talent for achievement. He redrew the map of Europe, created and abolished nations with a stroke of his pen, revised the legal system of France and thereby developed the fundamental principles of law still in use on several continents. And yet, his Leonine powers went astray as his anger raged beyond control and his determination led his followers to disaster. Much of the world was plunged into carnage by his ambitious schemes. Millions died as the price of his adventures. He attempted to reestablish slavery on the island of Haiti because human lives were less valuable to him than his own glory. He is the perfect example of a Leo in red boots!

Needless to say, few individuals from any segment of the Zodiac so completely betray their own best instincts. Dag Hammarskjöld (July 29) personified idealism. Bernard Baruch (August 19) was the epitome of dedication to business and service to one's country. Eminent Leonine women include Amelia Earhart (July 24), Emily Brontë (July 30), Lucille Ball (August 6), and Ethel Barrymore (August 15).

In government, Leonine luminaries have included Presidents Benjamin Harrison (August 20) and Herbert Hoover (August 10), Senator Estes Kefauver (July 26), and Simon Bolivar, the Liberator of South America (July 24).

Just as the Apostle John became a writer and evangelist, many other Leos have graced the world of literature with their talent. Among them are George Bernard Shaw (July 26), Booth Tarkington (July 29), John Galsworthy (August 14), Ogden Nash (August 19), and Sir Walter Scott (August 15). The inimitable James Fahey (July 23), humanitarian and author of the famous *Pacific War Diary,* has combined both the creativity and the dedication of Leo in his work. In music, composer Sigmund Romberg was born on July 29 and Claude Debussy on August 22, while Rudy Vallee was born on July 28 and the great Count Basie on August 21.

Two of America's most famous sons were Leos; and both demonstrated the Leonine inventiveness, which, combined with equally Leonine determination, eventually brought them success. Henry Ford, who found ways to bring the first mass-produced autos to people, was born on July 30; and Orville Wright, co-inventor of the first airplane, was born on August 19.

The tremendous potential of Leonine minds for scientific inquiry is evident in the careers of such diverse thinkers as Izaak Walton (August 9), the early English naturalist; Carl Jung (July 26), one of the founders of modern psychology; Dr. Louis Leakey (August

7), the famed anthropologist; Dr. Denton Cooley (August 22), perhaps America's foremost heart specialist; and Dr. Benjy Brooks (August 10), the very feminine Texas surgeon whose work in pediatric medicine has made her name known and loved around the world.

You who live under the sign of the Lion certainly have quite a roster of successful men and women to take as models for your own efforts! You have as well the negative example of Napoleon and a host of lesser Leos who lost their chances for enduring achievement and personal happiness when they misdirected their gifts and distorted their mission on earth. Remember that the good and evil available to Leos are also accessible to us all. With that encouraging yet chastening lesson in mind, let us see how each of the nine divisions within the sign of Leo serve, like variations on a theme played by a masterful composer, to embellish our world with disparity and enliven our relationships with a never-ending assortment of vivid personalities.

LEO–FIRST DIVISION *(July 28, August 1, 10, 19)*

Leos of the First Division have one of the most favorable planetary combinations of the entire Zodiac. In the early period of their lives, they will be forced into several detours away from their intended goal, but once they become aware of their potential and adjust their sights accordingly, they are sure to succeed. If you are a Leo One, your prominent characteristics include:

- excellent disposition
- emotional involvement
- ability to win honors
- intuitive avoidance of trouble

Your disposition—sunny, outgoing, ever enthusiastic—is your strongest point. You are invariably "up," as they say, cheerful and expansive. People are drawn to you upon their first meeting. Casual acquaintances, as well as close friends, frequently give you gifts as expressions of their esteem. Those who work for you are usually willing to make an extra effort on your behalf without being asked, and their compliment, delivered by deed instead of words, has a strong effect on you. The eagerness of your subordinates increases your own drive and is a great help to you on your road to success.

Your weak spot is a tendency to deal people out of your plans.

You may feel others are not capable of staying the course and meeting your high demands, but unless you learn to let them down gently, you will unintentionally hurt them. Even the grandest adventure needs the slow and plodding aid of average folk. If you appreciate their work as much as you recognize your own talent, you will include them in your efforts, both professional and personal.

Face the fact that your magnetic personality will bring emotional involvements in both your private and public affairs. Whether involving relatives, colleagues, or loved ones, these relationships can be meaningful and enjoyable. For example, you can feel the most intense loyalty to your boss, the greatest sympathy for relatives in need, deep affection for your colleagues, total dedication to the well-being of your family. In short, you can feel what we all feel, only in stronger form. And as long as your sensitivities are kept within reason, you will be ennobled by them and others will bless you for the richness you bring to their lives.

The danger in your special gift of emotional ties with others lies in the area of romantic attraction, especially while you are between the ages of twenty-five and thirty. For it is then that friends of the opposite sex will most frequently recognize your personal merits, and it will be all too easy for your affections to escape the control of your prudence. In other words, your best emotions can cause your worst problems. Guard against that outcome by distinguishing between sympathy and love.

Part of your attractiveness to others is your confidently relaxed attitude. Honors and trophies seem to come naturally to you. You don't push your way around people in a hurry to succeed, but do whatever work comes your way as well as you can. Perhaps you are sometimes surprised when casual acquaintances at a party wish to get to know you better. If so, you are underestimating your personal appeal, and that may be all to the good. That touch of modesty becomes you.

Like all Leos, you have trouble controlling your temper; but more than your fellows in any other division of your sign, you Leo Ones have been given ample ability to restrain your roaring. Another special talent that characterizes your division is an intuitive sense of impending trouble. Time and again, this has allowed you to anticipate problems before they appear, and has repeatedly given you an advantage over your competitors. Learn to sensitize yourself still further, not being gloomy about the future but honestly opening your mind to whatever vibrations come your way. If you do have a special receptivity to those signals, then you have been blessed in a special way and must learn to use your talent for the good of those around you.

If you combine all these Leonine characteristics we have discussed with your ambition, conscientiousness, and sense of achievement, it is no wonder that you are fated to reach heights in whatever field may be yours. And you will do so, just as John did, at a remarkably early age, well before your middle years. That means that you will spend an unusually long time already established as a success. So plan ahead while you are still young to assume responsibilities early and to reap the emotional rewards of a lifetime of service.

COLORS: For the regal Leo, apparel and surroundings should tend toward golden and yellow tones. Dress in colors as tawny as your namesake, whether the light fawn of a lion cub or the highlighted brown of its sire's mane. These shades are doubly appropriate for you because they subconsciously represent your first-place achievements. Admit it, you have a gold medal or ribbon put away somewhere as a memento, don't you? Moreover, the lighter golds, approaching the radiance of dandelions, reflect your sunny disposition and cheery outlook on life. By the way, humble yet sturdy as it is, the dandelion is a fitting flower for you to wear. Even if it draws curious stares, there is no more appropriate blossom for a Leo. Its name comes to us from the French and means "tooth of the lion"!

MONEY: The stellar combination that governs your financial life is excellent. Your rare money problems are most likely to occur in your early years, as you choose a career; and you must not let them discourage you from pursuing your dreams. Once you settle down, you will be able to pay off old debts rapidly and make your way to comfortable economic circumstances.

HEALTH: Here, too, your prospects are superb. Only in your childhood and teen-age years will you suffer from ill health of any serious nature, and even that is preventable through proper clothing and attention to your diet and sleep. Later in life, you will enjoy the long-term benefits of your sound constitution and overall good health.

RELATIONSHIPS: Family, friends, and colleagues will admire and respect you, although there will be occasional hurt feelings if you don't assert your sensitivity over your Leonine temper. Generous and loving, you will never lack friends; you earn their loyalty by your own faithfulness.

Let me repeat here what I have already said about your personal relationships in romantic situations. You will have much to offer the fortunate individual with whom you decide to share your life, especially after you reach your higher levels of accomplishment, around the age of thirty. It is sad but true that there will always be some individuals who seek to exploit the merits of others and bask in the reflected glow of hard workers and talented stars. Make sure that the one you love returns your love for the right reasons and would be willing to stand by you in bad times as well as good.

LEO—SECOND DIVISION *(July 29, August 2, 11, 20)*

Public prominence awaits Leos of the Second Division. If they cooperate with God's plan for their lives, they are well suited to be the showmen and public figures of this world. The reasons are summed up by their personal characteristics, for they are:

- self-expressive
- intellectually acute
- sensitive to the dramatic
- personable

If you were born within this division, your chief asset is the innate ability to speak your mind, not just with words but with the shading and nuance of meaning that sometimes convey our messages better than the phrases we say.

The indications of the stars reveal that the right career for you involves either writing or speaking to the public. You probably became aware of this trait at an early age and by now should have sensed that you are drawn toward a life in the limelight. Even so, you are apt to dismiss the idea as preposterous, a daydream. Besides, you may feel you are too old to start on the long path to fame. Banish that negative thinking! It is not too late to develop your talents and to move into a harmonious career. Do nothing rash, but consider carefully how you might expand your horizons and then proceed, one cautious step at a time, to do just that. Does your community need a civic spokesman? Does your local newspaper need articles of neighborhood interest? Do your children enjoy the tales you make up for them? Why not write them down in book form? Why not try your hand at letters to the editor? Why not speak your mind at the next citizens' association meeting? All those means of creative expression could be points of departure for a new career, or a supplementary one, in mass communication.

Leo Twos often gullibly put their faith in stories of instant stardom, like the tales of chance discovery by Hollywood press agents. If those illusions go unchecked, they can prevent you from exerting the effort that alone can bring you success. Every prominent performer I know has had to work hard to get started and then work even harder to keep the momentum going. My good friend Hildegarde, the inimitable chanteuse, spends as many hours today rehearsing at her piano as she did years ago when she first started on the ladder to the top. She still fills a nightclub with her performances, but there is nothing accidental about the ovations she receives. She has earned them.

Those are the hard facts, but you are well equipped to deal with them. All that talent with which you have been endowed was not meant to be wasted on fantasies. Remember that success is not an end in itself, but rather a life-style that results from building one accomplishment upon another. Begin now with what can be done in your immediate circumstances. That first step is the most crucial. How often we have heard the old adage, "A journey of a thousand miles begins with the first step." Another way of putting the idea was shown in a conversation between my husband and a small child, who asked how he could become a bishop. Jimmy replied, "That's easy. You just become a priest, then hang around long enough. The hard part is becoming a priest." So whatever your Leonine ambitions, stick with them!

No matter the level of your formal education, you are by instinct an intellectual. You recognize the truth in most arguments, even when fine words try to conceal it. You understand the difference between wisdom and learning and know that the former is, by far, more important. By all means, don't take your intelligence for granted. Develop it, whether by institutional education or self-study. There is no surer way to contentment.

Despite your formidable assets, you prefer not to compete. You can be in a crowd but not of it, and you don't relish fighting for the spotlight. Nonetheless, your talents may make you the center of attention, the one whom crowds gather to hear. Chin up! You will find it possible to have a public life and yet remain an essentially private person.

Your flair for the dramatic is a fine asset in catching the attention you need to present your ideas. In more intimate circumstances, dealing with a few individuals rather than a group, your magnetic personality will serve you well and secure the cooperation of those whose agreement you need. Even when you are not in the limelight, you are fastidious about your appearance. Your clothes, though not necessarily expensive, are clean and cared for; your grooming is impeccable, though not maintained at great cost. As you move up in influence and exposure, you will find that this simple wholesome appearance makes a better impression than overdone ornamentation or jaded elegance.

John must have shared many of your instincts. He knew that as a preacher of a new way of life, he had to attract the attention of masses of people and hold their interest to explain the message of his Gospel. For him, as for most Leos, it must have been easy; for John's record of success throughout the provinces of Asia Minor was spectacular. Perhaps he was something of a showman. Certainly the visions he recounted in the Apocalypse were more dramatic than anything ever written before or since. They still bring a chill and an abrupt sense of discovery when we read them. And yet, so many years earlier, when he was walking over the stony hills of Palestine, he never dreamed of the work that lay ahead of him. You, too, may have no idea of the important tasks that await you.

COLORS: The use of color is important to you, and you may already have discovered that all shades of green flatter your appearance, from the almost luminous sheen of new grass in the spring to the deep gloss of holly leaves in the fall. At those moments when your dramatic inclinations must be satisfied, try teaming green with vividly contrasting golds and yellows, as if you were a sun-loving lion in lush foliage. For a more subdued appearance, especially in your intellectual pursuits, cream, white, and even the off-shade of oatmeal can suggest your deliberate advancement in matters of the mind.

MONEY: It has been ordained that you will generally be lucky in money matters, but there will be ups and down in your fortunes, especially in your youth. Too openhanded at times, you find yourself short of funds when you need them. Your most secure earnings will come from intellectual rather than business ventures. For example, consulting fees or tuition payments will come your way more often than stock options or executive bonuses.

HEALTH: You tend to avoid intense physical activity, and your health suffers from your failure to get sufficient exercise. Your digestion is often poor, as is your circulation; and although you wonder what you can do to feel better, you are loath to change your settled habits. For a rapid return to vim and vigor, eat less of everything, especially of those rich foods you favor, and manage to work some moderate exercise into your daily routine.

RELATIONSHIPS: As a charmer, you are destined for a long and happy family life, a satisfying career, and numerous friendships. But there is a dogmatic quality about you that irritates others. You already know you have strong opinions on any subject worthy of your attention. Try not to force your views on others, who may have given as much thought to matters as you have, perhaps even more.

In romantic relationships, your insistence upon your opinions can be especially disruptive. Try this for an experiment. Sometime, when you and the one you love are in disagreement over a matter of fact, purposely give in, even though you know you are right. I do not mean for you to make a show of it, grudgingly admitting that the other party may be correct. Actually try to show that you respect views contrary to your own and that you see the error of your ways. Believe me, once you learn to do that, you will never want to revert to your old habit of dogmatic bluntness. For you will have discovered what we can learn only from experience: a gentle agreement is more powerful than forceful discord. This is true in business and in politics, but it is a thousand times truer in marital affairs.

LEO—THIRD DIVISION *(July 30, August 3, 12, 21)*

A driving ambition is the name of the game for Leos of the Third Division. You are a boiling kettle of get-up-and-go, and your ambition is an appropriate and constructive release valve for all that energy. To understand why you are a child of success, consider the impact of your astrologically determined personality. You are:

- a natural leader
- an achiever

- naturally adept in whatever areas interest you
- diligent

That is a potent combination of qualities, and it is no wonder that you are unable to settle for second best. Knowing you are capable of meeting most challenges, you relish responsibilities as much as most people turn from them. You shoulder burdens that others shun because you need to be in the center of the ring, the eye of the storm, wherever the action is.

Whether or not you try to assume command, others look to you as a leader; and those in authority, seeing the need for things to be done, are usually ambitious people. A healthy streak of selfless ambition characterized the Apostle John, who also needed to be involved wherever matters were most urgent. He had been a follower of John the Baptist before he met Christ; and at that time, the Baptist was one of the most controversial figures in Judea. When the young man did at last meet the Messiah, he soon became His favorite disciple and, three years later, was the unnamed youth who, as Scripture reports, still followed behind his Master even after He had been arrested.

Like you, John was an achiever. Even as youngsters, you Leo Threes wanted to be at the head of your class and frequently were. There were several reasons for that early success, as there will be for your accomplishments later in life. In the first place, your immense drive goads you to climb higher, to learn faster, to build better, to know more. In addition, you actually enjoy work because of the psychological pleasure you attain by being skilled in your pursuits. Whether they be exceedingly complex matters or rather simple chores, you derive an emotional and intellectual satisfaction out of doing work well. There is no greater asset in the adventure of life!

You have been blessed with yet another bonus: your diligence. People are sometimes amazed by how much you can accomplish in a day. Their amazement is an important part of the delight you obtain from keeping so busy. You enjoy the stunned looks on their faces when you announce that the project has been completed and you require more assignments to keep you occupied. No wonder you will rise rapidly in your career.

Your friendship is valued by many who regard you as honest, trustworthy, and dependable. Indeed, you possess those virtues in a world that greatly needs them. But there is a pitfall in your merits. They lead you to take on too much responsibility for others. You allow the weak to lean on you and transfer their problems to your load of worries. If you don't guard against this, if you allow yourself to be exploited emotionally, you will be sorely disappointed by friends who demonstrate none of the personal strengths you thought you saw in them. Perhaps, at the present time, you are still too loyal to your comrades to admit their faults. Perhaps your sense of duty prevents you from thinking frankly about the matter. Your faithfulness in this regard is like John's, except that his loyalty was not directed toward a flawed hero. He was the only Apostle at Calvary, and the reward for his fidelity was Christ's commending of His mother to John's care.

Let me give you one word of warning. You are so often right that you may think you can never be wrong. Your weakness lies in your too rigid opinions, many of them formed years ago. Beware lest your adamant views circle around your vision and close your mind to fresh ideas and new discoveries. By maintaining a reasonable openness to contrary opinions, you will forge ahead, aided by criticism and corrected by dissent. Because you give so much of yourself to others, your own growth as an individual will continue through life. What a happy future to look forward to!

COLORS: Although you neglect the use of color in your rush to your goals, your magnetic vibrations would be greatly enhanced by the golden yellow of a stunning sunset and by the entire palette of purple. In your loyalty, you reflect the demure pastel of hardy lavender; and in your leadership, you rightly assume the rich violet of a Roman emperor's robes. Reward your diligence and industry with the occasional use of lavish color in your dress and your home; even if you are not used to doing so, it will prove flattering, and harmonious with your commanding personality.

MONEY: Because your interests will lead you into many different areas, people will come to you with a variety of investment projects. Be guided by your intuition, for you have an uncanny instinct for discerning trends of the future. On that basis, you will make wise financial decisions; but by trusting implicitly in friends, no matter how well meaning their advice, you can undo years of thrift and industry.

HEALTH: With the proviso that you must watch your diet, I see nothing in your life pattern to indicate that you will have anything but good health. Because of the business and social commitments mandated by your life of success, you will eat out, at dinners and banquets and parties, with greater frequency in your middle years. Ease the burden of all that rich food by taking light nourishment during the day. Even a Leo can't afford to eat like a lion.

RELATIONSHIPS: Leo Three parents tend to expect too much from their children, perhaps because they themselves are exceptionally gifted and ambitious. Enormously proud of your offspring, you will probably spend more than you can readily afford to provide them with a head start in life. But what they will need most is your love and gentle encouragement. Remember that they must use their own talents to realize their hidden potential, and their interests, both intellectual and commercial, may not match yours.

Your most precious relationships can only be endangered by your dogmatism and your habit of assuming the burdens of others. Be generous with advice and with personal assistance in moderation, but leave to others the responsibility for their own lives. Above all, don't endanger your marital happiness with domineering assertions of your opinions. Remember that the best leader is always willing to learn, and the one you love will be the best teacher.

LEO—FOURTH DIVISION *(July 31, August 4, 13, 22)*

Leos of the Fourth Division stand on the razor's edge between positive and negative aspects of the sign of the Lion. The planetary combination governing their birth gives them ample potential for a happy and fruitful life, but also allows them to choose the route that leads to frustration and sadness.

More than any other Leos, you of the Fourth Division need all the self-control you can muster to restrain the raging lion within you. A careless attitude about the feelings of others or about your own future could swamp your good traits in the rolling wake of your bad ones. The responsibility for seeing that the ship of life sails on, proud and worthy, to its appointed destination is yours alone, for your strengths are more than sufficient for the task. You are:

- independent of mind
- unconventional
- charming

- sentimental

Yet each of these traits has a corresponding negative quality, and you can be:

- eccentric
- impatient with everyday matters
- patronizing
- nostalgically rooted in the past

You are as independent as a haughty lion, foraging alone in the wilderness. This autonomy of mind makes you highly original in your thoughts and words, which can be an asset in your career but a handicap in personal relationships. If those with whom you deal don't follow your random line of reasoning, or if you substitute brilliance for logic, you run the risk of becoming an eccentric, talking only to yourself. Especially among those you care about, your independence may make you appear disdainful and arrogant. Even friends and relatives will accuse you of being inconsiderate and intolerant because you so often disagree with them.

John had a degree of independence about him, but solved his problem in a way that might serve you as an example. He was frequently alone, both personally and in his role as a preacher. Thus his decision making, his brilliant choices of tactics in his evangelistic career, didn't disrupt the lives of others who were dependent upon him.

Your unconventional views, often concerning religion and the meaning of life, can cause you grief. For although there is nothing wrong with your search for truth, it betrays the wisdom it seeks if it leads you to abuse others for their own sincere views. Your lack of respect for convention will irritate many traditionalists. It isn't enough for you to disavow attempts to convert them to your own views. You must, in addition, try to accept them as they are.

You can do it, for you were born a charmer. Most things are yours for the asking, at least the first time you make a request. As you mature, you will find that people are most susceptible to charm when it comes in small doses. They resent being patronized or flattered or overwhelmed with pretty words. If you turn on your charm only to secure from them whatever you desire, they will surely sense your insincerity.

Once again, follow John's example. By traveling, he brought his message to hundreds of thousands of souls, many of whom must have been charmed by his boyish enthusiasm for the Gospel. Perhaps your personality will serve you best if your work takes you to many places to meet many people, none of whom will have an opportunity to tire of your pleasant ways. Perhaps you will be happiest as a roving lion, basking under a different tree every day.

Finally, another positive trait of your character is sentimentality. Make no mistake about it: it *is* an asset. Our personal ties with the past are vital reassurance as we walk into the future. You love family reunions and other opportunities to talk over old times. You pore over old photographs and enjoy meeting people who knew you as a child. The danger inherent in that attitude is the possibility that you will not be able to let the past go. You must not try to live in it. Leos are doers and operate well in today's world, not in the dreams of yesterday. So by all means, treasure your memories and maintain old ties, but look to tomorrow's challenges and the needs of this hour.

COLORS: When you feel your reverie drawing you back toward the past, alert yourself to the delights of the present with the liberal use of sapphire blue, as bright as the jewel. The typically Leonine colors of gold and yellow will work wonders for your morale by strengthening your positive characteristics, especially your lack of convention. No matter how you employ color, however, it will be up to you, not your apparel, to banish the negative aspects of your personality.

MONEY: Your Leonine independence and wanderlust will turn you away from the financial security most people crave. You are naturally attracted toward schemes to get rich quickly, and more than once you will be disappointed in them. Business partnerships are not for you; they would be disrupted by your need to make all your decisions for yourself. Like the lion that is your astral symbol, you prefer a short, swift chase to a long, dogged pursuit of your quarry. Short-term projects, therefore, will be more successful than long-range plans. Your investments should be made accordingly, and they will be especially rewarding if you have some personal managerial or supervisory involvement in whatever you are financing.

HEALTH: Your moods affect your health, and your weight often indicates the mood you are in. When everything is going well, you are apt to be overweight, enjoying your food perhaps more than you should. When affairs are going badly, you lose weight and are too preoccupied to attend to your physical needs. The solution is to work at maintaining a steady balance, for those fluctuations of weight could make you susceptible to either heart trouble or flus and viruses.

RELATIONSHIPS: To maintain your best friendships, stay at arm's length from your associates. Their overexposure to your deadly charm will lead them to resent your glib talk, despite their initially favorable reactions to it. Limit the way you spread yourself around so that you will not train the full brilliance of your smile on the same people too often.

In family matters, your habits are better understood, and so you can expect fairly loyal attachments. Because of your potential for eccentricity, your marital situation deserves your greatest attention. Instead of giving your beloved gifts, give understanding and tolerance. Don't flatter the one you love. Instead, learn to listen to his or her ideas and appreciate their wisdom. By doing this on an intimate basis, you will soon find yourself able to extend the same measure of sympathetic receptivity to others.

LEO–FIFTH DIVISION *(July 23, August 5, 14)*

The stellar influences which cast the life pattern for Leo Fives provide them, from birth, with creativity and excellent judgment. If you number yourself among Leos of the Fifth Division, you are inclined to be rather hasty in acting. Others may think you precipitous in reaching shoot-from-the-hip decisions. They do not understand that your mind is unusually alert and analyzes a situation with the speed of a computer, so that your choices are simultaneously impulsive and sound. Your quick mind will lead to frequent and abrupt changes in your life, both in terms of where you live and what you do for a living. You are:

- constantly seeking new challenges
- fast-thinking
- fond of movement and speed
- enthusiastic

Your search for new experiences and willingness to travel in pursuit of adventure are paralleled by John's constant journeying as part of man's greatest adventure. Just look at his career changes! From a fisherman, he became a disciple of John the Baptist, then a follower of Christ, and later a traveling preacher and writer, teaching in his old age a second and third generation of young Christians. Alterations of the most fundamental sort were as much a part of his nature as they are of yours.

Your speedy mental processes can, however, cause pain both for you and for others. You will often make a snap decision involving others, doing what you consider both necessary and right, without uttering one word of explanation. You feel that you need not explain your motives and conduct to anyone, even those affected by your actions. Learn now that it is folly to expect people to accept this pattern of behavior. If they cannot order you to change your ways, they will nonetheless resent them and eventually work against the fulfillment of your plans. Even though your decisions rarely have negative effects on others, they could damage some of your relationships. So learn to explain your intentions ahead of time. A good leader lets his troops know the direction in which they are marching.

Your love of challenges, combined with your hunger for movement, produces a need for rapid physical exertion, whether running or dancing or racing cars, planes, or speedboats. Once you find your own purpose in life and pursue it to fulfill the Creator's plans for you, life will move ahead at full speed toward your goals. That success will be facilitated by your enthusiasm. You tend to have short-lived passions for novel ideas; but while your attention to them lasts, you become totally immersed in them. That drive is a huge asset in any project, but be sure to let your superiors know about your zeal. When it is allied in a constructive way with your creative abilities, you are virtually unstoppable.

COLORS: For someone whose mind is continually flitting from one idea to the next and operating at a blurring speed, pastel shades are doubly useful. They not only capture the lightness and delicacy of your intellect but also can prove soothing when your enthusiasm runs away with you. Light shades, from the pale blue of sea-faded linen to the creamy white of a snowdrop petal, can remind you that your constant hurrying is more akin to the darting flight of a hummingbird than to the rapacious speed of dark birds of prey.

MONEY: Your financial status will improve steadily throughout life, thanks to your ingenuity in creating new ideas for products and services. That Leonine alertness gives you a head start over your competitors, and the typical Fifth Division personality pursues success as relentlessly as the King of Beasts chases his quarry. Like the charging lion, you, too, can run into a snare. So never invest or purchase on an impulse. Even in your case, quick decisions and money don't go together.

HEALTH: Your impatience with occasional illness can be a worse threat to your health than the sickness itself. You hate staying in bed to rest. You avoid your doctor and dread hospitals; to you, they represent a waste of precious time. You minimize injuries because their proper treatment might keep you from your all-important work. You are intelligent enough to know better, and I suggest you accept the responsibility for your own well-being. This applies even more emphatically to your love for speed. Unless you exercise the greatest caution, both at work and at play, your hurry will bring you hurt. Slow down, as the traffic warnings say, and live!

RELATIONSHIPS: Fast mover that you are, you attract others without effort. Members of the opposite sex are dazzled by your energy, charm, and daring; but few of them can maintain your pace. Even so, you are destined to find one who can and to marry happily. As long as you settle down with a like-minded person, your partnership will be enduring. Before that lucky outcome, however, you run the risk of experiencing several short-lived romances, each broken up by your desire for new horizons and fresh ideas. You will seem fickle, though in fact you are not. Remember that few people can change their life-style as painlessly as you. With due regard to the emotional needs of others, you need never be responsible for a broken heart.

LEO—SIXTH DIVISION *(July 24, August 6, 15)*

A Leo Six is emotional. That simple statement sums up most of your personality if you were born within this division. The planets governing your birth made love a vital factor in your life. You are:

- consoling
- affectionate

- gregarious
- up-to-date

Generous and sympathetic by nature, you strongly reflect the charity of the Apostle John, giving freely of your time and talent as well as your material goods. Fortunately, you have great emotional reserves; for you need them, day after day, as your loving nature provides comfort to those in need of solace. You are always there, it seems, with soothing words and sympathy when we need you most.

Your authentic affection will automatically attract numerous friends of both sexes. Occasionally, a member of the opposite sex will misunderstand your intentions; but once you make clear your own high ideals concerning home and family, the problem will disappear. This situation can most readily occur if you pursue a career in medicine, social work, counseling, or a job demanding personal contact with the people you help. Of course, that is no reason to shun those professions, which would be among the most rewarding for you of the Sixth Division.

You crave social life and love crowds, especially when you are entertaining large groups of guests in your home. Perhaps you have already discovered that your sensitivity to the needs of others enables you to perceive hurt feelings and damaged egos where others see only smiles and chatter. That may be why your guests feel close to you, even though many are only casual acquaintances. Rest assured, there is such a thing as instinct; and if you notice the hidden emotions which others ignore, then you have been gifted with the power to read hearts and to see unspoken pleas for help in the eyes of the lonely and the fearful.

Because of your finely tuned appreciation of human emotions and your fondness for large gatherings, you should consider a career in the performing arts. Think for a moment: don't you at times wish you could take to the stage and then dismiss it as nonsense because it troubles you that there are so many people near you in need of your help? Only you can answer those questions for your particular case. But I offer this advice. If you come to realize that you react best to the approval and delight of crowds, then your next step is to explore your God-given talents in creative endeavors, whether singing, acting, dancing, or writing. There may be more potential within you than you have dreamed.

Young people are especially attracted to Leo Sixes because your attitudes are seldom old-fashioned or stuffy. Like Peter Pan, you seem never to grow old. If this aspect of your personality is combined with your penchant for the performing arts, you might find yourself working with youngsters, writing children's stories, serving as a school librarian or as a member of the local children's theater. Whether as your paid profession or as a volunteer pastime, helping fledgling performers discover the wonders of the arts will help you to discover your own gifts.

Among your adult acquaintances, you will attract many unconventional people, drawn to you because you sympathize with their problems and never hurt their feelings through criticism of their eccentric ways. This could baffle your earlier friends, who will wonder at your new, uninhibited companions. Friction among your many admirers could lead you to the extreme of changing your residence so as to leave their squabbles behind you.

COLORS: The blue and gold colors that suit most Leos are equally appropriate for you. Indeed, because you live with the misfortunes of so many other people, you will need the vibrance of color to lift your own spirits, as you so heroically lift theirs. When that happens, splash on the colors of an ocean sunset, wildly mixing aqua with flaming orange. And for your moments of dramatic expression, the deep blue-black of a raven's wing can combine with the reddish luster of old coins to bring out the performer in you.

MONEY: There is a limited possibility of wealth and fame for you, and it is related to your prospects for becoming a performer in the arts. Not all Leos of the Sixth Division can reach that goal, for economic and familial circumstances may prevent them from experiencing their creative gifts. Even so, you are assured of an economically comfortable life, with generally good luck in business and money matters.

HEALTH: Like the Apostle John, who lived almost a century, you possess an excellent constitution and prospects for a long life. Your planetary combination is especially beneficent in health matters. The only exception concerns your fondness for animals, which may lead to minor injuries. No matter how lovable, the beasts of this earth can be even more unpredictable than people; and that is saying quite a lot!

RELATIONSHIPS: With a heart as big as yours, you will win, as you already have, the affection of all those who know you. Who could resist your selfless concern for their happiness? Your family will be especially blessed with your kindness and eagerness to help others, as long as you remember that charity properly begins at home.

The danger created by your emotionally receptive personality will encourage some people—for there are always a few who want to spoil a noble endeavor—to try to exploit your concern for them. Be vigilant against the wiles of ravenous wolves masquerading as lambs in need of your help. Your home is too precious to be imperiled for the sake of cunning charlatans who want to cry on your shoulder.

LEO—SEVENTH DIVISION *(July 25, August 7, 16)*

You Leos of the Seventh Division will repeatedly undergo tests of your faith, your confidence both in yourself and in God. More than others born under the sign of the Lion, you must remind yourself that your Creator placed you on earth for a purpose. Seeking it out despite recurrent disappointments, you will know, with the certainty that only God can give, when you discover your true goals. To assist you in your pilgrimage toward spiritual fulfillment, you have been given:

- a sense of humility
- an artistic and spiritual personality
- an introspective nature
- strong self-reliance

Your kind of humility is often interpreted by the unknowing as lack of ambition, for you seem not to want the good things of this world for yourself. In fact, you want a great deal and are determined to have it, but not in terms of material possessions. Because you are a born do-gooder, you are always willing to work for the general welfare, drawing your psychological benefits from the happiness of others. Slaving over a community project, you will bring it to success and then be inclined to think it would have done equally well without you. You are piling up your credit in Heaven while, here on earth, your own deprecating assessment of your efforts could even convince those you have helped.

I know you're not looking for praise, but I must point out to you that you owe yourself more recognition than you've been receiving. When you fade into the scenery and fail to claim credit for your accomplishments, you prevent others from seeing your merits and thereby from helping you develop them further. Because you are interested in using your talents to their fullest, you must bring them to the attention of those with the experience and ability to advise and encourage you. So speak up when you are proud of your work!

Your personality is, let us say, purist. By that I mean that you would rather listen to a recorded symphony at home, alone, than attend a concert with a group of friends. Your most enjoyable visits to art galleries are made alone. Closely related to this artistic sensitivity is your religious impulse. You probably pray, and I advise you to add regular meditation to your devotions. But you would never do so in public. Moreover, any display of religious fervor repels you, as though public piety were a contradiction in terms. Your religious emotions may be strong but they are utterly private.

Despite your introspection, you strangely refuse to recognize the psychic gifts with which you may be endowed, as if your sense of humility were blocking your appreciation of your natural powers. I urge you to look deeper into your mind and so to see the inexplicable talents your Creator has placed there for you to develop and use wisely. I feel an obligation to tell you that you carry your modesty too far when you allow it to smother gifts of the spirit.

Although you are genuinely fond of many people, it is hard for you to express your emotions freely. So you may develop the reputation of being impersonal and cold, although you are neither aloof nor unfriendly. Don't blame others if they fail to understand your subconscious gestures of affection. You will have to learn to be more explicit in conveying your goodwill. You are not truly shy or a loner, but you are an interior person. Your deep reserve and sense of privacy keep your inmost thoughts and feelings to yourself. Your allegiances are never worn on your sleeve, and even those you love require time to realize the depth of your commitment to them.

To find the part you have been assigned in the universal drama of man's return to his Maker, you must look beyond, as well as into, yourself. Though your self-reliance is commendable, you need not turn away from others. For it is in the intersection of daily life that we find our calling and step, one day at a time, closer and closer to our preordained destiny. I suspect that you will feel more fulfilled, both in your work and in your spiritual life, as you allow others to enter your private world and permit them to draw you out of it occasionally. To put the matter simply: make better use of yourself.

COLORS: Avoid somber hues that would reinforce your habit of withdrawing into your own mind. If you are reluctant to go to a party, for example, your spirits might be bolstered by wearing an outfit vivid with sapphire blue, bold orange, or vibrant green. Try it, and the odds are you will have a more enjoyable time than you had hoped for. If you think that such daring colors are inappropriate for your moments of prayer, consider the way people around the world have filled their places of worship with the most stunning array of brilliant colors. Indeed, many of the Lord's most marvelous creations come in the gaudiest shades.

MONEY: Your only monetary difficulties will be caused by your lack of effort to earn more. Part of your humility is the sense that you are already paid sufficiently for your work, and so you don't seek higher wages or a better position even when you deserve them both. If you choose not to change your self-effacing attitudes, then don't expect great wealth to come your way. You can, however, anticipate having enough money to meet your needs, and this will satisfy you. In addition, you will usually be part of a two-income family, which will help eliminate financial hardships.

HEALTH: Although you are not exactly physically robust, you are hardier and more enduring than people who look rough and vigorous. When you withdraw into yourself, you tend to be careless about your diet; but as you recognize that excessive introspection wastes your talents, you will circulate with more people and pay more attention to what you eat and drink. The result will be a noticeable improvement in the way you feel and an upsurge of energy.

RELATIONSHIPS: Once you come out of your shell, you will enjoy life so much that you will wonder what could have been so attractive to keep you bottled up in your private world. Marriage will come late for you, if it comes at all; but in either case, you will not be unhappy. Your best prospects for marital success will involve someone who shares your quiet commitments to the appreciation of artistic beauty and the contemplation of religious truth. If your love is directed to someone who is both more sociable than you and yet patient with your tendency toward isolation, then your romantic involvement will help you move gradually and painlessly into a broader social world.

LEO–EIGHTH DIVISION *(July 26, August 8, 17)*

The lives of Leo Eights are marked by contradiction. Their star-set pattern makes them persons of extremes. Their commitments are total. They are either fire or ice, but never lukewarm. Their opinions are known to all, for Leos of the Eighth Division are not shy about expressing themselves. And when their views change, the shift is complete, from one end of the spectrum to the other. If you are among these most definite of the Leos, you are perhaps nodding your head in agreement with that brief description of yourself, and you may not be at all surprised to be told that you are:

- generous
- warm
- stubborn
- mercurial

Most of the time, you are good-natured and generous to an extreme. Your ambition is to do your work well rather than to promote your fame or aggrandize your fortune. Strangers are drawn immediately by your warmth and openness. Helpful as this is in business matters, it can cause difficulties in a commercial partnership or in any project, academic, civic, or cultural, in which you are part of a team. Your colleagues may think you are putting on a public relations act to steal the show with clients and customers, although actually you are just unleashing your most personable characteristics.

It may be advisable for you to strike out on your own, to handle one-man projects and those aspects of your business in which you are solely responsible for their operations. Your friendly approach with everyone should not be stifled by the limitations of joint ventures.

Despite your Leonine affiliation, you are not easily provoked. That's because your self-confidence makes you too secure and assured to flare up at challenges or affronts. When seriously annoyed, you soon recover your composure. But you can reveal a fierce temper on rare occasions. Some have already learned that fact in their dealings with you.

Strange to say, through your generous and amicable personality runs a wide streak of stubbornness. Sociable and sensible to the feelings of others, you nonetheless are confident of your values and ideas to such an extent that it is virtually impossible to persuade you to disavow them or even compromise them in the interest of group harmony. Though a form of conceit, it is justified in part by the fact that you are usually right. Even so, try to be more objective about matters that concern you. Learn to step back from situations in which you are involved to gain a more balanced view of them. Most important, discover the distinction between vital principles and negotiable tactics so that by occasional compromises, you are able to forward your goals rather than disrupt them.

Indeed, reaching your goals is so important to you that when a relationship or project is not going well, you are apt to become despondent and walk away from it, despite your usually optimistic outlook on life. Later, you regret abandoning your efforts, and recalling all the little failures of your life, you may sulk into a state of depression. That is foolhardy. Even when you cannot go back and pick up the pieces of a shattered plan, you learn from each disappointment and will deal better with future situations. All setbacks are apportioned us for our own good so that by occasionally losing, we will be better prepared to win when it most counts.

An Eighth Division Leo is likely to possess certain psychic powers. You may often introduce a spur-of-the-moment subject into conversation, only to have someone exclaim, "I was just thinking of that!" Learn to recognize those little indications for what they are; and if you do sense some underutilized indications of intuition within you, by all means develop them as another wonderful asset of your pleasant personality.

COLORS: Your magnetism is attuned to purple and deep shades of blue. It may take time to learn to employ different shades of those lush colors to their best effect, but experimenting with them is enjoyable in itself. If you have a conference on your schedule, perhaps a pale violet tie or scarf, rather than a flaming magenta one, might put you in a less adamant and more conciliatory mood. If you are entertaining guests who are as reserved as you are outgoing, they might feel more relaxed in a softer-colored background than in a room vibrating with heliotrope and turquoise. However, if the language of colors fails you, you can always fall back on your innate sociability to convey your spirit of goodwill.

MONEY: Your financial prospects are patchy. While you have all the attributes for economic success, you could imperil your rise in the world by walking away from problems rather than seeing them through. During your early years, you will have periods of unemployment; they could sorely depress your spirits unless you turn them to your advantage by launching new ventures and striving for self-improvement. Women Leo Eights are impulsive shoppers, whose household purchases are apt to be expensive and ill considered. All those in the Eighth Division, men and women alike, must learn to keep their wallets closed until they reassess their financial decisions.

HEALTH: Sleep is a cure-all for Leos of the Eighth Division. You are blessed with the ability to sleep through your ailments. If you take that habit for granted, you will eventually learn that most people would pay dearly to be able in that way to short-circuit the misery of their sicknesses. In fact, this recuperative somnolence of yours is a very favorable aspect of an unfavorable habit of sleeping instead of rising early to face your problems. Some Leo Eights are hypochondriacs, and others ignore their ills. That peculiar pattern is typical of the all-or-nothing habits which lead you, in matters other than health, to extremes. You may have already discovered your vulnerability to allergies in your teen-age years. Cheer up: you will outgrow them.

RELATIONSHIPS: Preferring to proceed one day at a time rather than planning ahead, you let matters of the heart run their course without trying to steer them to a specific destination. That is, your romantic life is not aiming toward an early marriage with a certain someone. Your intentions, however, are not the controlling factor. Because you are so affectionate and outgoing, you will one day be surprised to find yourself on the brink of marriage. Your partner having made the decision for you, the arrangements will have been completed. You will only then decide, at that crucial moment, whether your happiness will be secured by going ahead or stepping back.

Your friendships will be many, if you practice the art of compromise to subdue your stubborn insistence upon being vindicated, and as enduring as your generous affection.

LEO–NINTH DIVISION *(July 27, August 9, 18)*

You have the heart of a crusader, Leo Nine. Your keen sense of justice and corresponding sensitivity to injustices make you sympathetic to the cause of the mistreated, the deprived, and the underdog. You probably began to exhibit your devotion to fair play at an early age, just as the Apostle John became a disciple of John the Baptist when he was scarcely beyond his teens. Leo Nines are often politically active in high school, running for office in clubs and student government—not for the honor of election but for the sake of having a voice in maintaining or improving the rules they live by. Even though you are not delighted by your role on center stage, you will do your duty as you see it.

Indeed, with the recent changes in our political affairs and the lowering of the voting age, more Leo Nines are becoming involved, not just in school politics but "the real thing." Teen-agers of the Ninth Division can frequently be found these days distributing campaign literature door to door and manning banks of telephones to get out the vote.

You will always be outspoken and direct in your dealings, including your political dealings; but you will find through experience that candor is not necessarily the same thing as bluntness and that honesty does not require you to attack people with the truth.

Despite your commitment to justice, I do not see politics as a way of life for you, at least not full time. Although you have little intention of pursuing a career in public affairs, you will be pressured by those who admire your convictions to assume leadership in civic campaigns, even to run for office. Voters looking for an outspoken candidate, with honest convictions and the gift of self-expression, will be quick to support your Leonine qualifications. But once you have managed to correct abuses, improve a troubled situation, or secure the legislation needed to right a wrong, you will leave the political arena to return to the mainstream of your life. You should be prepared, however, even after you drop out of active campaigning, to be recruited for service on innumerable committees dealing with minority groups, international relief, and the welfare of children and the aged. In fact, you might even make a career as a staff member of private or public agencies in those fields.

You will socialize with a broad circle of friends, for there is not an ounce of prejudice in you. Despite your strong convictions, you are sensitive to the potential of others and respectful of their ideals. Accordingly, many of your friends are unconventional, and you go out of your way to help them realize their unusual potential for accomplishment. Perhaps you sense the injustice of the way society sometimes shuns those with special talents, as if their insight or their criticism or their inventive ideas threatened the comfortable complacency of less daring minds. Whatever the reason, your concern for people who are slighted because of their eccentricities is commendable, but your tolerance must not become a threat to your own well-being. Remember that some unconventional individuals are themselves as prejudiced as those who oppose them.

You are inventive and clever with your hands, and that gift can help you relax with hobbies and crafts. Life is not entirely a crusade. You need occasional diversion from your noble causes, and anything from working in wood to pottery to knitting to motor repair will draw your mind away from this world's inequities. Because of your relish for projects, both civic and mechanical, your home buzzes with activity. Your children profit immensely from exposure to your high principles and your fascination with new frontiers of learning.

COLORS: Even the colors of your magnetic vibrations reflect your active spirit. Electric blues and shimmering greens convey the constant alertness that comes with your love of life. If you have occasion to prepare political literature or campaign posters, those forceful shades will help convey your message of hard-hitting honesty. Crusader that you are, the boldest red is your best accent color. Reminiscent of the scarlet crosses worn by the medieval crusaders, it can be a flashing reminder of your emotional commitment to justice and fair play. Of course, as a Leo, you favor the golden hue of an imperious lion. Put all those colors together and it should be obvious that your favorable spectrum is as wide as the horizons of your career, as ample as the roster of your friends.

MONEY: You will not enjoy financial security until you are nearly thirty. Your early years will border on deprivation because you will spend your money, as well as time and energy that could have been directed toward profitable ventures, on an array of noble causes. Later in life, you will live in modest comfort, but not luxury, which is the way you will like to live. The success of your campaigns for social betterment will always mean more to you than economic rewards.

HEALTH: Your splendid constitution guarantees you generally good health. Blood pressure problems, however, await you in your middle years if you allow your pursuit of high ideals to monopolize your attention and disrupt your moments of relaxation. You run the risk of serious accidents because you fail to concentrate on everyday matters. Despite those tendencies, you can enjoy your health unimpaired. You need only reserve a place in your life for peace and quiet with your family. Total relaxation is an art, which you must learn and practice. The effort is surely justified by the results.

RELATIONSHIPS: As I have already indicated, many of your friendships will be rather odd; for by championing the underdog, you will meet and be attracted to many dissenters and dreamers. But their offbeat idealism should sustain you in your commitment to a better life for all.

Your family will adore you, even if you do not provide them with the material things you wish you could give them. They are enriched by your example; and as long as you don't push your children into active imitation of you, they will of their own accord recognize the nobility of your endeavors and try to assist you with them. More than the children of the wealthy, your offspring are blessed with deep parental love. By guarding your health, you will be able to enjoy their accomplishments into your golden years.

You make an unexcelled marriage partner. Be sure that your life partner understands your passion for justice and is willing to share you with your many causes. That will continue to make your home life both a shelter from stormy public affairs and an encouragement to bring to others the happiness you radiate.

VIRGO—PHILIP

(August 23–September 22)

As we come to the sixth sign of the Zodiac, we reach the halfway mark in the circle of the heavens. This gives us an opportunity to reflect upon the astrological patterns we have been analyzing and to recognize the way each adds to each to form one cosmic whole. Think for a moment what life would be like if all humanity claimed one birth sign, if we all had the same strengths and weaknesses, likes and dislikes. How drab and tedious human affairs would be!

The diversity of mankind, which often brings problems of discord and misunderstanding, is actually a blessing. Our differences in appearance and in character are the Creator's own signature of authorship upon us, like the inimitable brushstrokes that identify the masterpieces of one painter above all others. No two flowers in God's garden are exactly alike. So whether we are towering sunflowers or demure creeping periwinkle, whether we blossom early like the crocus or late like chrysanthemums, we can be rightly proud that our talents and virtues are necessary to make this world complete.

It should be clear by now that that is the reason Christ chose twelve varied personalities as His closest associates. Each had something distinctive and irreplaceable to offer, just as each sign of the Zodiac endows those born within it with certain traits which cannot be duplicated. I am repeating that lesson here for a definite purpose. As we study the sign of Virgo, we must be aware that all the divisions of the Zodiac are cumulative in their impact. That is, they keep revealing new aspects of the humanity we all share; and, no matter what our own sign may be, each of the twelve, from Aries through

Pisces, opens to us new insights and understandings about the human spirit and its divine destination.

So, if you as a Virgo want to read this chapter first, be sure that you later read all the others as well with equal attention; for you will find it is as helpful to learn about the star signs of your fellow earthlings as it is essential to know about your own astrological makeup. And you who are not Virgos should be aware that to ignore this or any other Zodiac sign is to overlook one-twelfth of the human race! How foolishly we would be depriving ourselves and the world of one-twelfth of its humor, its courage, its wisdom, and its beauty.

With that in mind, let us attend well to the lessons that await us all in the sign of Virgo and in the life of its Apostle, the little-known townsman of Bethsaida named Philip.

As I have already explained, on the day of my spectacular vision concerning the Zodiac and the Apostles, not all of its details were immediately clear to me. I had been given an overall view of the special relationship between the twelve followers of Christ and the corresponding number of star signs. And, most graphically, I had glimpsed their opposing force, the negative power with which each Apostle, and each of us, has to contend—the dynamism of evil, symbolized by militantly marching red boots.

As time passed, each segment of the Zodiac diagram and the inset figures of the Apostles became clear to me, although I must admit that I had initially been puzzled by Philip's representation of the sign of the Virgin. If there had been women among the twelve Apostles, surely this sign would have been expressed by Mary or by any one of the many pious women who are mentioned in Scripture. But as it was, with the Apostolate a male fellowship, so to speak, Philip did indeed sum up the Virgoan character and makes a most fitting archetype for the sixth sign of the Zodiac.

Philip emerges from the few Scriptural references to him as the business manager, as it were, for the Apostles. Discriminating, analytical, painstaking, he demonstrated all the qualities necessary for someone whose job it was to find lodging, arrange meals, and function almost as a publicity-organizing officer for the early troop of evangelists. It was typical of him, and of the Virgoan character he embodied, that when Christ asked him how they could feed the five thousand people who were following the Master, Philip replied, probably shaking his head from side to side, that it would take a small fortune to buy the provisions. Read the story yourself in John's

Gospel, Chapter 6, Verses 1 to 6. He was the practical one, the organizer, who may have thought it was very unbusinesslike of Andrew to bring to Christ a small boy with five loaves of bread and two fish. His reaction to what happened afterward, when the assembled multitude were amply fed with those skimpy resources, can only be imagined.

It was significant that Christ turned first to Philip to ask what should be done even though, as the Gospel explains, "He knew Himself what He would do." For you Virgos are usually the ones people turn to when they have a problem. Your part in the universal scheme of things is as an efficient manager, and people depend on you to play that role. Knowing He would perform a miracle, Christ simply gave Philip, always the practical Virgo, the chance to say that there was no other way to handle the situation. Like you Virgos of today, Philip was levelheaded and realistic. He wasn't going to take any miracle for granted, or even ask for one! He sums up the sign of the Virgin to his self-reliant core. In this regard, he was the perfect aide-de-camp to his Teacher, a position in which Virgos usually excel.

Virgos often achieve great wealth and fame through their unflagging competence; but ironically, they don't regard either of those rewards as very important. They tend to think that money and renown are secondary to the satisfaction of doing a job well, and so they rarely seek recognition or recompense for their efforts. I suspect that a great many Virgos who read these words will nod their heads in agreement; and if that does apply to you, know that you are fulfilling your responsibilities and living up to your potential under Virgo's sign.

Christ's selection of Philip as an Apostle should teach us all that success isn't a question of position but of performance. It inspires us to excel in the everyday chores of life and demonstrates the value of any labor performed with dedication and care. Surely Philip made immense personal contributions to the work of the Twelve; yet he is not even mentioned in the first three Gospels, except for being listed as one of their number. The message for all Virgos is clear: whatever you do, do it well and forget about public acclaim. If you are a Virgoan housewife, for example, your fulfillment will come from cooking nourishing meals for your family rather than from competing for celebrity status. Remember that all of us, from all segments of the Zodiac, are most successful when we combine our best efforts with our inborn capabilities.

Even without intending to, you Virgos can become prominent in several careers. Your retentive brain can pick up and analyze data like a computer that equips you for any kind of work that demands a superb memory. More surgeons, for example, are born under this sign than under any other, especially during the September segment of it. Their work epitomizes Virgoan traits. They must be exact, deliberate, and meticulous, able to draw instantly on a mass of medical information and capable of organizing an operating room team around them. The same abilities, directed toward different ends, are essential for speech therapists and tour guides, as well as economic planners and construction foremen. To put it simply: a great many Virgos are needed in this world!

Because you can concentrate with ease for prolonged periods of time, you make excellent researchers. Any complex, detailed, and long-lasting project will profit from your involvement. Highly observant, a Virgoan housewife can walk through her home and spot at a glance anything that has been moved. Statistical errors which most people could not hope to discover appear obvious to you, and you therefore make good copyreaders and invaluable inventory clerks.

I know a Virgo who does statistical typing. Once when she showed me a sample of her work, I couldn't believe my eyes. There were pages of figures arranged in columns, all neat and accurate. It must have required the most intense concentration. That kind of personal discipline and concern for detail qualifies some Virgos to be critics, whether in the arts or in industry as quality control specialists. Your only shortcoming in this regard is that you may turn your critical acumen against yourself, seeing no reason why you shouldn't demand perfection from yourself before expecting it from others. By setting unrealistically high standards for both yourself and others, you run the risk of allowing your meticulousness to become a petty fussiness. Focusing too closely on trivia, you can ignore the broader view of things. In intellectual matters, this can lead you to ignore the important questions of human existence and to debate instead less significant matters of fact. Figuratively put, you can rely too much on the spirit's microscope and too little on its telescope.

Virgos are generally fortunate in romance. The obvious association of this Zodiac sign with the qualities of the Virgin scarcely needs explanation. You are modest and restrained in matters of the heart. You don't give your affection easily; but when you do, it is for life. It isn't easy for you to express your feelings about others, even when you really wish to. But once you recognize that this inhibition is not always beneficial, you learn to break through it when it no longer serves your purpose.

Your romantic life may be complicated by the fact that you don't judge people on face values. You must know people a long time before you even decide whether you like them. It is difficult for you to feel close to anyone who doesn't share your artistic and intellectual interests. Moreover, you tend to be conventional to an extreme, and any relationships beyond your present cultural orbit seem too eccentric and bizarre to take seriously. Over the long run, your habit of "making haste slowly" in romantic decisions will lead you to a happy marriage, for you won't rush into a wedding. Consequently, your marital commitment will be total and will thereby strengthen and secure your home life.

An interesting trait of Virgos, perhaps attributable to their sign's image of purity, is their concern for hygiene and health. You are often enthusiasts for physical fitness, and your obsession with your diet can lead you to total vegetarianism.

As children, you were esteemed by your teachers. Your books and desks were models of neatness. You probably asked the right questions in class, were diligent about your homework, and seemed unusually tidy and quiet. As a parent, be careful not to become distant with your children. Especially with small children, who need reassurance of parental affection, you must avoid aloofness and learn to be more demonstrative of your love.

It is apparent that the sign of the Virgin has much to recommend it. Its virtues are those which our world seems to need now. If you develop those positive traits with which you were endowed at birth, you can rightly be proud of your consequent merits. But Virgos, as well as any other humans, are susceptible to the allure of those red boots I saw in my vision. I need only mention that Jesse James, the most famous outlaw of the Old West, was born on September 5, 1847.

On the positive side, there are famous Virgos in every field of human endeavor. In politics, they include President Lyndon Johnson (August 27) and Governor George Wallace (August 25); in science, Lee de Forest (August 26), the man who invented talking pictures and television; in art, the beloved Grandma Moses (September 7). The superstar of the 1936 Olympic Games, Jesse Owens, was born on September 12; composer-conductor Leonard Bernstein on August 25; and Queen Wilhelmina of Holland on August 31, the birthdate also of Arthur Godfrey.

Literary Virgos whose works I have enjoyed include O. Henry (September 11), H. L. Mencken (September 12), Theodore Dreiser (August 27), and John Gunther (August 30). Some of my favorite movie stars share the sixth sign of the Zodiac: Ruby Keeler (August 25), Fredric March (August 31), Maurice Chevalier (September 12), and Claudette Colbert (September 13).

That is quite a roster of talent! But none of those individuals reached their heights of success without developing, at great personal effort, their special gifts. Remember this as we now survey each division within the sign of the Virgin.

VIRGO—FIRST DIVISION *(August 28, September 1, 10, 19)*

It is a paradox that Virgos of the First Division are driven primarily by love and yet, in one of many astrological ironies, are among the least-equipped people to convey affection to others. Your love isn't centered around sexual attraction, or even parental duties. It is rather a simple, warm affection for others and, above all, an awareness of God and a readiness to serve His purposes. But with all that powerful emotion bottled up within you, you are inhibited from revealing it. If you ever summoned the courage to wear your heart on your sleeve, you would probably put it on the inner lining so it couldn't be seen.

Despite my light words, your reticence is a serious matter, because it prevents a fine human being from communicating noble sentiments to others. It deprives them of your lovable qualities and robs you of much happiness. By concentrating on your admirable traits, you should find ways to let others recognize them in you. Then they will know that you are:

- modest
- loyal
- careful
- willing to serve others unselfishly

You have all the characteristics of a Virgoan organizer. Like your Apostle Philip, attending to the living arrangements of his fellow disciples, you are willing to submerge your own interests for the good of others. Your self-effacing tendency merges with the

Virgoan strains of modesty and intellect. You would never shout at a slow waiter in a crowded restaurant. You are not the center-stage extrovert who plays practical jokes or leads the chorus at a football club outing. And because people notice your restraint, they rightly say of you, "Still water runs deep."

You do have deep emotions which you must learn to bring to the surface. There is no need to play the quiet mouse all your life. I know a young mother of two who spent her early life in England. She had been quite content to take a back seat in family matters and in her marriage. When she moved to America, she was forced to make new friends and adapt to new living arrangements. The change in her was amazing and beneficial. She seemed to have left behind the straitjacket of her inhibitions. "I never knew what I was missing," she confided to me. "I wish I had branched out into all these social activities before."

That's the way with all Virgos, especially those of the First Division. Once you make a decision to alter your life-style, your talents enable you to effect the changes completely. There are some things, however, that you never change: the persons and principles to which you are loyal. Your fidelity is of the best kind: quiet, unassuming, enduring. It is often your way of expressing without words the deep regard you have for someone else.

Fortunately, your faithfulness is rarely blind. Though you are no vocal rebel, neither are you a gullible follower of every glib leader. You are as careful in your personal relationships as you are in matters of financial or social administration. That is, you attend to details of character, good or bad, as closely as you supervise the minutiae of business matters or the data of your studies. In that regard, we can all learn much from your caution.

We can also learn from your willingness to assist those in need —and not necessarily financial need. Whatever the affliction—emotional stress, family problems, personal disappointments—you do your quiet best to relieve it. While this is a plus, I want to remind you that it is possible to continue your selfless altruism while simultaneously putting more zest into your life. In fact, a greater enjoyment of the world's good things will actually strengthen your ability to bring comfort and consolation to the troubled and the fearful.

COLORS: The bold use of color can help you make the transition from Virgoan shyness to a more relaxed expression of your warm emotions. If you haven't yet discovered them, begin to experiment with bright poster colors. Think how you could release your inner glow through the dazzling yellow of spring's first daffodils; how you could proclaim your love for the world through reds as gay and bursting as ripe cherries. In your moments of healing, when you mend hurt feelings and bind up the wounds of rancor or betrayal, don't revert to somber hues. Instead, emphasize the new life of forgiveness and optimism with vivid greens. Perhaps you can socialize best if your living room is as lushly colored as a Vermont meadow in summer. If you are hesitant to express your feelings for a particular person, let the colors you wear around him or her say the things you can't put into words.

MONEY: Thanks to your meticulous habits, you will usually know where your money is and where it is going. That is a fine start on the road to significant saving and investment. I see you within a broad range of earning: anywhere between the lower-middle levels and the near-top. Wherever you find yourself in terms of income, you will use your money cautiously. As a consequence, you should reach financial security by middle age, and will be content with it. Lacking the driving ambition to become very wealthy, you will settle for comfort as opposed to luxury; and that is probably a wise decision.

HEALTH: Your physical tendencies are toward nervous complaints, especially skin problems and gastric disturbances, and perhaps even an ulcer in the later years of middle age. Your health is generally sound, when you stop fretting about it. Because of the precautionary instincts which mark all your activities, you are likely to become a worried eater, tempted by fad diets and cure-all regimens. A wise course would be to stay with a simple diet of familiar foods and maintain the exercises you enjoy so much.

RELATIONSHIPS: Your friendships seem to take forever to solidify; but once forged, they last for years. If you want to expand the circle of your acquaintances, practice, little by little, the graceful art of making others feel important. This will also help you lower your own barriers of emotional reticence, since it will take your mind off yourself and let your reactions come more naturally.

Your relatives will always be a source of comfort to you, and your marriage will be the rock upon which your life rests, secure and enriching. Your dominant characteristics make you an excellent marriage partner, and your spouse can count on even stronger marital ties as the years go by. The only possible danger I see for you in the area of romance is the outside chance that your innate sympathy for the troubled could lead you into an amorous relationship with someone who exploits your concern. But be reassured: your customary caution should alert you to that unfortunate circumstance if it should arise.

VIRGO—SECOND DIVISION

(August 29, September 2, 11, 20)

For those born under the planetary combination governing the Second Division of Virgo, a strong tendency toward wanderlust is indicated. You relish change as something good in itself; and even though it is usually beneficial for your spirits, it also can cause instability in your relationships and consequent unhappiness.

To help you maintain an inner center of stability and calm in a world filled with change and movement, you have been gifted with typically Virgoan traits. You are:

- imaginative
- loving
- creative
- reserved

Your imaginative power is the firstborn offspring of your intellect, and it should be a fertile and liberating force in shaping your life. Often, however, it doesn't flower as it should because Virgo Twos are modest and desire quiet lives. So you may have a grand idea, wildly innovative and spectacularly offbeat, and yet fail to pursue it because your personal reserve inhibits you from pushing ahead with it. A boss or colleague who doesn't recognize your true qualities will dismiss your potential by deciding you lack the ambition vital for success.

Don't allow that to happen. If you are determined to remain in the business world, prove your first-rate ability as a creative thinker by training yourself to speak up when you would rather be silent, to offer advice when you prefer to take orders, to propose reforms even if you blush from shyness. And if you find the pressures of commercial competition too disruptive of your mental composure, consider the alternative of an academic career. Perhaps in a classroom or library or laboratory, your privacy would be less invaded by social and professional intrusions. Whatever your work, put yourself in a position where others will judge the end products of your labor, not the outward appearances of effort and industry. By relying on the final results of your talents, you are resting secure on Virgoan thoroughness and practicality.

There is a persistent dilemma in your love life. Despite your great capacity for love, you probably don't know how to show it. Many of the persons you most cherish have no inkling of your fondness for them until you go to their aid when they are in need. You could be far more popular than you are now, especially with members of the opposite sex; but you don't seek their affection and, instead, wait for them to express interest in you. As a result, you aren't likely to marry during your twenties, when most people settle down, because your emotional timidity steers you clear of romantic involvements. This can be an advantage rather than a handicap. A late marriage is actually better for Virgos because it allows time to indulge your wanderlust and adjust your careers before you take on the commitments of a home and family.

An important sidelight on your character is its inclination toward agricultural activity. The virgin who is the symbol of your segment of the Zodiac is usually depicted holding a plant of some sort. This indicates an involvement with the earth's nutritive forces. Virgo Twos in particular have a strong affinity for the soil and enjoy gardening or farming. That doesn't mean you are prepared to make a living in such activities, but it does explain why, even in a high-rise apartment in the heart of a great city, you put plants in every window and love to visit parks and the botanical gardens. If you could combine your agricultural bent with your need to travel—perhaps as a consultant botanist or an agent for a florist delivery service—you could discover an ideal outlet for your creative spirit.

However you direct your talents, remember that you will increase your value to other individuals and to the entire community by outgrowing your self-effacing attitude. Stop sidestepping credit when it comes your way. We all need more than just a paycheck to let us know we're doing a good job. If one of your fellow workers or students was consistently underrated and unappreciated, you would be outraged by the injustice. Demand the same fairness for yourself.

COLORS: Choose clothes and home furnishings that will make you glow. Avoid dark colors that can only drive you deeper into your shyness. The mingled shades of a pigeon's wing, softly iridescent blues and grays and white, will complement your magnetic vibrations while expressing the soaring gentleness that rules your conduct. To help you feel more at ease in social affairs, pastel greens and equally airy blues will reassure you and invite others to know you better. These are, after all, the colors of growing things and life-giving water; and so they are naturally attuned to your Virgoan impulses.

MONEY: Your best chances for a good income involve freelance pursuits, especially in the arts and sciences, which enable you to give free rein to your creative inventiveness without the stifling supervision of a shortsighted employer. Virgo Two wives are likely to attain success in a career outside the home, although their love of plants often keeps them busy as full-time backyard gardeners. Because you are frugal, you seem to require little cash and, even on a pinched income, manage to save a little with your Virgoan prudence.

HEALTH: Only your diet stands between you and good health, especially when you are traveling. Then irregular meals and strange foods will make you vulnerable to sickness. Your exercise in active sports will help you stay fit, although you will probably never excel in competitive athletics because you lack the "killer instinct" required for physical contests.

RELATIONSHIPS: Your friendships will generally reflect your own personality: subdued, conventional, slightly intellectual, and extremely worthy. Without abandoning any of your present comrades, you might try to add spice to your circle of acquaintances by striking up less conforming relationships. If you find it difficult to meet people socially, your astrological interests can steer you to garden clubs and plant societies, to civic projects involving humanitarian aid, or to church relief work. Before long, you will discover that goodwill flourishes under your hand as readily as your favorite houseplants.

I already mentioned your romantic difficulty in having the

capacity for great love but difficulty in expressing it. Don't worry about it, for your concern can only drive you deeper into yourself. Remember, a relaxed spirit eventually finds its own way toward kindred souls. Though you may have to wait for the right person to appreciate your hidden reserves of tender affection, you will be rewarded with the most enduring love. Just as the greatest works of art require the longest time in creation, so does Virgoan romance move slowly toward perfection.

VIRGO–THIRD DIVISION *(August 30, September 3, 12, 21)*

Worldly success is the astrologically appointed destiny of Virgo Threes. Endowed with tremendous driving ambition and a restless urge to go farther, work harder, and be better, you are unfailingly:

- strong-willed
- fit for leadership
- ready to organize
- practical

You share the restlessness which led Philip to devote his life to the spread of his new faith, and you would be fortunate to find equally energetic ways to direct your strong traits toward noble purposes. In your early years, you must face a difficult choice: whether to pursue material rewards or seek the spiritual satisfactions you value more. Indeed, you may have already made up your mind which path at that crossroads to follow. It is probable that you are already moving along the route toward whatever ambitions you set for yourself in your teen-age years. With a will like yours, you are fated to reach them.

You will allow nothing to deter or to detour you. Without being vicious, you launch an aggressive attack on life. That direct determination bewilders your friends, who know you as a pleasant person whose dynamism seems out of control. Prepare now to face sooner or later the annoyance of some people who can't sustain your blistering pace and who resent your ascent to the top. Of course, you will gravitate there naturally, having set your sights on success; but inevitably someone will brand you as an opportunist, no matter how false the charge. That is one of the prices any of us must pay for prominence.

People are like water: they find their own proper level. While you are finding yours, remember that those you leave behind are no less important than those you will meet tomorrow. Those truly secure in their social or professional advancement have no reason to hurt another's feelings or belittle those whose pace is slower.

Because you are born to leadership, your tendency toward extensive participation in business and civic activities will probably occupy your time and attention. As a result, it would be wise to defer marriage until you become more confident in your career and less pressed with professional commitments. Happiness comes to Virgo Threes more from personal achievement than from matrimony. The wrong marital partner, unsuited to your ambitions, will find life with you a trial.

You *can* have a happy marriage as long as you don't rush into it. When you do make a definite romantic commitment, encourage your mate to become involved in social and cultural activities that will enable him or her to grow personally, just as you yourself are doing. As long as you both are working in the same direction, toward greater appreciation of broader horizons, you will remain together in a happy home.

Your qualities of leadership will be manifest not only in the way you seek and handle responsibilities but also in your skills as an organizer. In a corporation, you are adept at instituting production methods and sales programs. In governmental agencies, you excel in personnel administration. As a homemaker, you have the best-run kitchen and fullest freezer in the neighborhood, plan meals weeks in advance, and always know where the children's missing shoes can be located.

As a practical person, you are not given to utopian dreaming. Your fantasies have a peculiar air of reality about them because you feel you accomplish the goals you are hoping for. As another aspect of your practicality, you are skilled with your hands and enjoy learning the proper operation of machinery and household equipment. If you aren't already enjoying a hobby that calls for detailed knowledge and manual skill, you should discover one to your liking. It will provide essential relaxation from your hard-driving ambition.

COLORS: Perhaps because you are already so dynamic, the use of color is not important to you. Of course, the customary colors of leadership are appropriate to any commanding Virgo Three.

That may be why you occasionally wear a purple tie or scarf to a meeting without even thinking why you do so. In fact, the related shades of mauve, violet, and orchid can stress your natural aptitude for authority while toning down the abrasiveness of your zest for arranging things to your liking. Always practical, you may be reluctant to invest in clothes or home furnishings in any but the most conservative colors. If so, then use relatively inexpensive accessories in purple hues to accent the more authentic you.

MONEY: Impatient to climb to the top, you will fret over money more than is necessary. You will be hardly able to contain yourself with prudent investments long enough for them to bear fruit, and so you may have to learn the hard way that hasty profits are seldom lasting ones. Your two best sources of income will be your career, which promises to be lucrative, and your ownership of undeveloped land around the fringes of urban areas.

HEALTH: In your march to success, you are inclined to neglect yourself physically, treating your body as you would a machine. Your doctor is not a mechanic with a stock of spare parts for your burned-out faculties. While still young, learn to avoid the serious problems caused by a stressful life. Your star chart reveals a tendency toward diabetes. Annual medical checkups are therefore especially advisable, and will become vital as you approach middle age.

RELATIONSHIPS: In your friendships, don't throw the baby out with the bath water. As you scramble to the top of the heap, don't sacrifice your ties with treasured companions who may not share your ambitions. As a Virgo, you cherish your friends and relatives; and if one day you awake to find them lost in the wake of your personal victories, you will always regret your mistake.

Here's a hint that may help you avoid later remorse. Every week, on a regular basis, set aside a few hours to keep up with old friends, either in person or over the telephone. You can't spare the time, you say? On the contrary, you can't afford *not* to take time off and relax, and by keeping in touch with those who care about you, you will be forcing yourself to get away from the pressures that not only make you a success but also a candidate for serious illness.

I have already discussed your marital prospects, and will only outline them here. Expect to marry late, after you have laid a foundation for your lifetime of career success. By making sure that your partner shares your taste for challenges and your zest for command, you will establish a happy union which will crown your similar triumph outside your home. In the case of Virgo Threes, the couple who grow together stay together.

VIRGO—FOURTH DIVISION
(August 31, September 4, 13, 22)

Patience, my friends. Your planetary combination indicates that Fourth Division Virgos need the forbearance of Job to deal with the problems of life. You can survive them all—indeed, you can master every situation—if you keep in mind the fact that you are distinctly different from most people. Because you are so original and independent in your thoughts and words, you will feel out of step with the rest of the world.

It is you who hears a different drummer, as Thoreau once said, not everyone else. Accept that situation and learn to turn it to your advantage, and you will avoid the serious problems you would otherwise face. For your complex personality baffles people who do not understand that you are:

- highly principled
- outspoken
- honest
- creative

Many people of less exalted ethical standards can't believe that you Virgo Fours really accept the high moral code you profess. They wonder why you find it necessary to be so forthright and honest in your personal dealings, why you run the risk of antagonizing people by telling them unpleasant truths. They may even consider you a troublemaker or a fool, just because their own lives have never been illuminated by the brilliance of uncompromised principles.

On the other hand, I must admit that your vigorous pursuit of truth can cause you to blunder badly in your career, as in your social relationships. You don't hesitate to speak out, even when doing so harms your own interests. For example, at a staff meeting, you are tempted to answer your boss's question about company problems by telling him that the problem is him! When a vain acquaintance at a party asks your opinion of her outfit, you are apt to express all too frankly what you think of it. As a result, you may get the reputation for being quick on the lip. You certainly will not be advancing yourself among those you offend.

I don't mean to suggest that you are rude or vituperative. Far from it! Your Virgoan sensitivity makes it difficult for you to hurt someone's feelings; and when you realize the damaging impact of your outspokenness, you regret it. But you cannot bear to be false. Artificial compliments or silence in the face of wrongdoing are intolerable to you, and so you speak out with the best of intentions. The sad fact is that we live in a world in which phonies sometimes get ahead, at least temporarily; and so, because of your honesty, you may see glib talkers and professional flatterers advance beyond you.

Like you, the Apostle Philip used to speak his mind directly. At the Last Supper, as Christ coaxed His associates to realize what His life was all about, Philip blurted out, "Lord, show us the Father and it is enough for us." To which his Teacher replied, "Have I been so long a time with you, and you have not known me? Philip, he who sees me sees also the Father." It was as if Philip's impetuous speech had served God's purpose in setting up the conversation and so exposing the heart of Christ's message.

At your best, you do the same thing. Zeroing in on the essence of a question under discussion, your candor can elicit clear answers without embarrassing anyone. In doing so, you make life simpler for those of us who avoid the possibility of interpersonal conflict by keeping quiet. The problem with your honest inquiries is that you sometimes pin down a strutting pretender with perceptive questions and, without intending malice, antagonize those in a position to ignore your sound advice and to disrupt your most creative projects.

You can maintain your positive habit of striking at the heart of the matter and yet avoid its negative effects of discord and ill will. Try this simple alternative. Train yourself to use softer language and, without practicing insincerity, include justifiable compliments in your critiques. As an extreme measure, put your comments into writing. You will find that even harsh judgments, delivered on paper, are inoffensive compared to verbal denunciations. There is something about the written word that makes your acute analyses less personal and more acceptable, even to those who are criticized. Is that literary experiment beyond your abilities? Hardly, for Virgo Fours are gifted with the creativity that inspires those whose lives are focused upon high-minded ideals.

COLORS: Your honesty is as striking and bright as a star sapphire set in a golden pendant. Of course, few people can afford that kind of ornamentation; but all Virgo Fours can use the combination of brilliant blue and yellow in their apparel and home. To adjust your impact on those with whom you deal, adjust in equal measure the force of your colors. If you use one room of your house, a dining room for example, as a place for family or business conferences, tone down your impulses with walls of canary or lemon yellow, avoiding more emphatic shades that could exaggerate your forcefulness. For accent colors, you will find that the delicate shade of russet, halfway between rose and brown, expresses your streak of Virgoan sympathy, which all too often others fail to recognize.

MONEY: Success in your career will probably be slow in coming, so you will have money problems until your middle years. Your financial status will improve as a consequence of your gradually acquired skill in diplomacy and personal relations. As you develop tact and delicacy in expressing your principles, your superiors will increasingly recognize that your honesty and integrity are great assets in business, and your probity will be rewarded with economic security.

HEALTH: Because you have a remarkable ability to recover rapidly from illnesses, you tend to ignore precautions to safeguard your health. Although you generally can afford to be less vigilant about your physical fitness than most people, the neglect of your diet can undermine even your sound constitution. Your Virgoan soundness of body can also be imperiled by your occasional defiance of the weather.

RELATIONSHIPS: Upon first meeting, your acquaintances are apt to think you more interested in defending your principles than in acquiring friends. If you give people a chance to know you, they will recognize your total lack of malice. To enjoy a full circle of warm friendships, learn to curb your tongue while preserving your integrity. It can be done.

Like all Virgos, you of the Fourth Division take time to find the proper romantic partner; but when you do, your marital prospects are excellent. In the case of Virgo Fours, you must guard against the possibility that your unrestrained candor could offend, and permanently alienate, someone who loves you dearly. Especially in matters of the heart, it may be better for you to let your eyes and actions speak more eloquently than your words.

VIRGO—FIFTH DIVISION *(August 23, September 5, 14)*

In both a positive and negative sense, Virgo Fives are the chameleons of the sign of the Virgin. Adaptable, changeable, versatile, you get along well with all kinds of people. You are equally at home in grave or festive situations. At solemn or riotous moments you are equally suited to the proceedings. Consequently, you succeed at almost anything you choose to accomplish. Your astrological characteristics give you this splendid pedigree.

These same gifts, however, have their drawbacks. You can be too versatile, keeping too many irons in the fire, both in terms of your career and in terms of your personal relationships. Because of your powers of adjustment, you may allow yourself to be too readily led by others, making changes in your life-style without sufficiently considering their implications. It is one thing to have the talent to master any set of circumstances, but another matter to have the wisdom to know which circumstances should be avoided in the first place.

Because of your splendid endowments of personality, you can slip into the deadly sin of pride. Knowing your versatility, you can court change for its own sake, as a daredevil tightrope-walker seeks more dizzying heights to traverse on his slender thread of life. And so you may be tempted to abandon your settled ways, your accustomed values, your traditional standard of behavior, to prove to yourself and others that you are as open to change as a crystal bead that reflects every color of the rainbow with the slightest movement. In the process, you can lose much that is valuable—in fact, much that makes you the admirable Virgo that you are.

Perhaps you have already sensed that possibility. Perhaps you have pleased your friends by keeping up with their latest fads but wondered whether you should be adapting to them or opposing them as foolish or dangerous. That is your true Virgoan character speaking. Heed its warnings. There is no reason why a Virgo Five can't be as definite and decisive as anyone else. Because your opinions and principles are expressions of your own personality, they are too precious to allow others to mold and alter them. There will always be, in the lives of all of us, some person or power trying to dominate our own judgment of right and wrong. Look more closely, however, and you are apt to discover that beneath their magisterial robes of ostentatious learning and pretended fairness, they wear another outfit; and it matches their red boots! Why should you, with your gifts, follow in their footsteps?

Make your adaptability a positive force. Make it further your ambitions and serve the needs of those around you. Harness it to a career that allows you frequent changes of place and of duties. The military would be a good field for younger Virgo Fives; and a position in sales, especially as a national representative, offers the lure of travel and new faces. At our real estate office, my husband and I once hired a temporary secretary from an agency. She was so competent in her work that we offered her a permanent job with us, but she turned it down, explaining, "I like a different job every few weeks. It keeps me interested, and I meet such nice people." Needless to say, upon inquiry, I discovered she was a Virgo Five. Perhaps you might follow her example.

A housewife of the Fifth Division of Virgo will find ample opportunities to direct her zest for change toward a happier, livelier home. Continually redecorating, experimenting with herbs and spices in her cooking, making alterations in her wardrobe, she can make her home a welcome and exciting place for her husband and children. Of course, Virgo Five partners should keep their fidelity toward each other untouched by their penchant for change. From the beginning of their marriage, they must recognize that love adapts well to every change, except a change of lover.

This same principle holds true in all aspects of your life. There is always one value, one goal, one enduring ideal which must be beyond change. In your profession, you may move from job to job and city to city, all the while keeping inviolate your desire for excellence in your work. In your leisure pursuits, you may switch hobbies every week and try your hand at every sport, but you must use each of them as a means to greater knowledge and more rewarding friendships. And within your family, you can adapt to every success and failure, every delight and heartbreak, without altering the fundamental commitment that sustains your life together.

COLORS: Because your life is an exercise in versatility, your personality is itself a rainbow of characteristics and emotions. Therefore, all colors belong in your wardrobe, and I suspect your home is probably a riot of shades and textures. In using the entire spectrum of colors, you are authentically expressing your own personal diversity. The only advice I would offer in this respect is to emphasize those colors which are most favored by those dear to you. By being happy with all hues, you will thereby also contribute to the happiness of your friends and family.

MONEY: As in most aspects of your life, there is no hard line pointing to your economic success. Many paths will take you to your goals, and you needn't be bound to a single career. I do think you will move into a creative form of self-employment in your thirties. This kind of work doesn't provide pension plans or stock options; so when your luck is running well, be sure to save a considerable amount, both for rainy days and for eventual retirement.

HEALTH: The source of your stamina is nervous energy, and it helps you cope with even the most rapid changes in your work and travel. But continual stress eventually leads to physical disruption, and it can become serious if you neglect your need for rest and diversion. There are two ways to avoid impairing your health. By settling in the right career early in life, you will spare yourself the tension of subsequent professional adjustments. But that is unpredictable, and so you might be better advised to seek restful holidays, even when you are young. Get into the habit of leaving work at the office. Use your free time not in challenging pursuits but in leisure and meditation. That practice will also help you distinguish between prudent changes and needless ones, and it will create a calm center in your busy life.

RELATIONSHIPS: Your open nature makes you an easy touch, both materially and emotionally. Perhaps because you are amenable to life's variety, you are apt to find some merit even in rather unpleasant people. That is commendable, but beware their tendency to exploit your tolerance for their selfish purposes. Especially in sexual relationships, you must guard against casual encounters, which will invariably leave you hurt and humiliated.

You have the potential to make an excellent marriage, but it will probably not come early in your life (although, even in this regard, your extreme adaptability could make a success of even a youthful marriage). Relatives will provide you with the emotional anchor and stability that may be lacking in your many friendships. Take care of your family; attend to their needs; cherish their time with you. For they are more precious to you than you might now realize.

VIRGO—SIXTH DIVISION *(August 24, September 6, 15)*

Much as this word is overused, I must nonetheless describe you Virgo Sixes as romantic. You are tenderhearted and susceptible to the charms of the opposite sex. Therein lie your strengths and virtues, as well as your weaknesses and potential faults.

Especially in your youth, your romantic spirit makes you vulnerable. You are attracted to older individuals, and this can lead you into emotional entanglements before you are sufficiently mature to handle them or sufficiently prepared to get out of them painlessly. If you are still a young Virgo of the Sixth Division, please recognize this liability now, before you walk innocently into a romantic snare that could leave your heart crippled for life.

It is during your youth that you will most likely come to the crossroads of your future. One way will lead to a quiet, contemplative life, in which religion will be a deep influence upon you and your family will always be close to your heart. The other way will bring your inner restlessness to the surface. You will feel compelled to break away from family ties and launch a life of active adventure. This second option, which many people choose, includes far more disappointments, especially in romantic relationships.

Even so, contradictory as it sounds, a Virgo Six will be able to develop bright prospects for happiness by following either path. Of course, the circumstances of that contentment will be different, but your Virgoan characteristics will enable you to turn them to your benefit. The choices you do make when confronted with that crossroads will depend upon many things, the most important of which will be whether you are, at the time, in love with someone. So great is the power of the human heart.

You Virgo Sixes have an affinity for animals. Indeed, the name of your Apostle comes from two Greek words—*philos* and *hippos*—meaning "fond of horses." This humanitarian regard for the creatures of the earth could act as a steadying and ennobling factor in your life-style. It is likely to lead you to work and reside outside urban areas, even in rather isolated places, perhaps as a naturalist, forest ranger, or game warden. Animal husbandry is an appropriate career for you; also veterinary medicine, positions in zoos and pet stores, even branches of teaching which involve the study of wildlife. Whatever your profession and wherever you live, you are likely to have pets in your home, even if you explain their presence by saying they provide good companionship and entertainment for your children.

Your planetary pattern gives you an enjoyment of artistic efforts. Even if a painter or musician isn't up to par, you sense the dedication to beauty inherent in their work. The way you yourself create in the arts and in literature will depend on your choice as a teen-ager. If you opt for a quiet life, your life-style will involve extensive exposure to and participation in writing, painting, and composing. The opposite path doesn't exclude you from artistic endeavors; but it is more apt to steer you toward the theater, television, or motion pictures, either in production or before the cameras. Whatever your present age may be, it is vital that you recognize within you the need for creative expression. Perhaps you have realized that your needlework is much more to you than a hobby, that your garden enables you to translate into material fact the immaterial aspirations of your spirit, or that your homemade outfits are actual works of art. Good for you! You are discovering that the daily life of each of us can be a symphony of commonplace beauties. Rest assured that sooner or later, you will know which artistic activities have been intended for you. By keeping your mind open on the subject, you will be ready to develop those talents which will lead to the success indicated in your astrological chart.

COLORS: Yours are the truest colors of the Virgin. A vibrant white will emphasize your essentially idealistic romanticism. It is as if the vibrations of your magnetism were visually akin to the appearance of a brilliant blue sky, with here and there drifts of the purest white clouds. Whether in a suit or on the walls of your study, white is best for you when accented by the blue of sky and water. It may be the dusty hue of a summer cornflower or the deep blue of a sailor's uniform. It may even be that special shade we associate with Renaissance portraits of the Virgin, as well as those by Poussin, whose name has been applied to that brilliant color. In fact, you may find that an old outfit of white and blue, even if it is bedraggled and worn, suits your creative moments and is especially comfortable when you practice an instrument, struggle with a sonnet, or fill your hands with the flowing clay on a potter's wheel.

MONEY: The indications for your fortune are good. There are signs in your astrological makeup that indicate scholarships and grants during your formative years, comfortable earnings later, and unexpected aid during economic setbacks in your middle years. Investments in property, commodities, and precious metals all offer you prospects of significant income.

HEALTH: You possess that basically sound Virgoan constitution. No major ailments appear in your stellar chart, and your hopeful mental outlook keeps you physically well; for the power of the spirit over our bodily health is tremendous. The only danger you face is the stress of a rapid life-style. Don't allow it to bring you to exhaustion. Like the animals you love, have sense enough to turn away from labor and exertion to rest or recoup your energy.

RELATIONSHIPS: As I mentioned at the beginning of this discussion, you Virgo Sixes are romantically vulnerable, especially during your critical early years. Chances for a happy early marriage are not good, and you should delay thoughts of settling down until your career is already under way. In that way, there will be less disruption of both your professional commitments and your home life.

Your family will always think highly of you, even if you choose to grow away from them in your search for the new and dramatic. Despite your tendency to doubt them, friends are loyal to you, recognizing the romantic spirit which governs you and makes you unpredictable at times. It will be to your long-range good if you shed your reservations about telling people how you feel about them. This will become especially vital in your late twenties, for it is then that you will make the personal commitments which will shape the rest of your life.

VIRGO–SEVENTH DIVISION *(August 25, September 7, 16)*

Interest in religion and in the occult is a major factor in the star chart of Virgo Sevens. There are astrological indications of your interest in areas of the mind which you conceal from friends and relatives. Because you sense the disapproval and mockery of those who are uninformed about the powers of the human spirit, you tend to keep your interests to yourself and study in private the little-known region where body and soul meet and interact.

The investigation of psychic phenomena cannot be hurried, and it will be years before you can decide with any degree of certainty whether you possess psychic powers beyond the usual capacity of all humans. As I have said before, all the talents God gives us, no matter how unusual they may seem, are precious gifts to be developed for His purposes. And so in contemplating the spiritual life and all the things in this world which laboratory science cannot analyze, you are pursuing higher truths than chemistry or physics can reveal to us. And in the process, you are fulfilling yourself by being true to your Creator's plan for you. It probably will come as no surprise to you to be told that you are:

- highly intuitive
- seeking guidance from senior individuals
- looking for mental satisfaction
- analytical

It is a great strength of Virgo Sevens, in all aspects of their life, that they are never too late to begin new projects. Frequently, they take music lessons in old age, as they were unable to do when they were young, and become adept at their instruments. This applies as well to your psychic development. Even if you are in advanced years, if you want to develop the intuition you know you possess, remember the future is still yours.

There are many groups, probably in your own community, that are interested in the links between religion and the mind. There you can find others with interests like yours, and through your common concerns you will be able to further develop the powers that are yours. In fact, you may be more advanced psychically than you realize because your previous interest and reading on the subject have already heightened your positive attitude and sharpened your personal awareness. The background you have already accumulated, together with your Virgoan analytical mind, will allow you to move forward quickly toward an appreciation of your gifts.

Your habit of seeking guidance from older individuals you respect is a symptom of a broader search in your life for security and wisdom. You are looking for an enduring faith. During your younger years, you are apt to enjoy the companionship of older people, especially when you enter into their discussions about man's past and future. In fact, when you marry, probably in your thirties, your spouse is likely to be several years older than you.

This fascination with the experience and sagacity of age leads you to seek mental rather than material goals. You don't gauge success by the number of dollars in the bank but rather by an individual's advancement in self-understanding and philosophical learning. Your greatest treasure is peace of mind, that satisfaction the intellect senses when it has discovered reliable and eternal truths.

The good news for Virgo Sevens is that the peace they seek awaits them for the taking. As soon as you recognize that fact, you will be enriched in spirit beyond any counting the world knows. The change could be dramatic. When Philip was called to Christ, he didn't debate the choice for several months before reaching a tentative decision. His reaction was immediate. Your own watershed could come as suddenly; and when it does, your astrological pattern indicates that you will make the right decision.

COLORS: Because of the psychic strain in your life, it is no surprise that shades of dove gray, soft and warm like the down of that lovely bird, suit your meditative personality. That doesn't mean your appearance, any more than your character, has to be bland. On the contrary, because your attitudes are affirmative and your outlook is positive, your magnetism is strengthened by the emphatic assertiveness of green, the bolder the better. Virgo Sevens are at their best when they accent a gray dress with an emerald pin, real or artificial, or when their gray business suit is brightened by a jade green tie.

MONEY: During your formative years, you will worry needlessly about money matters, just as you will be inclined to fret about many things you cannot control. Rest assured that your distress is pointless. You will stay in the black throughout your life except for short periods when your own uncertainties about yourself lead you to misjudge your investments and purchases. Even those setbacks will fade in your middle years, and your economic position will then be comfortable.

HEALTH: Self-doubt and excessive anxiety in your early years may well lead you to be overly concerned about your health. While I encourage a prudent concern for physical well-being, I must warn against the ill effects, both physical and psychological, of hypochondria. Once you emerge from your spiritual shell, finding in like-minded seekers after truth the fellowship we all need, you will enjoy glowing and carefree good health.

RELATIONSHIPS: Because of your attachment to older people, you will find that the occasionally cutting edge of competition with your peers is absent from your friendships. And so your social relationships will tend to be both happy and enduring.

Steer clear of casual sexual encounters, because you simply can't deal with them without acute and lingering pain. Your romantic attachments must be total and lasting, for no other kind will provide you the peace of mind essential to every Virgo Seven.

As I have already indicated, your marital prospects may involve someone considerably older than you, whom you will love not only romantically but also intellectually. A fellow seeker of wisdom, equally interested in the mind's psychic powers, will suit you best as a spouse. Be sure that the lucky person you select to share the calm happiness of your Virgo Seven life is respectful of your religious commitments.

VIRGO—EIGHTH DIVISION *(August 26, September 8, 17)*

Yours is a serious, studious, and reserved nature. Although your planetary combination has given you a pleasant and likable disposition, it has also made you restrained in initiating friendships. Although you treat people well, you make little effort to deepen acquaintances into something more personal. And those few people who are close to you are often puzzled by your seeming disinterest in them, although there is no unkindness about it.

There is a good reason for your attitudes. In your early years, perhaps through parental influence, you acquired a love for books; and the written word became a substitute for people as your companionship. You are:

- reticent
- oriented to work
- intellectual
- meticulous

The vibrations of the Eighth Division indicate that many of you within it will lead quiet, indeed restricted, lives until your mid-thirties. It may be that family obligations hem in your ambitions and circumscribe your opportunities for self-improvement and awareness of the world's wonders. Perhaps a lack of money prevents you from pursuing the one career you most yearn to follow. An early marriage, seldom a good idea for a Virgo, may have tied you down to someone possessive and domineering, who will not allow you the freedom to explore your gifts and find your proper role in this earth's endless cast of characters. For whatever reason, you will probably retire from the world until you begin your fourth decade. And then you will come into your own!

Because you are reserved about your opinions and feelings, you are unlikely to seek a glamorous career. It is more important to you to be happy in your work than to be famous because of it. Your diligence and honesty make you a most desirable employee, but your reticence will prevent you from demanding the recognition that should be yours. You are reluctant to advertise your virtues, even though your commitment to your job and dedication to your duties entitle you to special esteem, promotions, and bonuses.

It is possible that a change in your life, around the age of thirty-five, could alter that situation. Once recognition comes your way, once your efforts are properly rewarded, either at your place of employment or in your community, you will become more positive about your merits and more aggressive, while working as hard and as thoroughly as ever before. You will thereby find that you are only securing for yourself the justice you demand for others.

Your early love of books broadens your mind even more than usual among Virgos, who are generally an intellectual group. Like the Apostle who represents your astrological sign, you are likely to be the quiet mover behind the scenes. You can be immensely well informed but so quiet about your knowledge that few people guess just how erudite you have become through years of reading. Of course, your valuable gifts would be most appreciated in the publishing business, in library offices, and in certain research activities. As an editor, you can perform superbly the meticulous work that is needed to produce a first-rate newspaper or magazine. Your joy will always be in the way your work appears before the public free of errors rather than the expectation of popular acclaim.

As time goes by, you will find that your intellectual prowess is greatly valued by many people, some of whom want to learn from you. No matter what your field of special interest—a scholarly discipline like history or art, or a popular pursuit like gardening or carpentry or auto mechanics—it will provide opportunities for you to be instructive and helpful to others. It will also be of direct benefit to you in a surprising way; because once you discover how people need your tutoring and assistance, you will begin to lose that reticence that keeps you from being entirely relaxed around them. As is so often the case, you will find that in lending a helping hand by sharing your learning, you will also be helping yourself.

COLORS: Just as much else will change in your life when you receive delayed recognition during your middle years, your use of color will also be different after you leave your youthful reserve behind you. During your early years, you will probably choose dark and somber shades, as heavy as the old and faded bindings on the books you cherish. Those colors will do nothing to lift your horizons and extend your ambitions. But as you become aware of your potential and realize what you have already achieved in learning and skill, you will instinctively be attracted to colors better suited to your Virgoan vibrations. Pastels and vivid greens can lift you from your obsession with work and free your spirit as effectively as the slim volumes of poetry you keep close at hand. Light yellow clothing will express not only your kinship to the demure primrose flowers but also your intellectual affinity for the creamy parchments of a rare book collection.

MONEY: The restrictions of your early life will cause you to miss one or two golden chances for wealth. Always overly cautious in your investments, you are also too inclined to let others direct your spending to their purposes. It is one thing to sacrifice for those you love, but another to give up your creative and rewarding pursuits to subsidize the amusements of less industrious individuals.

HEALTH: Your psychological tendencies lead you away from physical activity and could turn you into a sedentary bookworm unless you guard against it. Balance your long hours of reading and meditation with brisk walks, even jogging. Before you curl up with that book of short stories, ride your bicycle over to the park and make a sunny lawn your reading room. Or combine your reading and your exercise another way by researching a new hobby. Collect and study some volumes on gemstones, for example, and then set off on a rock-hunting hike. Use your imagination to bring sufficient activity into your daily life to maintain your good health.

RELATIONSHIPS: A late marriage, even a second marriage in certain circumstances, will work out best for Virgo Eights. For as you mature, you will be less likely to accept a thoughtless partner who doesn't appreciate your instinctive thirst for ideas and information. Of course, even in the case of early marriages, there are Virgoan prospects for happiness as long as your lover is willing to share you with your books, your work, and your eventual entry into the spotlight of recognition for your accomplishments.

Virgos of the Eighth Division find children a source of great pride and pleasure. Whether they are your own or those you generously take into your care, they will especially benefit from the respect for learning you can instill in them. All members of your family will be closer to you than your friends; because unless you make heroic efforts to be more sociable, you will have few intimate comrades. Those acquaintances who do become part of your inner circle will usually do so because they and you both recognize your common appreciation of literature and the life of the mind.

VIRGO—NINTH DIVISION *(August 27, September 9, 18)*

You Virgos of the Ninth Division are the diplomats of this world. You are among those blessed peacemakers, so sorely needed in this period of man's history, of whom Christ once spoke so highly. In times of dispute, it is you Virgo Nines who are standing by to pour oil on troubled waters. You step between snarling combatants to soothe their anger with well-chosen words. No wonder so many people think you are worth your weight in gold! For you are:

- tactful
- a born manager
- acutely observant, especially in matters of personality
- spiritually calm

You may shrug your shoulders as you read this, thinking, "Who, me!" But remember all those times when people have asked you to arbitrate a dispute between them. They beg you to settle thorny questions, whether of property or of pride, and you can usually reach an equitable decision. Perhaps you have never considered that peacemaking, but it is every bit as important as the work of great diplomats. In fact, with a gift like that, it would seem that you should seek a career as a negotiator. Your heart is not in such professional situations, however. You are strictly an amateur conciliator, and I wonder if your talents for compromise would function as well in a formal, institutionalized arrangement, in which it was your official job to do what you usually do spontaneously.

Many Virgo Nine men are successful as architects, engineers, or foremen in construction projects. I suspect that their gift for bringing opponents together enables them to coordinate the vast and complex efforts of hundreds of individuals who together erect a building. Virgo Nine women find their best vocations in responsible business roles. They are frequently business executives, accountants, or those supersecretaries we call administrative assistants even though they often make more important decisions than their superiors. When they become homemakers, they are usually active as organizers and fund raisers in civic and charitable projects.

In all these activities, your innate Virgoan gift for harmonizing contradictory forces will be useful. An incident from the life of your Apostle demonstrates how Virgo Nines instinctively know the diplomatic way to handle whatever situation arises. Philip was called upon by some visiting Greeks to arrange a meeting with Christ. He himself didn't set up the interview they wished, however. Aware of his subordinate place in the fellowship of the Twelve and recognizing the limits of his own authority, he took the matter to Andrew. This was a small thing, but a correct one. And diplomacy is the art of doing small things properly. In all aspects of your life, it is the pathway to happiness for Virgo Nines.

One of the best traits of the Ninth Division of Virgo is an unwillingness to quarrel over trivia. Though you will take a stand for principle, you won't argue about slighted feelings or petty property disputes. Thus you create peace and calm around you, whether it is in your home, your office, or amid the bustle of a building enterprise.

I know a family in which both parents are Virgo Nines and their five daughters all were in their teen-age years during the same span of time. Scarcely a day could pass in their household without a disagreement among the girls over who was going to wear what clothing. Yet those parents handled the matter wonderfully. In true

Virgo Nine fashion, they would bring the disputing sisters together and ask each of them why it was vital that she wear a particular item on that particular day. After each daughter had explained her argument, all the girls would decide by vote which of them had the best reasons. Those girls are as close to their parents as any children can be.

Of course, there can be a drawback to your penchant for peacemaking, just as there surely is for every virtue. There is always a way for a noble quality to go astray or to cause trouble instead of delight. In your case, you will find that there are some circumstances in which your intervention, despite your good intentions, would be disastrous. Even your formidable diplomatic skills can't cope with the marital problems of your friends, and your impulse to mediate in complicated legal situations could cause personal troubles requiring the attention of a lawyer. We each must know the limits of our abilities. Don't push yours too far.

COLORS: Because you care about the way you present yourself to others, colors are already important to you, and your taste in selecting the right shades makes your home a pleasant environment. Indeed, your fondness for crimson and pink may turn your living room into a veritable rose garden! Those shades enhance your magnetic vibrations, especially when they are accented with white, cream, and other pale shades. In fact, I suspect that the bold way you interplay red with quieter shades subconsciously reinforces your stature as an authoritative peacemaker in the minds of those with whom you deal. People sense, from your free display of the color of the heart, that your intentions are sincere and your opinions judicious.

MONEY: Once your career begins to roll, you will always be solvent. I see no serious financial problems for you, and some Virgo Nines are destined for considerable wealth. Your perception and powers of observation enable you to see the facts of an economic situation, just as they allow you to ascertain the justice of a disputed issue. Because of your ability to bring hostile factions together in harmony, your talents will be sought by employers who need a peaceful work force. By keeping in demand, you will also keep your earnings high.

HEALTH: Your physical condition is unusually good. Virgo

Nines are blessed with a remarkable freedom from serious disease. Of course, any of us, no matter how protected by our astrological patterns, can imperil our health through carelessness and mistreatment of the wonderful mechanisms of our body. But if you follow the rudimentary rules of good health, you should be safe from sickness. With regard to accidents, however, you will have to take your chances with the rest of us and must exercise due caution.

RELATIONSHIPS: You are self-confident and rarely rattled. No wonder people are attracted to you. Some of them will expect you to work out their problems for them. However that effort may turn out, it is a fact that your own difficulties are usually handled with prudence and dispatch. Arguments rarely interrupt your friendships; and even when your family or relatives are squabbling among themselves, you manage to remain on good terms with all of them. It's quite an accomplishment, but that's par for the course for a Virgo Nine.

Although you don't make friends easily, you are seldom wrong in your choice of them and remain fervently devoted to them. Similarly, you bring Virgoan fidelity to your marriage and make an excellent life-mate. Your home is usually a place of calm, for you apply your talent for moderation and accord to whatever little problems are bound to arise between any man and wife. Just as with your professional work, you anticipate problems before they arise in your family, and so you are doubly prepared to minimize conflict and keep your love strong and vibrant throughout your years together.

LIBRA—BARTHOLOMEW

(September 23–October 22)

Through six signs of the Zodiac we have seen how the Lord of Creation gives each of His children certain talents with which to accomplish the work He has assigned them. The astrological division of human abilities recalls St. Paul's observation: "There are varieties of gifts, but the same Spirit; and there are varieties of ministries, but the same Lord; and there are varieties of workings, but the same God, who works all things in all."

Happiness consists in using our particular gifts for purposes larger than our own. The greatest misfortune occurs when we divert our powers to worldly ends. There is a tragic eloquence in the simple lament of Cardinal Thomas Wolsey when, in 1530, after a splendid career in affairs of Church and State, as he was being taken to London for trial on charges of high treason, he realized that had he served his God as diligently as he had Henry VIII, he would have left behind him true greatness rather than empty memories of glory and might. Stripped of his honors and deserted by his friends, Wolsey knew his talents had been misdirected, his God-given power misused. He sorely regretted his folly and mercifully died before his trial and probable execution.

We can avoid his remorse and look ahead with the same vision he saw only in hindsight. From the knowledge we gain by studying each segment of the Zodiac, each of us can understand the pattern and meaning of our own and of others' lives. That is why, whatever our birth sign, all of us have reason to learn about every astrological division. So let us now turn with undiminished interest to the sign of Libra, the Scales.

In the vision which led me to write this book, the Apostle associated with Libra was Bartholomew, who is also referred to in Scripture as Nathanael. Because of the confusion over those two names, they are often thought of as two different Apostles. In some ways, that was the case, as it is with many Libras. And that is why Bartholomew, a balanced character given to weighing both sides of a matter and sympathizing with all parties to a dispute, is an appropriate embodiment of Libra's judicious evenhandedness.

In astrology, the Scales are associated with the ancient Babylonian belief that the stellar constellation they represent was somehow involved in the judgment of the living and the dead. The ancient Egyptians believed that the god Osiris, king of the Underworld, weighed the hearts of men on his scales to decide their ultimate fate. Moreover, farmers in the land of the pharaohs weighed their harvest when the moon was full, in the astrological month of Libra.

It comes as no surprise that Libras are inclined to weigh matters for themselves. They rarely accept a fact without questioning it and, even with their natural human subjectivity, seek the detached view of every issue. Their two foremost attributes are a love of knowledge and high personal standards. In both respects, Bartholomew was exceptional. He was probably the best educated of the Apostles; and when Philip first brought him to Christ, their Master exclaimed, "Behold a true Israelite in whom there is no guile!" Those traits help to explain why Libras so often achieve great things. Only Ariens outnumber them in each year's Who's Who.

If you were born under the sign of the Scales, you probably find a remarkable kinship with Bartholomew when he first appears in the Gospel of John. He was at first skeptical of Philip's claim to have found the Messiah, just as you are usually wary of claims and promises. Having met Christ, however, he acknowledged His divine authority with some of the bluntest words in Scripture, saying, "Rabbi, thou art the Son of God, thou art King of Israel." What a typical Libra! You doubt reports and rumors, but, after checking the facts for yourself, reach an instant decision on the evidence. Even more important, when you follow your spiritual instincts, your snap judgments are usually correct.

You live by high principles, have very little of the rebel in you, and base your actions on reason and information. When another person wants to dominate a situation, whether at work or in your community or even in the home, you will recognize superior leadership, but only after that individual has demonstrated ability and honor.

That does not mean you are not a leader in your own right. You welcome responsibility as a challenge, not a burden, and can take command with such easy calm that others do not recognize how much you accomplish. Even when you don't receive credit for your achievements, it doesn't bother you. You prefer a wider view of human affairs, in which credit is not given here on earth, and that is only one of the charming attitudes that makes Libras such pleasant companions.

Because balance is the keynote to every Libran life, you have a strong sense of justice and have frequent difficulty in deciding upon a course of action that is not absolutely right. Given a choice between two less than satisfactory alternatives, you may choose neither and let matters slip by rather than compromise your principles. This can make you indecisive and too easily influenced by others, despite your Libran independence. Because you see whatever good there is in *any* position, the choice of good or evil, the choice between the values represented by your Apostle and those symbolized by the Devil's red boots, is blurred and difficult. Recognizing some merit in everyone, you could even look sympathetically upon Lucifer and recall that he once had been an angel!

A typical Libra does not ruffle easily. You almost always keep your temper under control, although when it does break out, it is apt to be as emphatic as your commitment to fairness and justice. Despite your enthusiasm for so much of this world's beauty and knowledge, you restrain your emotions to the point at which people may think you are disinterested, even in the things that most absorb you. Neat, almost fastidious, your home and personal attire reflect your concern for order. I suspect that if you have a garden, you know where each plant grows and can name them all for visitors.

Your concern for harmony and aversion for interpersonal conflict combine with your penchant for detail to make you a superb administrator. In hospitals, scientific foundations, and laboratories, the men and women responsible for teamwork and institutional goals are quite often Libras. In fact, all areas of science, with its guarded and undramatic ways, count a great many Libras as professional researchers and volunteer workers.

The same balancing of influences determines the romantic life of Libras. Although you are enchanted by the idea of falling in love, you are not the type to lose your heart at first sight. Although your personality is warm and your character outgoing, you rarely demonstrate your affections and, consequently, mistrust the motives of anyone whose approaches come on too strong or too soon. Idealistic and refined, you can be gullible when an unscrupulous person appeals to your lofty principles and uses them to cover his real purposes.

It is best for Libras to marry later than most; and as a rule, you will wed only once, even if that marriage comes to a premature end. With your temperate, level personality, your home life should be happy; and so it will be worth the wait to settle down. By looking to the future and not rushing into romances that were never meant to be, you will bring your love life into harmony with your astrological pattern and profit from it immensely.

Another factor in your personal relationships, perhaps involved in your marriage, is the likelihood that at some point in your life, you will take on responsibility for a close relative, either a parent, an in-law, or one of your children, who suffers from either a physical or mental incapacity. As always, you will see that there is a good to balance a bad situation. Although it will place restrictions on your life, your spiritual rewards in shouldering the extra load will be tremendous. And that matters to you. Unseen, inner growth is a vital concern for sensitive Libras. Actively interested in religion, you yearn to comprehend the underlying meaning of life. This can be the most profound and enriching aspect of your Libran thirst for knowledge; and, like all wisdom, it is best increased by being shared with others.

Your questing mind is apt to make you aware of whatever psychic gifts you possess, and it will be relatively easy for you to develop them through your calm and meditative attitudes. This aspect of your being will allow you to understand fully the mission you have in this world and to appreciate the eminent role assigned to you in the overall pattern of the universe. The chances are that you will find your place in it more quickly than most people do and that it will concern service to your fellow man.

This emphasis upon public service characterizes the lives of many eminent Libras. John Adams, second President of the United States, was born on October 19; and his long career was essential to the establishment of American liberties. In similar ways, both

Eamon de Valera (October 14) and David Ben-Gurion (October 16) served the people of their respective countries, Ireland and Israel.

Libran humanitarians include Frances Willard (September 28), founder of the Women's Christian Temperance Union, and Eleanor Roosevelt (October 11), whose lifelong concern for the unfortunate will be her undying legacy. Mahatma Gandhi (October 2) embodied the nobility of thought and action that is a common attribute of Libras at their best.

The inspiration of great music has been given to us by such Libras as Franz Liszt (October 22), Giuseppe Verdi (October 10), and George Gershwin (September 26). In literature, famous Libras include William Faulkner (September 25), F. Scott Fitzgerald (September 24), Eugene O'Neill (October 16), Noah Webster (October 16), who compiled the famous dictionary, and Kay Halle (October 13), the well-known Churchill scholar and author.

The inventor George Westinghouse (October 6) not only made railroads safer and more efficient but also devised over four hundred mechanical and electric inventions which improved the daily lives of millions. An earlier counterpart was Girolamo Cardano (September 24), the sixteenth-century scientist, mathematician, and astrologer. The educator who, more than anyone else, shaped public education in twentieth-century America, John Dewey, was born on October 20; and in an earlier age, William McGuffey (September 23) put together the reading texts which formed the basis of elementary education in a simpler America.

This star-studded array of Libras shows how far you can go with the talents given you by the astrological circumstances of your birth. Like the Apostle Bartholomew, you have qualities of greatness. To learn how to liberate them and apply them to their best purposes, we must now examine each division within the sign of the Scales.

LIBRA—FIRST DIVISION *(September 28, October 1, 10, 19)*

The role of a Libra One is to fight for justice. You have been endowed with virtues that leave you admirably equipped to succeed in many areas of life, but especially in the field of law, whether as a maker of it, a practitioner, or an enforcement officer. You are:

- sympathetic

- liberal
- fair-minded
- idealistic

In addition, you possess the ability to see clearly situations which baffle and mislead others; and you usually express yourself well, although in a subdued way characteristically Libran.

In your case, the scales of Libra are the scales of justice, like those represented by the blindfolded figure who symbolizes the impartiality of the law. Though this is a typically Libran relationship, it is especially strong within the First Division. And I would not be surprised if, from your childhood years, you have had a fascination with courtroom proceedings. Perhaps you were a judge in your high school's student court.

Your natural sympathy means that if you follow a career in the law, you are more inclined to side with the defense than the prosecution. Your loyalties might seem conventional on the surface, but they are to the establishment of law rather than to its institutions, personnel, or political representatives. I would not be surprised to find you chronically battling for the underdog in whatever situation you face, whether it concerns labor conditions, the rights of minorities, or the plight of underdeveloped nations.

This is your liberalism in action. You don't care about distinctions of class or creed or color, but about what is right. Although that is laudable, there can be negative effects. For example, your single-minded aid to accused and mistreated persons can make you forget that in some cases, the underdog is wrong and deserves to suffer penalties of law. You may develop a simplistic view of social and political affairs, in which certain individuals and interests are altogether good and certain others are totally malign. In short, your Libran scales can weigh falsely unless you exercise a vigilant objectivity in finding out the facts of each case.

Fortunately, your astrological influences give you a fairness of mind. That should warn you when your sympathies are being played upon by the unworthy. Indeed, this characteristic can be so strong in you that it can turn to your disadvantage. In an informal discussion or a formal debate, in business negotiations or a commercial transaction, your sense of fairness inclines you to point out to an opponent or client even those factors which work against your own interests. As an example, in selling a house, you would be sure to mention any defects, thinking it dishonest to do otherwise.

Some will therefore consider you a sucker; others of more refined ethical sensitivity will recognize the nobility of your conduct.

There is one blind spot in your idealism. You fail to see in advance how your involvement in controversial situations, seeking fair play for others, can cause potentially dangerous reactions against you and your loved ones. Remain true to your ideals, but at the same time be more cautious in your approach to them so that you don't defeat your own purposes.

In addition to work involving the law, there is such a wide variety of professional activity open to Libra Ones that my only advice would be to trust your own instincts. Even if the discovery of your most appropriate career comes late in life, don't be discouraged, but be prepared to make the changes necessary to secure a new start in life. This applies particularly to Libra One housewives, who are likely to receive job offers in whatever careers they were pursuing before they were married. Accept them, for things will have a way of working out for you.

COLORS: Helping to emphasize your personal magnetism are all shades of yellow and gold and, when you really want to stress the forcefulness of your words and ideas, orange and golden brown. These colors are appropriate for several reasons. Most obvious is the fact that you have a heart of gold and should let the world know it! In addition, your personal commitment to justice brings sunshine into the lives of many other people, if only in little ways that you yourself do not notice. In your attire, you may already be doing the same thing subconsciously, perhaps cheering up an office torn by personal disputes with your lemony scarf or tangerine sweater.

MONEY: This is a fairly bright aspect of your future. Although I can't say you will be wealthy, your prospects do seem fairly secure. Your income will usually come from intellectual pursuits, although many Libras enjoy manual work because they feel the close interaction between body and mind. The ancient Greeks felt the same way, and their wisest philosophers cherished the ideal of a sound mind in a sound body. Whatever your work, your income should rise steadily throughout your life.

HEALTH: You should remain active all your years, and there are likely to be a great many of them. As long as you retain your habits of exercise and alertness, you will remain in good health. A sluggish inactivity will not only bore you but will also weaken your resistance to infectious diseases. Your major health problems are apt to be accidents rather than illnesses, and injuries to your head or shoulders could cause considerable and lasting pain. Make caution your keynote, especially in driving and in rigorous athletics.

RELATIONSHIPS: Because your honesty and lack of guile leave you vulnerable, some of your business relationships will prove to be unreliable as you discover that associates, colleagues, and competitors are not always above exploiting you for their own selfish purposes. On a personal level, you will enjoy a few very rewarding friendships and a wider circle of more casual friends. You will find that those nearest to you share your emphatic feelings against injustice and mistreatment of the helpless.

A romantic by nature, you will never be able to love and leave someone. For you, a commitment of love is permanent, and you will read meanings into sexual relationships that are not always there. Be more guarded, or you will be hurt by those who do not understand that your affections are enduring. Exercise special caution to avoid confusing love with your chronic sympathy for the underdog. Make sure that the life-mate you choose shares your own ideals of justice so that he or she will understand the time and energy you will devote to various causes.

LIBRA—SECOND DIVISION
(September 29, October 2, 11, 20)

A Libra Two is the right person to have around in an emergency. With your amazingly quick mind and cool thinking, you grasp a situation immediately and reach the right decisions in seconds rather than minutes. While others are still exclaiming over a piece of news, you have already formulated a response to it. You waste little time in emotional reactions and prefer to do what you can rather than worry about what you cannot.

The Apostle Bartholomew's love of knowledge is deeply ingrained in you, and this helps you to cope with surprises and crises. Because you make a point of knowing in advance about a great many subjects, you know ahead of time what should be done in a given situation. When it arises, your course of action is invariably the most prudent and expeditious. You have been gifted in other ways, too. You are:

- able to inspire others
- dedicated
- diplomatic
- good-natured

I might say you do your homework. Amassing knowledge and exploring the unknown, you not only build your own confidence but also reassure others who are exposed to your intellectual resources. Without intending to do so, you inspire them to broaden their horizons, to seek for themselves the wisdom which you pursue all your life. Sometimes the best teachers are those who don't know they are teaching. This is your case, for even those who are unconcerned about learning sense your delight in it and feel your contagious enthusiasm for the wonders of knowledge.

If all of this comes as a surprise to you, if you think this analysis of your personality is too complimentary, that is just your natural Libran modesty at work. The plain, unvarnished truth is that you are an extremely likable person. People respect you for your intellectual integrity and admire your mental agility and competence, but they like you for yourself. Ever fair-minded, you are dedicated to your work, no matter what; and you display an obvious honesty that takes for granted that others will reciprocate with equal integrity. Even so, you don't put on airs as though you were holier than your fellow man. You are far too much the diplomat to do that. Besides, it probably never occurs to you that you are, in fact, holier than those who are less devoted to the truth and less concerned about moral principles.

Your tactful handling of people is a much needed ability in this world. You are diplomatic by instinct, both because you assume that even an unpleasant person can teach you something and because you are naturally cool and calm even in the face of aggravation. Willingness to listen to another person's point of view makes you a treasured conversationalist in a society that is given to shouting rather than discourse. Moreover, you are affectionate in both speech and manner, with members of both sexes, and praise aloud the efforts of others. No wonder people do their best for you, feel at home around you, and value your presence at social gatherings.

The principle underlying your behavior is even more admirable. You lead people to wish to better themselves, and you see it as your responsibility to help them in that attempt. This is a wonderful way of sharing your gifts with the world! Let me offer a personal example to explain the influence you can have if you choose to use it.

When I was a girl, I had a teacher who, I later discovered, was a Libra Two. She was criticized by her colleagues because many of her former pupils seemed to perform poorly after they left her tutelage, even though she gave them good marks and failed hardly anyone. Was she too lax in her standards for us? Not at all. She did not fail students because she did not need to. Her pupils enjoyed her teaching so much that they worked diligently to please her. Later, with less dedicated teachers, the same subjects seemed like drudgery instead of fun; and we girls, I'm ashamed to confess, put in less effort than we should have. We just didn't care as much about our work as we had with our favorite teacher, and the negative results soon showed in our tests. As a typically good-natured Libra Two, our former teacher probably saw the irony of the situation and must have enjoyed a quiet laugh over it.

Other Libran traits are a love of travel and a special sensitivity to water, which can bring out all the best in you. Your star pattern indicates that you will be happiest living or working near the sea or by a lake.

COLORS: Although colors are not especially important to you, on those odd days when your spirits need a lift, use shades that are as calm, open, and reassuring as you are. Bright greens, teamed with white or cream, will help your appearance convey to others the guileless affection you automatically offer to those you meet. There will be times when you will have to assume immense responsibility as others look to you for instant decisions and for a model of cool self-composure. It is then that you will find a sparkling white outfit, whether a woman's dress or, in the case of a male Libra Two, a bold summer suit, dramatically useful in expressing the authority thrust upon you.

MONEY: Your inherent modesty makes you all too willing to surrender your share of credit and applause to others, and this can be a factor in reducing your earnings, especially in the early stages of your career. Later in life, you will enjoy more fully the fruit of your labors. But avoid speculation or gambling, for you are one of Nature's losers when it comes to financial risks.

HEALTH: As a rule, you are not physically active and are susceptible to communicable diseases, especially those of the respiratory tract. Try to treat yourself to more frequent exercise, and I don't mean just carrying your beloved books to the library and back. Particularly in winter, eat carefully and cherish your health as much as you do your knowledge.

RELATIONSHIPS: You are not very romantically inclined, perhaps because you are so absorbed in the pursuit of learning. Unless you marry while you are young, it is probable you will not wed at all. Of course, there is always the chance that you might meet someone who shares your devotion to knowledge and your generous affection for the whole world. In that case, you will make a splendid pair.

One way or the other, your life will be full of affection, for people will reciprocate the warmth you convey both by words and by that inexpressible quality of making others feel at ease. Even if you remain single, you will never be lonely, although you may often find yourself alone. Libra Twos are among those fortunate individuals who carry around with them the whole panoply of human wisdom to serve as their constant companion.

LIBRA—THIRD DIVISION *(September 30, October 3, 12, 21)*

As a Libra Three, you are marked for the good life. You may have difficulty in choosing your career and life-style; but once you do, all is easy sailing. Your astral pattern indicates that you will be drawn toward a profession which allows you to help others, perhaps in medicine, charity work, a religious life, or a governmental body dealing with the aged or poor. Among your personality traits are:

- generosity
- a sunny disposition
- ability to work well with top people
- aptitude to fulfill your dreams and those of others

Wanting to help others, you are probably generous with your time, money, and energy. Perhaps you don't even realize the extent to which you devote yourself to the benefit of the needy. Perhaps you suppose that most people are as selfless in this regard as you. That is evidence of your Libran humility, taking your good deeds for granted, as if there were no other alternative but humanitarian action.

Needless to say, generosity, like any other virtue, has its corresponding weakness. You must guard against the tendency to deny your own loved ones the time and attention they deserve. Any magnanimity that sacrifices the well-being of your dependents is misguided. So, like a true Libra, balance your home responsibilities with your desire to assist others.

Your cheerful, outgoing disposition enables you to work well with people and attract many friends. Indeed, your popularity may be such that you will be plagued with an overly active social life. Being much in demand as a companion, you will have to carefully avoid offending all those whose repeated invitations you turn down. Rely on your native Libran tact to handle those situations. The best blessing your sunny disposition brings you is a happy home life, an excellent marriage, and loving children. No matter what setbacks come your way from time to time, as long as your family remains a contented oasis of mutual affection, you can conquer all adversity.

I don't mean to predict that much adversity will come your way. Far from it! Like the Apostle Bartholomew, you are a neat, smooth, unhurried operator; and so you work well with people from all stations in life. But the people at the top, the movers and shakers, so to speak, will especially recognize and appreciate your abilities and the way you deal with them. Polite but not stuffy, efficient but not brusque, direct but not rude, you are going to be a sought-after associate of the high and the mighty, and will make personal friends of people in positions of command, especially in religion and government.

The personality characteristics of Libra Three housewives are by no means diminished by their careers as homemakers. Active as they are in local politics and charities, leaders in church affairs, their outstanding ability to deal with authority makes them the natural spokeswomen for groups petitioning or protesting to public officials. And their buoyant spirit keeps their homes filled with harmony and compassion, despite the inevitable little disagreements of life. During their middle years, Libra Three housewives are likely to be offered a good job in some kind of philanthropic organization. You must consider carefully at that point your home situation and decide whether you are free to accept the offer.

Young Libras of the Third Division should be encouraged to

carry out their ambitions, no matter how farfetched they seem or how remote from the family's everyday life. Those born under their potent star combination often achieve a great deal of good for the world. And so when they are still young, they should be given every opportunity for study and travel to equip them for their later mission in life. This does not mean that a family of small means must send their Libra Three daughter to Paris. It means that she should be given the parental help, through appreciation of her talents, to do all she can with whatever is available to her. As I have said repeatedly, each of us has a special role to play on earth, and Libra Threes are numbered among the positive powers for good in the Zodiac. Remember and act on it.

COLORS: Your magnetic aura is subdued but nonetheless effective in impressing others with your good qualities. It can be emphasized with shades of mauve and purple, deep and rich or pale and delicate. Those hues will express compassion and sympathy for those who need your aid. Strange as it may sound, you don't need brilliant colors to express your good humor, for your sparkling disposition speaks for itself. In addition, you will find that as you move up the ladder of success with the aid of your prominent friends, your attire and your home furnishings will become less gaudy and more restrained. Ample use of lavender and lilac can combine both dignity and your lighthearted idealism.

MONEY: In the initial stages of your career, you will make only slow economic progress. Later, you will receive grants or an endowment which will enable you to continue your work in some special way. Needless to say, you will also benefit from investment tips from your influential friends, although even their best intentions can sometimes steer you wrong.

HEALTH: Your excellent constitution will improve steadily as you mature. In your early years, there is a potential for a lingering ailment, perhaps with your heart or bloodstream. However, it should exert no ill effects upon your later life. Do be careful in traveling, for I sense indications of an accident, caused by lack of attention. Like all astrological possibilities, it can be avoided through forewarning and care.

RELATIONSHIPS: Because you have the gift of making your own dreams come true through your steady progress toward success, you also have the power to assist others in going along with you. This means you will reap a tremendous harvest of gratitude. What is more important, you are so likable and comfortable in dealing with even total strangers that your friendships will be many and lasting. Of course, there are bound to be a few individuals whose affection will be feigned in order to take advantage of your talents. That is one small price for your terrific gifts.

Your marriage is apt to be a good one, weakened only by your occasional temptation to become involved in romantic affairs. There is no need for me to warn you against that folly. You know that those irresponsible dalliances are only for diversion, but they will grievously hurt your partner when they inevitably come to light. Your dreams of enduring bliss in love will come true through your concentration on your marriage as the sustaining center of your life. Use the asset of your radiant disposition to make your home a haven from the world's adversity and a delightful reflection of your own spirit.

LIBRA—FOURTH DIVISION *(October 4, 13, 22)*

The life of a Libra Four is a combination of travel and charm. You of the Fourth Division have a restless spirit of ambition, and it sets you apart from other Libras. You love to travel, and your flexible personality allows you to radically change your locale, habits, friends, career—all this without offending others or disparaging their lifestyles.

Your physical mobility is a sign of an internal quest. Like the legendary knights of antiquity who journeyed afar in search of the Holy Grail, you are seeking an unchanging ideal, an eternal set of values. In plain fact, you are looking for God.

Your spiritual search makes you one of Nature's discoverers. Constantly venturing into new places, exploring new philosophies and theories, ever in pursuit of things you do not know, you are a perfectionist and will not settle for second-rate principles or unworthy beliefs. Everything you see, hear, and experience you analyze and weigh on those scales which are the sign of Libra. And most of the time you decide that the world's easy answers don't balance with your exalted concept of the truth. Don't be disheartened. Your apparent rootlessness is not a sign of any inferiority on your part. You are restive because, whether consciously or not, you know there is something better for you. It is a noble idealism which leads you to give up a perfectly good life to hunt for an uncertain quarry, led only by the hint that what you seek will be better than what you leave behind.

Charming Libra that you are, you make friends easily; and no one would ever suspect that even in their midst, you are often lonely. Enjoying their camaraderie, you sense an emotional need which no number of friends can fulfill. That is why, within a year or so of making your latest set of acquaintances, you hurry off again to break new ground and meet new people. No wonder some folks will consider you a social butterfly, frivolous and changeable, even though that is not at all the case. It is not fickleness but idealism which impels you onward. Sometime in middle age, when you find the goals for which you have been searching, you will dramatically change. Suddenly, your roots will pierce deeply and permanently. Settling down like a block of granite, you will not even want to spend a brief vacation away from your newfound home. Your old friends will be astonished at your abrupt stability, and you will know you have arrived home at last.

Through all your journeying, both geographical and spiritual, you will carry with you a Libran delight in information and facts. That is why, if your finances do not allow you to travel, you relish travel brochures and magazines about exotic places. It is not enough for you to visit a city, stay in one of its look-alike motels, and make the quick tour of its famous places. No, you read about its history, learn its patterns of growth and development, and tour its neighborhoods and cozy gathering places. Needless to say, when you do settle down, you become an expert on your community's past and an informed observer of its present circumstances. Your knowledge in this regard, combined with your typically Libran reputation for fairness, will make you a valued civic activist and respected local spokesman.

As you can see, your life pattern is a rather good one, and you can rest easy in knowing that eventually your intellectual discontent will be cured. It might be advisable to seek a job in which you would be free to travel extensively. Sales or promotional work might suit you, especially because your wanderlust is equaled by your amiable disposition.

COLORS: The unfettered use of color can help to satisfy your desire for change. Use color combinations in gay contrast: bright red and yellow one day, a range of blues the next. Mix and match the shades of your apparel and your home furnishings so that each day you can feel a little different, a little unorthodox. For special occasions, when you want your magnetism at its strongest, try blushing pinks, as innocently pure as the reputation of Sir Galahad, your fellow seeker after the ideal. Accent those tender shades with a bold and vivid green, which represents in you, as it does in nature, the cycle of change, rebirth, and renewal.

MONEY: A financial high point will come in your early years, and money matters will thereafter decline until your early thirties. Then the trend will reverse, bringing you to greater prosperity. There you will rest comfortably for a decade or two until, late in your career, close to your retirement, you will again reach an economic acme. For your astrological makeup, sound investments will concern commodities, precious metals, and land.

HEALTH: You have a tendency to make yourself ill by suggestion. Especially during your travels, the expectation of sickness can actually hasten its onset by putting you in a moody frame of mind and eroding your spirits. Counter that tendency by remembering the exciting things you have to do and discover. Your natural energy and desire for activity will then keep you in good cheer and better health. Guard your throat and lungs, for those are the parts of your body which may be chronically weak.

RELATIONSHIPS: Because you appear flighty and changeable in the way you deal with people, you could experience misunderstandings from your colleagues at work. With a little attention, you can make your social relationships more durable, without necessarily being overly intimate. The benefits in harmony and goodwill, especially in your job, will be worth the effort on your part.

It would be wise for you to postpone marriage until later in life, for then you will have lost much of your restlessness. Your chances of a sound and enriching home life will be much greater once you have settled down intellectually as well as physically.

You may have already discovered that the charm of a Libra Four can win hearts without effort. Good for you; but remember that this gift, like every other talent we possess, has been given us for our benefit and the good of others. Use it wisely to seek out someone who is kindred to your questing soul, so that together you can enjoy to the fullest the journey of life.

LIBRA—FIFTH DIVISION *(September 23, October 5, 14)*

Lofty principles, devotion to duty, and strong convictions characterize Libras of the Fifth Division. Your planetary combination endows you with both strength of character and the ability to sacrifice your own desires to the mandates of your responsibilities and obligations. In a phrase, you live beyond yourself.

You are apt to be the member of the family to whom others turn when a relative needs aid or personal attention. You give care and support during emotional crises and lingering illnesses. And you do not feel rancor or resentment for the sacrifices you make. You do not pose as a martyr but, rather, take for granted that it is only right for you to give up your dreams for the good of others. Your beneficence also extends to persons outside your family, for you are:

- mindful of others
- interested in life
- adaptable
- peaceable

Those who know you may pity you because you seem to have so little freedom of action to explore the world and experience its delights. They think you sacrifice too much of yourself for the welfare of others. You may be stunned to read these words, for their attitude is totally alien to your spirit. Like the little Dutch boy who, in the old nursery story, held his finger in the leaking dike to save his village, you see your duty and you do it—no questions asked. That is a rare virtue in today's world, and so a Libra Five is a rare blessing in the lives of those you care for.

You regard all aspects of life in the same light. Intensely loyal to your friends, faithful to your relatives even when they are unworthy of your fidelity, you are above all devoted to your principles. You will never be a pragmatist, and I suspect that your favorite political candidates are those who refuse all compromises and prefer defeat to deception.

There is an important aspect to your personality which less sacrificing persons do not understand. Despite the curtailment of your freedom of action, despite the good times you give up to serve others, you retain a wide range of interests and activities, pursuing them in a quiet but intense way. Although you keep a low profile and don't aspire to leadership in your clubs, your athletic team, or your civic association, you are the proverbial willing worker, gaining the full flavor of life by enjoying its everyday activities.

Cultural affairs mean much to you. The theater, music, books, and art galleries are your treasures on earth, and much of your social life revolves around them. Needless to say, people who know nothing of those activities will consider you a homebound wallflower. Little do they realize that your world's riches make them seem paupers by comparison. Like Christ's devoted friend Mary, the sister of busy Martha, you have chosen the better part.

Both in your personal affairs and in your professional life, you Libra Fives are versatile and adaptable. You communicate well with all kinds of people except the coarse or vulgar. As a refined individual, you instinctively avoid any situation or person who might impinge upon your own sensibilities. All of this means that your abilities are wide-ranging, and you would make as good a cook as you would a carpenter, whether you are male or female. Because of your talent in getting along with the public, especially with those who share your artistic tastes, you would be more than happy teaching creative children, helping adults explore the world's storehouse of learning in a library, or acting as a salesperson in a music store or gallery.

Harmony and peace, at home and at work and in society, are most precious to Libra Fives. You cannot tolerate discord, and are able to work with even difficult or waspish people without conflict. You are skilled at giving orders because you know how to obey them, and women Libras of the Fifth Division are often gifted with an exceptional executive quality which prepares them for administrative positions in business. In both her career and her home, a female Libra brings a reassuring balance to her work.

Occasionally, your search for harmony will cause you to retreat from a position which you know is correct. You may find yourself sacrificing a principle to preserve peace, simply because you hate to be party to a nasty dispute. That same characteristic makes you a prized friend and counselor, for you bring a sense of healing to all your relationships.

COLORS: Light colors are best for Libras of the Fifth Division, and pastel shades are excellent in conveying the subtle force of your magnetic aura. Because almost any color complements your skills and gifts, you can decorate and dress with abandon, as long as you emphasize delicate tints more than somber hues. With your peaceable spirit, a roomful of reds seems pleasant. With your zest for art and knowledge, a gray office becomes a lively place. Treat yourself as well as you treat others. Wear those pastels which proclaim your kinship to all that is blithe and delicate in this world.

MONEY: Chances are that you will be a better financial adviser to others than to yourself. Your investment ideas are usually sound, but you seldom have sufficient cash in hand to apply them for your own benefit. I suggest you plan your economic future early in life, to avoid possible pitfalls as you grow older. This is especially important inasmuch as you tend to sacrifice so much for those you love.

HEALTH: For most of your life, you will enjoy good health. Your resistance to communicable diseases is excellent, and I suspect it has something to do with the indomitably positive attitude with which you approach life. Only a few digestive problems and a chest complaint are indicated as possibilities in your astrological pattern.

RELATIONSHIPS: I have already mentioned your prospects for strong and loyal friendships, especially among others who share your artistic interests. You owe it to your acquaintances to let more of them get to know you better. Their lives would be enriched by exposure to your lofty world of principle and ideals.

If you do marry, your partnership will be enduring and mutually rewarding. Whether you marry, however, will likely be determined by the responsibilities you take on. For example, if you assume the care and supervision of an infirm parent early in your life, your marital chances will greatly diminish; for you will be single-mindedly devoted to your loved one. On the other hand, if that special responsibility comes later in life, it is likely to involve one of your own children or a parent whom your spouse will welcome into your home. In either case, married or not, your personal relationships will reinforce your essentially spiritual attitude toward life and will assist you in your efforts to care for those dear to you.

LIBRA—SIXTH DIVISION *(September 24, October 6, 15)*

A Libra Six can be described as "personality plus." Your planetary combination has endowed you with remarkable gifts, making you one of life's most fascinating individuals. You command admiration and provoke envy in those less fortunate, for you are:

- personally magnetic
- sexually attractive
- entertaining
- affluent

Who could resist that package of charm? But because you have been so spectacularly blessed, you must be especially careful that your mighty assets do not turn into mightier liabilities. As I have said before, each virtue casts a shadow of a corresponding vice; each positive trait has its negative counterpart. Yes, you have wonderful powers, but that means you could wreak terrible harm if you should ever decide to wear the Devil's red boots. You must sit down and consider what you will do with your abilities. Will they be turned to the benefit of those with whom you deal, or will they master your aspirations and turn you away from your appointed goals? It is up to you, as it is, indeed, to each of us.

With regard to your career, however, you will have no difficulty in finding your way. Early in life, you will discover what you want to do for a living and, charmer that you are, promptly set about working for that end. Progressing rapidly through the necessary training, you are likely to do well from the start and become affluent at a relatively early age.

Loving to entertain, you are willing to spend considerable sums to do so properly. Libra Sixes have good taste, and so your social events are neither gaudy nor pretentious. You know that the secret of a gracious host is not excessive cost but personal attention, and your hospitable manners and good conversation make guests reluctant to leave your home.

In addition to party-giving, the field of entertainment has another meaning in your life, for show business would be a particularly apt area for your splendid personality. You could be successful as a producer, performer, perhaps even a writer. With your prospects for affluence, you might become a benefactor to actors and other gifted individuals. On Broadway, those generous sponsors are called "angels," and for good reason. Many a star's career is due to the interest and support of a particular "angel."

All these are fine and admirable qualities. Perhaps you are pondering how they could possibly go astray. Think for a moment. If everything in life comes to you easily, if you take for granted the blessings for which others strive and sweat, you may become blasé about your assets. You could look down on your fellows who populate the workaday world and who never reach your heights of popularity and wealth. In fact, from sheer boredom you could turn your charm and dynamism to the acquisition of power and the misuse of people.

That is why I earnestly advise you to consider planning your life; for despite our astrological influences, it is we as individuals who are ultimately responsible for our conduct and values. It is so easy to diverge from the path of principle, especially when those about us flatter our decisions and compliment even our errors. I urge you to stick by your better judgment and reinforce your ethical perspective by using your gifts to help others develop their own talents. This is a worthy way to express your gratitude for all the wonders with which your Creator has filled your life. A word of encouragement from someone as successful as you could transform the lives of those struggling to achieve and aspiring to great things.

COLORS: Amber and topaz suit your magnetism. If you own jewelry made of those stones, they are apt to be your favorite pieces, even though other gems might be more expensive. There is something in their rich brown tones, sparkling with gold and orange and the luster of antiquity, that sums up the richness of your life and the warmth of your personality. The same colors can be equally effective in your wardrobe and your home if you don't care to wear jewelry. Your flair for dramatic décor and emphatic expression of your emotions through your attire will guide you in the effective use of color.

MONEY: Your intuition in money matters is formidable, and you will usually invest wisely. Your personality will be your greatest asset in dealing with business partners and the public, but you must pay the price which comes with success. That is, you must be wary of those opportunists who would seek your backing for their projects with false claims and exaggerated promises. Learn to evaluate people, especially if you become involved in show business, with a calm and reflective judgment.

HEALTH: Apart from occasional infections, your health will be glowing. You possess great powers of recuperation and a high resistance to most contagious diseases. Exercise is vital for you, not so much for your physical fitness as for your mental relaxation. Your busy life demands that you take time to unleash your energies in strenuous action, so that your tension does not build up and unsettle your professional work.

RELATIONSHIPS: Your ability to inspire others and draw out the best in them socially and professionally will win you loyal friends. Your reputation for gracious entertaining will keep you surrounded by a large social circle. Your only problem will be to separate the wheat from the chaff, to remain on good terms with exploitative acquaintances without yielding to their pressures for your favors.

There are some danger signals for your romantic life. Because of your personal magnetism, many people, especially young people, will assume that your interest in them is more than platonic. This can lead to a number of destructive love affairs and more than one unhappy marriage.

Your marriage will need to be worked at as hard as you would work on a business project of the first magnitude. Your dynamic nature can be trained to strengthen and enliven your home life instead of threatening its stability. If rifts should develop within your family, you can in fact heal the wounds by applying the same natural graciousness you use in your social life. Patience and understanding can make your marriage as rich as your bank account.

LIBRA—SEVENTH DIVISION *(September 25, October 7, 16)*

A Libra Seven is best described as unconventional. You fit no pattern, adapt to no specific mold, and so your life is hard to describe with any great precision. Your combined planetary influences make you strong-willed and consequently able to steer in any of several directions. At the same time, you are willing to make sacrifices for others. All combined, that leaves you considerable leeway in being whatever you want to be. You are:

- reserved
- a loner
- impulsive
- intellectual

Your introspection makes you appear shy, even timid, with casual acquaintances. In fact, you are only reserved, sensing a certain propriety in not exposing your feelings and emotions. Perhaps our society has become accustomed to the great and the lowly baring their souls and discussing their private lives and deepest values, but it was not always so. And you are one of those individuals who would rather return to more formal days, when a person of breeding and character maintained a certain closed realm of mind and spirit which was shared only with a few intimates.

You are a deep thinker, and casual theories and fancies mean nothing to you. Perhaps because of the critical reaction you may receive for your apparent aloofness, you have some feelings of inferiority which are really unjustified. The fact is that you have different values from your fellows and march to a different drummer. You are instinctively a loner who wishes a certain seclusion to pursue your own goals and make your own decisions—in short, to do your own thing.

This can create a problem with those close to you, who can be hurt unintentionally by your desire to get away from people. The difficulty is caused by lack of understanding on both sides. You are apt to go off with a book during a family party and think nothing of your departure from the group. Your relatives will naturally be upset, as if you were deliberately insulting them. Perhaps you could try to explain your need for a brief period of meditation. Once you understand that your seemingly odd behavior offends people, you will surely correct it, for you are by no means rude or thoughtless. This is just one of those cases in which a little more communication can avoid ill feelings.

In finding a career, take time to explore and to plan. You are inclined to be impulsive and liable to make several false starts. You desire, and perhaps should find, a career that is offbeat, one that allows full use of your abilities without requiring too close an association with colleagues. Before you commit years and great expense to one profession, consider possible alternatives carefully.

These same precepts apply to marriage as well, especially for those occasional Libra Seven women who marry only to escape an unpleasant situation at home. An extended courtship can give your beloved ample time to get used to your characteristics, both pleasant and unusual, and together you can make realistic decisions for your future. If your partner shares your desire for a certain personal privacy and is equally reserved, then you may be perfect soul mates, creating a universe full of wonders within the narrow limits of your mutual affection.

Like the Apostle Bartholomew, Libra Sevens operate best alone. Like him, you prefer to sit and study under your own fig tree, so to speak; for he was doing just that when Philip came to him with the news about Christ. Imitate his example. Use your quiet times alone for good purposes, restoring your spirits and fortifying your mind to face the world's demands upon you. When you return to the public world of interaction and responsibility, you will speak more wisely and act more effectively. You will be able to communicate with others gently and with humor. In this way, your moments of reserve can liberate you for moments of dynamic intellectual leadership.

You are profoundly intellectual in ways you may not even realize. Remember that the life of the mind does not necessarily involve extensive formal education. Rather, it involves a respect for learning, an appreciation of people who seek wisdom, whether from philosophy books or street-corner conversations. Many humble people of little repute are much more intellectual in this regard than famous professors. Through your interest in all kinds of knowledge, you can expand not only your own horizons but also those of your friends and family.

COLORS: Your best colors are those we usually associate with isolation or remoteness: the whole range of grays, from a dove's gently shadowed white to the somber emphasis of charcoal. But they don't have to be moody, especially if you set them off with accent colors, like the deep cream shade of buttermilk. Use this and touches of electric white to state clearly your streak of idealism, for it cuts through your intellectual pursuits like lightning knifing through a dark forest.

MONEY: This straitlaced advice will seem old-fashioned to you; nonetheless, I suggest you avoid financial speculation. Libra Sevens are too impulsive to take economic chances, especially those involving large sums. Your level of prosperity is apt to fluctuate wildly because of your changeability. I suggest you buy government bonds in good times as a safeguard for later rainy days and your retirement years.

HEALTH: Your astral pattern indicates that you may experience ill health in your middle years because of a mistake in medication. This possibly dire occurrence can be avoided through commonsense measures. When you feel ill, see a doctor. Do not rummage through your medicine chest, trying some of this and a little of that. More important, restrain your impulsiveness around machinery and, above all, on the highway.

RELATIONSHIPS: Although your reserve makes it difficult for you to strike up casual friendships, your intellectual interests can be focal points for positive social interaction. Book clubs, museum groups, discussion forums, and similar gatherings in a hundred different fields all offer opportunities for you to meet people who share your interests and appreciate your virtues.

Take your time before you commit yourself to someone romantically. You may be enchanted with the idea of falling, as they say, head over heels in love, but you are so impulsive that the experience could leave you with emotional bumps and bruises.

It is probable that you will marry well when you are in your late twenties; and although your partnership will not always be smooth, it will, strangely enough, be a long and happy one.

LIBRA—EIGHTH DIVISION *(September 26, October 8, 17)*

Libra Eights are among the world's doers and achievers. Knowing almost instinctively how to get things accomplished, even how to change what seems inevitable, you proceed to do so while others stand around, wringing their hands in despair. You expect turmoil in life and have learned to shrug it aside. A quiet, complacent existence is insufferable to you. As long as there is a challenge to meet, you are eager to test your strength and dare the impossible.

Whatever does become the main interest in your life, it will be all-absorbing, so much so that you become one of those hardy individuals who works around the clock. You are:

- active in reform
- indomitable

- concerned for others
- fair-minded

You see no logic in letting things remain as they are because they have always been so. When there is cause, you figuratively pull out your trusty soapbox and shout your protests to the world. Especially with regard to social issues, you are a persistent reformer, going from one campaign to the next. With that attitude, you are used to running into opposition, but you are seldom daunted by it. It usually only adds another layer to your emotional armor, so that subsequent criticism, even insults, are deflected by your indomitable sense of purpose. This does not indicate that you have become unfeeling, only that you value your ideals more than the casual opinions of uninformed critics.

Your activities to correct wrongs and improve life for others are not sparked by selfish motives; you realize your own limitations and don't pretend to have all the answers. You are, on the contrary, a crusader in the best sense of the word. I realize many of you Libra Eights may be shaking your heads as you read this, sure that it does not apply to you. Perhaps you have never given a speech, never walked a picket line or signed a protest petition. Perhaps your reformist efforts will never make the evening news broadcast on television.

There are subtler, and frequently more effective, ways to fight for justice. It may be your work as a dogged foot soldier in local civic improvement efforts; it may be your campaign to improve conditions in your child's school; it may be your privately given aid and advice to a friend or relative with self-destructive habits. Whatever your current cause, you commit yourself to it without even realizing the sacrifices you make to further it. And sacrifices there will always be. Like the Apostle Bartholomew, you will have to pay the price demanded from all idealists. Just as he met the most severe tribulations with coolness and dignity, so you can cope with lesser troubles in patience and fortitude.

You may have reason to wonder from time to time what you have done to deserve the hostility of occasional opponents. Take heart. The only reason you become the target of their ire is that you disturb their consciences and expose their misdeeds. Some people who rest easy in their complacent toleration of evil resent your reminding them of their obligations to fight it. Naturally, they will disparage your motives and distort your true principles.

None of that will stop your progress, both in your social concern and in your own career. I sense that you are headed for the top like an express elevator. This professional success will cause you to change your residence at least once, whether to pursue a better position or because you can afford a grander home. For many Libra Eight women there are indications of a change in life-style in their middle years. This could be caused by a return to their premarital career or by the development of an entirely new one through their social concern and community action.

Whatever your work, even if it does not deal directly with people but involves machinery and ideas, you will always be more gratified by what it does for others than by what you gain from it. For example, you can observe a mass-production assembly line and think of the millions of families who will be able to purchase the inexpensive goods it produces. Less insightful persons see only a factory and hurried workers, for they overlook the human application of all labor. So it is that you can be happy in almost any position, for you know it in some way contributes to the common good.

COLORS: Your most effective presence is gained by using a combination of white with dark, heavy colors. It is as if the contrast expressed your own balance, so typical of Libras. You see the evil in the world, and yet you use your talents to make things better, in much the same way that a dazzling white scarf changes the whole meaning of a black dress. Or a dark blue business suit can be changed from an expression of conformity to one of determined exuberance by a plain white handkerchief tucked jauntily in its breast pocket.

MONEY: Because of your rapid ascent up the ladder of success, you may experience periods in your middle years during which you will be short of funds. Sound paradoxical? Not at all, for your increasingly affluent life-style may outpace your rising income. So take it easy with lavish purchases. Because many of your best efforts will involve charitable endeavors, you may not be sufficiently reimbursed for your work. But money from an unexpected source should provide you later in life with a level of comfort previously unknown to you.

HEALTH: Because you will be under considerable pressure from your reform activities, be sure to guard those moments of rest and relaxation you know you need. Without those breathing spaces to recharge your physical and emotional batteries, you will be courting ailments. No matter how pressing a crisis may be, you need occasional leisure to keep your morale high and your stamina strong.

RELATIONSHIPS: Relatives will prove the best anchors for your friendships because many so-called friends will attach themselves to you only to exploit your rise to prominence. Sexual relationships will naturally result from your magnetic personality and driving enthusiasm, and you must beware of allowing your romances to become casual affairs that will later cause you regret and depression.

Marriage at an early age is not recommended for Libras of the Eighth Division. Although you do need the aid and encouragement of a partner, you will be so concerned with your life's work, especially while you are young, that you will not find time to sustain a satisfactory home life. A later marriage, especially if your spouse shares your fervor for reform, will have brighter prospects.

LIBRA–NINTH DIVISION *(September 27, October 9, 18)*

The Ninth Division of Libra is governed by a combination of planets which can influence those born under it in either of two opposite directions. So it is that worlds of difference seem to separate Libra Nines from one another. They may find it impossible to believe they are astrological kin to such contrasting individuals. Perhaps you have already experienced this ambivalence, this tendency to go off in two directions at the same time. You can be either:

• ebullient		• meek
• tactless	or just the opposite:	• diplomatic
• overpowering		• subdued

You tend to be in the first category; and so, despite your good intentions, you frequently irritate the very people you wish to help. Your task is to harness your natural enthusiasm. There is no denying that you are fun to have around, both at social affairs and on the job, but you would be even more of an asset if you would occasionally relinquish center stage to someone else.

You are inclined to be too blunt in stating your views. I don't mean that you are arrogant or domineering, for those faults are absent from your character. You simply fail to understand that many people cannot take criticism, though they love to give it.

With the best of intentions, you can sorely offend those persons who need compliments and agreement to make it through each day. If you stop and consider how many people fit that description, you will admit I do not exaggerate.

Without malice on your part, you often find yourself in some bewilderment when your casual remarks have sparked an argument. You are always ready to apologize even though you may not sense just why you should be sorry. Frequently, it is not you who should express regrets but your offended opponents, who mistake your forthrightness for rudeness. Even so, it does no good to realize that you are only partially to blame for occasional disputes. Look at it this way: what difference does it make if you are blameless when your overpowering approach to problems prevents you from solving them? To achieve your goals in life—and you certainly have the ability to do so—learn to tone down your personality. Practice listening, just as you would practice your golf swing or your needlepoint. Learn to pay compliments without overdoing them. Learn to bite your tongue, either literally or figuratively, when you feel the urge to put an uninformed "expert" in his place.

Think of yourself as the spice of life, for indeed you are just that to a great many appreciative people. But your gifts, like all spices and herbs, are best used in small measures. Otherwise, they overpower all other ingredients. So don't add too much pepper to an argument or too much cinnamon to a romance. Think about this and you will understand what I mean.

At the other extreme, some Libra Nines are altogether too meek and diplomatic for their own good. If this applies to you, you might consider yourself a pallid opposite to your ebullient cousins in the Ninth Division. Intelligent, affectionate, outgoing, all of you have great assets. But one group of you lacks the diplomacy to be an effective ambassador for your own ideas, and the other group has ample tact but insufficient forcefulness to put a point across.

At each extreme, the remedy should be obvious. Retreat to a middle ground. Just as an intense and demonstrative Libra Nine must learn restraint, so, too, a diffident and humble Nine must learn self-confidence and directness. If you feel too subdued, learn to push yourself—your ideas and your projects—as you would any good product. Charming and refined, idealistic and organized, you can relate well to most people once they get to know you. It is up to you to give them that chance.

COLORS: For you ebullient Libra Nines, I recommend pastel shades to mute your showmanship and calm your emotions. To be specific, when you know you are going to have to deal with some rather unpleasant people at a conference or a party, a pink tie is preferable to a red one, and a light blue suit is less harsh than a navy pinstripe.

For you who are at the opposite extreme and want to become a little more emphatic in your relationships, I suggest the liberal use of poster colors, bold, even gaudy, especially in the room you use most for entertaining. Perhaps a few massive pieces of modern painting, exclaiming in tones of orange and magenta, will set the stage for a more dynamic you.

MONEY: Your intelligence and talent indicate that you will hold several positions of authority and responsibility. The key to the spectacular success that could be yours is to develop, simultaneously, your tact and your showmanship. If you can make the two forces run in tandem, then you can set the world on its heels.

HEALTH: In your youth, you are apt to be delicate and to experience trouble with your teeth, your skin, and your chest and lungs. However, a new cycle of good health will begin in your twenties, and I see no further prospects of serious illness for you. There is the possibility of danger from fire or firearms, so it behooves you to exercise great care around both.

RELATIONSHIPS: No matter which extreme of the Ninth Division you identify with, you are a warm and appealing person underneath your exterior appearances, and among your friends you are known as a thoughtful and gracious host. The same characteristics keep your family loyal to you and protective of your feelings. That blessing alone is enough to guarantee a happy life.

But it is not your only blessing. Your marriage, probably in your early twenties, will be a great success. Your only handicap in marital adjustment will be your initial inability to demonstrate your affection openly. An understanding partner will make light of that; and as time goes by, you will discover the innumerable little ways to express your feelings, with or without words.

Your astral chart indicates the possibility of a second marriage for you very late in life. Of course, whether or not that comes to pass, now is the time to think of the immediate future only and to search for someone who will appreciate your Libran virtues.

SCORPIO—THOMAS

(October 23–November 21)

There is quite a contrast between the characteristics of the sign of Libra, which is inclined toward gentleness and abstraction, and those of the next sign, which tends toward intensity, determination, and passionate command of concrete situations. Indeed, no other segment of the Zodiac endows its children with as much wit and cunning, as much feeling and ardor, as Scorpio. Those born under it are psychologically akin to their symbol, the scorpion. Like that hardy, adaptable creature, they are alert and quick, sometimes stinging, and always on their guard.

Because of their endowments, Scorpios are like the Apostle who, in my vision, is associated with their sign. Dynamic, decisive individuals, they play a pivotal role in the lives of many other people. Capable of great achievements, only they can determine whether their work will be for good or ill. When they have faith, they can lead legions under their banner. When they deny, they can impose doubt on others by their power of suggestion. Scorpios are true replicas of the Apostle Thomas.

Before we see how closely Scorpios of today resemble that headstrong, sharp-tongued follower of Christ, it is important to understand, no matter what our astrological sign may be, that the lessons of Scorpio apply to us all. Just as the experience of Thomas was the cumulative wisdom of his fellow Apostles, so, too, are the characteristics of Scorpio, in a way, the cumulative potential, both positive and negative, of all of us. Scorpios are also pivotal characters, capable of turning abruptly from one direction to another. To some extent, that is true of every human, for each of us ultimately faces the choice which Thomas faced. Sooner or later, we must turn decisively to follow the best ideals of our better nature or to tramp along the paths of misery in alluring, but entrapping, red boots. That choice is especially emphatic for Scorpios because their gifts are especially great. So it is that whenever Scorpian talent serves noble ends, it can win the world to its banner. When it turns to unworthy goals, it can destroy the dreams of mankind.

Perhaps you are wondering how this applied to Thomas. After all, most people know nothing about him other than his initial refusal to believe that Christ had risen from the dead and returned in reality to His followers. We recall the phrase, "doubting Thomas," which has entered our language as a cliché for a habitual skeptic. Of course, the tendency to doubt demonstrates an important aspect of Scorpian personality that resists domination by the opinions of others while asserting its own authority as final judge of disputed matters.

There was more to Thomas than his disbelief in Christ's rising from the dead. If you check through the Gospels, you discover him a man who always knew his own mind, who was utterly loyal to his Master and never averse to saying so in the bluntest language. He seems the kind of person who wins your heart by his unrehearsed enthusiasm and straight-from-the-shoulder frankness. All this, too, is Scorpio at its best.

Even in his doubt, Scorpian Thomas was fulfilling his intended purpose, unconsciously using his inborn skepticism as part of the Creator's plan for him. By refusing to believe in the Resurrection until he could touch the risen Christ, he was expressing the doubts which millions of Christians would later experience; and because Thomas spoke as he did, and later was so visibly convinced, all later generations of believers are indebted to him for setting the record straight, once and for all. This may be a blunt way to express what he did; but after all, in discussing Scorpio, bluntness may be appropriate.

Thomas offered us a perfect example of the interaction between good and evil. It was not especially laudable for him to declare that he would never believe Christ had returned until he could feel for himself the wounds He had suffered. But out of Thomas's adamancy came powerful reassurance of the faith of the early Church. Of course, if Thomas had continued in his disbelief, if he had invented reasons to disregard the evidence he saw, then his Scorpian character would have gone to its negative extreme. Then he would have shown the world how powerful those red boots could be when a Scorpio wears them. In fact, he did just the opposite. What is a valuable lesson for Scorpios is also an essential truth for us all. Without temptation, there is no virtue. Without the risk of failure, there is no glory in success. Without the power to choose evil, we would not have free will to choose good. At some time in life, every reader of this book must share Thomas's dilemma. Let us hope we all decide as happily as he did.

By knowing your astrological traits, you Scorpios can maximize your positive impact and minimize your negative potential. And you do indeed have negative traits, as we all do. Your astuteness and canny sense of judgment can render you too suspicious, and thus alienate you from friends and disrupt your family life. Your determination to accomplish your goals can turn into obstinacy and can tie you to erroneous opinions and lost causes out of sheer pride. Your delight in maintaining a certain independence and privacy can change into an obsession with secrecy and furtiveness. So much good can be twisted to its opposite.

No wonder Thomas is an appropriate representative of your sign! In Scripture, he is on occasion referred to as Didymus, which is a Greek word meaning the same as his Hebrew name: the twin. Indeed, Scorpios are often twin personalities, having two sides to their natures. One is practical, given to action, brash and even domineering. The other is spiritual, concerned with ideas, devoted to the truth, compassionate and introspective. When made to work together, like two powerful steeds running in joint harness, they are an irresistible combination.

Thomas was both a practical man, earning his living from his craft, and a seeker after truth. Consequently, he was not only susceptible to being influenced by others but also able to impress his views upon them. You Scorpios may find it easy to express yourself in speech and writing, although your ideas are frequently not your own. You are intellectually discriminating, and can recognize good arguments when you hear them. So often your role will be to explain eloquently the ideas which more original thinkers cannot get across to the public.

This ability to interpret and express others' ideas as well as your own will be a major factor in your life. You could be a writer by profession, and most likely in the field of history. Another obvious choice for you is the religious ministry, explaining complicated theological truths in everyday terms for average folk. You could be a wonderfully sensitive teacher, bringing the greatest thoughts of mankind to your pupils in vivid and fascinating ways. Needless to say, you will have to be careful of your personal and professional associations; for the very fact that you are quick to respond to others presents the risk of aligning your talents with someone less honorable than you, whose true purposes may be hidden from you.

Younger Scorpios are drawn to political and social causes which they think will benefit their communities. Underestimating the complexity of contemporary life, you may devote your gifts to groups whose simplistic solutions will only worsen problems. Keep your true goals clearly in mind, and if your associates appear to be deviating from them, be prepared to leave them abruptly. This could save you from a rude awakening later on.

Because you are idealistic and want to be useful, you can be duped by anyone unscrupulous enough to exploit your single-minded enthusiasm. That is why many idealists become bitter skeptics; they have seen their dream betrayed by its chief advocates. Don't let that happen to you. Your twin nature does give you the capacity to see both sides of a question, if only you will look for them. You could be qualified as a negotiator, a compromiser, or a mediator, in both your professional and private relationships. Instead of totally committing yourself to one political faction, you can be the instrument for bringing enemies to a common ground of agreement. You will never know until you try.

Always remember that your Zodiac symbol is a scorpion. That means that your ready facility for self-expression can be manifested by stinging wit. So if you are called upon to act as liaison between opposing parties, steer clear of personal comment. Although you mean no harm, an imp of mischief sometimes leads you to show people their errors in sarcastic language. Your sharp tongue can not only cause pain and hostility but also dilute your considerable abilities to calm troubled waters.

Thomas was like you in this regard. A person of conviction and courage, he could not tolerate timidity. When Christ heard of the death of His friend, Lazarus, in Bethany, He proposed to hasten there, despite the possibility of violence from His enemies. His followers were alarmed by the proposal and feared to face persecution.

Thomas, however, was confident that Christ knew what He was doing, and was annoyed with his fellows' reluctance. He forcefully told the other Apostles, "Let us also go, that we may die with Him." Their reaction to Thomas's unequivocal statement of loyalty is not recorded, but we can imagine that some of them were sheepishly embarrassed to compare their own fears with his bold faith. He hadn't meant to offend them, but they must have been stung by his rebuke.

Was this the same Thomas who later questioned the Resurrection of Christ and who ever after was called "doubting"? Yes, it was the same vehement Scorpio, as absolute in his moments of faith as he was in his times of disbelief. Notice how you Scorpios seem to live a double life in many respects. You are likely to have two careers at once, with two incomes. While you are single, you are apt to have two romances at the same time, although I will not predict how well you will be able to sustain that burden on your heart.

This duality makes you astrologically akin to Geminis. Many Scorpian housewives are working mothers from choice. They sense that their single role as homemaker is not sufficient to occupy their taste for diverse challenges. They frequently use their outside employment as an outlet for their aesthetic or spiritual energies, while their cooking and cleaning and washing satisfy their need for the practical. They may teach dance or a musical instrument, and some serve as substitute teachers and evening librarians.

Professional Scorpios of either gender could be mechanics or engineers who also have the ability to paint well enough to sell their artwork at a handsome profit. They could even be actors who, in their spare time, build custom-crafted furniture! While still students, they might earn their tuition by playing with a professional musical group. The possible combinations in Scorpios are endless.

As a Scorpio, your duality may cause you to postpone concentration on your major career; and by thus spreading your interests, you could court financial hardship early in life. After you launch your second, supplementary career, your finances will probably improve. But you must keep a close watch on your pocketbook because your enthusiastic nature makes you too eager to invest in people and projects before they are thoroughly investigated. You may already have learned the folly of relying on the word of others in money ventures. Remember that warning whenever you are approached for loans or speculations.

As you mature intellectually and spiritually, you may well discover an interest in the occult. If so, in your middle years, you will quite abruptly find that your powers of intuition, which you had noticed only vaguely before, have increased greatly. This realization will make your daily life go more smoothly. Commonplace experiences will take on a happier quality. Old friends will reveal new aspects of their personalities, and you will find new insights into your long-held views on religion and in politics. These discoveries will lead to more serious exploration of the occult, through which you will probe the psychic powers given you by the Creator for His work on earth. Once you learn to use them for His purposes, you will be on your way to greatness.

It is probably not accidental that Thomas has always been considered the Apostle of India. From the earliest times of the Church, it has been traditionally believed that he traveled through the Middle East and Persia to preach the Gospel in southwestern India, the area now known as Mysore, Travancore, and Goa. That land of mysticism and fascination with the occult would doubtless have been susceptible to his persuasion, especially if he had used the psychic powers so frequently found among Scorpios.

The terrific potential of Thomas's astrological cousins has enabled many of them to achieve success. President Theodore Roosevelt was born on October 27, Presidents James Polk and Warren Harding on November 2, and Robert F. Kennedy on November 20.

The intensity of Scorpio was apparent in the lifelong scientific passion of Madame Marie Curie (November 7), the Polish discoverer of radium and two-time winner of the Nobel Prize, and of Anton van Leeuwenhoek (October 24), the inventor of the microscope. In the arts, equally intense dedication to excellence was shown by the painters Pablo Picasso (October 25), Jan Vermeer (October 31), and Claude Monet (November 14), as well as by goldsmith and sculptor Benvenuto Cellini (November 1).

Scorpio's strong interest in the human mind has been demonstrated in the varied careers of the Russian novelist Feodor Dostoevski (October 30), who was a pioneer in the development of psychological fiction; Hermann Rorschach (November 8), whose name is still applied to the ink-blot tests he devised; the Reverend Billy Graham (November 7), whose work links the mind and the spirit; and Dr. F. Regis Riesenman (November 10), one of the foremost psychiatrists in the Washington metropolitan area.

Scorpian composers include Georges Bizet and Johann Strauss (both October 25), and John Philip Sousa (November 6). Their Zodiac sign is shared by such writers as James Boswell (October 29), John Keats (October 29), William Cullen Bryant (November 3), J. P. Marquand (November 10), and Robert Louis Stevenson (November 13).

Two of the world's favorite entertainers are Scorpios: Dale Evans (October 31) and her husband, Roy Rogers (November 5). The full variety of talents available to men and women of the Scorpion is evident in the diverse careers of explorer Richard Byrd (October 25), General George Patton (November 11), playwright Moss Hart (October 24), the philosopher Voltaire (November 21), actress Katharine Hepburn (November 9), Supreme Court Justice Louis Brandeis (November 13), and frontiersman Daniel Boone (November 2).

From that long roster of Scorpian talent, it should be obvious that those born under the eighth sign of the Zodiac are peculiarly favored for fame and accomplishment. To see how each day within that sign offers its own combination of advantages and drawbacks, let us now explore how the traits of the Apostle Thomas are reflected in all nine divisions of Scorpio.

SCORPIO—FIRST DIVISION
(October 28, November 1, 10, 19)

A zestful energy invigorates the inventive ideas of Scorpios of the First Division and makes them natural leaders. They relish challenges to their considerable skills and consider each moment of every day a fresh opportunity to strive and to accomplish. Just to be around them is to feel their enthusiasm for life, for they are:

- highly creative
- energetic
- bold
- ambitious

In some creative livelihood, you will find your best fulfillment, combining, as Robert Frost once said, your avocation and your vocation; that is, you can make your living by doing work you enjoy. It need not be the kind of labor we usually consider artistic, for you are blessed with the vision that enables you to see the creative potential in baking a cake, farming a rich and well-ordered field, dreaming up a new project for your industrial company, or carefully crafting a piece of wood. If the tradition is correct that Thomas was, like Christ, a carpenter, we can imagine how his work was not only practical but was also an aesthetic experience. The well-shaped panel, the finely fitted plank, the neatly carved ornament are all creative opportunities, as much as the formal sculpture that fills our museums. The important thing for you is to experience the satisfaction of producing something that is original, something that is your own.

This trait, of course, applies to Scorpian women as well as to men. In my real estate work with my husband, Jimmy, I meet every year more and more female Scorpios in executive positions, as architects, contractors, and engineers. This is, in part, related to changing conditions in our society, but it is also due to the assertiveness of their Scorpian creativity. In fact, the construction industry and related businesses are well suited to the tastes of Scorpio Ones, because you think in bold, sweeping patterns. A high-powered originality pushes your suggestions through, and can result in large-scale plans for urban renewal projects, housing developments, or extensive highway systems.

Your kinship with the elemental forces of Nature makes you sensitive to contemporary environmental problems, and your high principles lead you to make contributions of your time and money to ecological projects. Perhaps it involves joining your high school neighborhood clean-up campaign, or you may be one of those unsung heroes who always leave a public picnic ground cleaner than they found it. Whatever your means, you try to preserve our earth's delicate beauty.

The same boldness and daring that motivate your work can disrupt your relationships if you are not careful. Remember that many people like to be coaxed along, both in professional dealings and in romance. They can be overwhelmed by your habit of taking charge of situations and expecting people to follow your leadership. And leader you are, for your ambition is often the strongest facet of your complex personality. This combines with other characteristics—determination, aggressiveness, a critical spirit, and keen observation—to make you a driving force for progress. Your charisma can be impaired, however, by the tendency of your wit to run toward sarcasm. This can hurt the very individuals you want to lead. To your credit, the offense is usually unintentional, and when you perceive the resulting ill feelings, you are quick to apologize and restore interpersonal harmony.

Confident in your own abilities, you can inspire confidence in others, too. Don't be surprised if, in school or at work or in your community, you find yourself drafted to serve on committees and to run for offices. Your associates are apt to discern your inborn executive ability even if you are not aware of it.

COLORS: Because your powers are already supercharged, the use of color is not very important to you; but that's no reason to ignore it. To match your apparel to your zest for living, make sure your wardrobe has much bronze and sunshine yellow. Your boldness is a helpful, beneficent quality, so don't confine it with drab browns and blacks. If a male Scorpio One feels awkward in a yellow suit, he can achieve the same exuberant effect with a lemon shirt or a gold tie. And for those quieter moments—for even a Scorpio has some restful times—surround yourself with comfortable greens the color of mossy rocks.

MONEY: Your major money problem will not be making it but holding on to it. You will probably earn considerable sums. How could you help it with all your talents! But you will spend it too quickly, entertaining too lavishly, giving too generously to charities and to needy individuals. You would be wise to secure a financial manager, especially when you climb the heights of success. Otherwise, you could reach the top with empty pockets.

HEALTH: In your teen-age years, you are apt to be subject to respiratory diseases. The common cold will plague you, in and out of season. But as you reach your middle twenties, your health should improve dramatically. Maturity should bring you a vigorous constitution, as hardy as the indomitable creature that is your Zodiac symbol. You can hasten the development of your inborn resistance to illness by starting young to watch your diet and to avoid intoxicants. With your exuberance, you surely have no need of them.

RELATIONSHIPS: Just as your powerful personality attracts friends, so, too, your waspish wit can drive them away. It is up to you. Why not explain in advance to your intimates that if they are ever offended by anything you say in jest or in earnest, they should let you know immediately so that you can dispel ill feelings? By doing this, you will not only prevent painful antagonism, you will also impress your friends with the sincerity and warmth of your affection.

A Scorpio One makes a good marriage partner and parent. Your problems in the home will take the form of the inevitable squabbles which occur in almost all families. Of course, there are apt to be several strong-willed personalities under your roof, and so the incidence of skirmishes will be high. Use your natural abilities as a leader and organizer to calm such situations, especially when they involve your children. Remember that the best lesson for them is the one you set by your example.

It is probable that you will be tempted toward extramarital romances, because your commanding spirit makes you attractive to anyone looking for an authority figure. Especially in your thirties, opportunities will occur for you to indulge in a prolonged affair. Perhaps as you move toward the top in your career, you will think that the restraints of your family life are irrelevant. There could be no greater folly, so condition yourself to avoid by instinct any threats to your marriage.

SCORPIO—SECOND DIVISION

(October 29, November 2, 11, 20)

A Scorpio of the Second Division is one of those rare individuals who seem to have complete freedom of choice in all of life's major decisions. Your astrological influences give you what might be called an "open-ended" horoscope. Your personality combines a strange package of qualities, and they free you to develop yourself in any number of diverse ways. You are:

- extremely sentimental
- imaginative
- given to fantasies
- analytical

You are a softhearted romantic; and because you find this world so unsatisfactory in so many respects, you love to daydream your way out of it. If your immediate surroundings are unpleasant—a dirty street, a noisy office building, a decaying neighborhood—you tune them out and use your imagination to escape to nobler circumstances. This is especially true in matters of emotion. Your sentimentality causes you constant hurts. When an old building is torn down, you think of its tenants who had lived there all their lives. When the city begins a drive to remove the hordes of suffering stray animals that have resulted from the carelessness and cruelty of pet owners, you mourn for every dog and cat, although their present life in alleys is even more tragic. You treasure faded mementos and save old letters. In fact, you probably wish you could have been born in another century, but I suspect that your sentimentality overlooks much that is good now and much that was evil in the past.

There is nothing wrong with either sentiment or a creative imagination. Indeed, they can become the components for a soaring spirit that sees a reality deeper than the daily news headlines. The danger in them is that they can lead to habitual fantasizing, and you do, in fact, tend toward that form of intellectual escapism. You might daydream about what a tremendous lover you are, especially with that special someone in your class or office. Fine, but what about letting that certain person know how you feel? You may pretend you are a prominent and powerful political figure, reshaping society with your votes in the Congress. But when are you going to take the first step and volunteer as a precinct worker in a local campaign?

The point I wish to make is that fantasy can be a creative form of thinking. It can encourage us to strive for great things. It can liberate us from the restraints of disparaging critics and naysayers. But all that depends on what we do about our fantasies. If we work to make them come true, then they strengthen our lives. If we use them as excuses for inaction, then they undermine our powers.

But you, gifted Scorpio, need not dissipate your creative talents. Turn your imagination to the disciplined daydreaming that produces musical compositions and literary beauty. If you like to build castles in the air, try constructing them on paper, in poems or short stories. Once you enter the wonderland of a piano keyboard or the seemingly lifeless strings of a violin or guitar or harp, you will forsake fantasies for the inspiring reality of music and art.

It seems contradictory, but an imaginative Scorpio Two is also factually analytical. You look at problems dispassionately and envision all their possible ramifications. Perhaps this is just the better side of your penchant for fantasy. Under controlled circumstances, it enables you to apply your searching zeal for improvement to any number of professions. If you train yourself to keep to statistics rather than dreams, your unusual vision will be valued by dynamic corporations and rewarded accordingly. First, you must trust in your own judgments and assert them as boldly as you would in your loftiest daydreams.

In romantic matters, it is especially vital that you not let the dreamer within you rule your conduct. Women who are Scorpio Twos are especially liable to have someone else pick their dates for them, while they themselves pine for some dream lover they have never met. Sometimes, they proceed into a marriage knowing that they are not truly in love but nonetheless fascinated with the storybook version of romance. Eventually, the brute facts of everyday life must be faced, and the result is misery.

Marie Antoinette, Queen of France, was a Scorpio Two. When she was told that the peasants were starving because they could not afford bread, she is supposed to have answered, "Let them eat cake." Her inability to cope with the immediate needs of the real world finally brought her to the guillotine. But you can escape the little guillotines of life—the heartbreaks and affronts and disappointments—by directing your free will toward the mastery of events. Through one decision at a time, you can reassert your own powers to shape your future and the world you live in.

COLORS: Because Scorpio Twos need to realize that their lives can be as bright as their daydreams, sparkling greens are appropriate to heighten their awareness of their vibrant life-force. Because your insight can be as brilliant as a maharaja's emerald or as delicate as a holly leaf draped with winter's snow, express yourself with their colors. Imagine the appearance at a business meeting of a male Scorpio Two, attired in a cream-colored suit with an apple green tie which fairly shouts to the world that its wearer is in charge. If a woman of the Second Division appears at a social gathering in a gown of violet, as tender as her feelings, accented with emeralds either real or artificial, she will have no time for fantasies; her admirers will keep her far too occupied.

MONEY: Because of your initial indecision, you will start slowly in the race toward wealth. Your early years will be marked by financial fantasies, leading you to spend more than you have. Once you break that habit and live within your means, your growth in intellect and discipline will be matched by the growth of your bank account.

HEALTH: Because you are not usually physically active, you are probably not robust. Sometimes your escapist fantasies involve imaginary illnesses, which can be as troublesome as real ones. Be reassured, however, for there are few indications of major sickness in your astrological chart. And once you come to grips with reality and make yourself its master, you can dispel even those threats to your well-being.

RELATIONSHIPS: Your task must be to project yourself more forcefully in discussions, in business dealings, and especially in romance. Make your own decisions; you will be more respected for them. Grasp life with two hands, and all your relationships will be enriched for it.

Your family is good and loving toward you. Your married life can be a delight as long as your intended partner understands your need for occasional quiet contemplation to chart your inspirations. It will help if your spouse is a strong decision maker and appreciates the wonder of your imaginative view of life.

SCORPIO—THIRD DIVISION
(October 30, November 3, 12, 21)

The hardiest characteristics of Scorpio are evident in the Third Division, and those born within it are virtually assured of success in their work and prominence among their contemporaries. The pattern of their planetary influences makes it quite clear just how their prospects were shaped in that direction.

If you are a Scorpio Three, events in your early life gave you a maturity that is rare among the young. You can look back to experiences that put you "on your own" at a tender age. Usually the circumstances were physical rather than intellectual. Perhaps one or both of your parents died. Perhaps they were divorced, with the result that you felt you had lost them both. Maybe a family financial crisis forced you to work part time while you were still in grade school.

Less frequently, the critical experience for a young Scorpio Three is purely emotional, consisting of some awareness, some sudden realization leading to virtually overnight maturity. It may be a bad shock, a premature romance, or even a religious experience. Whatever the root cause, the result is the same. You were out in the world, coping with its demands and facing its challenges, long before your peers of the same age. No wonder you have a huge head start over them, for already you have:

- learned to shoulder responsibility
- developed self-confidence
- become a dynamic worker
- survived a major test of your will

Suddenly thrust into the great, cold world, you learned that the only way to survive with dignity and control over your own life was to shoulder responsibility for yourself. You aren't afraid to make decisions and to stand by them under criticism. It is incomprehensible to you how some gifted young people, born with every advantage, cannot accept accountability for their actions. When they complain of being powerless to shape their future, you reply that the lazy and the timid are always helpless. Because you didn't have the carefree life of contemporary teen-agers, you never had time for an identity crisis. You were too busy struggling for an education and overcoming obstacles to success.

That effort has made you a finer person, unusually mature and wise in the ways of the world. You have a quiet confidence in yourself. All your life you have proved your abilities. You know there is a tremendous difference between getting the job done and getting the credit for it, and you can spot a braggart even before he speaks.

You will make a superb administrator in any type of business and have all the assets for executive leadership. Your superiors must already have recognized your dynamism on the job. Ready for any task, glorying in the quality of your work, you will base your career not on contacts or flattery but on performance. No wonder you are destined for a rapid rise in prestige and income.

Even with all these admirable qualities, you might have succumbed to pessimism and despair if your zest for life had not survived a major test of your will to carry on. This probably involved your adherence to your principles when you were tempted to set aside your ethics to gain an immediate goal. Because you refused to do so, your best virtues have been tempered like metal that is made stronger by being subjected to heat or pressure. The result is that your character dominates all your dealings, and there is no greater asset in life. Both in romance and in business, your integrity will be your best recommendation.

There is a drawback in all your abilities. You are inclined to overextend yourself, attempting always to do more and to do it better. You may not realize that even your shoulders cannot assume unlimited responsibility. So learn to delegate authority. Otherwise, you will be the kind of supervisor who does the work of your underlings to make sure it is performed correctly.

This same failing carries over to family matters. When you assign tasks to your children, you may give them such precise instructions that they wonder if you trust them with the work. You should realize that your own offspring can't grow up to imitate your virtues unless you allow them a measure of independence, just as you were given a very large dose of it when you were younger. Teach your children to get more out of life by initiating their own projects and accepting either credit for their success or blame for their failure. By doing this, you will bless the world with more people like you, for you will be able to raise sons and daughters who share your energy and continue your integrity.

COLORS: Although you pay little attention to their use, the proper colors can accentuate your spirit of accomplishment. Like any individualistic leader, you were born to wear purple; its regal overtones are appropriate to your life of success. However, because you should learn to reassure and welcome those who might be overwhelmed by your dynamism, it is advisable to use lighter shades of that color. For example, your colleagues already know what a powerhouse you are; but when you sit down to a conference with a lavender jacket or tie, they can sense, perhaps for the first time, your tenderness and vulnerability. Mauve and pale violet are similarly suitable for letting people know that there are moments when, despite your forcefulness, you are indeed the quiet woodland violet, in need of affection.

MONEY: The lessons of your youth have left lasting impressions on you, and you spend money reluctantly. Your thrift will provide the basis for sound investments in land, antiques, and government bonds, and your honest industriousness should guarantee you ample salaries from appreciative employers.

HEALTH: As if your splendid character were not strength enough, your planetary combination endows you with patterns of good health. Your astral signs all indicate an excellent physical constitution and a long life.

RELATIONSHIPS: Perhaps because of the lonely experiences of your youth, you have a reserve that inhibits you from displaying affection; but this needn't be a serious problem. In fact, many of your associates think your streak of shyness is attractive. You may be addressing a large group with perfect ease and then, when approached by someone for whom you deeply care, become flustered and embarrassed. Though it may be an awkward experience, it's an endearing one.

Be careful to treat business colleagues with respect. Your tendency to monopolize decisions can be interpreted as an aspersion on their abilities. They will not care for your underestimation of their talents.

You will marry later than average and will make an excellent partner and a somewhat overprotective parent. Of course, the reason is your memory of your own early years. Let your children know why you want to shield them from the rigors of the world and then allow them a greater measure of freedom.

SCORPIO—FOURTH DIVISION
(October 31, November 4, 13)

Three entirely different paths lie open to a facile, adaptable Scorpio Four. The attitudes you develop over a period of years will determine which road you choose to follow through life. Of all Scorpios, you face some of the most difficult choices, and your future happiness depends largely upon your self-control. You could devote your considerable abilities to any one of these:

- investigative work, in the broadest sense of the words
- illegality and the pursuit of illegitimate profit
- sensuality and the gratification of your selfish appetites

What startling choices! And what radically different futures are available to you! Needless to say, only the first is likely to bring you either peace or fulfillment. By investigative work, I don't mean sleuthing. Although your Scorpian inquisitiveness and acute eye for detail do qualify you for criminal investigations, there are innumerable other areas in which to develop your talents. For example, all the sciences, especially medicine, need your questioning mind and alert analysis. Similarly, the field of insurance could not function without well-placed Scorpios to supervise its tremendous mass of detailed data. In industry, the creative work of product development needs the spark of Scorpian wit and, particularly, the inexhaustible inventiveness and originality of Scorpio Fours.

I could continue to list ways your assets can be pointed toward achievement, but you probably have already thought of your own interests and may want to enlarge upon them. As with any good thing, there is a danger in carrying it too far. For as you explore your capabilities, you will discover that they enable you to make great profits in short order if you use them to evil purposes. Even within a legitimate career, there will be ample opportunities to pursue illegal deals and fraudulent arrangements.

I must be frank about this. It is a rare person who never sees a chance for a dishonorable venture, although most people resist the temptation to pursue it. I'm not suggesting that you of the Fourth Division are less ethical than the rest of us. I'm only explaining that your great talents will bring you correspondingly greater opportunities for good or for ill. So when your temptations come, they will be correspondingly greater. And your astral pattern enables you to follow your inclinations as only you see fit to do.

A third alternative for you is an obsession with sensuality, which will lead to short-term success and long-term failure. Both male and female Scorpios of the Fourth Division are unusually attractive individuals, and their personal magnetism wins the hearts of the opposite sex. You will discover your potential as a great lover; but if you allow it to dominate your life, you will also learn how painfully lonely a life of pleasure-seeking can be. Eventually, all the banquets end; all the toasting stops; all the luxury and affluence wither away. You will be left with a hangover for your body and bitter recriminations for your spirit. If you should decide to explore the path of sensuality, be prepared for the mournful circumstances awaiting you at its end.

To avoid that dire outcome, concentrate on the ennobling aspects of your positive traits. You have a strong sense of purpose, so give it free rein to direct your labors to their best ends. Instinctively loyal, once you have decided on your allegiances, you will make significant contributions to them. All this depends upon one thing: your system of spiritual values.

Notice how Thomas handled this problem. At the Last Supper, when he was confused by Christ's declaration that He was going away to His Father, Thomas blurted out that he and his companions didn't know where He was going. How then could they find the way to follow Him? Thomas was taking no chances. Knowing that one way alone could bring him happiness, he urgently sought after it. You can do the same thing. You can begin now to ponder what you have already learned from the experience of life: that your tremendous gifts of intellect and personality bring you lasting contentment only when they serve your loftiest aspirations. Fortunately, your chances of choosing that happiness are every bit as great as Thomas's were.

COLORS: Throughout life, your inspiration to keep moving along the path of creative self-fulfillment will come from your deep, and deepening, faith. But you can sustain yourself in troubled times and energize your spirit on all occasions by the judicious use of color. Because there is nothing tentative or hesitant about a Scorpio Four, there should be nothing equivocal about your clothes and your home environment. On you, a sapphire dress or sweater or tie looks natural and appropriate, while it would appear gaudy on someone else. The brightest reds reflect both your intellectual acumen and that burning streak of emotional passion which makes you a warm friend and ardent lover. Especially in the rooms you use for entertaining, express your bold command of life with colors as rich as your imagination, as strong as your wit.

MONEY: Fourth Division Scorpios, especially those born on the November dates, must be careful in money matters. You work best alone, and so you may have to finance your own ventures without outside assistance. Because your schemes tend to be daring, they may provoke occasional financial emergencies. These can be overcome as long as your initial plans aren't unrealistic deals to get rich quickly. Your fascination for promises of instant wealth can only hurt you, both personally and economically. For you, the true route to wealth is hard work and dedication, which are inborn Scorpio virtues.

HEALTH: Illness comes to Scorpios of the Fourth Division only as a consequence of their mental and emotional attitudes. When you allow disruptive elements—whether anger or envy or resentment—to rule your relationships, then you are prone to suffering from nervous disorders, stomach complaints, and circulatory trouble. By maintaining a bright outlook on life, however, you can preserve both your stamina and health. By adapting to your surroundings and to your associates, rather than by trying to change them to your own tastes, you can attain both a peaceful mind and a vigorous body.

RELATIONSHIPS: Your tendency to run to extremes in emotional matters can cause obvious difficulties in your interpersonal dealings, especially outside your family. Your loved ones will recognize the pattern of your boisterous reactions, while more casual acquaintances will not realize that your strong words don't necessarily indicate animosity or bitterness. Another stumbling block is your tendency to hold grudges. There is no sillier way to waste your time and your psychic energy! Stop brooding over slights, for your resentment hurts you more than anyone else.

You have probably discovered already that your personal magnetism is exciting and attractive to members of the opposite sex. You could easily come to relish sexual escapades, not for their romantic potential but for the sheer adventure of the illicit and the daring. That irresponsibility can make you ruthless about the feelings of those who assume that your attentiveness to them is an expression of real concern.

Although the powerful currents of your emotion can be dangerous, they can be equally forceful in healing hurts, encouraging the weak, and loving one lucky person with a total commitment. That happy alternative is yours for the choosing.

SCORPIO—FIFTH DIVISION *(October 23, November 5, 14)*

Scorpios of the Fifth Division carry over many of the traits of their astrological kin of the preceding division, but in a rearranged pattern that stresses both their emotions and their psychological need for success. Like all your fellow children of the Scorpion, you Fives are veritable engines of energy and are able to direct your physical and intellectual prowess into several different channels. You are:

- passionate
- imaginative
- persistent
- determined to make your mark in society

Because your emotions are among the strongest of any segment of the Zodiac, you must learn to treat them with respect, as if they were a powerful and unpredictable animal. Like those Yellowstone Park bears, at once so lovable and so dangerous, your feelings are best kept at a distance. Under control, they can excite you to noble achievements and the warmest devotion. When they control you, however, the damage they do to others is exceeded only by the harm they bring to you.

In contemplating my vision of the Apostles and their Zodiac signs, I realized that the Apostle Thomas had traits similar to yours. Like you Fives, he was a man of fire and thunder, of passion and drive. But he seems to have realized that his weaknesses could also be his strengths. He didn't bottle up his passion until it would explode at an awkward moment. He didn't stifle it and allow it to turn into bitterness and malice. On the contrary, he liberated his feelings, sharing them with the thousands of strangers to whom he preached his good news of Christ's message. Rather than frustrate his astrological nature, he turned it to the best cause.

That is what you Scorpio Fives can do with your passionate spirit. Team it with your imagination, and you will make a superb artist, creative thinker, even an inimitable dress designer, a vibrant home decorator, an inspired landscape gardener. In short, you are one of the sparks of this world, and you can ignite whatever you choose. Like fire, you can be either a blessing or a curse. Your warmth can comfort chilled hearts, or it can sear tender feelings; it can enlighten dimmed vision, or it can blind with its brightness. As I have said repeatedly, the choice is yours, as it is with each one of us. When your creativity begins to boil and your Scorpian wit whistles like a teakettle, then your decision is most acute. Either the thunderous tread of the Devil's red boots or the fiery eloquence of Thomas's evangelistic mission will set the beat to which you march through life.

And march you will, for there is nothing timid about a Scorpio Five! Persistence is the hallmark of everything you do. This trait probably surfaced when you were little, and I suspect your parents had a difficult time keeping you from whatever household objects fascinated your infant curiosity. In your adult years, this same characteristic can appear either as diligent pursuit of your goals or as obstinate adherence to self-destructive habits. At your best, you are the student who keeps working on a difficult math problem until it is solved, the athlete who trains heroically until a record is broken, the housewife whose patient determination helps her children overcome handicaps. At your worst, well, let us assume that your better side is so attractive that there will be no need to even consider its alternative!

An interesting result of your persistence, no matter what form it takes, is that you are determined to leave your mark on the world in some extraordinary way. Even if you achieve financial success, you will be restless until your name is known and some measure of fame secured for your memory. If you find that impossible in your professional situation, you may strike out in a new career, go into politics, even dally with illegal adventures. For, sad to say, many of the cleverest, boldest criminals are Scorpios! The same attention to detail and foresighted overview of a situation that make you succeed in your work enable some of your astrological brothers and sisters to lead notorious and daring lives.

I don't think I have to tell you which course will bring you enduring happiness and which will leave you as miserable as a desert scorpion without shade at midday. If you have any doubts, you might find them answered in the life of your fellow Scorpio, Thomas.

COLORS: With attention to your clothes and home décor, you can tone down your emotions, especially your occasionally violent temper. Calming pastels, especially in delicate shades of blue and green, can balance the forcefulness of your personality. Plan ahead. If your day is apt to involve taut encounters, soothe both yourself and those with whom you must deal by wearing something in cream or dove gray. In romantic situations, you can express your passionate nature, without unleashing its wilder aspects, by combining both a light and dark shade of the same color. For example, a Scorpio Five male in a pale blue suit need only add to it a turquoise tie, as bold as the native turquoise in the rocks of the scorpion's natural environment. Then there will be no doubting either his tenderness or his zeal.

MONEY: Although you have a burning ambition to succeed, you don't necessarily intend to accumulate money. You desire a comfortable standard of living, and will usually reach it by your middle twenties. Thereafter, wealth will hold less enchantment for you than the prestige and power that come with it. Yet it will continue to come your way, almost as an accidental result of your achievements. All of that leaves you with little to worry about financially.

HEALTH: Because of your intensity and passion, you have the potential for ulcer trouble and for severe migraine headaches. In addition, there are astral indications of a possible liver or kidney complaint in your later years. Most of these problems can be minimized, or avoided altogether, by commonsense precautions, especially by staying away from highly spiced foods and heavy drinking. For someone of your electric nervousness, regular sleeping habits are essential in order to restore the energy you burn up so prodigiously.

RELATIONSHIPS: You may already have a reputation as a mercurial companion—very good company when your spirits are high but morose and unpleasant when things go wrong. Despite this, your vigor is greatly attractive to members of the opposite sex, and your adventuresome tendencies will lead you into a number of casual sexual encounters unless you are prepared to steel yourself against them.

Your marriage can suffer from your sometimes unreasonable attitudes. If so, the marital disruption will be more your loss than anyone else's. Learn now to avoid that outcome by utterly abandoning the pride that keeps you distant from your loved ones. Once that is done, you Scorpio Fives make excellent parents, and will find in your children the surest way to make your marks upon the world.

SCORPIO—SIXTH DIVISION *(October 24, November 6, 15)*

Blessed with an auspicious combination of planetary influences, Scorpios of the Sixth Division can enjoy both happy and effective lives. Their own contentment is related to the benefits they bring to others, and the only serious handicap with which they must contend is their tendency to flounder in romance. Before I explain that drawback, let us observe that you Scorpio Sixes are:

- lovable
- talented in many fields
- unselfish in helping others
- easily influenced

You are as cuddly as a teddy bear, even if you sometimes put on a gruff exterior to mask your tenderness. Self-sacrificing and self-effacing, you are devoted to your family, and probably learned at an early age to give up your wishes to please them. Like the Apostle Thomas, you are always ready to serve others, even at great personal cost. This means that you are likely to set aside your own plans and ambitions to do the bidding of others. That could be noble, but it would also be a foolish loss for the rest of us. You Scorpio Sixes are gifted with varied talents, and if you don't develop them, if you allow others to divert you from your true goals even for selfless motives, then you will deprive the world of the best services you can offer it.

Your wide-ranging capabilities could lead you into any one of several professions. By nature, you are attracted to areas of service, whether to a community, an organization, or your country. You would do well in medicine, either as a physician, a lab technician, a therapist, nurse, or researcher. A religious mission overseas or among the unfortunate in our own country would suit you; so would a position in a philanthropic organization. On a more personal level, Scorpio Sixes make fine librarians and public information specialists.

The reason you deal so well and tactfully with people is simple. You enjoy helping. In a sophisticated and blasé world, that seems almost childlike, and perhaps it is. We could all do with a lot more of it! In your case, you don't wait for people to prove themselves worthy of your affection but give them the benefit of the doubt. You like them on the spot; and only later, if they should betray your kindness, do you shut them from your heart.

Your altruism, your tendency to help others without question of reward, has already cost you time and money. For even when young, Scorpio Sixes are often involved in projects, whether organized or individual, to assist the needy and comfort the afflicted. You may suspect that this is nothing rare, that everyone shares your impulse to help. Unfortunately, that isn't true, and one of your greatest contributions can be to teach others to imitate your selfless spirit.

And now to your weakness! You are susceptible to romantic disappointments. Because you instinctively like people, you are apt to fall in love too easily. You lack the touch of hardy skepticism that helps us distinguish between love and superficial attraction. This makes you vulnerable to repeated heartbreak, as the objects of your affection prove unworthy of it. Indeed, sometimes they will not even realize your deep regard for them; you may think they have jilted you, although they never realized your relationship had become serious. The only reason you haven't been gravely hurt by this is that most people sense your inner goodness and don't wish to abuse it. Once you recognize this tendency of yours, you can correct it in part by deliberately slowing down your emotional reactions to people. You can take your time about falling in love, just as it takes a long time for you to dislike anyone. As a result, your romantic relationships will be more enduring and more likely to lead you to a happy marriage.

If you are a young and unencumbered Scorpio Six, it may be advisable for you to seek your career away from your home and friends. Your talents may flourish best without the stifling demands of relatives who want you to follow a predetermined path to their goals. On the other hand, if you are presently contented and fulfilled, then your home situation is bringing out the best in you, and you would be foolish to abandon it.

Let me sum up all the positive attributes of your division with a personal anecdote. I have a friend, a Scorpio Six, who was a famous actress for many years until her vision faded and she no longer could move with confidence on the stage. She learned to read in Braille and volunteered to make recordings for the blind in her splendidly dramatic voice. She once told me, "Not only can I read Braille, but I can read it out loud." Needless to say, I was moved by her selfless enthusiasm for life. It is characteristic of you Sixes: you love out loud.

COLORS: Just as you are lovable to most people, so, too, your dominant color is everybody's favorite: blue, in all its variations. The airy, spiritual quality of a Madonna blue expresses your selfless devotion to the well-being of others, and you may prefer that shade in your home and office surroundings. However, there are times when you must be more assertive, especially in dealing with individuals who would exploit your better nature. When you do feel the need to be your own person and follow your own mind, a rich navy blue or bright royal blue can convey and reinforce the stronger aspects of your character.

MONEY: Although you care little about money, you can do as well in financial matters as you wish. In business or government, the diversity of your talents points you toward the executive level. In a profession, whether law or medicine or scholarship, the same abilities will bring you renown. But be sure you have an efficient administrator or colleague to see that your bills are sent and paid on time. You haven't the heart to demand the payment you deserve.

HEALTH: Scorpio Sixes usually have strong constitutions and rarely suffer serious problems with their health. Later in life, guard against putting on weight, or it will lead to grave coronary difficulty. Remember that the animal which serves as your astrological symbol is lean, fast, and alert. A fat and sluggish scorpion wouldn't survive the rigors of the desert.

RELATIONSHIPS: Continue to be loving and giving, but be more selective about the recipients of your affection and your aid. As I have already explained, you are likely to misjudge hasty romances; and so you should be wary of early marriage, especially if your engagement has been brief. Your best chances for marital happiness are with someone you have known and respected for a long time, someone who has repeatedly demonstrated trustworthiness and reliability.

Most of your friends are loyal and sincere, and you will make a superb parent, especially if your marriage is entered into prudently and with considerable forethought.

SCORPIO—SEVENTH DIVISION
(October 25, November 7, 16)

The planetary combination governing the Seventh Division of Scorpio bears strongly on the mental faculties and endows those born under it with intelligence and psychic powers. You are:

- unconcerned about material things
- a lover of solitude
- a natural supervisor
- purposeful

You are the most spiritual of all those born under the sign of the Scorpion. Your primary need is for mental and aesthetic stimulation. A life without ideas is to you less than life. Pursuing knowledge, theories, new facts and old beliefs, you neglect material goods and are unconcerned with money. At your best, you use some small part of your intellect to arrange your financial affairs securely but do not seek any more wealth than you need to sustain your life of the mind. Indeed, so rich are your mental powers that you will not need to tax your resources to make a comfortable income for you and your family.

Another reason you are reluctant to enter the race for financial success is your love of peace and quiet. An intensely private person, you enjoy solitude, perhaps even more than you should. Your reserve comes not from shyness but from the fact that intellectual challenges are much more rewarding to you than social ones. And so you may seem uninterested and preoccupied at a party, and some may consider you withdrawn or a snob.

The truth is a far different matter. When you meet someone who shares your interests, who has ideas and wisdom to share and relishes the exploration of unknown frontiers of learning, you are an ardent conversationalist, very verbal, even witty. When you know that the guests at a social gathering are fellow seekers after spiritual enlightenment, then you can become the life of the party.

Your career opportunities are indicated by the combination of the two factors we have just discussed. With great intellectual powers, you are suited for all sorts of research; and with an aversion to casual mingling, you would be most effective in a supervisory position, in which your relationships with other workers would be pleasant but not intimate.

An excellent memory will aid you in whatever you undertake; and I suggest that if you are young, you discuss with knowledgeable advisers at your school or local businesses just how your talents might be employed both in the immediate future and after the completion of your education. You must realize that you have much to offer and you mustn't resist working your way up the ladder of success. You needn't be avaricious, but you must not disdain financial rewards. After all, one day you will find that the demands of family life require you to come down to earth and provide necessities for those who depend upon you. That should be no problem for you. The same purposefulness which leads you to extensive research and prolonged contemplation will lead you to steady work as well. Your progress will come gradually, not spectacularly. Without your seeking prominence, it may eventually be thrust upon you because of your years of effort and achievement.

Some people may be surprised by the way an abstract thinker like you is also a dutiful and energetic employee even in jobs requiring little mental activity. They don't realize that intellectual accomplishments come about the same way as athletic ones, through sustained effort and long practice. Throughout your life, you will be told how lucky you are to be blessed with a strong mind. You will smile and thank them for the compliment, knowing all the time that your astrological gifts would have come to nothing if you hadn't spent those lonely hours in strengthening your intellect.

The same holds true for your psychic powers. You may have been neglecting them all your life, or you may have realized their potential even in your childhood. Whatever the case, you of the Seventh Division have abilities that demand respect and nurturing. It is impossible for me to say with precision just what those powers are. Perhaps you have precognitive dreams; perhaps extrasensory perception; perhaps a special sensitivity to the unspoken emotions of others. I leave to you this wonderful and most rewarding aspect of your personality.

COLORS: To emphasize the unworldly facets of your character, dress frequently in cream and white. This holds true equally for men and women of the Seventh Division. A man who is not afraid to wear a splendidly white suit to a business or social meeting can communicate his immaterial, intellectual values to those around him without saying a word. And because you are not totally divorced from reality, because you employ your wisdom in your profession and in your appreciation of artistic beauty, accent your light attire with brilliant greens, especially the color of an emerald. To my mind, that is uniquely appropriate because your love of learning is like a glowing jewel, shining in your private vision to illuminate the lives of others.

MONEY: Caring little about money, you will be concerned only with the security it can provide. Living modestly and frugally, you can enjoy an independence rare in modern life. Your children will realize one day that although you didn't give them every rich present they wanted, you gave them far more precious gifts: respect for learning and a hunger for truth.

HEALTH: A Scorpio Seven is not apt to be strong physically, but you will compensate for this by applying your ample store of information to health matters. Recognizing the importance of your physical well-being, you will read widely in biology, nutrition, and related fields, so that you can apply that learning to your own life.

Consequently, your careful diet and avoidance of dangers will keep you safe from serious ailments.

RELATIONSHIPS: Your personal relationships will lack drama, and that will work all to your good. Moving cautiously around new acquaintances, you are slow to develop warm ties and even slower to let anyone enter your private realm of study and meditation. But when your friendships are solidified, they are splendid. Perhaps you, more than any other individuals, realize the full meaning of the old saying that a good friend is like a good book. Indeed, you have the best of both of them!

The same is true of your marriage. It is likely to be a success because you will enter into it slowly, with prolonged consideration of alternatives. That would have been the usual advice in days gone by; interestingly enough, it is also the wisdom revealed in recent sociological studies, which prove that the most enduring marriages are those in which the partners have known each other for years before their wedding.

Your home life will be quiet, as you like it. You will probably have only one child, who will be both gifted and introverted. Be sure you reinforce the talents of your child or children by showing them how to cope with the world rather than retreating from it.

SCORPIO—EIGHTH DIVISION
(October 26, November 8, 17)

A Scorpio Eight has been given a strong and stubborn will. You will require much discipline to keep it under control and make it serve your best interests. For years, you may think the world is out of step with you, until you realize someday that you must adjust your own wants to the realities of everyday life. You are:

- headstrong
- argumentative
- discerning
- secretive

That may sound like a bad-tempered package, but actually it isn't. Scorpio Eights are, in fact, usually likable, good-natured, highly individualistic people. Your problems are brought about by errors in judgment, not by defects in spirit. Once you set your mind to something, you are like a horse wearing blinders. You see only your predetermined goal and will not be deterred from it.

Is that a bad trait? It depends on what your goals are! If you are pursuing exalted purposes, then your dogged willfulness can be admirable. The danger, of course, is that you will ride roughshod over anyone in your way. You can have the best of both worlds by maintaining your headstrong dedication to your objectives while learning patience and tolerance. That will be difficult, but possible; and with those qualities perfected, you can conquer the world and the hearts of everyone in it.

As I have said before, we each have a special part to play in this world. Your role should be obvious. There are so many worthy projects, so many vital endeavors, which languish and fail because they lack direction and drive. Fund-raising campaigns fall short of their mark because no one could organize them well enough. Community clean-up efforts bog down because no one was available to supervise them. Complex business deals stall because no one takes responsibility for pushing them through. You have the initiative and persistence to handle such matters. This is the positive side of your stubbornness, and you must make the most of it.

In the process, beware of the tendency to look for disputes. If there is a ground of disagreement, you will stand on it. Although you are neither nasty nor rancorous, you are argumentative and don't like to pass over little differences for the sake of compromise and harmony. On the contrary, you relish debates and are probably fond of political rallies at which rival candidates speak against one another. That is your kind of entertainment!

As with most traits, this can be either good or bad, depending on how you use it. Thomas, the Apostle of Scorpio, was like you in this regard. Quick to speak, combative in discussions, he found that his talent for debate could convince thousands of people to change their lives for the better. He could pick out the weak spots in arguments against Christianity and dispel them. He could explain to others why their excuses and exculpations didn't justify the things that were wrong with their lives. In short, he remained argumentative, but he spoke out for worthy purposes.

You can do the same thing. Your determination can inspire others to follow your leadership in any number of positive projects, and your verbal spunk can incite them to accomplish great deeds and reform their lives. Or, if you choose to wear the red boots of discord and malice, your eloquence can sow dissension among others, setting them against one another for the benefit of no one except the master of all red boots.

How can you tell which paths lead you to your happiest goals and which will bring you to a bad end? Luckily, you Scorpio Eights have no trouble distinguishing between them. In fact, you are unusually perceptive and make uncanny judgments based on obscure facts which others don't notice. Just as you instantly detect the differences in quality between two pieces of cloth or furniture, so can you discern the faults and flaws in a theory or an alibi. This characteristic would make you a fine quality control specialist in a factory or on an assembly line, and also enables you to be an investigator in police work and related fields.

Like the furtive animal which is your astrological symbol, you Scorpio Eights are secretive. By instinct, you are reluctant to share private information, even when it is harmless. You suspect the motives of anyone who pries into your personal background. This habit can make you overly distrustful if carried to an extreme. On the positive side, it makes you a splendid counselor, for you never divulge confidential information. People in need of a sympathetic but very private hearing could find in you just the person they need. Keep this in mind when you are considering career alternatives, for the very traits you take for granted are those which might be most valued by a potential employer.

All in all, the Eighth Division of Scorpio can be a powerhouse, producing dynamos like you. Your intelligent choices alone will decide whether your electric impact illumines or shocks, energizes or short-circuits the world.

COLORS: The careful use of color can help you dilute your dogmatic tendencies and control your emotions. Soothe the angry vibrations that sometimes surround you by wearing pastel shades, especially rose and pink, which are the lightest versions of your most appropriate color—red. Of course, you must be careful how you handle that powerful hue. It will exaggerate your strongest characteristics, and most of the time that isn't advisable. But in romantic situations, when you have come to the conclusion that one certain person must understand how you feel, then ample use of red and crimson may finally get your message across. It is worth trying.

MONEY: There is no middle path for you in your economics;

it is all or nothing. In your early years, precious little money will come your way. As you mature, and as you learn to control your combativeness, your career prospects will dramatically improve. With your combination of brains and talent, you could become quite wealthy.

HEALTH: Temperament governs your physical condition. In youth, your discontent can bring on such ailments as indigestion, skin trouble, and even elevated blood pressure. Frustration at not getting your own way could lead to misuse of alcohol and other drugs. That is why it is essential that you learn self-control as soon as possible and that you emphasize the better side of your personality. With the passage of time, you will mellow, and your health will surely improve.

RELATIONSHIPS: Once again, the extremes of your temperament can lead you to either war or peace. An undisciplined Scorpio Eight is overly sensitive to well-meant criticism and feuds with business colleagues. A more mature Eight turns disagreements into creative confrontations and is respected for rising above petty differences.

Because you attract members of the opposite sex through your fiery personality, you may have a succession of lovers. This could break up your marriage if you wed early. It may be prudent, therefore, to settle down later in life, after you have curbed your seesawing emotions.

You will be a good and, for you, strangely tolerant parent, to the point of indulging your children's every whim. Once you conquer your disruptive tendencies, you have real potential as a marriage partner.

SCORPIO–NINTH DIVISION *(October 27, November 9, 18)*

The best way to describe the personality of a Scorpio Nine is to say that you would make a great cheerleader. You are:

- aggressive in a positive way
- good-humored
- an organizer
- well intentioned
- inspiring to others

Somehow you have managed to collect all the aggressiveness of

Scorpio at its worst and to neutralize its venom into a pleasant, engaging directness. You can stir up people in the best sense of the phrase and bring out the best in their efforts and spirits. That's what I mean by calling you the cheerleaders of the world.

I suspect that your inborn modesty prevents you from appreciating the value of this trait. You applaud the work of those who plan a project and supervise its execution, but you should also recognize that their best schemes would come to nothing without the enthusiasm you can generate. That's why you should expect your employers to put you in charge of high-priority ventures. Be flattered by their confidence, but at the same time, understand that you do, in fact, merit it.

You have many of the best characteristics of Scorpio: executive ability, gregariousness, and imagination. Warm and vital, unswerving to your duty, you should set your sights high, both in your career and in your personal relationships. As long as you take nothing for granted, as long as you keep your eye on your noblest goals, you can expect a stellar life, filled with accomplishments and spiritual satisfaction.

Perhaps the most important assets you have been given by your astrological influences are an unflappable good humor and organizing skills. As the pressures of daily life in this electronic age increase, persons like you will become even more valued. Just imagine all the little situations you encounter each day—on your way to work, in your neighborhood, while shopping or working or dining—in which your harmonizing abilities could be helpful. If your days are at all like those of most Americans, the list would be endless! We need Scorpio Nines to straighten out snarls, to soothe hurt egos, to use a joke to break up a quarrel. You do all this instinctively. Small wonder people like to have you around in tense situations!

It is characteristic of most Scorpio Nines that you are well intentioned, even when your actions prove ill advised. Even when colleagues doubt the wisdom of your proposals, they don't question your motives. This means that you can have disagreements, even serious ones, which will not become personal; that's a tremendous help in any field of activity.

No wonder you inspire others. Usually unintentionally, you set high examples for them to follow. Even in school, you may have helped many of your friends to stick with their studies or their athletic endeavors just by showing them what hard work and determination can accomplish. By all means, take this wonderful ability of yours into account when you choose a career. It is too valuable to waste, especially in a world where so many people search for direction and need the inspiration of your personal contact.

With your talent for getting to know people and putting them at ease, you could be a social worker, a parole officer, or a splendid investigative journalist. A peculiar factor that may determine your occupation is the planetary influence indicating your propensity to work with cutting tools of some kind, very much like the Apostle Thomas and his carpentry instruments. You could be a surgeon, a lumberman, a butcher, a woodworker, even a superb chef. You may be a full-time housewife who limits her culinary masterpieces to occasional dinners on special occasions, but the zest you put into your work will identify your Scorpian attributes.

Even if your social life is busy in your youthful years, it will become more so as you grow older. It is apt to center around your good marriage. If other couples like to bask in the glow of your happy home life, let them. You were born under a loving star, and you might as well share its benefits.

COLORS: There is no sense hiding your light under a bushel, to use the old metaphor. You are a walking sunrise, bringing fresh light into darkened lives and urging people on to a fresh new start. Your magnetic vibrations are as blunt and emphatic as red, ruby, and garnet, and all those jubilant shades will match your appearance to the effect you have on others. For your private moments, or those shared with one or more very special persons, you will enjoy wrapping yourself in very dark, cool blues, whether as apparel or as home furnishings. These give you a peaceful respite from your hectic days.

MONEY: The economic pattern of your life shows a steady improvement after your late teen-age years. After hearing about all your wondrous talents, you shouldn't be surprised to be told that financial security and consequent comfort are assured you by the time you reach your middle years. Of course, like all good things, they, too, depend upon your willingness to develop and properly employ all the gifts you have so generously been given.

HEALTH: Accidents, rather than ailments, are a potential threat to Scorpio Nines. Disease will seldom bother you, perhaps because your continually optimistic spirit adds vigor to your active body. But you must be careful in handling firearms and electrical gadgets. Your extensive traveling may recharge your psychic batteries, so to speak, but it also presents hazards to your safety; so do take care. Anyone who works as hard as you must set aside ample time for rest. Otherwise, both your health and the quality of your endeavors will be imperiled.

RELATIONSHIPS: Your birth stars gave you an affectionate nature, and so your life is filled with friends. You take that for granted and wonder how solitary, gruff individuals manage to settle for anything less. Your creative and generous spirit wins hearts without even trying, for most people can sense your selfless intentions by instinct.

Your chances for a splendid marriage are so good that you would have to make deliberately wrong choices in romance for anything to go wrong. The only advice I would give you is to make sure the person whom you choose as your companion in life fully appreciates your worth. You have too much to offer to fritter it away in a prideful, self-centered partner. By seeking someone who shares your dedication and cheerfulness, you will be guaranteed loving children who will be able to change the world into a better place.

SAGITTARIUS—
JAMES (THE GREATER)

(November 22–December 21)

In the cyclic progression of the Zodiac, the intensity and passion of Scorpio are followed by the relaxed exuberance of Sagittarius. Thus the influences of the stars turn human nature from one set of characteristics to another, and the result is variety and contrast. A popular song of a few years ago advocated "different strokes for different folks," and surely the abrupt change in temperament from the Apostle Thomas to his Sagittarian fellow demonstrates the wonder of mankind's diversity.

The Apostle revealed in my vision as the embodiment of everything that pertains to Sagittarius was, like all those born under that sign, jovial and optimistic, self-confident and frank, dependable and forceful. He was the older brother of the Apostle John, known to history as James the Greater, to distinguish him from the James of Gemini, who was shorter in stature.

Not much is recorded concerning James. Together with his brother, he was called by Christ a "Son of Thunder," because, like you Sagittarians, he was a strong and direct person, never afraid to express his views. His personality can explain why the symbol of Sagittarius is the centaur-archer, part horse and part man, armed with bow and arrow. In his conversation, James was as sharp and swift as the flying arrow, yet as warm and appealing as the graceful steed. His responses were sometimes as delicate as the taut bowstring, sometimes as heavy as the centaur's hoofs. While his spirit aimed at the stars, his feet were rooted to the ground. Aspiring to great things, he was down to earth in practicality.

He shared your tremendous confidence and didn't hesitate to speak up for himself. One day, he unabashedly asked Christ if he and his brother John could sit on either side of the Lord when He established His kingdom. Apparently, James hadn't yet realized that his Master's kingdom would not be an earthly one. That was why Christ replied by cautioning James that he could share the glory only if he shared the pain and sacrifice of His mission to the world. True Sagittarian that he was, James took up the challenge. In fact, he was the first of the Apostles to die for the new faith that Christ had left them.

Indeed, it is characteristic of you Sagittarians that challenges make you great. You love the excitement they generate. Like the centaur's galloping hoofs, your mind races while others walk. That's why you always seem to stand out ahead of the crowd, both literally and figuratively. It is common for you to pass by other people who can't keep up with your sidewalk pace. In conversations, you frequently break into others' comments and finish their sentences for them even before they know what they were going to say. Mentally and emotionally, you are faster on the draw.

Because you approach a subject with the head-on precision of the archer's arrows, you have no patience with anyone who beats around the bush or who doesn't know what he or she is talking about. Your own speech tends to be very much like your thoughts: rapid-fire, almost staccato. With the cool deliberation of a computer, you choose your words well, though effortlessly; and if you've been working awhile to develop your vocabulary, you find you can say a great deal in a very few words. It's as if you communicate by shorthand. Needless to say, that can be a tremendous advantage in business. No one expedites a committee meeting better than you, when you cut through the verbiage to get to the heart of the matter in a sentence or two. Beneficial as that can be, you must be aware of its drawbacks. When you are bored by small talk and bothered by vague or evasive speakers, you can be brutally honest. Your frankness can alienate and offend those whose cooperation you need, and it can wound those whose only fault is that they lack your gifts for self-expression.

This damage can be done despite your good intentions; and, rest assured, your motives are usually the best. The reason you react so vigorously to expose even little deceptions is that your sense of justice commands your conduct. Strongly advocating law and order, especially for your own behavior, you are grieved by injustices and angered by unpunished misdeeds. That's an admirable trait, and you can rightly be proud of it. But don't allow it to get out of hand, for even the Sagittarian Apostle had trouble in this regard.

James shared your quick temper that occasionally leads you to act against the very principles you want to uphold. Earlier, I referred to the day when the Apostles were entering a town in Samaria, and the local residents were hostile to them. Infuriated, James and his brother asked Christ if they should pray for the wrath of God to destroy the village! Their Teacher's rebuke was gentle, reminding them that He had not come to earth to harm people but to change them. Of course, James had known that before; but when he allowed himself the luxury of an angry moment, his temper overruled his beliefs. You are prone to the same difficulty, especially when you are spiritually depressed and brooding about the ways of the world. Then you are most apt to slip into the red boots you find conveniently at hand; and on you, they can be especially damaging. The symbolic steps you take are as powerful as the hoofbeats of your astrological sign. Thundering across the skies, the shooting centaur can be as forceful for evil as it usually is for good. I keep telling people from every segment of the Zodiac, the choice is yours alone. By keeping a close rein on your temper, you can throw those pinching boots back at the diabolical bootmaker who crafted them with such cunning and guile.

The peculiar composition of your star sign assures that you can gain mastery of all your impulses. For the centaur, half human and half beast, is an ancient symbol of the balance within all of us between raging nature and reasoned intellect. It sums up the duality of your Sagittarian nature, which makes you kin to those born under the signs of Libra and Gemini. At your best, you combine your two halves to see both sides of a question and to recognize that truth is usually fragmented and divided among all the parties to a dispute. When your arrows are aimed at the stars, you are fair-minded to the point of sacrificing your own views out of respect for the opinions of others.

Permeating your whole life, this dualism means that you may switch your allegiances without deliberation, sometimes recklessly. It is as if you had outgrown the framework of your beliefs. Sometimes you merely crave intellectual exercise; and like a horse too narrowly penned, you knock down your restraining bars to run free toward another pasture. You could be the politician who changes parties, the clergyman who changes denominations, or the scientist who abandons his career to become an artist. Or, more commonly, you could be the office worker who takes on an extra job as an auto mechanic just for the vigorous activity it offers. You might be the busy executive who still finds time to tend a large vegetable garden, or the housewife who, in her spare time, maintains a thriving little business in her home.

Don't be surprised if your occupations involve you with animals. Even if your life-style doesn't permit you to have pets, you have probably always felt a special appreciation and understanding of them. I'm not a Sagittarian; but I do love all animals, especially dogs, and all too often bring forlorn strays in need of a meal home with me. The man to whom I entrust them for training and grooming is a Sagittarian, and I marvel at the way he handles them and communicates with them.

Like a true centaur, you Sagittarians love the outdoors and are usually skillful in hunting and camping. I know a charming woman in New York City who is a consultant to the diamond industry. Elegant, poised, knowledgeable, every summer weekend she goes to her cabin in the Poconos, where she spends hours, hip-deep in a river, casting for fish. This might seem out of her character, but she is a typical Sagittarian, with dual interests and the self-confidence to indulge herself in both of them. In fact, women Sagittarians are usually the nobler of their astrological kind. Men of the centaur seldom have sufficient patience for the everyday petty tribulations we all face, but your sister archers usually do. By mastering the minor events of the day, they learn control over the major ones.

Perhaps because the archer shares Cupid's identification with arrows, many Sagittarians of both sexes marry on impulse and subsequently regret it. It is the women, however, who work to salvage faulty marriages. Loving their homes, devoted to their children, they sacrifice so much for them that they often manage to restore to health an apparently dying marital relationship. Women Sagittarians usually possess a high sense of honor and duty. This makes you the kind of wife who persuades a reluctant husband to attend PTA meetings, who shepherds her family to church regularly, who reads the political literature that floods the mailbox in order to keep informed on civic issues. You are the kind of mother who helps a toddler to brush her teeth morning and night, making sure it is done properly. Granted, you can sometimes be overly solicitous and want to do too much for your loved ones. But in general, you are a treasure, and they know it!

With the qualities that are your birthright, many Sagittarians have risen to power and fame. Like James the Greater, they recognized in themselves the Creator's gifts to them; and, for good or ill, developed their powers to reach their goals. The same path can be yours; for, as with every archer, it is your prerogative to aim your arrows where you please, knowing that you alone are responsible for their flight.

That is the lesson in the lives of Winston Churchill (November 30) and President Zachary Taylor (November 24); of Benjamin Disraeli, the architect of the British Empire under Queen Victoria (December 21); of John Jay, one of the founders of the American Republic and first Chief Justice of the Supreme Court (December 12). Their careers in public affairs were equaled, indeed, in some cases surpassed, by the glorious and tragic life of Mary, Queen of Scots (December 7).

Among contemporary political leaders, two dynamic individuals exhibit the forcefulness and charm typical of Sagittarius. The ever youthful Senator Strom Thurmond was born on December 5. Helen Delich Bentley, Chairperson of the Federal Maritime Commission and one of the most powerful women in American government today, celebrates a birthday on November 28.

The women of Sagittarius are seldom shy, and many of them have shot to prominence as surely as a well-aimed arrow. Former Senator Margaret Chase Smith (December 14) was the only woman in the U.S. Senate. Dr. Janet Travell (December 17) became known to millions of Americans as the lady doctor—and every bit as much the lady as the doctor—who helped President Kennedy with his back problems. Famed anthropologist Margaret Mead (December 16) needs no introduction; nor does Caroline Kennedy (November 27), from whom we can expect truly Sagittarian accomplishments.

Among creative Sagittarians have been composers Beethoven (December 16), Berlioz (December 11), Friml (December 10), and Sibelius (December 8). Sagittarians who have turned their intellectual facility and way with words into literary careers include Louisa May Alcott (November 29), Mark Twain (November 30), Maxwell Anderson (December 15), Jane Austen (December 16), and Willa Cather (December 7).

Some of you children of the centaur will find yourselves interested in the occult, and this will be a natural outlet for your surplus mental energy. Perhaps that was the case with the great psychic and seer Nostradamus (December 14), whose predictions, made four hundred years ago, are still being fulfilled today.

In religion, the qualities of Sagittarius gave us the beloved Pope John XXIII (November 25) and Junipero Serra (November 24), the builder of the beautiful missions in California.

The creative restlessness of your astrological character can lead you to important inventions and discoveries, as it did Eli Whitney (December 8), who perfected the cotton gin, and Christian Doppler (November 29), the Austrian astronomer who formulated the principles for measuring the motions of the stars.

Just as Doppler charted outer space to understand the interactions of the heavenly bodies, so we can chart our own lives to fathom the ties between us and those usually unseen planets which, in part, shape our futures. To do that, we need now to look at the many variations within the sign of the Archer. For whether or not we are Sagittarians, their personalities must concern us all because, like planets passing one another in the cosmic void, we all interact on our journeys through life.

SAGITTARIUS—FIRST DIVISION
(November 28, December 1, 10, 19)

Life is good and promises to be even better for Sagittarians of the First Division. Your acute mind is matched by a warm heart, so that your intellect and your emotions work in tandem to develop and express your pleasant personality. You have:

- a sunny disposition
- generosity
- enterprise
- ambition

As a born optimist, you seldom stay downhearted for long. Even when you confront serious disappointments—as we all must from time to time—you stress positive elements and hope for the best. You know it is possible to be cheerful without being giddy. That is why so many people enjoy having you around, especially when they must deal with weighty matters. Like the sun that breaks into a dark room and suddenly transforms its gloom into a wonderful interplay of light and shadows, you can exercise a rare magic in the daily lives of your family and associates.

Apart from your contagious delight in each day's living, your contributions to the welfare of others are significant. Thanked or not, you are persistently generous, helping someone out even when you yourself need a hand. Perhaps you have already learned the ancient wisdom that whatever you give in a spirit of selfless sharing will come back to you tenfold. You will find in the contentment of your evenings and the vibrance of your mornings the richest blessings that Heaven saves to reward openhearted givers like you.

There is a different kind of generosity, involving not material sharing but intellectual tolerance. It is the generosity that allows others to disagree with us without rancor. A Sagittarius One usually extends this special consideration to opponents. Lacking distorting prejudices, you can see people and situations by their true light. Your strong intuition assists you in this. That is why you have less than your share of family arguments and tiffs at work. That is why a younger Sagittarius One seldom participates in the efforts of his fellow students to shun those youngsters who are different or nonconformists. You learn at an early age that the most valued generosity—as well as the most difficult sometimes—is that which shares affection and respect.

I don't mean to suggest that you of the First Division are patsies for exploiters and rogues. When someone tries to deceive you, your tolerance stops, although your reaction doesn't usually involve the fiery anger characteristic of some other divisions of your sign. You set the record straight, defend your honor, and refuse to brood about disappointments with people. You have too much on your mind to bother about recriminations.

Just what is on your mind at a particular time is impossible to say, because you leap from one subject to another like a frisky centaur. Seeing all sides to a problem, you may stop midway through a project and begin anew in a different way. This flexibility is a priceless asset both in your schooling and your later employment. Of course, that spirit of enterprise, constantly searching and changing and pondering, must be complemented and brought to fulfillment by the hard work that can be generated only by ambition. Fortunately, that is another of your traits. Diligent in your pursuits, you very much want to succeed in them, no matter the prestige or disregard usually attached to them. Unlike the ambition that devours its practitioners, yours is benign. It doesn't distort your values, nor does it harm others to achieve your purposes. On the contrary, it is based on the accurate assumption that the most enduring success is won by being cooperative and persistent. That is why you are pleased at the success of others and enjoy your own triumphs most when their benefits can be shared.

You usually choose a career early in life, train properly for it, and settle into a steady progress of personal advancement by the time many other people are just beginning to select their life's work. This early start enables you to satisfy the dualism in your personality, because once you are well established in a job, you have the time and security necessary to branch out into another field. By your middle years, you will probably have two trades, two offices, or at least a weekend avocation that serves as a second career, whether for profit or not. You never feel completely at ease when concentrating all of your ample energy into one channel of employment.

As time goes by and you become more prosperous and comfortable, you might find it most rewarding to give up any secondary jobs you have taken on and to substitute charitable and humanitarian work for them. This effort will provide the diverse activity you relish. It will also keep the arrows of Sagittarius aimed at their true celestial targets.

COLORS: The centaur is a powerful and amiable influence upon you, and you therefore share the good-humored nature of James the Greater. To express that cheerfulness, the royal colors of gold and yellow, purple and violet, are most appropriate. Consider yourself a light-footed, prancing horse, bedecked with the gayest trappings of a ceremonial occasion; for that is the spirit of the centaur of antiquity, wreathed by woodland sprites with yellow daisies and sprays of lavender.

MONEY: Your emphasis on living life to its fullest means you are no hoarder of money, although your inborn abilities virtually ensure that you will earn considerable sums. Some speculations will turn out poorly for you, probably involving a risky loan; but you aren't the type to hold a grudge over it. Working harder than ever, you will come back to recoup your losses.

HEALTH: A splendid constitution is another of the blessings bestowed upon Sagittarians of the First Division. Your greatest danger comes from taking that gift for granted. By overworking yourself, you can be like the horse which gallops at its owner's urging until it falls from exhaustion.

RELATIONSHIPS: Your strong drive for sexual expression makes you romantic and affectionate, and with an appreciative partner, your marriage will be enduring. The cheer you bring to each day's living can keep alive the dreams of youth and the spark of yesterday's happy memories. Male Sagittarians of the First Division are naturally adept at conveying their affection, whether verbally or by the many little gestures that make them such desirable lovers.

Their female counterparts are usually the best neighbors on the block, warm, discreet, and helpful. The same qualities make their children feel comfortable at home and reluctant to give up its supportive security for the false sophistication of teen-age fads. The result is great family harmony in a home that remains the center of everyone's life.

SAGITTARIUS–SECOND DIVISION
(November 29, December 2, 11, 20)

Your part in the cosmic drama of humanity's return to its Creator is a religious one. All the astrological influences upon your birth point to the same thing: a deep spirituality and profound philosophical outlook on life. This means that religion either already plays a vital role in your affairs or will soon do so, even if you now seem uninterested in it.

Your commitment may not be to a formal religion or a denominational creed. It might simply be a serenity of soul, an inexpressible communication with nature. You must find your own ways to express it, for it is such an essential element of your spirit that to suppress it would be to smother yourself and to live without purpose. You have been given:

- little desire for material things
- psychic faculties
- great creativity
- a compulsion to travel

Money and fame mean little to you, even when they come your

way almost effortlessly. It is to your credit that your successes don't change you in either attitudes or manner. Friends from your early years, who might not get as far in life as you, will still feel at ease with you. They know that your progress can't disrupt your ties of affection with them or replace your personal values with vain ambitions.

As you grow older, spiritual matters will become increasingly important to you, so much so that if you had lived in a different time and place, you might have become a hermit, contemplating the wonders of creation in your desert solitude. Today, however, the world needs your talents and your zeal. You are too valuable to shrink away from a troubled society, even when you find its materialism distasteful and its egotism offensive. We need you!

This may come as a surprise, but one of the reasons for your vital spirituality is the fact that you possess certain psychic faculties. Did you think such powers only come to a few, very special people, none of whom ever enter into your life? Quite the contrary! There are many individuals who have unusual gifts but who fail to realize how they have been blessed. Maybe you dismiss peculiar incidents of foresightedness as being mere hunches, good guesses, or lucky breaks. Don't be fooled. If you explore your psychic abilities, you can strengthen and apply them to problems in your own life and in the less fortunate lives of others. Your special powers enable you to guide others with prudent advice. I suspect you are already valued as a counselor by many people who ask you for your opinion about their most personal troubles. They may sense in you what you yourself don't yet see: a talent for anticipating the consequences of various decisions. In fact, the gift of prophecy has frequently been found among Sagittarians of the Second Division.

To make the most of this, and of all your other powers, you will need more confidence in yourself. Remember that the abilities you take for granted are prized by those with whom you deal, and so you should take pride in them. You are inclined to be submissive, following leaders who may not have the insight you possess. If you allow the seed of doubt to sprout and flourish in your mind, it will soon overgrow your better judgment and choke your personal independence. So cultivate faith in yourself; that confidence is necessary to the full utilization of your creative energy.

And creative you are! You may never compose music or poetry, may never paint or sculpt, but the appreciation of beauty and eagerness to participate in its development mark your work and your leisure. A Sagittarius Two will make original garments with a unique verve, turn a tiny backyard garden into a matchbox-sized Eden, have a hundred recipes for making great dishes out of hamburger. In all the little things of life, you apply your fancy for a better way, a fresher approach, an innovative method. And the result is an unpredictable flowering of creative spontaneity.

I don't want to encourage you to be artificially aggressive persons, but I do suggest you give your creativity its just due by being more open about your abilities. Step gracefully into the limelight when it comes your way. Remember that all your assets come from God, who didn't endow you with them so they could remain hidden. By denying your gifts, or neglecting them, you fail to do your part in accomplishing His plan for the world. So submerge your misgivings beneath an authentic sense of mission. Be bolder; in doing so, you will become more relaxed and outgoing.

Another trait you share with your Apostle is the urge to travel. As the Roman occupation of ancient Palestine worsened, thousands of Jews scattered across the lands around the Mediterranean Sea. Several of the Apostles traveled to the same places, keeping contacts in Jewish communities overseas, as well as establishing Christian churches among peoples of every language and nationality. James journeyed far, through incredible hardships and dangers, to carry Christ's message to anyone who would listen. Legend has it that he eventually reached Spain, the Roman province of Hispania, where he was martyred. To this day, he is the patron saint of that country, and in every Spanish-speaking land there are cities named after him: Santiago.

Today, you can travel with greater ease and may not even notice the religious drive behind your journeys. But you are apt to enjoy visiting shrines and probably find a special satisfaction in seeing for yourself the holy places of your faith.

COLORS: Your special combination of energy and quiet diffidence presents a visual poem: a mighty white horse resting peacefully in a lush green meadow. Use those colors to convey your personality to others. As a child of the armed centaur, express your spirit with mingled cream and moss, white and emerald, snow-bright boldness and grass-cool calm.

MONEY: Your indifference to material wealth makes you unconcerned about riches. But your concern for the needs of others can lead you to raise large sums for their benefit. So there should be no doubt about your abilities either as a wage earner or as a fund collector. Your financial dilemma is rooted not in your skills but in your will. Once you make up your mind to be prosperous, once you want to enjoy economic security, you will do so.

HEALTH: As is so often the case, the health of Sagittarius Twos reflects their attitudes. As long as you continue to repress your personality in favor of the dominance of others, you will be prone to minor illnesses and accidents. You are likely to be a food faddist, indulging in popular diets without heeding your doctor's advice. Once you set your mind on your own course, you will notice a new vigor in both body and intellect.

RELATIONSHIPS: Your introversion makes it difficult for you to pursue close relations with members of the opposite sex, and when you do attempt to force yourself into a more dynamic role, you are apt to bungle the effort through embarrassment. You may have to rely on friends to do your romantic groundwork for you, arranging introductions, and so forth. There's nothing wrong with that, and it can greatly assist you in preparing to strike out on your own.

Once you find someone who appreciates your merits, who is sufficiently sensitive to perceive all the good you keep hidden within yourself, you will be a loyal and sincere marriage partner. Your life together may not be exciting, but it will be enriching and ennobling. Within the chrysalis of your ideals, there is a spectacular butterfly waiting to take wing!

SAGITTARIUS—THIRD DIVISION
(November 30, December 3, 12, 21)

Yours is one of the brightest divisions of the Zodiac. It is filled with promise and potential, and all you have to do is use them. This doesn't mean you are guaranteed prominence or power or fame. It means only that they are within your reach if you have the will to grasp for them. You are:

- a leader
- enthusiastic
- dependable

- competent
- unmindful of yourself

A Sagittarius Three thrives on responsibility. Your role as a leader has been assigned to you from birth. Now you must apply your talents to the tasks for which they were intended. It may be easier to let others take the initiative, to avoid the responsibilities that come with positions of command; but you will never be happy that way. Your astrological character must be in the forefront of things for you to feel fulfilled.

The Apostle James was like you in this. He, too, was a leader, although not so able as Peter; and he enjoyed and sought after responsibility. Do you recall what he was doing when he saw Christ for the very first time? The son of Zebedee, the owner of a small fishing fleet, was down at the water's edge helping the hired hands mend their nets. It is the sure sign of a successful leader that he can perform the duties he assigns to others, that he readily takes up the slack they leave, that he considers no work too lowly for him. Because you share James's willingness to lend a hand and do more than your part, you can share as well his later role as a shaper of lives giant among men.

The best asset of any leader is a contagious enthusiasm. It doesn't drive followers on; it leads them by inspiration. It incites them to follow your example, and encourages them to outstrip your own efforts. That is why you will not rise to success over the devastated hopes of your colleagues. Rather, they will lift you to prominence willingly, as proud of you as you are grateful for their assistance.

Have you had the experience of being asked by your superiors to take on extra duties? Perhaps your teachers request your participation in extracurricular projects; your employer wants you to work overtime; your neighbors insist you represent the civic association at the town council meeting. In all these cases, those who know you recognize your dependability and overall competence. Once you establish a reputation for being reliable, it will precede you into new situations—a new job, an incipient romance, new business projects. That is one of the benefits of your determination to meet your obligations and fulfill your commitments.

You are able to live up to your reputation through your fine sense of organization. That is why you thrive on a career which requires you to juggle several factions, ventures, or ideas at one time.

Many Sagittarians of the Third Division find their best contentment in engineering, design, and construction because of the innumerable details that enter into every decision. Your strong points are coordination and synchronization, by which you bring together the mass of data and fit it effortlessly into a working whole.

For all those strengths, you do have one vulnerable weak spot. Though you are skilled at organizational tasks, you are often unable to organize the vital interests of your own life. Relegating your plans and dreams to a back burner, so to speak, you take life as it comes without a blueprint. You would never do that in building a construction project, but you tend to do it in building your future. But life does have a blueprint, whether we care to use it or not. In fact, this book is intended to make that very point and to direct you to the source of our life's true plan. Once you learn how to interpret it, then you will bring your own purposes into conjunction with your Creator's goals for you, and every good dream will come true.

COLORS: Third Division Sagittarians appear at their best when surrounded by blue; that color is both as strong as your leadership and as calm as your competence, as electric as your enthusiasm and as bland as your dependability. If it seems that blue can be all good things to all people, then you should accept that as a compliment! Remember that the shades of blue must be adjusted to your daily needs. A rousing speech at a political rally will require you to wear the forceful colors of a tumultuous sea, while a romantic occasion should be enhanced by your use of pale blue. And for your most dramatic moments, when your leadership is at its best and your words must fly swiftly and unerringly as the archer's shafts, try an outfit of midnight blue, accented by white, just as the midnight sky, brightened by light, reveals the constellation Sagittarius at its best.

MONEY: Your prospects are not poor, but neither can they be taken for granted. You must plan ahead early in life, or by the time you are looking forward to retirement you will realize that your lifestyle has eaten up your resources and left you economically insecure. Save your money, invest it in long-term projects, and consider land and transportation as suitable areas for your interest.

HEALTH: In general, you share the rugged constitutions of most Sagittarians. Few physical ailments will bother your early and middle years. But by your sixth or seventh decade, you will find your resistance to disease lowered. And if your economic situation is then worsening because of carelessness and inattention on your part, your financial burdens will interact with your illnesses to complicate your worries and intensify your distress. So it is essential that you take stock now and rearrange your finances toward increased frugality. Your mental and physical health will benefit from the changes.

RELATIONSHIPS: You are a natural teacher, and people will eagerly listen to you for hours. At a party, your conversation acts as a magnet to surround you with friends. Like all leaders who are generous with their advice and information, you will never lack for company.

At the same time, contradictory as it sounds, you will be bothered by the same shyness which troubles several other divisions of Sagittarius. You may be a charismatic personality in your official dealings, but in your intimate relationships, words may come slowly and emotions may be restrained. Even so, that will not seriously impair your romantic prospects. Like the archer's arrow flying unerringly to its target, you will meet and marry the partner you've always dreamed of, and the union will live up to all your hopes.

SAGITTARIUS—FOURTH DIVISION
(November 22, December 4, 13)

For Sagittarians of the Fourth Division, success will come like the arrow of the Archer who is your Zodiac symbol: swiftly, silently, and unexpectedly. It will be your responsibility to snatch it as it flies past. And you will, as long as you haven't taken your considerable talents for granted. By knowing yourself, exploring your strengths and weaknesses, you can increase your chances of knowing when and whence the arrow of advancement will fly at you. And the surest way to catch it is by being prepared to use its benefits for the general good of humanity.

That should be easy for you, for the list of your personality traits makes clear your potential for worthy contributions to the common good. You are:

- clever and intellectual
- imaginative

- independent
- withdrawn
- psychic

Your many positive characteristics are interrelated. For example, your alert and witty mind naturally makes you imaginative and daring, and those qualities in turn give you an independent spirit of intellectual and emotional autonomy. It seems as if you can hardly help but make your mark!

Even if your present work isn't an essentially mental endeavor, your intellectual precision helps in its execution. That means you can be a superb auto mechanic or repairman or chef, for the same cleverness that enables some Sagittarius Fours to solve scientific mysteries allows others to solve the intricate riddles of a malfunctioning engine or a complicated recipe. Have you ever watched a really good repairman approach a mechanical problem? He doesn't poke around to see what's wrong, but carefully considers first the possible causes and their remedies. He processes that information on the spot and arrives at an astute decision. No matter what field you choose, Sagittarian cleverness will be a priceless advantage.

All your talents combine to make you an independent sort. You like to think that you don't need the supportive encouragement of others, even those close to you. Relying on your mental powers, you seldom ask for others' opinions or their assessment of your work. This frees you from following the standards of other people, and in that respect it can be a liberating trait. But it can also trouble your life if you allow it to overrule your innate need for companionship. Here is your weak point! All your positive powers can combine to make you withdrawn from the world, and this can frustrate the Creator's purpose in giving you those gifts in the first place. Here is a fine example of the delicate balance between good and evil. I'm not suggesting that you are wicked, not at all! But, like all of us, you are free to turn your merits into vices. It is as if the devious fellow in the red boots has said, like one of the fairies at the christening of Sleeping Beauty, "Here is the gift I give, and its influence will negate all the other good ones." He has connived so that all your blessings can be dissipated by your tendency to lock yourself away in a private world of your rich imagination. Do that, and you will never realize your full, God-given potential.

It should be a consolation to you that James had to make the same decision. It may have been easier for him because he had a very determined brother to help him go the right way. Your first step should be to recognize candidly that you have powerful qualities which are not fully developed. The second step is to take reasonable measures to turn those abilities outward, to put them at the service of those around you. Finally, in order to maximize your impact on others, learn to speak a little more forcefully. You have been whispering your demands for freedom of thought and action. Start to shout them! Walk onto center stage once in a while. Display your real personality; and then when happiness or love bursts upon the scene, you will be prepared to seize them as they come. You will snatch the arrows of fate right out of the air!

It is likely that you have already been endowed with a power that can make others sit up and notice you, a power which can lead you out of your intense privacy and bring out your best traits. You probably have great psychic gifts. Of all Sagittarians, you are most likely to be involved in occult pursuits. Even if you denigrate your gifts and feel uneasy about their effects, even if you are embarrassed to admit that you possess unusual abilities of vision and perception, those powers will not go away. You may realize that your odd dreams were actually warnings of future events, that your anticipation of a surprise visit or an important communication was no coincidence. Once you face up to your gifts and explore their impact, then you will take over the limelight and use all your abilities as they were intended.

COLORS: Here is a perfect way to bring yourself out of your shell! Think of your mental abilities as the golden arrows of the archer-centaur. Think of your emotions as his bronzed hoofs, churning the sky with their spirited gallop. Then use the whole range of yellows to remind yourself of your powers and to escape the stultifying withdrawal that can weaken them. Even in your private moments, a lemony tie or buttercup scarf or golden wallpaper in your living room can alert you to the stimulating benefits of social involvement.

MONEY: At best, your income will appear in intermittent spurts. Your casual attitude about savings will repeatedly bring you to hard times, because money won't always appear when you need it. This is especially true when you play the shrinking violet and fail to push yourself forward to success. I suggest you do two things to better your economic prospects. First, be more aggressive in securing the financial rewards that are rightfully yours. Second, invest in long-term secure projects when you do have money. That will tide you over when the going gets rough.

HEALTH: Unlike your fellow archers, you probably don't enjoy a vigorous constitution. Respiratory and digestive ailments are your most frequent ills. But watch for abrupt improvement in your health once you decide to take the world by storm. The determination you can bring to your affairs can simultaneously strengthen your physical condition and relieve, almost overnight, your chronic complaints.

RELATIONSHIPS: No man or woman is an island. As long as you attempt to withdraw from relationships, you will feel frustrated and restless. Your purpose in being on this earth is to help unify mankind into one tremendous brotherhood of the spirit. So come out from your mental corners and unleash your talents. Once you begin to reveal them, you will have no difficulty in making friends.

Romance is difficult for a retiring Sagittarius Four. But as you mature, especially after your thirtieth birthday, you are apt to present a new face to the world. And your marriage after that age will be a good one, even if an earlier attempt at wedded life has failed you. An appreciative spouse, who recognizes the wonders of your intellectual vitality, will make your long wait for a happy home a small price to pay for its benefits.

SAGITTARIUS—FIFTH DIVISION
(November 23, December 5, 14)

The confluence of planetary forces at your birth has given you, at least potentially, a giant of an intellect. Your inherent brilliance is balanced, and could even be outweighed, by a restless and far-ranging spirit. You probably have great difficulty in pursuing any single interest for any length of time. Both your mind and body are always on the move. Mentally, you leap from one subject to another. Needless to say, this can dissipate your brain power. It can fritter away the priceless gift of intelligence on a variety of incomplete projects.

Your success in life will relate directly to your ability to apply yourself to the task before you. You already know that when you want to, you can bring tremendous concentration to your endeavors. Learn to extend that time span. Learn to work at one chore an extra hour, then two, until your impressive mental faculties can be concentrated in prolonged attention. One day, you will wake up and realize what a formidable weapon is at your disposal. For in addition to your acute mind, you are:

- ambitious
- impulsive
- impatient
- romantic

Your best incentive to concentrate on your work and curb your intellectual wanderlust will be your ambition. Sooner or later, you will realize that unless you buckle down to serious effort for a career, you will not attain your rather grand goals in life. Your ambition would be even stronger than it now is if it hadn't been blunted in your youth. You were probably so much better equipped than your teen-age contemporaries to deal with life that you came to take for granted your effortless early advancement. It won't always be so, however, so you'd better prepare for the day when you begin to fall behind.

If you now look at your career and feel you are not as far along the road to success as you should be, blame the shortfall on your restlessness and impulsive nature. Think back over the last few years and remember those many occasions when you have judged a person, for good or ill, too quickly. Recall the situations into which you have rushed, unsure of their details and disregarding the possible complications. Individually, these mistakes may not be disasters; you can get over them, extricating yourself with your powerful mind. But cumulatively, they can slow down your march to happiness. They can weigh you down with so many little burdens that you stagger under their load.

By the same token, your restlessness can be directed outward, demanding from others the same hurried rush through life. Your impatience can not only disrupt your health; it can also damage relationships, for few people will be willing to accept your demands for speedier service and a more hectic reaction. Worst of all, you may sorely offend those who can't keep up with you intellectually. Disdaining their slowness, you may scorn them as unworthy of your attention. By doing so, you will free yourself from their tardy pace but will also lose much of the peace and most of the beauty of life.

In love, you are more fortunate. You are a softy at heart, a real romantic, who will go to great lengths to please someone you care for. It is as if, in matters of the heart, you find a respite from the driving ambition of everyday life. Your romances are oases to refresh your spirit, haggard as it is from the impulsive zest with which you charge into every challenge. Although an early marriage is a mistake for you, you will usually continue wearing the same rose-colored spectacles to view your spouse as you wore to view your sweetheart. I think you understand what I mean, and I know your wedded life will be tolerably happy.

All in all, we might say that you have a positive attitude toward life, as long as life doesn't take too long about things! Think of ways your energy, once harnessed, could be directed to the noblest causes. With you in command, a charity fund drive will surpass its goals. Once you learn to accept the shortcomings of others, your commitment to advancement can make you the rare teacher who incites students to push ahead faster than they think they can. And through it all, your romantic spirit will soar over every obstacle, certain that if love doesn't conquer all, then at least nothing has yet conquered love!

COLORS: Colors can help to curb your instability. When you must focus on a single task, surround yourself with a single color. It might even be a good idea to have one small room of your home totally decorated in one light, pastel shade; there you could more easily accomplish those chores you've been postponing: finishing your tax reports, reading that novel, writing the dozen letters you should have sent last month, completing that half-sewn suit, even thinking through those vague ideas you want to explore to their ultimate conclusions. I suspect you will find that a pale, blushing violet combines both the quiet you need and the hint of passionate impulse in the real you. So use it generously, both in your clothes and in your home décor.

MONEY: Sagittarians of the Fifth Division almost always make money in large amounts because they have excellent intuition concerning investments. But you seldom respect the real value of your wealth and spend it altogether too freely. By restraining your financial excesses now, you will be able to anticipate a comfortable old age. Recklessness today, on the other hand, will bring sorrow and need tomorrow.

HEALTH: Other than certain dental problems in your middle years, you should face no serious ailments. I sense that your eating habits leave much to be desired, and they may have something to do with your later oral trouble. To avoid it, closely examine your present diet, as well as your impulsiveness at the table. Your tendency to bolt your food and rush for the door will lead to digestive complaints in your late thirties.

RELATIONSHIPS: Beware of the way you exercise your wit at the expense of others. Your quick mind can lean to sarcasm, partly as a form of intellectual amusement. But it can make you enemies, for even those who admire your gifts can be offended to the quick by one of your clever, but unfeeling, remarks.

It may seem peculiar that that handicap is not present in your romantic affairs. You wouldn't think of turning your inventive humor against the one you love. There is a deep reason for this, and it can help you all your life. When you are with your beloved, you feel perfectly secure. There is no need for you to perform, to demonstrate your mental prowess. Accepted as you are, you can let your calmed nature come through. Now, if you can just apply that to the rest of your life, your brilliance can subordinate your restlessness and send you darting toward the target of your dreams.

SAGITTARIUS–SIXTH DIVISION
(November 24, December 6, 15)

Your life promises to be pleasant and easygoing, because your personality attracts friends and admirers who bask in the sunshine of your cheerfulness and charm. You are one of the nice people, who help the rest of us get through a difficult week with your conviviality and spark. You are:

- a mixer
- a good host or hostess
- a lover of travel
- a community focal point

Your talents as a social star have a peculiarly advantageous trait: you tend not only to mix well on your own social level but also to get along with celebrities. It is as if you not only remain at ease around the great and famous but your relaxed approach to them also puts them at ease and reassures them they won't be gawked at or treated with unnerving deference. That's why you are never intimidated by bosses, never cowed by teachers, and don't hesitate to ask the most popular person in your class for a date.

I believe you share this characteristic with the Apostle James, for his father, Zebedee, was a prominent individual in his community. And he must have introduced his children while they were young to the great men of the land, so that by the time James accepted his mission from Christ, he feared no man and dared to preach his faith to the mighty as well as the lowly. Because James was adept at handling people in different situations, he was a natural leader among the Apostolic band; and in the Scriptural listings of their fellowship, he is always listed among the most important three or four of them.

Considering your combined astrological and Apostolic pedigrees, it is no wonder that you are a superb host! Even if you have little money, your taste is the best. Your home may be sparsely furnished with secondhand goods, but their colors and styles harmonize nicely. You are that special individual who even in old clothes retains a dignified bearing; you know that a person's worth comes from within rather than from external display. And if you have money, your life-style may be elegant but never extravagant. Your menus may be rich but not garish; and, most important, your friends may be poor or powerful, but they will rarely be boorish or arrogant.

I believe that the reason your social sense is so acute, the reason you can put almost anyone at ease with a handshake and a smile, is that you are a lover of peace, not only in the world but in your personal relationships. The hint of antagonism is enough to concern you. Ignoring arguments, forgetting offenses, you can make unpleasantness disappear and even bring old enemies together, at least when you are at your best. I needn't remind you of the lesson which James heard taught by Him who originated it. You peacemakers, blessed as you are, have a special role to play in human affairs; and it brings you special rewards.

There is a dualism about you. Women of the Sixth Division often marry twice, sometimes radically different partners. Their male counterparts frequently have two incomes, and their relaxation is apt to be a far cry from their daily work. For example, those who work in offices may spend their weekends in the most arduous pursuits, even climbing mountains or shooting the rapids. It is quite common for Sagittarius Sixes to have two residences, perhaps a vacation cottage in addition to their regular home. Why a vacation cottage? Because you Sixes love to travel! Even the Apostle James, traversing the ancient Mediterranean in his mission of enlightenment, didn't exceed your passion for moving about and seeing new sights. It is quite possible that you will marry someone from another land. It isn't unusual to meet a Sagittarius Six with a Deep South accent whose mate speaks with a Yankee twang. In a way, you bring disparities together and make a harmonious whole of them.

Having heard all this, you shouldn't be at all surprised to be told that you have the capacity to be a community focal point, the center of neighborhood action and the energy source for innumerable civic projects. Because you think quickly and in unconventional ways, always respecting intelligence in others, even if they lack formal education, you can bring together a team of very different individuals whose combined talents can be invincible.

Of course, this touches upon your role as the host or hostess with the most or mostest. Persons involved in social and professional events appreciate your hospitality, even if it involves only a glass of lemonade shared with your bridge club while discussing local school problems. I see your home as the meeting place for inquiring, challenging minds. No wonder you love to bring them together!

COLORS: The appropriate use of colors can be a great help to you in your vital activities as a peacemaker and social leader. Even a modest party on a tight budget becomes a spectacular affair when your wit and verve run free in decorating your home with the colors that magnify your personal aura of dignified exuberance. The real you is as emotionally lavish as a rose-red sunset, as coolly in control as the deep purple sky that nightly puts out the sun. I suspect that females of the Sixth Division already see their best color schemes; and if it is difficult for you men to appear in crimson or violet suits, remember that your tie, your scarf, even the flower in your buttonhole on special occasions can all convey your Sagittarian spirits.

MONEY: Especially in the early years of your career, money problems will be far from your mind. Later on, when you realize you have been too lavish with your good fortune, economic difficulties will be unavoidable. Even large sums of money, coming to you through marriage, legacies, and gifts, will not keep you from regretting your excessive expenditures unless you start now to prepare for a rainy day.

HEALTH: Your excellent constitution can be weakened only by too much high living in your youth. It is possible for even a strong fire to burn out by being too bright. It is wise for you to have frequent medical checkups, for your busy life-style and extensive socializing can lead to digestive trouble and a disposition to illnesses.

RELATIONSHIPS: Your inner need to feel free can lead you to range widely in your choice of friends and lovers. You must be cautious in your choice of a partner, for your social whirl will bring you into contact with a great many attractive and desirable people. It's possible to be blinded by sexual attraction, and you of the Sixth Division are especially susceptible to that handicap. Remember that your spouse will have to be not just physically delightful but also a match for your intellectual leanings.

You relate best to people who can offer you a challenge and teach you new things. Most of your friends fall into that category, and your best marital chances follow along the same lines.

SAGITTARIUS—SEVENTH DIVISION

(November 25, December 7, 16)

As a Sagittarius Seven, you not only stand at the crossroads of life, you practically live there! Your development is a series of crucial decisions, most of them pertaining to the recurring choice of being either a doer or a dreamer. If you choose your direction early in life and stay with it, you will not go astray from your appointed path, no matter which direction you follow.

In the pattern of things, you are equally useful to God's design for the world as doer or dreamer, as activist or contemplative. I want to stress this point because it is often not understood that a life of vigorous accomplishment isn't necessarily preferable to one of quiet meditation and unspoken aspirations. You are one of those rare persons who can try on both life-styles for size and pick whichever fits you more comfortably. Your birth planets have made you:

- submissive or aggressive
- gentle or tyrannical
- dependable or irresponsible

To confuse matters still more, you can't be assured of receiving a neat personality package of all the first or all the second qualities. You might be both submissive and irresponsible or a dependable tyrant, if you see what I mean. The arrangement of those items, as flexible as the choices in a family-style Chinese dinner, is up to you. And it is likely that your pattern will be set, although not rigidly, early in life. You needn't live out your days frozen into the pattern you so early adopted, however. Whether you are inclined to a gentle and poetic view of the world or to a commanding insistence upon your own desires, you can temper your attitudes to reach a more moderate position, what the ancient Greeks called "the golden mean."

In fact, the gentler aspects of your nature need to become bolder, for you are all too often swept off your feet by a stronger personality. In romance, this can be heartbreaking. In business, it can lead to bankruptcy. Worst of all, whenever you allow another mind to do your thinking for you, you waste your best talents. If you stand at your many crossroads waiting for someone to pick your direction, you will miss your appointments with destiny. Part of the triumph comes from finding your own way, relying on others for their advice but reserving the final decisions for yourself.

On the other hand, when you feel yourself acting as a petty master, ordering others around without regard for their wants and opinions, you must loosen up a little on the archer's bowstring. You will find that your nerves also loosen, and with the greater relaxation will come a better appreciation of the rights and feelings of those you would otherwise tyrannize.

I hardly need to explain your other set of contradictory traits. When you are dependable, there is no one more faithful to duty and obligations. You can be the secretary whom the bosses allow to virtually run their company in their absence or the parent whose children are the most secure in the neighborhood, knowing that their every need is understood and attended to. On the other hand, if you repeatedly succumb to your irresponsible leanings, you can be a plague to your colleagues at work, pushing your chores off onto them. Your family situation will be still worse, for your loved ones will find that your commitments are like poorly aimed arrows, launched by a rather giddy centaur. Beware of this habit, for someday those erratic darts might gravely wound someone through your careless disregard of your responsibilities.

At your best, you can prevent that from ever happening. Indeed, at your very best, you can rise above all the bother and enmities of the world to shape your future fearlessly and independently. Seeking out the unusual, especially when you dare to be the dreamer you were born to be, you will arouse suspicion and jealousy. I recall the case of a Sagittarius Seven who, as a boy, decided to become a professional ballet dancer. His youth would have been easier if he'd professed an intent to overthrow the government! But he survived opposition and mockery both from his family and from strangers, worked as a newsboy and supermarket clerk to pay for his lessons, and now is a prominent choreographer. His wife is proud of him; for he has always been, first and foremost, true to himself. Learn from his experience.

COLORS: As with several other divisions of Sagittarius, the whole range of purples, light and dark, flatters your appearance and emphasizes your magnetism, whether you are in a gentle mood or one of your more aggressive phases. I do recommend for you dual spirits of the Seventh Division a special expression of your ambivalent nature. Jade green is especially favorable for you, but ever so much better is actual jewelry made of real or simulated jade.

This requires some explanation. The next time you have an opportunity to examine a piece of jade—a necklace, tie pin, ring, or statue—look closely at its delicate marbling. At first, you may not even notice that it is not a solid color but a subtle blend of lighter and darker shades, sometimes streaked through with white. In its deep recesses is the symbolic representation of your shifting dualism. For both men and women of the Seventh Division, it is an apt sign of their astrological character.

MONEY: Your income will probably be derived from unusual sources. Although you will be on a payroll from time to time (and would be wise to use that security to prepare for less comfortable circumstances), you are likely to receive occasional payments, in significant sums, from another source. They may be royalties or lecturing fees or patent rights. We should allow the dreamer in you to find out the reason for those windfalls.

HEALTH: A Sagittarius Seven is usually high-strung, and this can affect your health adversely. If you've been suffering from headaches, defective vision, digestive problems, and dental pain, by all means see your physician. And if he tells you you must relax and give your nervous system a rest, remember what I told you about making sensible decisions at the crossroads of your life.

RELATIONSHIPS: Your relish for the unusual will lead you into several rather odd friendships, but their variety and eccentricity will add spice to your other acquaintances. In your aggressive moments, you may drive off people who just cannot cope with a commanding personality. It is especially important in your career that you remember to harness that domineering stallion within you. Those with whom you work, even in the arts and other expressive fields, won't tolerate a tyrant for long.

Your strong sexual attraction may lead you into amorous relationships which in hindsight will seem humorous and frivolous. But at the moment, they will be troublesome and embarrassing. In this respect, you must learn, perhaps the hard way, to restrain that impulsive centaur of Sagittarius.

Marriage can be a wondrous experience for you or a disaster. The outcome depends on how well your mind and your partner's are adapted to each other's needs. Your physical relationship will not be a problem, but it is more vital that your intellectual liaison be mutually rewarding. Remember that the next time you are swept off your feet by a pretty face or a ruggedly handsome suitor.

SAGITTARIUS—EIGHTH DIVISION
(November 26, December 8, 17)

Life can be a long, hard road for Sagittarians of the Eighth Division, but you in that sign are eminently equipped to deal with the problems that arise. And at the end of your arduous journey, you will find rich rewards of personal growth and spiritual harmony. Your astrological pattern indicates rather difficult early years at the start of your career. You may think there will never be an end to the obstacles in your way, and it is even possible that you will give in to despair, that "carrion comfort," as the poet Gerard Manley Hopkins called it.

That would be the worst action you could take, and I will trust in your common sense and persistence to get you through the bad times into the sunshine of your better days. There is every reason for you to push ahead, for your characteristics indicate an ability to reach in time whatever goals you set for yourself. You have:

- great endurance
- conscientiousness
- thoughtfulness
- reserve

There are, of course, different kinds of endurance. There is the stamina that keeps some people running in a marathon race despite their pain. There is the emotional hardiness that allows others to take abuse and disappointments without renouncing their commitments to persons and ideals. And there is a subtler kind of endurance, which strengthens you, not just in moments of crisis but over long periods of doubt and uneasiness. Although you are probably blessed with all the varieties, the last is your specialty. Through years of slow progress, during which your dreams fade away and your youthful hopes wither, you can keep on keeping on, as if you know you will eventually move into a second youth.

And indeed you will! Unlike some adventurers who searched for the Fountain of Youth, you know that your character, more than your dress or language, determines your age. As long as your principles are fresh and untarnished, then your words and deeds have the force of teen-age vitality. That's the lesson you can teach others through your diligence. Conscientious to a fault, you think of others' needs before considering your own. You may not even know how much your kindnesses have been appreciated; all too often people don't express their thanks with words. Perhaps it's just as well; you would prefer that no one fuss over your virtues. You just take for granted that everyone does what he or she can.

Sometimes, however, you do more than you should. Admirable as your concern for the feelings of other people is, it inclines you to too great a sensitivity, too rapid concessions, too much compromise and conciliation. Your valid interests can be sacrificed, and your fear of offending others can make you indecisive and erode your confidence. That would be tragic, for your positive characteristics need to be emphasized and contributed to the general good, not hidden under the bushel of your uncertainties. By all means, continue to be thoughtful and considerate, but also be optimistic about yourself. Do you keep apologizing to your colleagues or fellow students, as if every mistake that happens is your fault? Subconsciously, you are trying to maintain harmony within your group, and you are offering up your own self-esteem as a sacrifice for peace. That's a case of splendid intentions and foolish decisions. Believe me, the best avenue for your thoughtfulness is not reticence but boldness. Be more forward in offering your help and more insistent that your assistance is valuable.

Sagittarius Eights usually succeed in their chosen professions through their qualities of diligence and endurance. No wonder! In an age when many people have rejected what they call the "work ethic" in favor of concentrated leisure, you are a prized employee and an excellent supervisor. You know how to encourage others to work hard through the best incentive: your own example.

The same qualities will ensure your marital success. You will work at making a happy home; and while the marriages of more glamorous and debonair couples crumble apart, yours will flourish like a well-rooted plant exposed to twenty-four hours of sunshine. True to your customary form of being well prepared, you are the kind of individual who studies books about marriage, including its physical, psychological, and economic problems, long before you meet the person you intend to wed. Because you are always prepared for the worst, you can not only cope with it, but also with the best when it comes along.

It is your habit to back away from arguments. You anticipate unpleasantness and avoid it. That's a solid asset, because your pattern can be contagious. Those associated with you can pick up, as if by instinct, your way of minimizing rancor. That's why your relationships, slight or serious, tend to be altogether harmonious.

There is an important piece of advice hidden in your star chart. The years between your twenty-fifth and fortieth birthdays may find you occasionally depressed, feeling that your goals are slipping farther away from you. At those times, keep up your spirits! Persistence will lead to a radical change in your situation. Let me put it this way: don't stop reaching for the stars, for the stars are reaching for you. And when your years of hard work do pay off, all the long endeavor will have been worth the effort.

COLORS: Your endurance shows even in the colors that best suit your personality: the substantial yellow of hammered gold and the rich tone of freshly smelted bronze. Your reserved nature, however, will keep you from being too free with those shades, and you'll feel more comfortable when you balance them with darker colors, especially a purple as deep as your own kindness, as lush as your generosity, as princely as the gift of your concern. Centaur that you are, if you have ever seen a performing circus horse, decked out in trappings of violet and gold, you will know exactly how to express your powerful presence through the dramatic combination of your best colors.

MONEY: The typical pattern for your astrological combination is to accumulate money slowly but steadily. You handle finances conservatively, although in your youthful days, you probably had some memorable spending sprees. An exception to your caution is your habit of loaning money to relatives. Here your thoughtfulness takes command over your prudence, and you may well be stuck with one or more uncollectable debts. Later in life, when you are more than comfortable with your income and savings, you will be a particularly tempting mark for those who want to exploit your good nature. While you can continue to be kind, you must learn to be careful, too.

HEALTH: Although your constitution is generally sound, your resistance to emotional stress is low. The resulting upset when you must face prolonged tension or cope with personal bitterness can cause you digestive and skin problems. Just take life a little slower, relaxing more than you now do, and watch your health flourish in the physical hardiness that is the natural condition of the centaur.

RELATIONSHIPS: Because you avoid friction and conflict, you may be ignored by people who would find your companionship delightful. Of course, some others are merely contemptuous of anyone who doesn't stand up to them, and they aren't worth your worry. But do be more positive in your dealings with others. By insisting upon more respect, you will earn it and will find new, warm friendships as a result.

Your marriage prospects are excellent, but your courting days may be somewhat difficult. Your reserve makes you wary of anyone who seems too interested in you, and you may walk away from potentially happy relationships because you fear their emotional entanglement. Take your time. Your caution ensures that you won't wed on impulse, and that will be all to the good over the long run.

SAGITTARIUS–NINTH DIVISION
(November 27, December 9, 18)

The Ninth Division is the powerhouse of Sagittarius. You who were born under its influence are suited for life as a leader. As you will be the first to take command, so will you also be the first to attract hostility. You tower above your fellows, not only like a mighty oak but also like a lightning rod; and so you must expect to get more than your share of jolts!

Because of your superabundant energy, you will sometimes be considered reckless and headstrong. Look into yourself and you will see the better truth. What some people mistake for bullishness is really a sense of mission, a determination to fulfill your purpose in life. With all your powerful characteristics, there is every reason to expect you will indeed do so. You are:

- ambitious and forceful
- coolheaded and determined
- outspoken and diligent

The reason for your success, whether already achieved or waiting for you in the future, is that you apply your ambition to worthwhile causes. There is something deep within you that tells you whether the particular goals you are pursuing will ennoble or degrade you, and as long as you adjust your sights accordingly, there will be little that can halt your progress.

More than most people, you feel acutely the need for challenges, both intellectual and physical. The sports you most enjoy are those demanding rigorous discipline of both mind and body. Whatever you do, whether it's playing a tennis match against a pro or putting golf balls in your backyard, you must do it with total involvement. Nothing less than perfection is your standard for yourself. No wonder you can hardly be prevented from reaching whatever heights you aspire to.

A necessary adjunct to your insatiable urge to strive and accomplish is a cool mastery in emergencies. Like Moses before Pharaoh, you are unafraid to speak your mind, politely but firmly, especially if you see an injustice. You would walk up to the principal of your school and register a strong protest against unfair regulations. You would tell your superiors in the armed forces why you disagree with their decisions. You could sit before a Senate investigating committee and, without batting an eyelash, tell its members why they are wrong. Needless to say, you are often involved in controversy, and you love it! To you, it is only another form of challenge, and you approach it with the same confident sense of being in charge that a skilled lion tamer feels when he enters the cage of snarling beasts.

Because of your determination and need for new horizons to explore, you enjoy travel and engage in it as much as the Apostle James. In another age, you would have been one of those daring adventurers who discovered new lands, always ranging farther afield than was considered wise. In today's world, you might be a researcher in a laboratory, always looking a few steps ahead of the latest scientific data, or the volunteer fireman who is always first on the scene of a fire. Whatever your occupation, your venturesome sense of discovery keeps you a little out in front of your colleagues. You would be unhappy anywhere else!

Of course, your outspokenness can reach an extreme, as can any good thing. It is one thing to raise your voice in protest when a serious injustice is perpetrated; but when you raise a fuss over every minor irregularity—every one of life's innumerable inequities—then, like the boy who cried wolf once too often, you will lose your credibility, and your ideals will suffer for it.

In all your traits, you Sagittarius Nines are like your Apostle. Ambitious James, who had once sought a special position in Christ's kingdom, was so determined to spread the Word of the Lord that he traveled throughout the known world, carrying the Gospel with him. Undaunted by the high and mighty, facing the most severe retaliation for speaking his mind, he could be silenced only by death. Ignoring all threats, just as you do at your best, he adhered to his mission.

Today's Sagittarius Nines aren't likely to be called upon for such a sacrifice, although in this rapidly changing world we live in, who can tell what challenges you may face tomorrow and at the end of this century? In any case, you are always willing to pay the price for your ideals; and sometimes the cost is ostracism, scorn, mockery, even hatred. In a way, that is today's martyrdom, and you gladly accept it to preserve your principles.

It should be obvious that your great qualities of moral and physical courage are the key to why you were put on earth. As a leader, you are also meant to be an inspiration. Your part in the mosaic of human life is especially important, because once it slips into place, many other pieces will find their proper positions as well. What that means is this: by your example, you can teach others to reach out for the great and good things you yourself pursue. Sounds simple, doesn't it? But the doing, as you know, is never as easy as the saying!

COLORS: Of course, your colors reflect your magnetic traits. For several reasons, your best shades are vivid red and crimson. For one thing, those are the colors of passion, and your life is certainly streaked with it. Those are also appropriate expressions of your tendency to wear your heart on your sleeve, so to speak, vocally sympathizing with every victim of injustice. Though your coolness under fire doesn't give out scarlet vibrations, your determination to stand up for your beliefs certainly does. You are today's Christopher Columbus, forging ahead into new worlds with a blazing banner like the one he carried, the crimson flag of Queen Isabella.

For days when you feel more subdued, and for occasions when you realize you must restrain your more enthusiastic tendencies, by all means mute the spectrum of reds. Use rose and pink, even peach, to make both your words and your emotions gentler. This applies to both men and women of the Ninth Division, for a male Sagittarius Nine may be especially helped by the mildness of a pink tie or a rose sport jacket.

MONEY: Every astral indication shows that you will do well financially. A new and unexpected enterprise, in which you are likely to invest during your middle years, will quickly succeed and enable you to sell out your holdings at a great profit. Because, in general, you perform better in dealing with ideas rather than products, try to choose a career which will test your intellect rather than your personality or strength.

HEALTH: Those Sagittarius Nines born on the two December dates of this division face more health problems than their brethren born on the single November date. Always needing to be doing something, you tend to neglect your own well-being. You postpone doctors' appointments and often neglect to take prescribed medication. You will appear to be in top condition as you enter your forties, but then your health may wear down rapidly as the unnecessary strains of your youth catch up with you. That scenario of later sickness can be avoided. All you need to do is to start now, by pacing yourself more slowly, to preserve your centaur's vigor through relaxation and rest.

RELATIONSHIPS: You will earn the respect of those who know you and the animosity of those who do not. Your shining success is bound to provoke jealousy from petty souls, while noble individuals, no matter what their social and economic status may be, will wish you well because you treat them with dignity. Forget the criticisms of professional grumblers. Take comfort in the many solid friendships you have, even among people who disagree with your views but admire your selfless defense of what you think is right.

Your marriage will probably be a good one—or two. There is a definite chance that you will share your life with more than a single person, whether your first union is disrupted by divorce or death. That's just a possibility, of course, so don't anticipate the worst! Your perfect mate will be someone who loves to travel and enjoys a hectic pace through life. It will be helpful if he or she relishes company as much as you do because your home will always be a social center. That's only to be expected when its resident is a widely known leader in both professional and civic endeavors.

CAPRICORN—MATTHEW

(December 22–January 19)

Just as the patterns of the heavens are ever changing and yet ever faithful to the designs of their Creator, so do the innumerable personalities of mankind always provide us with something new, something different, while reflecting their Creator's intention that His glory be revealed in each of them. So it is that as the astrological influences of Sagittarius wane in late December, a very different combination of forces takes their place. The exuberance and joviality of the shooting centaur give way to markedly contrasting characteristics under the sign of Capricorn.

This is the sign of the horned Goat, and that symbol is most appropriate for those born under its sway. For they are apt to be alert, calculating, prudent, a little aloof, austerely independent, sometimes haughty, and frequently rigid in their adherence to set customs and traditions. They walk the most difficult pathways of life with the ease of the mountain goat, nimbly leaping from crag to crag. They scale the heights of success with the effortless assurance of the Alpine chamois, that delicate creature which romps around the mountaintops to the amazement of exhausted human climbers.

The person whom I saw in my vision as the embodiment of Capricorn's traits and attitudes was Matthew, and his presence among Christ's followers provided not only diversity but controversy as well. Matthew was the least likely candidate for an Apostleship that his contemporaries could have imagined. Though he was a Jew, he worked for the Romans, gathering their taxes from his own people. As you can imagine, this made him a social outcast. He not only collaborated with the invaders but also gathered money from his own people to help the hated occupying forces. Perhaps his ambition, typical of Capricorns, led him to seek official favor. Perhaps his desire for financial success, another trait of his Zodiac sign, explains his conduct. Perhaps he merely decided that someone had to do the job, or else the Romans would do it themselves much more harshly. Whatever the reason, Matthew must have been startled when Christ approached him at his table, probably in a marketplace customs post where he was collecting official levies from travelers or merchants. Christ didn't let Matthew's background dissuade Him from extending His solemn invitation. Knowing there was something more to this unpopular tax man, He called him to learn His words and thereafter to teach them to the world.

Much the same thing can be said of you Capricorns of today. There is more to you than meets the eye. You are the proverbial still waters that run deep. It's as if you are perched high on a craggy precipice, like the contemplative Angora goat of the Caucasus Mountains; only you and others of your mystic tribe know the location, amid your frozen rocks, of the remains of Noah's Ark. Keeping your secrets to yourself, you disregard the judgments others make about you and pursue your own goals in your own misunderstood ways.

No wonder, then, that you are individualists, independent in your views, determined in your decisions once you have made them in the privacy of your mind. This doesn't mean you are headstrong or reckless. For those absolute choices of yours, fixed and final, are reached only after extremely prudent debate with yourself. Like a mountain goat standing for hours on a cliff's edge, silently eyeing the best possible footholds and pitfalls, you take great time to assess your direction and then suddenly leap toward your goal. Just as naturalists marvel at the goat's ability to traverse seemingly impassable walls of stone, so, too, people marvel at your talent for jumping over obstacles and scrambling over opposition or resistance.

Capricorns have a special liking for money and great ability in handling it profitably, usually turning it to noble purposes. They therefore make superb managers for investment companies and administrators of estates. Always ready to take a chance, you may relish gambling and rather risky speculation, not so much for possible profits as for the excitement and test of your wits. Because of your shrewd and calculating nature, even chancy ventures usually prove successful.

That means you are usually on the lookout for a promotion or salary increase. You may hop from one job to another, always looking for better financial remuneration, just like the capricious mountain goat leaps from rock to rock, higher and higher up the slope, in search of the next juicy patch of grass. In fact, the very word "capricious" is related to the Latin *"caper,"* meaning—you guessed it!—goat.

This needn't be a weakness, for your usual pattern is to select your most successful career rather late in life. If you hadn't explored the whole mountain, you would never have come across those opportunities which enable you to make the fullest use of your talents. Remember that Matthew never dreamed that his accounting books would be put aside in favor of a religious mission to all mankind. He took the chance of giving up the security and wealth of his job and, in so doing, gained a much richer future than he at first understood. In the same way, your best achievements will probably come from an unexpected career in rather unusual work.

I'm assuming, of course, that you will be alert for your opportunities when they come. Remember this: no mountain goat can leap safely from height to height wearing red boots! Their leaden weight would trip and hobble every jump. At those times in your life when you imagine yourself perched on the brink of tremendous decisions, as you gaze out over the eternity before you, make sure your agile feet are free of entrapment. For if you try to climb to success in those glamorous, but clumsy, boots, you will suffer the fate of a foolish or reckless Ethiopian ibex. When you reach for the starry heights, you will slip and fall into a horrendous gorge. And just as the world is diminished by the loss of even one of those almost extinct princes of the animal kingdom, so, too, would humanity be poorer by losing you.

Although Capricorns are individualistic and sometimes isolated persons, they nonetheless make excellent hosts. Especially when you are entertaining a large number of guests, your social skills are at their best. You would rather have a seated dinner for twenty than a brunch for four. It's as if the challenge of the affair is more important than the occasion itself. Not surprisingly, many Capricorns function superbly as the social directors of resort hotels, as chefs in hotels, and as professional advisers for the large-scale soirees that are becoming too rare in our society.

That doesn't mean you are a social butterfly; far from it! Your gatherings must have a purpose in addition to eating and chatting. Idle small talk isn't your pastime. Your parties may advance your business dealings, your social causes, your political interests, or your cultural concerns. You will be promoting a certain candidate, arguing in favor of various civic improvements, learning details of the current financial situation, even exploring unusual fields of knowledge with your guests who are expert in them. Many of your entertainments are actually fund raisers, and it is those which most satisfy you; for then, even your amusements contribute to worthy efforts. Later in life, as you approach your goals, you will find that your associates, your hosts, your guests are persons who rank as celebrities in their respective fields. You will, of course, entertain them as graciously as you always greeted your guests, no matter what their background or status.

Matthew did just that. Upon Christ's invitation to follow Him, he quit his post as tax collector, renouncing its lucrative benefits, and threw a party at his house to celebrate the change in his life's direction and meaning. Naturally, his new Teacher was the guest of honor. The events of that party are important for your self-understanding. Many of Matthew's friends were collaborators with the Romans, for most patriotic Jews wouldn't associate with him. These were the persons invited to his banquet for Jesus. Imagine the reaction of the other Apostles! Several of them, like Simon the anti-Roman Zealot, were probably furious. The general public must have raised a ruckus to learn that the distinguished one from Galilee, of whom great things were reported, was feasting with turncoats and traitors. To explain His purpose for being there, Christ declared, "It is not the healthy who need a physician, but those who are sick." We shall never know how many of the guests listened attentively to Him and questioned Him about His teachings. We shall never know how many lives were radically changed through those conversations, how many individuals were put on the high road to Heaven through that one Capricorn's party!

This should make you aware of the great, though often unnoticed, influence you can have over others. You probably scoff at the notion that people hang on your words, waiting for direction for their lives; but many do, especially those who want to climb the ladder of success with you leading the way. You must bear this in mind when you expound on controversial subjects, for there is a Capricornian tendency to advocate a position not from total conviction but from momentary fascination with it.

You love the intellectual exercise of a debate, as if you were leaping from peak to peak, scaling sheer ideas and mounting difficult slopes. Young emotional people are especially swayed by your silver tongues. Some Capricorns realize that and use their power for its maximum effect. The results can be disastrous. I need only point out that Hermann Goering, Hitler's air force commander, was a Capricorn. On the more positive side, some of you use your gift of eloquence responsibly. You understand what people need to hear from you and know as well what you must, in truth, tell them. The ancient Roman orator Cicero, who was probably the greatest public speaker of all time, was your fellow Capricorn. Take his magnificent orations as your examples. There has never been more masterful political discourse than his.

As a rule, Capricorns marry well, especially if their marriage comes later than usual. Seek a husband or wife who can be a good companion, even when you seem to be isolated atop your mental mountain peaks. It won't be enough for you to secure an amorous lover; your personality also demands a creative partner who can keep pace with your fleeting mind, a loyal defender who will sometimes retreat with you to the spiritual remoteness of your meditation. If you have children, they will be more likely to take after your mate than you. You may be the deciding factor in the household, but your offspring will resemble, both physically and in their mannerisms, their other parent.

Because you yourself are determined to climb heights and scale impossible barriers, you shouldn't be surprised to learn how many of your brothers and sisters born under the sign of the Goat have done so in the past. Four American Presidents were Capricorns, and surely that sign's determination was evident in all of them. Woodrow Wilson (December 28) so insisted upon ending the First World War in such a way as to make another war impossible that he ruined his political position and destroyed his own health. Millard Fillmore (January 7) and Andrew Johnson (December 29) both worked their way up to national power from modest backgrounds as apprentices to shopkeepers. In fact, Johnson was illiterate until his wife taught him the wonders of reading!

Perhaps the most famous of all our Presidents, from the perspective of the next generation, will be that very typical Capricorn, Richard Nixon. Born on January 9, he has shown repeatedly the persistence and stamina we associate with this sign. Especially in his several political comebacks, he has been the rather lonely climber of mountains. Indeed, he and several other notable Capricorns of my acquaintance remind me of yet another goat that may serve as a symbol of Capricorn's free spirit. There used to be in the National Zoo in Washington, D.C., fairly near my home, a very large and unbelievably lovely blue goat. His lush coat had a definite blue tint to it! This superb specimen was a rare animal from the Mediterranean island of Crete, and it had been sent to the United States as a gift to President Truman from the people of Greece. They thereby thanked him for his aid in their struggle, after World War II, against guerrilla forces which attempted to seize their country. Just as that exotic creature was a symbol of liberty, so, too, the goat of Capricorn should symbolize your determination to use your talents for your own spiritual freedom and for the intellectual liberation of mankind.

The rebel instincts of Capricorn may have inspired several of the Founding Fathers; for Paul Revere (January 1), Benjamin Franklin (January 17), Alexander Hamilton (January 11), and John Hancock (January 12) all shared this sign. Their fellow rebel, who might be called one of America's Founding Mothers, was Betsy Ross (January 1), who is credited with designing and making the first American flag.

A rebel of a different kind was Clara Barton. Born on December 25, she founded the American Red Cross and pioneered new careers for women long before they became fashionable. General Billy Mitchell (December 29), now hailed as the father of the United States Air Force, defied the thinking of his superiors and insisted upon the need for this country to build up its air power. For his Capricornian independence of mind, he was court-martialed, although the course of history proved him right.

The diversity of Capricorn's gifts can be illustrated by the fact that December 25 was the birthdate of such disparate individuals as Conrad Hilton, Isaac Newton, Humphrey Bogart, singer Gladys Swarthout, and painter Maurice Utrillo. J. Edgar Hoover, the boss of the FBI, was born on January 1; and Danny Kaye, a gentle favorite of mine for the joy he has brought to millions of children, was born on January 18. Needless to say, you children of the Goat are exceptionally facile people.

Evidently, you Capricorns share an unusually strong need to be of service to the human community. Louis Pasteur (December 27) used his God-given scientific genius to free millions from the scourge of disease. Albert Schweitzer, the saintly missionary doctor, was born on January 14; and Joan of Arc, the Medieval warrior who was executed for her visions and her faith, was born on January 6. Perhaps you Capricorns feel that you, too, have a special call to unusual work or creative leadership.

I won't disagree with you. I will only note that because I am a Capricorn, you don't have to explain your feelings to me. Together let us examine the many divisions of our sign to understand better the gifts we have received and the mighty benefits we, and all humanity, can enjoy from them.

CAPRICORN—FIRST DIVISION
(December 28, January 1, 10, 19)

The route to success for Capricorns of the First Division is unusually difficult, for you tend to choose goals which seem almost unattainable. And yet, because of the characteristics of your astrological makeup, you are well equipped to reach your seemingly unreachable ambitions. You want only the best, not necessarily in terms of material possessions, but in quality, in performance, in attitudes. You therefore demand from yourself your best effort, feeling that anything less than that would be unworthy of you.

This can be an unbeatable combination and can make you an achiever, a setter of records, a winner of gold medals. That was the way it was with the Apostle of Capricorn, Matthew. He had been financially successful as a tax man. Despite the animosity of his neighbors, he had risen to the top of local society through his Roman contacts. But that wasn't the end of his ambitions or the pinnacle of his dreams. By renouncing his one career, he was able to initiate a much grander one as a messenger to all mankind. You Capricorns of today share his traits, for you are:

- level-headed
- persistent
- thorough
- slightly reserved

By calling you level-headed, I mean that you are extremely practical people. Even so, most of your associates will tell you that your goals in life are far beyond your capacity. But look into yourself, and you'll know better! Even as late as your middle years, you may have to admit that the successes you have been working for are still as far away as castles built in the air. But that won't make you surrender your dreams—at least, not as long as you refuse to wear those dream-killing red boots I've been warning you about.

On the contrary, when you realize how distant your goals still are, you will only become more determined. This is perhaps your major trait, and it explains why so many Capricorns of the First Division may be found in high positions, although they began life with few advantages. Your persistence is as great as a bulldog's; and if you've ever seen one of those feisty little creatures in action, you know what a compliment that comparison is. Rely on your willingness to work hard to give you that added boost you'll need to surmount the final hurdles between you and the achievement of your dreams.

Because you are so serious about everything you undertake, both in your job and in your private life, you probably already have a reputation for thoroughness. In high school, you are the student whom others rely on to prepare the final report of laboratory experiments; they know you will omit no detail, ignore no conclusion. In social affairs, you often find yourself managing the catering of parties, the scheduling of car pools, the logistics for a community dinner. This is the way you will advance in all fields. Progress does come, even if it comes slowly at first.

Capricorn Ones are private people. You enjoy being alone and frequently turn down social opportunities in favor of staying at home by yourself. Others find this torturous, as if they couldn't stand to live with the person they've become. You, on the other hand, commune with your mind, and this brings you the great personal calm which less fortunate individuals try to find through drugs and alcohol. I hope you are sufficiently confident of yourself not to find your habit odd, for it can be positively enriching, both intellectually and emotionally.

I should make it clear that you are no hermit, and I don't recommend that you withdraw from the strengthening interchange of social contact. You mix with people well and don't feel ill at ease in large gatherings, but you rarely give much of yourself beyond the limits of your home. The few lasting friendships you have are usually the result of efforts by others to maintain their close ties with you. Consider this a moment: do you suddenly stop seeing a particular person, or group of persons, without any explanation and then, months later, just as suddenly resume your friendship with them as if there had never been any period of distance or silence between you? Perhaps you need those times of self-sufficiency to recharge your psychic batteries and to accomplish the projects you've been building so diligently. Remember, though, that many people will be baffled, and some hurt, by your abrupt closing of the door of communication between you. Try to let them know you aren't cutting off your ties to them, only taking a little vacation of the spirit to rearrange the furbishings of your mind.

You probably hate to ask for favors. It's as if doing so opens you to rejection, makes you vulnerable, exposes too many of your needs. At the same time, you are always willing to offer help. Aren't you the person who picks up the restaurant tab, who helps with the dinner dishes when you are a guest somewhere, who feels it is important to do something kind for someone who is kind to you? All that is admirable, but my advice is that you let others participate in the activity too. Let them grant you a favor now and then; and when you really need help, don't be so shy about admitting it. That, after all, is why God made so many of us: so that there would be plenty of helping hands around when someone needed one!

Because you are highly moral, you tend to avoid any situation where your principles might be challenged. And yet, you will find as you move slowly toward your goals that true success usually involves facing, and overcoming, some fundamental threats to your values and standards. It should be comforting for you to know that with your persistence, there should be no problem in being true to the best aspirations of your spirit.

COLORS: Perhaps because your mind is focused ahead on your plans and dreams, you usually care little about colors in your surroundings or your wardrobe. With a little experimenting, however, you will find that they can help you in all aspects of life. I suspect that shades of yellow and gold would most enhance your magnetism, because in your rather reserved privacy, you are like one of those aloof Alpine mountain goats, standing silently on a peak to await the first brilliant beams of sunshine from the East. Let that radiating yellow, as bright as the gold coins which Matthew collected so assiduously, bring you out of your reverie and give you added zest in your daily work.

MONEY: Frugal and cautious in money matters, you may never be in debt in your entire life, not even through the use of the credit cards that seem to have become a necessary part of modern living. Your sense of independence abhors borrowing, although your habit of helping others may make you a too generous lender. These traits will be especially beneficial in your early career, for it isn't likely that you will have much money then. And so you will plod along your course, slowly but surely accumulating the capital which many others earn early and spend even earlier! When substantial cash does come to you in your middle years, you will be the most prudent investor ever known. Your simple tastes will not be replaced with luxury. You will look on your wealth as a source of security, not of ostentation. That's why you will enjoy it more, in the long run, than those who are fantastically rich and always uneasy.

HEALTH: You can preserve your natural store of vitality as long as you don't undermine it with drugs and alcohol. Popular as they are, they aren't for you of the First Division. In your middle years, bad weather may affect you in various ways: chills, rheumatism, arthritis. It may even be advisable for you to seek a high, dry climate to avoid aches and pains. Fortunately, if you ever should want to do so, your early habits of industry and thrift will probably have made it possible for you to enjoy the luxury of a sudden move to more pleasant surroundings.

RELATIONSHIPS: Like the household cat that disdains too much meddling in its affairs and walks alone, you will attract some people to you by your independence. Despite the appeal you have for others, and although you find members of the opposite sex quite attractive, you tend to have only business dealings with them. It is as if you regard romance as a waste of time. Many of you Capricorn Ones decide early in life that marriage would be a handicap in your career, and so you never get around to deciding upon a mate. The best way for you to discover a spouse may be in the mutual pursuit of a hobby, which will slowly bring you together until you find that personal affection has triumphed over more practical considerations.

Whether you marry or not, you will find your best associations within your family circle. There you feel free to express your emotions and admit your dependence upon others. Your home will also serve as a relaxing oasis of contentment, which will help you deal with the stress of your persistent drive to the top.

CAPRICORN–SECOND DIVISION
(December 29, January 2, 11)

The life pattern of you Capricorns of the Second Division reminds me of a line in one of John Denver's songs about poems and prayers and promises. That could stand as the summation of your astrological analysis, for you are:

- a highly promising talent
- suited to literary work
- sensitive
- religious

More than any other Capricorns, you of the Second Division are highly imaginative and intuitive. Gifts of imagery, of description, of comparison and debate have been given to you; and by developing them, you could become a superb poet or author.

This can be true even of individuals who don't think of themselves as literary people. Perhaps you've never had the experience of writing beautiful words, even if they come slowly and with great effort. Perhaps your poetic talent is more suited to the composition of lyrics, which your own voice or others turn into music. Perhaps your poetry is the spontaneous sort of speech which the Irish call blarney. Written or not, it touches the hearts of those who hear it and converts doubters to your ideas. You tend to be a born communicator, especially in language that is rich and throbbing with feeling.

Your language only reflects your spirit, for you are acutely sensitive, both to beauty and to the less pleasant aspects of human affairs. You are too easily hurt, and your feelings are bruised even by unintentional slights. When someone offends you, it's as if you shrink into yourself and take solace in what you might have done or said in reply, if you had only thought of it. Despite your brilliance with words, you don't react with instant verbal retaliation; your first impulse is to cover over your feelings and retreat with your dignity. In most cases, that's probably the wisest course.

You could find writing an outlet for your sensitive appreciation of life. Especially in the area of fiction, with its limitless range of possibilities, your imagination would be free to roam to its creative contentment. For a more practical literary slant, you might try journalism. Its very personal nature would enable you to right some of the wrongs that offend you. But first, I suggest you develop a thicker skin; journalism is no profession for the emotionally vulnerable.

Matthew, the Apostle of Capricorn, had an experience that may soon come to you. I sense that he never intended to be a writer; but when he realized that Christ was saying such wonderfully wise things that mankind had never heard before, he recorded them so they wouldn't be lost forever. Perhaps he would sit down each night, at the end of their travels, and jot down whatever the Master had discussed that day. However he did it, Matthew compiled a book of sayings, the record of Christ's own words, and this soon was extended into the Gospel of St. Matthew, the first of the four Gospels of the New Testament.

Although it was, of course, written after the death of Christ, it was probably compiled years before the accounts of Mark, Luke, and John. Matthew's version was being read in his own time, by his contemporaries. It was he who saved for succeeding generations the Beatitudes, that code of perfection which Christ gave His followers. It was Matthew who saved for all humanity the Lord's Prayer. This writer-by-chance, this spontaneous scribe, left the world a literary legacy which excels all others. Perhaps, on a lesser scale, you will be able to do what he did on the grandest scale of all. Perhaps you will just discover yourself involved one day in writing important words. The wonder will be in finding your own best opportunities for self-expression.

Remember that you don't have to seek a strictly literary career. So many famous men and women of letters were part-time authors, devoting their daily work to a quite different profession. You may find a special happiness in writing homemade children's books for your own or your neighbors' little ones. You may even prefer to submit anonymous devotional pieces to your church publications.

In fact, it is in religious literature that you are apt to have a singular success. With your ambition for the noblest ideals, you of the Second Division are especially attracted to religion. Considering its activities and objectives worthwhile outlets for your energies, you search through life until you match your special sensitivity to the particular commitments of your faith. This is the dynamo which sustains your talents and directs them to their most rewarding purposes. It is also the source of the additional strength you need to guard your tender sensitivity; for once you realize the spiritual dimension of all human interaction, you will be less concerned about your injured feelings and more aware of the contribution you can make through your unimpaired gifts. There is far too much you have to say for you to keep quiet.

COLORS: To embolden your vibrations and emphasize your spiritual nature, I suggest you liberally employ white, cream, and pale green in your personal appearance and your home environment. Strange as it may sound, the ample use of white will express your allegiance to the written word, for all your life will be a page and everyone you meet will be a character in your story. More seriously, we might consider that white is the color of abstraction, of immaterial thought as opposed to dominating material concerns. It is, therefore, particularly appropriate for someone of your spiritual nature. It reflects the sensitivity, the openness to others, the innocence that underlies all your talents for expression and communication.

I think you will find very useful, for entertaining and for all your more exuberant moments, a warmer white, verging into cream. When your action must be forceful and your words pointed, by all means remember the great horns of the markhoor goat of Afghanistan. Let your white world mellow into ivory and adjust your personal appearance accordingly. As a host or hostess, you would look your best in a cream-colored suit with dashing accents of pale green; then you will most seem, in the subconscious perception of astrological kinship, like a pale young chamois grazing on tender mountain grass.

MONEY: Your major interest in money is to secure the personal independence that frees you from depending on others. Your concern isn't for selfish individualism. Rather, you don't want to be a burden to anyone, even when others are glad to give you a hand. You will earn a comfortable income, even though literary work is a rather risky business. I fear you will spend your earnings too lavishly and will extend your purchasing power too carelessly to less industrious friends. If I were your financial adviser, I would tell you to be true to yourself. You will thereby be true to others and, what is equally important, ensure that they are true to you. Since you keep your own economic counsel, however, I will leave it to you to exercise more prudence in the handling of your resources.

HEALTH: There is a paradox in your health. You are basically a hardy individual, like the vigorous goat that serves as your astrological symbol; but you are prone to minor maladies which could, in later life, become very serious ones. What's the explanation for that apparent contradiction? You must remember that frustration and tension cause as much sickness as viruses and germs. That's why you are susceptible to various complaints. An offense to your feelings may also injure your stamina. An affront to your ideals, when you allow it to disrupt your mental focus, can cause you physical discord as well. You needn't suffer headaches, stomach upset, and other discomforts as a result of your emotional trials. Train yourself to need less approval from other people, and learn especially how to distinguish between those who are worthy of your attention and those whose negative opinions are rooted in bigotry or ignorance. You can't please all the people all the time, and there is no use in trying to do so. By becoming a little more intellectually independent, you will also become healthier. And that bonus will enable you to write better and longer in whatever literary pursuits you undertake.

RELATIONSHIPS: Because you seek admiration and esteem, you may make some sad mistakes in judging friends. You may be attracted to unworthy individuals and repulsed by critical, but altogether noble, acquaintances. I would suggest that you give everyone more of a chance, while at the same time being more independent of their opinions of you. After all, with your gifts for beauty and feeling, you don't need their pats on the head. I'm expressing this strongly because of my deep feelings about your excellent potential.

Your romantic life will be on the upswing in your thirties. Expect to come across someone who truly appreciates your marvelous literary abilities. Neither of you may expect love to develop out of your mutual admiration for each other's writing; but in more ways than one, you will create beautiful poetry together. Your family will remain as the central joy of your life and will greatly comfort you in all the troubles of life, little and large.

CAPRICORN—THIRD DIVISION
(December 30, January 3, 12)

A Capricorn Three is a dynamic individual, aggressive and forceful in every plan, every desire, every ambition. Your problem in life is that you can be overwhelming. The same personality traits that get things done for you can also earn enemies and win you a reputation for being ruthless. Your first order of business should be to develop a low-keyed tactfulness that will guarantee the effectiveness of your powerhouse spirit. You are:

- sometimes highhanded
- reliable
- enthusiastic
- analytical

I doubt that you Capricorn Threes are ever intentionally offensive; but your way of handling people, especially in critical situations, can be both abrupt and inconsiderate. The problem is usually not in your words but in the manner and speed with which you say them.

This may explain why you are sometimes puzzled over the reactions of your colleagues when you are determined to do a good job. It's as if they resent your drive for excellence, as if they are jealous of your perfectionism. There may, however, be a little more than that to their response. Have you ever told them what a grand job they are doing? Have you ever asked their advice about your own tasks? Or have you been a frequent critic of their performance—just for their own good, of course? Learn now that most people won't appreciate your negative assessment of them, for their good or for any other reason. You've heard the old saying that molasses catches more flies than vinegar. Take a moment to consider how that axiom can improve your own relationships. To make that generalization a little more particular, reflect upon what we have already learned concerning your Capricornian kin in the Second Division. How would you handle their extremely sensitive nature? The answer should be easy: a little diplomacy, a kind gesture, an occasional compliment. Keep that in mind, no matter whom you are dealing with.

The reason I advise you not to assert your own superiority over others is that it's unnecessary. Your solid merits need no amplification. Foremost among them is your reliability. This trait has probably been yours from childhood years, and it applies to your private affairs as well as to your career. When a friend asks you to handle matters for him or her, there is simply no further question about them: they will be promptly attended to. When your loved ones need your assistance or comfort, they seldom even have to request it, because you're the first to be on hand with an open heart. The best part of this characteristic is that you take it so much for granted that you don't expect the beneficiaries of your aid to cover you with gratitude.

What keeps you going in good times and bad, in your occasionally highhanded but always reliable embrace of all that life can offer, is your enthusiasm. It's an innate relish for doing, accomplishing, and daring. You are the exuberant mountain goat that leaps up the sheerest cliffs for the sheer joy of the journey. This is the key to the success that lies ahead of you, for it teams perfectly with your reliability to give you just the right balance of zeal and charm. Your task must be to keep the two in tandem, plodding ahead carefully with your work while bounding ahead joyously in your attitudes and eagerness to succeed.

A relatively rare asset is also yours; for Capricorn Threes usually possess analytical minds, capable of reducing complex situations to rigorously reasoned patterns in no time at all. You tend not to see a difficult personal situation as an emotional poem to be contemplated, but as an intricate engineering matter involving people instead of machines. And so you seldom let raw emotion interfere with your decisions, which is usually to the good. Indeed, its greatest benefit is in its application to yourself. For by turning your analysis upon your own conduct and attitudes, you can see your own flaws, evaluate alternatives to them, and promptly act to correct them. To put this metaphorically: an analytical Capricorn Three will astutely measure, to a millimeter, a pair of red boots and will discover that they would fit so poorly that there is no reason even to try them on! That, at least, is my hope for you and, indeed, for all of us.

Let me offer a personal example of the way your qualities combine to produce an admirable individual. A good friend of mine, a Capricorn Three, once told me that a college professor had asked her why she wanted to be a teacher. When she replied that she loved children, he declared that a poor reason for choosing a classroom career, because the youngsters would disappoint her and walk out of her life as casually as they strolled out of her classes! He advised her to become more casual about her charges; but when she followed his advice, she quickly became the most disliked teacher in the school. She was denying her inborn gifts as a Capricorn Three.

Her analytical mind, so very like yours, was able to perceive what was wrong. She set aside her newly assumed attitudes and reverted to her authentic self. She treated students as interesting individuals who could share her Capricornian enthusiasm. Most of all, she reinforced her reputation as a reliable teacher, colleague, and friend. She covered classroom assignments meticulously and taught her pupils to be equally thorough and dependable. In short, she provided them the best possible lesson: her own example. And now, she looks back upon a long and happy career; and some of her closest friends are her students of twenty-five years ago.

Notice how the same pattern is revealed in the life of Matthew, the Apostle of Capricorn. He made much the same kind of adaptation, leaving the highhanded practice of tax gathering for a more enriching career in the service of others. The same option is open to you and to all your fellow children of the astral goat.

COLORS: You would be wise to emphasize your irrepressible enthusiasm for all that life has to offer by using shades of purple in your dress and in your home. For some people, that color might seem a little strong, even garish; but for you, it's the natural complement to your vivid and vital commitments. You of the Third Division are as reliable as the hardy highland violets which, spring after spring for thousands of years, crop out on the same rocky ledges in the Alps. So use their hue liberally to state your personality as boldly as you usually state your views. And because there is a quieter side to your nature, experiment with shades of delicate green to see if their pastel invocation of meadow plants and mountain lichens brings out the Capricornian essence in you.

MONEY: Prepare to handle large sums of money at various times in your life, whether they are your own or someone else's. In your career, you will probably face problems over money matters from those whom you antagonize unless you learn to handle them more tactfully. Your personal finances will steadily improve over the years, as long as you avoid taking on too much work in trying to gain instant wealth.

HEALTH: The greatest danger to your physical well-being is overwork. Even the strongest patriarch of a wild goat herd can attempt too much. Make sure your leaps over chasms, in your career and in your private affairs, don't strain your stamina. Especially during your middle years, you could impair your health permanently through foolish overexertion. Learn to consider your job as being less important than your fitness of mind and body. Your family will appreciate your wisdom in doing so.

RELATIONSHIPS: Marriage is often a problem for Capricorn Threes because their personalities can be not just dominant but domineering. Your partner may have to bear with the fact that to you, your career matters more than your home life. Of course, none of this need be true. You can make those adjustments in your behavior and values that will put your family first and your profession second—or even third, ranking behind your health. Confidentially, I hope you do just that.

It would be advisable for you to marry late, certainly not in your teen-age years, and to choose a spouse who will have both an understanding of and respect for your work. Love is great, but it usually needs to be bolstered by mutual interests or, at least, tolerance of each other's diversities.

Your romances before your marriage will tend to be short-lived but intense. In matters of the heart, as in everything else, you leap ahead with a passion.

It is likely that your parents will always be dear to you, and you to them. This relationship may well be the most rewarding of your entire life. Be sure your intended mate, should you decide to marry, respects and appreciates them. Otherwise, you would find yourself caught in a distressing situation between your parents and your lover, and there's no way to escape that dilemma without great pain and anguish.

CAPRICORN—FOURTH DIVISION
(December 22, 31, January 4, 13)

Personal independence is the most prominent characteristic of Capricorn Fours. You who were born within this division were endowed at birth with a highly original and self-sufficient nature, just like that of your Apostle, Matthew. You are:

- eager to strike out alone
- serious
- romantic
- determined

If the home situation in which you grew up was not conducive to innovative ideas and offbeat attitudes, then you may have had an awkward childhood. On the other hand, if your family environment was unconventional, it may have been wonderfully supportive of your attempts to explore the unusual and try the unique.

In either case, by the time you are a teen-ager, you are apt to be chafing at the bit, eager to be out on your own, making your own decisions. You yearn to be a free spirit, to let no one arrange your affairs, to set your own life-style. As a general rule, you are anxious to rebel against the tenor of your upbringing, whatever it may have been. For you, the substance of the rules by which you were raised is less important than the fact that there were any rules at all!

Your independence is, by itself, neither good nor bad. It depends on the use you make of it. Indeed, your urge to be different is only a symptom of your great talent. You want the world to know about it, and you can't be blamed. You feel you must make your mark; and with your astrologically set abilities, I don't doubt that you will do so. You must carefully consider, however, whether you can best succeed by indulging in unconventional behavior for its own sake.

Being unusual mustn't become an end in itself for you. Your gifts of mind and spirit can be undermined by faulty motivation. Even the noblest of characters can be brought low when tripped by the influence of the red boots. Your creativity is a fine instrument for expression and understanding. It can make you a valued counselor to others who are trying to fit their differences into the overall pattern of society. But it could also bring you to grief if you allow your values to become subservient to your talents, instead of the other way around.

That shouldn't present any great difficulty for you, however; you Capricorn Fours are serious and determined people. You are concerned about the wrong you see in the world, and you take upon yourself the responsibility for setting it right. You are aware, often from your childhood years, that very talented people have a special obligation to use their gifts for purposes more profound than self-gratification and making money. Your awareness of this serious dimension of life may even have made you seem a little odd through your high school years, when you were too concerned with the problems of mankind to participate in the frivolous concerns of your fellow students.

There is a danger in all those good intentions, however. You will find, if you haven't already, that significant changes on a large scale take years to accomplish. You may be soon discouraged when, after a short period of struggle, you assume that nothing can be accomplished and that further effort is pointless. You may retreat to the comfortable but cowardly position of saying, "The world is in a mess, and to show that I'm not part of it, I will break entirely with conventional society." I'm sure you understand the phenomenon I'm describing. There are many idealistic people today who have allowed their aspirations for a better world to turn sour and, what is worse, to make them bitter.

In any particular instance, your true motivation is known only to you and to God, so I won't attempt to meddle in matters of individual conscience. When you know that your commitments to bold ideas and new principles are founded upon selfless ideals, you should hold fast to them. When you suspect that your defiance of convention is really self-serving, meant to make you seem heroic, then let your serious mind dissuade you from any further waste of your emotional resources.

Because of your determination, there should be no question about your potential success in whatever career you mark out for yourself. But determination without insight becomes merely blind force, like the charging power of an ox. Remember that your Zodiac sign is not an impetuous bull but a calculating goat. Keep your determination prudent and informed so that as you forge ahead, you will constantly readjust your sights and reorder your personal priorities.

Your determination also means that in the event of personality conflicts, you may break entirely with the people involved. Many of you Capricorn Fours leave home at an early age to live elsewhere. This doesn't mean you abandon your family but, rather, that you feel a certain independence from it. Although the separation is apt to be difficult and more painful than you realized, you will feel compelled to go through with it, just to prove that you can stand by yourself.

As a hopelessly romantic individual, you form emotional attachments—it might be more accurate to call them entanglements—even when you suspect in advance that they won't work out. You love the idea of being in love and are willing to take foolish risks to enjoy the giddy feeling of being swept off your feet by an attractive member of the opposite sex. Like every gamble, this one has certain drawbacks. Because you delight in defying rules and escaping the restrictions of convention, you may allow your romances to become irresponsible, both sexually and emotionally. If so, your romantic spirit will suffer most of all; for at heart, you are seeking enduring appreciation of your worth and lasting commitment by the one you love. This is a matter to which you should turn your seriousness, which may have been given to you precisely for this purpose: to balance your romantic impulses and lead you to a greater happiness.

COLORS: Your powerful magnetism suits the whole spectrum of colors. You could wear a rainbow and make all the colors match. As a romantic, you can express your gentler side by emphasizing blues and grays, complemented by soft pastels. These shades can convey to others your inner readiness to accept them, even when your exterior demeanor conveys an opposite message. Because your life has been characterized by the determination to strike out on your own, you may like to wear rather unusual hues, especially in situations where they will be least expected. Perhaps you are already in the habit of appearing at a business meeting in a shockingly bright suit or attending a formal affair in a brilliant red gown or a green velvet tuxedo. As long as you are conveying your authentic feelings without being garish, I applaud your daring.

MONEY: Expect the unusual in money matters. Your early desire for influence and power will probably bring you sizable amounts of cash well into your middle years, but you may spend it just as fast as you accumulate it. Many of you Capricorn Fours, having achieved what you longed for, step out of the spotlight and give up the high incomes you wanted. When you decide to escape from the rat race, be sure you have first made prudent plans for investment and retirement. It's never too early to plan ahead, for financial security is the basis for the personal freedom you have always sought.

HEALTH: Your tremendous energy enables you to escape common illnesses. Like the bounding white goats that rule the precipices of the Rocky Mountains, you seem to have endless vitality. But like them in another way, you face the danger of accidents in your travel plans. As they do, look before you leap, especially if your journeys take you to exotic places with, let us say, less reliable forms of transport. There is also an indication in your astrological chart that you could be injured in a public disturbance. This can be avoided through foresight, so take care to minimize the chances of such an unfortunate occurrence.

RELATIONSHIPS: In your love life, relationships are likely to be many and casual, although they will never seem that way when you are involved in them. You will always think that your present favorite is the only one in the world for you. Perhaps you would be able to realize the truth if you made a greater effort to communicate with the person you think you love. Especially in very personal relationships, you find it difficult to express your feelings, and so your partner may be totally misunderstanding your intentions. Save yourself several broken hearts by learning to put your cards on the table and by expecting your loved one to do the same.

Your best marital prospects are in a late marriage. Your earlier experiences with imperfect love will prepare you to appreciate the more mature commitment of two people who respect each other's principles and admire each other's aspirations.

Try to maintain your ties with your parents. You will find as time goes by that when your contemporaries turn against your unconventional beliefs, your family will be more understanding than you previously imagined them to be. Even if, years ago, you were eager to leave them, you may one day be just as eager to return; and you will discover that it is not they who have changed but you.

CAPRICORN—FIFTH DIVISION
(December 23, January 5, 14)

Long-term planning is your key to success. You are apt to be a success no matter what you do or don't do, because you've been so richly endowed by the stellar influences over your birth. Even when you act on impulsive decisions, you have a better than even chance of landing on your feet. If you do decide to lay out a plan for your life, as opposed to a year-by-year approach to whatever fate offers, then you will quickly scale great heights. You are:

- widely talented
- intellectually active
- openhearted
- religious

If it is possible to be overly talented, then that is your problem. It is difficult for you to make up your mind just what you want to do with all the gifts you've been given. You find even in your childhood that you can learn science as well as art, that you can succeed in scholarship as well as athletics; and this makes you approach life as though it were some giant smorgasbord to be nibbled at with a carefree appetite. You choose one hobby or career, then another, knowing that you are likely to triumph in all of them.

And what's wrong with that? It hurts no one and delights you greatly. Look at it another way. You have the potential to do much more than merely succeed. You have the talent to reach greatness. If you don't focus it, if you don't develop and concentrate it at its strongest points, then the world will lose a leader and receive instead a prominent person. And in the process, your loss will be greatest of all, because you will forfeit your chance for that excellence which alone will satisfy you fully.

That's why I urge you to be more selective in your enterprises. Choose carefully which projects are most worthy of your attention and then give them the full benefit of your intellectual prowess. Your mind seeks new ideas, new mental exercises to perform. Because you easily handle a half-dozen different responsibilities at the same time, you are probably ideal material for a top executive position. Be sure you don't fritter away those excellent prospects by chasing after minor ambitions while great ones slip away.

It's good that your success will bring you monetary rewards, for you are a philanthropist at heart, giving of both yourself and your earnings. You are deeply touched by acts of kindness and want to return favors. This humanitarian quality may combine with your restlessness to enable you to travel on missions of mercy. That was the case with Matthew, whose journeys spread the Gospel of brotherly love while probably satisfying his own need to be on the move. Goat's feet are seldom still; in your case, they run to those in need.

I hardly need list those professions in which you could put these tendencies to good use. With your wide range of gifts, you could as easily be a physician as a clergyman, a nurse as a U.S. senator. Add to that your love of travel and you could be a high functionary for an international relief organization. While you are thinking of a dozen other alternatives, remember that they all require extensive training, and you can't postpone forever your choice of a major career to the exclusion of lesser interests.

When you do focus on a primary goal, it may well have something to do with religion, for the life of the spirit will always be important to you. Whatever your faith, you tend to be diligent in its practices and participate in your own private devotions as well as the formal services in your church. The inner observances of religion are as vital to you as the external ones. And so you probably murmur a silent grace before your meals, whether at home or in a restaurant. The best aspect of your religious personality is that you are well equipped to share this interest with others. Your intellectual talents enable you to convey to friends and strangers alike the joy you have found in your faith. This opens tremendous opportunities for your personal fulfillment, because you will be able to help those in need not only through material assistance but also with far more powerful aid in the sharing of your religious inspiration.

Those Capricorn Fives born on the January dates of their division are usually not only pious but also interested in the occult. You probably have latent gifts of psychic perception, although you are the only one who can really discover them. Once you take the time to analyze your life, to evaluate your reactions to events and to persons, you will understand the role your special powers have already played in your affairs. Their future impact upon your life is in your hands. By ignoring them, you will waste splendid talents. By abusing them, you will trade lasting happiness for passing notoriety. By developing your psychic gifts according to the Creator's wishes, you will transform all other aspects of your being into an ongoing poem in praise of the Lord of the Universe.

Home life means much to Capricorn Fives. Even when you are affluent, you prefer to do your own cleaning and cooking rather than hire a servant. Your instincts for making your dwelling your own very personal home are very strong. No wonder your living environment is usually immaculately clean and warmly comfortable.

You are particularly blessed in opportunities for personal and professional growth, which will continue throughout your long life. If you ever feel that you have reached a permanent plateau and learned enough and experienced enough, then you'd better take a closer look at your affairs. For you of the Fifth Division are not intended to settle down in comfort as long as there are more mysteries to explore, more wrongs to right, and more broken hearts to solace. Many of you will refuse to retire until very late in life, if at all; you sense that your part in the pattern of mankind is to be active, to help others, and thereby to enjoy your fullest flowering.

COLORS: Pastel shades are unquestionably best for you, perhaps because they express the ever airy atmosphere in which your mind functions. As a creature of intellect, flitting over ideas as daintily as a darting butterfly in an overflowing garden, you can inform others of your constantly changing interests by wearing light and subtle shades, reminiscent of the hues of blossoms, shifting their colors slightly with every change in the sunlight. I sense that blues are especially good for you, expressing your religious interests and your emotional ties to the great canopy of the sky, even when it is punctuated with clouds. For both men and women of the Fifth Division, a suit of blue, like the color of a summer sky full of brightness, will help you in your efforts to bring more sunshine into the lives of others.

MONEY: Your early years will be lean because you will be searching for the best outlet for your talents. Rather than earning whatever you can, however you can, you will pursue more than a few dreams until the right one catches you. When that happens, your financial future is assured.

You dislike being in debt, and will actually deny yourself the necessities of life in order to avoid bills. You are equally cautious in your investments, and will consequently miss some good opportunities for sound profits. No matter! Your forward progress will be steady, and you should be relatively affluent before your middle years.

HEALTH: Your sensitivity to your emotional environment will make you react physically to undue pressures, to sudden setbacks. Although you are active and vigorous, you can't guard against every disappointment. Train yourself to ward off despondency before it seizes you. When a leaping mountain goat stumbles, it immediately rises to its feet and resumes its pace. By learning to accept life's defeats as well as your far more numerous victories, you will enjoy overall health. Be careful of minor digestive and tooth maladies. Even a touch of arthritis could result from inattention to your well-being.

RELATIONSHIPS: You will be a close, trusting, and affectionate marriage partner. If you are already married, I'm sure your spouse knows what I'm talking about. Involving yourself in the affairs of others, but only with their approval, you wholeheartedly try to help them. Of course, they love you for it, because they sense in your selflessness no touch of egotism or taint of personal advantage.

Your idea of a good time socially is a quiet dinner party at home—naturally, at your home, for nowhere else are you so at ease—with only a few close friends and your loved ones. To your business associates and acquaintances, you seem a bit reserved, though always sensitive to their unspoken messages. They assume you understand what they want or need or fear without using words to tell you. The fact of the matter is, you usually do!

CAPRICORN—SIXTH DIVISION
(December 24, January 6, 15)

The Sixth Division of Capricorn is the astrological home for a great many exuberant, extroverted people. Those born within it are personable and attractive, because their character emphasizes expression and relationships. If you are a Capricorn Six, you already know you are:

- romantic
- happy to be in the limelight
- disciplined
- patient

Romance is the key factor in your life. Throughout your life, you will have to cope with it, for better or worse. It can bring you happiness heaped as high as the Alpine habitat of mountain goats, or it can make you wonder whether there is any good in life. The difference lies in one vital lesson: that romance, like a warming fire, must be kept under control. Once it spreads beyond its proper limits, this great blessing becomes a threat to everything you hold dear. If you enjoy it prudently in your youth and, once married, restrict romance to your happy home, then you won't be burned by it.

The root of your romantic nature is your need for the approval of others. There can be many reasons for that emotional requirement; and to explore them, a psychologist might be more competent than an astrologer. Like all of us, you hunger for affection; but in order to receive it, you are often too willing to take risks with your heart and ignore the warnings of your intuition. Seeking the approval of others, you will give them attention, flattery, applause, even love, always hoping to receive the same in return. Sometimes you will be lucky, and sometimes you may cry yourself to sleep at night. Forewarned is forearmed. I don't want such grief to come to you.

What most disturbs me is that your searching for approval through hasty romances is utterly unnecessary. Capricorn Sixes are well endowed with talents, both useful and charming, and it's foolish for any of you to sell yourself short. Are you not imaginative, creative, charismatic? Do you suppress your artistic tendencies in order to avoid the chance of criticism? Do you keep your inventive ideas to yourself so that no one can contradict them? My advice is simple: stop it! A Capricorn Six has no reason to feel inferior. Look into yourself and you will see why.

I rarely approve of a mother's putting her child on the stage at a tender age, but that's the place for you of the Sixth Division. Perhaps it provides you opportunities to show the world your splendid gifts; perhaps the reaction from audiences assures you of the affection you need. You love the limelight, either literally in the theater or figuratively, lecturing in a classroom, preaching from the pulpit, speaking in a political campaign. For that brief while, when you are the center of attention, the world seems to slip into its proper order, with you in the headlines and everyone else reading about you!

Unfortunately, we can't all be public figures, but I like to think that there is a spotlight for everyone in this world. I recall that a father-and-son team of carpenters in Nazareth spent decades in their own very private spotlight, making the best furniture they could. All that matters is that we do the best we can. By recognizing your abilities and developing them, you will inevitably come upon your own stage, your own limelight. It may not be before an immense audience in a grand atmosphere, but it will allow you at least to contribute all your efforts to a world that sorely needs them.

That is a far better way to satisfy your romantic yearnings for approval than by escaping your real circumstances through short-lived affairs. Remember that the recognition that most matters is that which you extend to yourself. When you wake up in the morning and look into your mirror, knowing that the person looking back has useful and challenging work to do this day, you will no longer seek acceptance in the easy compliments of others. Then your daily chores—whether they involve building skyscrapers, ending wars, performing heart transplants, or changing diapers—will provide you with that private stage you've always needed for your best performances.

You will find, sooner or later, that you have the will and individuality to break free from the need for temporary affections as a substitute for mature independence. Many of you, in fact, will actually turn your tremendous discipline to performances under very real spotlights. Your self-control can be marvelous, enabling you to endure the long hours of rehearsals in music or dance or drama. To the uninitiated, your career will seem like monotonous drudgery. To you, the discipline will be a source of order in your life and will free your powerful creativity. Where there is no discipline, art becomes anarchy, but that will never happen to your talents.

The reason it will never happen is that you possess the inherent patience to wait for the maturing of your talents. This is a natural adjunct to your discipline. You were probably a most uncomplaining child, seldom throwing temper tantrums when hungry or uncomfortable. As an adult, you can bear with waiting, knowing that your self-control will see you through to the good things that await you.

Matthew must have had the same trait as he sat there in the market collecting taxes, suffering the scorn and insults of his countrymen. He must have patiently waited for some radical change, some sudden improvement in his life. And when he entered into the limelight as an Evangelist, he stayed there, forever. What an encouragement his example should be to you!

COLORS: Although your personal magnetism is already vibrant, indeed, stunning in its dramatic impact, you can better direct it and emphasize its positive aspects through the astute use of blue. As a romantic spirit, you appear at your best in midnight blue. As a natural performer, more electric shades suit you, especially in your home décor. For there, in the intimacy of your living room, you can make your own stage, focus your own spotlight, by the unrestrained use of aqua and baby blue. Your show business personality is complemented by that showiest of flowers, the tall spikes of delphinium, and its special shade of blue should go on stage with you. In situations that try your patience, however, especially in dealing with unpleasant people, I recommend the liberal use of turquoise, both the color and the stone; that unique blue hue has been compounded over endless eons, and so is a perfect expression of your remarkable endurance.

MONEY: Once you learn to control your relationships, you will also be able to control your finances, much to your banker's satisfaction. Look to the future, not the day after tomorrow. As you make yourself less dependent on the opinions of other people, as you respect yourself more and appreciate your own gifts, your economic instincts will become more reliable. In fact, for a mature Capricorn Six, there is a distinct chance of amassing great wealth in short order.

HEALTH: Expect generally good health throughout life. Speed, however, is a threatening factor. Your concern for your personal relationships, your worry about the opinions of others, even your romantic fascination with someone traveling along with you, are likely to take your mind away from the dangers of a journey in a car. Take care with your driving.

Be as practical as you must be cautious. Make certain that you carry ample insurance to cover both the medical costs of a possible accident and the income lost during recuperation. Although you can prevent disasters through alertness and prudence, you should also be prepared to cope with them if they do come your way.

RELATIONSHIPS: I can't stress too greatly your need to avoid short-term romances. Marry, and you'll be happy. You of the Sixth Division seem to have an infinite capacity to love, and a stable marriage will give you ample opportunity to give and, equally important, to get affection. With that secure anchor for your self-esteem, you won't need self-defeating flings to excite, and eventually frustrate, your romantic impulse. Settling down to a productive and fulfilled life, you will keep your family close to you. In their company, you will find your best audience, your kindest critics, and your most appreciative fans.

CAPRICORN—SEVENTH DIVISION
(December 25, January 7, 16)

Because the Seventh Division of Capricorn includes the date on which Christians observe the birth of the Lord, I feel obligated to explain that although each of the Apostles can be identified with a different sign of the Zodiac, their Master cannot. The date customarily used to honor His coming into the world is, of course, not a definite matter of historical record. The Child of Bethlehem may or may not have been born on December 25. What is important is that we understand that He was not subject to particular astrological influences. On the contrary, He was subject to none of them because His Divine personality combined every imaginable good into an intimation, in human terms, of things beyond the comprehension of mankind.

With that exemption understood, we can examine the characteristics of the Seventh Division, applying its wisdom to all those born under its stars. Perhaps I should say, born under the *movements* of its stars, for Capricorn Sevens are extremely mobile people, both in the physical sense of travel and in the intellectual sense of restless searching for new ideas. You hunger for change, for innovation, for things you've never seen or heard or tasted before. Especially in your mental fascination with undiscovered thoughts and hidden theories, you are the true mountain goat of Capricorn, forever leaping upward to obscure crannies in the rock until, with one final heroic leap, you join your astral constellation in the sky. But let us leave figures of speech for a moment to note that you are:

- active
- unsettled
- prudent
- persevering

A routine life seems to you not worth living. If you are to develop to your fullest, indeed, if your intellect is to survive in all its natural vigor, you require constant change. This doesn't necessarily demand geographical travel, but it does mean that your mind must never be allowed to stand still. If it does, it will stagnate. Should you find yourself unable to travel, whether for financial, family, or professional reasons, there are many compensatory devices to take the place of journeys. The three I recommend most highly are reading and reading and reading, if you get my point. On the most meager budget, you can escape into the endless world journey of the public library. On its shelves of old and new books, silly and profound books, solemn and jovial volumes, you will find the truest liberation available on this earth.

Even so, it is likely that you will change jobs and residences more frequently than most people, and your friends are apt to be somewhat offbeat—not unpleasant by any means, but rather unconventional. Delighting in the strange views and eccentric visions they bring into your life, you will travel, as it were, through their sometimes bizarre experiences.

Another symptom of your active nature, in both body and mind, is your concern for physical endeavors. You are forever tidying the house, tinkering with the car, or fiddling with the garden. Even if you don't participate in sports events, you enjoy watching them. On a picnic, you like to hike through the forest; at a party, you love to dance; in school, the highlights of your courses are your field trips. There seems to be no end to your appetite for action.

When disciplined, your mobility can accomplish much good. However, there is a fine line between being active and being unsettled. I admire your vigor, but caution you against its excesses. Remember that even a rambling rose has roots. In your travels, as in your intellectual wanderings, it is important that you retain your ties with people and places that really matter to you. Then, when you feel the need to draw strength and determination from a sense of stability and continuity, your personal roots will provide you emotional nourishment.

Try to harness your energy through a career that will gratify your psychological inclinations while it meets your financial needs. You might be happy as a travel agent, a courier, a deliveryman, a writer of travel guides, or as an employee of an airline or cruise ship. Once you learn to journey in your mind, rather than geographically, you can be a superb librarian or aide working with youngsters who are learning to read. Indeed, you might combine all aspects of your active personality by becoming a traveling book salesman!

Above all, find a position that will enable you to save a bit of money as you go along, for you are apt to change jobs frequently and need some reserves to fall back on during difficult periods of transition. This shouldn't present serious problems for you of the Seventh Division because you are unusually prudent folks, even for Capricorns, most of whom are shrewd and calculating. As children, you seldom took the foolish risks in which your playmates indulged. You were careful in traffic, cautious around strangers, and prompt with your homework. As adults, you steer clear of both financial and romantic risks. The major decisions in your life—marriage, buying a home, the values by which you raise your children—are made only after great deliberation and soul-searching. This is all to the good, for all those matters will be affected, favorably or unfavorably, when you move from job to job in pursuit of fulfillment.

I don't doubt that you will discover what you seek. So strong is your perseverance that you need no encouragement from me. You are the barnyard goat at his most determined, butting against the gate for hours until it breaks open and sets him free. That's the way you approach the challenges of life—hammering away at them long after others have resigned themselves to failure. Although you will not always succeed, your persistent belief that you can is a powerful weapon in turning that faith into fact.

COLORS: Because your spirit is sufficiently restless by itself, it isn't necessary to provide further stimulus through shocking shades of exotic colors. Wherever you travel, you may find it wise to make your living room a calm image of the most peaceful aspects of nature. Create for yourself a woodland setting with much green and gray, as if your home were amid a clump of aspens high on a rocky slope. Those are colors of permanence, of endurance, and they will not only temper your zest for constant activity, they will also reflect and strengthen your prudence and perseverance. They will root you to the best in yourself by tying you to the best in nature.

MONEY: Wanting little money, needing even less, you are interested in profit mainly as a means to finance your travel. And so you feel free to change jobs, even incurring considerable losses in pension benefits and company seniority. You will be able to pay your bills, especially your traveling expenses; but you must look to the future. The demands of family life can't be financed on a shoestring, especially one that is constantly walking to new places! Your best investments will be in real estate, but be sure you are prepared to settle down before taking on the responsibilities of managing parcels of land.

HEALTH: After a somewhat shaky start, you will strengthen with age. Your youth is likely to be delicate, your middle age robust. It's as if your perseverance rewards you with added health each time you overcome a disease. Be especially careful of respiratory ailments and infections, for you will be vulnerable to both of them during your travels.

RELATIONSHIPS: Your tendency to pull up stakes and move on will make it difficult to form lasting friendships. You will know and like hundreds of people, being esteemed by them in return; but most of those relationships will be superficial. In romance, be prepared for a number of affectionate attachments. Even in love, you are persevering, being loyal to several of your former flames long after your grand passion for them has subsided to a cooler appreciation of their merits.

Your stars indicate a strong religious influence upon your later years. This will affect your friendships and bring you into intimate cooperation with a circle of associates whom you may not yet have met. In their company, as in the love of a calming and gentle spouse, you will find the intellectual and emotional answers for which you have searched all your life.

CAPRICORN–EIGHTH DIVISION
(December 26, January 8, 17)

A Capricorn Eight should learn early to accept the knocks life gives without being felled by them. Your road to success will not be an easy or a direct one; but you must be assured from the outset that though the way is long, it is no dead end. Your bumpy ride through life will never lack excitement, though it will bring disappointments. You must learn to look on your progress toward your material and spiritual goals as a pilgrimage, not a pleasure trip; and you should always be encouraged by the certainty that with effort, a Capricorn Eight can match Matthew's greatness and enjoy the delight in life which characterizes the gamboling goats of the rocky highlands. Their paths, like yours, are neither soft nor level; but your journey, like theirs, can be both proud and determined. You have:

- ebbs and flows of misfortune
- a mercurial temperament
- resourcefulness
- great mutual attraction for members of the opposite sex

If you think that life will be kind to you, I must regretfully advise you to think again. The odds are that it will not be so beneficent. Decisions you will make or have already made in your late teens will prove the pivotal factor in determining your future happiness. If you decide wisely and then have the heroic determination to stick with your youthful choices, you will emerge unharmed by misfortunes. Time after time, however, you are likely to feel as though your life is mired in the quicksand of bad luck. The advice I give to you is the same warning given to explorers who step into real quicksand: don't panic or thrash about. Ease your way out of the predicament. Above all, don't despair; for each time you make your way through the swamps of trouble, you will be stronger, your way will be easier, and your goals will be nearer. Each test of your courage will be a reconfirmation of your eventual triumph.

Note well that it will be essential for you to throw off despondency, to recharge your mental and emotional batteries, and to get back into the game of life. In my meditations upon the vision which led me to write this book, I sensed that Matthew experienced a major crisis in his life just before he met, and immediately followed, Christ. He was despairing of his status among his people. Fearful of his neighbors' wrath, uncertain of the future, he could have given himself up to pure greed and self-satisfaction. Instead, he held to the hope that something would deliver him from his sorry circumstances. Indeed, he was rescued—although probably not as he had expected—and thereafter he rose steadily upward in personal contentment and public fame. Let his fantastic experience be both an example and an incentive to you.

Your greatest weakness is a mercurial temperament. One day, you are walking on air, as the ancient Greeks thought Mercury, the messenger of the gods on Mount Olympus, strode across the sky on his errands. The next day, you are down in the dumps, moody and melancholy. This is especially likely to occur when people you admire and trust let you down, and I'm afraid that that phenomenon is all too common in our world. But that's no reason to allow the shortcomings of others to govern your own moods. Don't make the mistake of becoming emotionally dependent upon anyone outside your inner circle of family and friends. Those you love deserve your trust even when they fail you; the bonds of long affection can survive even a betrayal. Even a family rent by dissension can close ranks when threatened by an external danger. So put your faith in your own, and don't rely on acquaintances and business associates to honor their commitments.

I don't mean this to be a gloomy assessment; on the other hand, I don't want you to impair your abilities and productivity through the gloom of hurt feelings and shattered dreams. You have too much to offer, too much to accomplish, to waste time sulking. Look at the matter in another light or, shall we say, through another metaphor. Your life will be like a roller coaster, with rapid ups and downs. You can let this erratic progress discomfit you so much that you slow your life down to a crawl, or you can take advantage of the ride's forward momentum to climb that next hill and race around the final curves to your goals. As in every other sign of the Zodiac, the choice is up to you Eighth Division Capricorns.

Do you think you can make it? I *know* you can! For your astrological characteristics include a powerful resourcefulness. Like your cousins in the Fifth Division, you are serious and intellectual, always directing your learning to the practical purposes of your ambitions. The reason you are so frequently faced with challenges is that your gifts of mind and spirit lead you to take on many projects and tasks which others shun as hopeless, only to see you, battling against fantastic odds, prove that the deed can be done, the cause can be saved, the ideal can be achieved. If life were a fairy tale, you would be the knight who slays every dragon to rescue distressed damsels.

The mention of handsome knights and fair maidens brings us to another salient characteristic of yours. Like Capricorns of the Seventh Division, you are strongly attracted to, and attractive to, members of the opposite sex. Even if your hair isn't in shape, attire not the best, your eyes a little bleary from too much work, you have that vague appeal which brings admirers to you like bears to a honey tree. Of course, your romantic affairs will share the same up-and-down pattern as the rest of your life. So be prepared for occasional heartaches and surprises. Just be sure that in the process, you aren't responsible for someone else's sadness. In the long run, that assurance is the best guarantee of your own contentment and peace of mind.

You can expect your rocky road to level out by the time you are approaching your fortieth birthday. Suddenly, the stamina and insight you have gained from confronting so many challenges and mastering so many threats will make you virtually indomitable. The world will fall into place; and like the triumphant mountain goat standing on a pinnacle, watching the distant sunrise long before the lowland creatures can see its rays, you, too, will be king of the mountain!

COLORS: To subdue your mercurial extremes of giddy delight and moping despair, include in your wardrobe and home furnishings much gray. Now, I realize that that shade will not, by itself, keep you from sadness; but it will calm your emotions and help you think things through. Especially helpful will be those pale shades reminiscent of the softest underfur of a baby goat. And for dramatic occasions, when it's time for you to claim your credit and take your bow, use the royal shade of gray: silver! That is, after all, the color of mercury, and it will endow you with wit and words as quick and flashing as the silver wings on the heels of the legendary god Mercury. And for a powerful accent color, as emphatic as your prospects for ultimate success, jolt the gray world back on its heels with shocking sapphire, freely flaunted!

MONEY: Hardship during the early years of your life is apt to keep you financially lean thereafter, but you will adapt your life-style to your restricted circumstances. By putting away modest amounts of money, either in savings certificates or material investments like antiques and real estate, you will one day realize that the hard times of your youth were worthwhile in the long run. In addition, you may be pleasantly surprised by a windfall enrichment in your fifties. My only criticism of your finances is that your generosity can be extreme, and I hope you will guard against insincere friends in search of loans.

HEALTH: Especially in your developing years, depression can take its toll of your health. Because the body reacts to psychological conditions as well as to physical ones, your occasional gloom is nothing to joke about. Learn to live with setbacks, but without grieving over them. Take special precautions against the chance of an auto accident, which could result in spinal injury and lasting back trouble. An alert eye can preserve your safety.

RELATIONSHIPS: Your personality will be toughened by adversity, and so you could sense yourself becoming somewhat callous by your middle age. There is no need for that hardening of your emotions. People love you for your persistence in the face of adversity. They esteem your brave spirit. They rejoice in your triumphs. What's more, they need the attention which only you can give them.

Because you are both serious and militantly honest, you are unlikely to enter lightly into sexual affairs. There is, however, the chance of your foolishly undertaking one last fling in your late thirties, purely for the adventure and thrill, as well as for the reassurance that your youth is not entirely behind you. I will assume that thus forewarned, you will evaluate the treasure of your happy home and devoted spouse; both are too precious to imperil.

CAPRICORN–NINTH DIVISION
(December 27, January 9, 18)

You Capricorns of the Ninth Division swing on the pendulum that swiftly arcs between greatness and disaster. What an exciting message that is! Let me explain.

For every positive influence of your Apostle Matthew, there is a corresponding negative influence from the master of the red boots. We are all subject to those opposing forces, but you are especially sensitive to their extremes. Why? Because you are so forcefully endowed with the traits of mastery and accomplishment that, one way or another, you must make your mark on the world. My fervent hope is that you choose to do so the way Matthew did. You are:

- extremely ambitious
- highly capable
- self-confident
- strong-willed

You are almost certain to have an eventful life and to achieve great things. Only if you retreat to a desert island can you avoid the success destined for you; and even there, I suspect that you would probably discover some lost civilization in the wilderness. From time to time, however, circumstances over which you have no control will intervene to cause you sorrow and pain. It is at those moments that you can win your best victories by reaffirming your ideals and pushing on with the work at hand.

You will never be satisfied with anything but the top rung of the ladder. In fact, that's where you belong. Bold in your ideas and in their execution, loving adventure and excitement as much as others crave peace and security, you remain, at least outwardly, calm and confident. In short, you are the perfect executive.

Well, almost perfect. It is true that you don't react visibly to stress and deadlines. But inwardly, you may be a bundle of nerves. You are rarely frightened, even more rarely insecure. But because you see situations so clearly, you perceive all the dangers as well as all the opportunities. So your bland, confident attitude gives your colleagues a feeling that everything is surely under control—under your control, that is! All the while, you know that a contract is not final until the signatures are affixed. You know that a building is not finished until the tenants have moved in. You know that a million and one little things could go wrong to upset your plans.

This is, in professional terms, a definite asset. It makes you a prized employee and a leading candidate for top management posts. You should set your sights on big business or government. Don't be afraid of the pressures there; you can handle them just as surely as Matthew did. Remember that even before he met Christ, he was handling tremendous responsibility in the collecting of Roman taxes. Wealthy, powerful, envied, he eventually found ways of turning his talents to better purposes. As you climb to the top of everything life has to offer, remember that your enduring happiness depends on your willingness to use your success for more than your betterment alone.

In terms of your private well-being, that asset can be a handicap. If you allow your career worries to disrupt your personal life, then you will later pay a heavy price in the impairment of your health and the sorrow of your family. If you can keep your business troubles away from your home life, fine. If not, realize now that fame and fortune are not worth the sacrifice of love and harmony.

As a self-confident powerhouse, you may even have the reputation for being a bit cocky, for staring the world in the eye and winning every time. Granted, you can deal with almost any crisis that arises. One thing you can't take with equanimity is criticism. You have a quick and volatile temper and can be both dogmatic and headstrong. A thousand professional, social, civic difficulties you can handle, settling controversies as you go along; but the moment you are personally attacked, you may take out your anger on the world.

This trait has ruined a great many promising people. If the general public, in whose eyes you are a masterful leader and thinker, should see you lose your cool, as they say, your prospects for continued success, much less respect, would be dashed. Because you have worked long and hard to get where you are today, it would be tragic to lose the stature you've been building. You deserve the admiration and affection of hundreds; don't fritter it away in a needless tantrum, no matter how much you are stung by your critics.

My vibrations in meditating upon your astrological charts indicate that some of you Capricorn Nines will go down in history, but in what roles is entirely up to you. I have to warn you that you are easy prey for yes-men. You relish flattery and often can't tell when compliments are genuine or false. This is a common shortcoming among the very talented, and you are no exception. At the height of your success, the day may come when you feel surrounded by enemies, even though there isn't a foe in sight. Look more closely at your underlings, especially at those who never dare to find fault with your decisions. Your eventual place in history will be determined by how well you select your assistants and partners. Choose carefully. So much depends upon it because so much depends upon you!

With all your marvelous gifts, it is no wonder that you are strong-willed. Knowing the right way, you are impatient with talk of any other way to do something. I admire your insight and eagerness, but that doesn't excuse your occasional tendency to ride right over others when you feel you are correct. You may have to learn the hard way that a successful executive listens patiently even when he is hearing folly. More important, a winning administrator keeps his team together, even the weaker members of it, with generous compliments and rare rebukes. Once you try a gentle but firm word of advice, instead of a roaring command, you'll never want to resume your overly dynamic treatment of your workers.

In your fifties or sixties, you run the risk of a serious setback in your career. It could fundamentally change your life-style. Remember in your youth that if you can look back over a lifetime of good deeds and private kindnesses, no misfortune of money, no loss of prestige, no fall from fame can destroy your true riches, your immaterial treasures.

COLORS: In your electric world, always speaking with the force of your personality, you don't need the boost of special colors. And yet, I strongly sense that in the lives of innumerable individuals, some of whom you don't know well, you are like a rare and hardy rose, as red as Santa's suit, blooming in their heart's garden in the dead of winter. You can explain what that means better than I can. At any rate, you would be wise to use dramatic touches of red and rose, both to break up the monotony of your clothes and to add vibrant flames of spiritual fire to your home. Perhaps if you wear a single small rose on special occasions—and this applies to both men and women—you could let it symbolize the usually controlled passion that swells within you and motivates you ever onward to the top.

MONEY: Your middle years will see the accumulation of great sums of money. By then, you will have gained a position of responsibility and will decide how considerable amounts of cash are invested or spent. I needn't tell you how prudent you must be in these matters, for most of the capital will not be your own. The way you handle these dealings will crucially affect your career.

Personally, your fortune will be assured, even if your later years find you in reduced circumstances. No matter what you lose, you will retain more than enough to continue on in comfort.

HEALTH: Your constitution is as splendid as your prospects! Hardy from birth, you've always been able to shrug off ailments because you simply could not take the time to be sick. Lucky you! I hope, however, that your vigor will not lead you to abuse this gift. A reckless disregard for your health while you are young will cost you dearly later on. Start now to avoid possible heart trouble and blood disorders by taking time to rest, no matter how busy you are, and by occasionally withdrawing from the pressures of competition and accomplishment.

RELATIONSHIPS: I fear that in your overpowering drive to the top, you will make more than your share of enemies. Some will be merely disappointed opportunists, but others will be sensitive people whose feelings you have disregarded. Treasure loyal friends, even when they criticize you, for that may be the best evidence of their faithfulness to you. In business, you can't be too careful of flatterers, because your star chart reveals that a money matter or land deal in which you are involved will come under scrutiny later, with possibly unfortunate results for you.

In your love life, you will want to form several romantic liaisons, all of them designed more for convenience than for lasting love. By marrying around your thirtieth year, you will marry well, although you will have to work hard to maintain a happy family life. Your career will tend to draw you away from your loved ones. That would be especially unfortunate because, in times of trouble yet to come, your family can be your best source of consolation and sound advice. So make a deliberate effort to maintain and tighten your closest ties, even when you must sacrifice your professional triumphs to do so.

Let that be your secret key to the mighty happiness of Capricorn. By building your life around those you love, you build not only for today but also for eternity.

That advice applies not only to a Capricorn but also to every one of us. And so, with those words in mind, let us turn to the next segment of the astral cycle, the sign of gentle and charming Aquarius.

AQUARIUS—JUDE (THADDAEUS)

(January 20–February 18)

As the order of the heavenly bodies brings us away from aloof and canny Capricorn, we enter a very different segment of the Zodiac, one characterized by a generous, sensitive, unconventional personality. All those traits combine in the sunny spirit of Aquarius, the water-carrier, the sign that has, during the last few years, become a symbol of the new world of peace and harmony that is waiting to be born.

Obviously, mankind hasn't yet moved into the Age of Aquarius. We stand on its brink. We glimpse its rich potential for humanity's liberated talents. Its beneficent atmosphere of fellowship and kindness gives us hope. But each day's news headlines remind us that we have a long way to go before reaching that new astral era.

In the meantime, as we each make our own way through life, the lessons of astrology can help us in the search for our special gateway to Heaven. Of course, it is our responsibility to approach that portal, and only the one Lord of Creation can open wide the door for us. No constellation of stars can do that, but our knowledge of their influences upon us can make our task easier and our journey happier. That is why, no matter what our own Zodiac sign, we should all be interested in the way human nature is developed and displayed in the personality of Aquarius.

The same holds true for every division of the Zodiac, especially the last, the one that follows Aquarius. For there the powers of good and evil, of nobility and shame, of greatness and defeat are most strongly concentrated. But I'm getting ahead of myself! For the present, let's attend to those charming individualists who are, in astrological terms, the children of the Water-Bearer.

In a spiritual sense, Aquarians are related to one of the least known of the Apostles. Sometimes called Thaddaeus or Lebbaeus, he was the brother of James the Less. His name was Jude, a variant of Judas, a common name at that time, and in my vision, he appeared as the embodiment of the positive characteristics of all Aquarians.

Jude was perhaps the most lovable of the Apostles. Indeed, his nicknames were expressions of endearment and affection. Thaddaeus is derived from the Hebrew words for "breast-child," and Lebbaeus comes from the words for "heart-child." These names were well chosen for him, as they are for all Aquarians who realize the best that is within them. Like Jude, they can not only draw the love of those who know them but also give their own great love to all the world.

You who were born under the sign of Aquarius are highly sensitive. Your intuition is keen, your feelings tender. Quick to perceive distress or sorrow in others, you are equally quick to be hurt or saddened yourself, especially when someone for whom you care fails to return your affection as intensely as you give it. Then you are apt to immediately break off your relationship, as if you had been deliberately offended. To say the least, this can be puzzling to those who know you. Without intending to wrong you, they can find themselves on your blacklist. You must remember that not everyone has your ability to love to the outermost limits of human sentiment. What might seem lukewarm affection to you, to others might be a major effort of the heart to demonstrate its feelings.

Keep that in mind the next time a friend fails to respond emphatically to your kindnesses. After all, Jude didn't give himself his nicknames. They were bestowed on him by others, who appreciated the constant charity he practiced. That is Aquarius at its best. At its worst, you might eventually reject most of those you claim to love just because they don't meet your exalted standards of total love. Each time you turn away from someone, though, you not only diminish them but also lessen your own capacity to love. And so it is that even the very positive and humane traits of the water-bearer can generate negative personal vibrations. Like a pebble tossed into a tranquil pond, those vibrations can carry small waves of bitterness throughout the human community.

If you have been reading this book chapter by chapter, you

probably know already what I am going to say next. Yes, even you Aquarians can wear red boots! Though your love is powerful, it is not omnipotent; and if it is directed toward selfish purposes, if it becomes possessive and domineering, then rest assured that the master of the red boots can find a pair of them in your size. Once you put them on, the cool and clear waters of Aquarius will turn acrid and muddy as the lively spring of your living nature becomes stagnant with pride and self-concern.

You Aquarians must remember that all over this planet, water is a symbol of life and of rebirth. As the water-bearers of astrology, your true role on earth is to refresh the parched spirits of those who thirst for a kind word and helping hand. In the words of the old childhood rhyme, you are like Friday's children, loving and giving. How absurd it is for any of you ever to march around in those misdirected red boots! Encumbered with their malign weight, you couldn't also carry the overflowing water jar of love.

Let us begin, then, with the understanding that you will always be like Jude: humane, warmhearted, a friend to those in need. Your ample talents will ensure you success in a worldly sense, but you will modestly allow others to take credit for your work. As a small example of that trait, it is interesting to note that at least some of Jude's writing in the New Testament was copied in part by another of the inspired authors. Jude's Epistle forms the basis for the second chapter of Peter's Second Epistle. In other words, Jude was something of a ghostwriter!

You Aquarians resemble Jude in that your satisfaction comes from a job well done, not from seeing your name up in lights. This doesn't indicate a sense of inferiority, for you are usually too outgoing and personable to brood about your possible shortcomings. Rather, you are quietly confident and don't need public acclaim to assure you of your abilities.

An even stronger factor in your reluctance to take credit for your accomplishments is a natural kindness, a willingness to allow others to enjoy glory. An inveterate humanitarian, always looking out for someone else's good to the neglect of your own, you tend to function as a kingmaker, a power behind the throne, in both your career and your personal life. By that, I mean that you will delight in the success of your colleagues, your spouse, your children, knowing that their advancement is largely your doing. It is as if the happiness of others is your one uncontrollable passion.

Do you reach for your purse or wallet every time you hear a hard-luck story? While visiting an Aquarian friend, I noticed that her recently delivered mail was mostly solicitations from charitable organizations. I commented, "You must be on every mailing list in the country!" Her reply was poignant. A few years ago, she had made a donation to one charity, and now she was practically going broke trying to help them all. As the appeals for aid poured in upon her, she couldn't resist responding generously. When I cautioned her that she was not the World Bank and should restrict her gifts to a few favorite causes, she insisted that the hungry and sick and orphaned needed her help, whether they were in Mississippi or Uganda, India or Chicago.

I had been wrong: she *was* the World Bank, at least emotionally! There could be no limits to her generosity, even when it disrupted her own life. And although I deplored her vulnerability to requests for assistance, I deeply admired her selfless and sympathetic spirit. No wonder Aquarians usually enjoy the fond esteem not only of their friends and family but also of casual acquaintances and virtual strangers who have heard about their generosity.

Almost as admirable as your openhearted giving is your masterful tact. Dreading arguments and disputes, you bottle up your own opinions rather than directly challenge those of a less informed or less astute person. You shy away from debates, even friendly ones, for fear that serious issues may provoke unpleasant emotions. But for all your reticence in the face of controversy, people seek out your views, draw out your opinions, insist upon your advice. The reason should be obvious to you. Most people are wise enough to know that wisdom is more often silent than noisy, and so your avoidance of verbal wrangling sets you apart as a prudent counselor and an insightful student of human affairs.

There is a slight drawback to that characteristic, and that is your tendency to go too far in compromising and conceding for the sake of peace. You are too likely to tell people what they want to hear rather than explain how you truly feel. In minor matters, this habit makes little difference; they are pleased with your response, and you avoid the interpersonal tension which invariably upsets you. But when a really important issue arises, you must be willing to demonstrate your intelligence and judgment by telling the truth in plain terms. On matters of principle, it is occasionally necessary to run the risk of argument to defend one's beliefs. After all, isn't that how you want others to behave? Don't you expect them to be honest with you, even when they disagree with your views? I'm sure you do. So reciprocate, defending your most cherished ideals with gentle words and kind insistence.

Good relationships with those with whom you live and work are especially vital to you. In fact, you may have already discovered to your dismay that your studies suffer in a disorderly classroom, your work is more difficult in a bickering office, your housework takes longer whenever you have had a family tiff. That is why you instinctively protect your most essential ties, preserving harmony and affection in your home as the highest priority for a happy life. The secret of your general success in this regard is an emotional versatility that allows you to adapt easily to the psychic vibrations of those around you. None of this means you are always eager to preserve every relationship. When your dealings with a particular person repeatedly turn sour, when you are more than once disappointed in someone's character, then you sever ties as decisively as you would otherwise act to reinforce them. You rarely regret breaking off with such characters, and you are right.

Like Jude with his three names, you often seem to be more than one personality. Aquarians are apt to hold down more than one job, to socialize at quite different levels, and to pursue a broad range of interests and activities. Preferring quiet and solitude, you will follow your career among groups of strangers, whose company you will enjoy. It is as if you can exchange one mind for another, functioning as quite a different person when the need arises.

In your early life, your world of action and accomplishment is outside your home, leading you to explore distant paths and seek unknown treasures, both material and intellectual. That trend, however, will reverse later in life, as you increasingly find the spiritual resources you need within your family circle.

Many Aquarians find it advisable to go into business on their own, having complete freedom of action to initiate their sometimes radically innovative ideas. Even when employed by others, they often find an extra job or civic commitment which will allow them the creative independence they need to keep their wits and acumen at their best.

Because, like Jude, you shun the spotlight and let others take the bows that are rightfully yours, many of you become the trusted aides to top executives and celebrities. They rely on your competence, admire your principles, and sense that you won't steal the limelight from them. How right they are! Your greatest satisfaction will come from making your employers appear brighter and wiser than they really are. There will be occasions, of course, when you can't escape the spotlight, even when you run from its admiring glare. Your talents will sometimes take all choice out of your hands, as you find yourself on center stage. It is revealing that Aquarius has been the predominant sign of members of the United States Congress. So often the children of the Water-Bearer are pushed forward into the public eye, whether or not they seek a life of leadership and glamour.

Because your astral influences make you creative and questioning, often unconventional and sometimes defiant of custom and tradition, you may feel a strong, if unexpressed, desire to unleash your genius upon the world through art, literature, music, or drama. When you pursue any of those fields, however, publicity and attention will inevitably come your way. Don't worry; as long as your work remains true to your personal vision, even the most brilliant spotlight won't reveal any flaws in it. Whether in the spotlight or off in the wings, you alone will decide whether the drama of your life is comedy, tragedy, or an ennobling play of wit, pathos, and enlightenment. Remember Shakespeare's maxim, that all the world's a stage; but be sure you realize that, unlike most actors, you are free to write your own part and determine your own ending.

Knowing that, you can set your sights as high as you wish. After all, four Presidents of the United States were fellow Aquarians: William McKinley (January 29), Franklin Roosevelt (January 30), William Harrison (February 9), and Abraham Lincoln (February 12). Two more political leaders who nearly made it to the White House were Adlai Stevenson (February 5) and Wendell Willkie (February 18). Among the current roster of potential occupants of the Oval Office is Ronald Reagan (February 6).

Musical Aquarians have included stylists as different as Jerome Kern and Mozart, both born on January 27. Schubert (January 31), Victor Herbert (February 1), and Mendelssohn (February 3) all shared the creative influences of the astral water-bearer. The same holds true of their astrological brethren who turned their powers of expression to literary channels: Lewis Carroll, author of *Alice in Wonderland* (January 27); W. Somerset Maugham (January 25); Charles Dickens and Sinclair Lewis (February 7); and Jules Verne

(February 8), whose fiction reveals both technical genius and possible psychic powers of foresight.

Susan B. Anthony, the mother of women's liberation in America, was born on February 15. Thomas A. Edison, who, in a manner of speaking, made his own spotlight to perform under, was born on February 11. A man all America loved and all America still respects in our fond memories, Charles Lindbergh, celebrated his birthday on February 4. Some Aquarians just could not avoid public attention, so great were their accomplishments.

One of my own personal heroes, in addition to Mr. Lindbergh, was the astronomer of the Renaissance, Galileo (February 15), who turned his Aquarian search for a better vision, a deeper truth, toward the heavens. In doing so, he revolutionized man's concept of the heavenly bodies and of his own place in the marvelous universe.

But what of our place in the universe today? What role do Aquarians have to play in the unfolding mysteries of God's cosmic will? Those questions must be answered by each one of us for ourselves. So let's turn now to review each division within the sign of the Water-Bearer so that our knowledge of human variety can lead us to the sure realization of mankind's one purpose, one goal, and one Lord.

AQUARIUS—FIRST DIVISION *(January 28, February 1, 10)*

Personal independence is the foremost character trait of Aquarians of the First Division. Though you are as humane and sensitive as others born under your star sign, you are also acutely aware of your own need for freedom from social and intellectual restrictions. You are seldom concerned about what others may think of your behavior and ideas. The very people whom you would never deliberately hurt may be shocked, if not outraged, by your defiance of their standards. And that, you would contend, is their problem; for they must not try to fit you into their patterns and molds. You are:

- aloof
- generous
- original
- friendly

Independence is a trait we all admire. Who can help but esteem the movie version of the self-contained cowboy, shaping his own life and answering to no one else's call? Even in your school years, your companions probably recognized that you were the rare individual who didn't follow fads but pursued your own goals in your own ways. In adulthood, you are the forcefully opinionated person who goes against the current of public opinion polls and who is willing to stall a jury forever because you believe the accused man is innocent.

All that is to your credit. You must learn sooner or later, however, that few of us live on the rugged frontier these days. As social beings, we have certain obligations to others. In business as in schooling, in civic affairs as in your family, people must feel that you are approachable. Like it or not, you will need the cooperation of others if you are to reach the top. Sometimes the water-bearer's overflowing jar becomes too heavy to carry alone. So be prepared to compromise your independence for the sake of accomplishing your goals.

Aside from a few Capricorns, there aren't many people who can match your ability to do without the approval of others. Remember that in all your dealings, both professional and personal. You may like to walk alone, but those who depend upon you still need a helping hand and an encouraging word. Let them know you need them, even if it pains you to express your emotional dependence upon them. If you fail to do this, you will gain a reputation for being not only aloof but also arrogantly superior in your attitudes. That will make you few friends, and could even alienate those who love you. If this sounds familiar to you, if it is happening to you already, it isn't too late to turn things around. Use a little diplomacy. A few kind words, perhaps seeking someone's opinion of your work or your ideas, can undo in an instant the emotional damage of many months of neglect.

Even when your aloofness runs to extremes, it rarely impairs your generous spirit. Strange as it may sound, you can simultaneously be distant from your fellow man and yet warmly committed to his well-being. You are the type of donor who avoids charity parties while sending in your checks by mail, and so your reputation may not do justice to your giving. Indeed, the people who consider you uncommunicative or haughty don't know that your openhanded sympathy has more than once imperiled your bank account. Toward those who are in distress, you can be as free and easy with your money as the water-carrier is with his ample jug, spilling stars across the heavens.

Those who know you best are those who know the best you. Your acquaintances who are willing to let you exercise the creative independence you crave are rewarded with the warmth and loyalty of a devoted friend. You are tolerant of their failings and supportive of their virtues. This is the side of your personality you should show to the world more often. I assure you, it is possible to extend the same friendliness toward those who don't yet understand your need for personal autonomy. Indeed, by doing so, you will find new ways to strike out on your own and fresh approaches to the independent life which delights you.

Because you have, from your youth, formed your own opinions, you tend to be highly original in your thoughts. Your self-sufficient attitude makes you a great innovator, finding new and clever ways to express yourself, verbally or artistically. You will often be regarded as unpredictable because your thought processes don't run in the ordinary channels. For this reason, you can change a dull committee meeting into a lively exchange of ideas just by proposing new insights into old problems. Your children can especially benefit from exposure to your mental independence. It can do more good for their intellectual development than squads of teaching specialists. By endowing them in their childhood with your own love of self-gathered knowledge, you will give them a legacy far richer than monetary wealth.

In sum, you Aquarians of the First Division march to a different drummer, but there is no need for you to walk alone all your life. By explaining your beliefs and values to others, you may find that they wish to follow along your way. With their cooperation and support, your fine mental abilities will be even stronger and your work more successful. Surely, those prospects are worth the effort it will take to reconcile your own independence with your social obligations.

COLORS: The way you dress and the appearance of your home can help to warm your personality. Let the truly generous person behind your aloof exterior shine through to the world with the exuberant colors of aqua and sea green. Like the hues I saw around the Apostle Jude in my vision, those shades are natural expressions of the flowing magnanimity characteristic of the water-bearer.

You shouldn't hesitate to be as original in your use of color as you are in your handling of ideas. What might seem bizarre in someone else's living room will, in your home, appear as the appropriate expression of an unpredictable spirit. For your favorite room, whether the kitchen or den or bedroom, you might surround yourself with white, like the foam of ocean breakers, accented only by the deep and shifting colors of a storm-tossed sea. And don't forget that a golden ornament can be a physical manifestation and symbol of your innate generosity, which enriches others as it doubly rewards you.

MONEY: You are the archetype of the successful entrepreneur, and should be successful in any enterprise that allows you to go your way toward success alone, or at least unsupervised. Because you are not only confident but also sufficiently objective to calculate risks and assess realistic possibilities, your investments should be prudent and beneficial. By the time you reach middle age, you should have accumulated a comfortable nest egg. Your financial reserves should leave you free to enjoy the many leisure pursuits you have been long postponing if—and this is a major proviso—you decide early in life to reach the wealth that awaits you.

HEALTH: Although your health will be generally good, your lungs and heart are prone to ailments. So be careful of minor chest infections. Regular exercise, mild rather than arduous, will be the best insurance policy against coronary problems.

RELATIONSHIPS: Your aloof glamour fascinates members of the opposite sex, and so you will never lack for companions, whether for frivolous socializing or for serious bonds of affection. Your fidelity as an extremely loyal marriage partner is a constant joy to your mate, even if you aren't demonstrative with your love. Try to choose a partner who understands that your emotions run deep, even though your words don't reveal them. When your spouse knows that your affection is as enduring as it is silent, your home life will be both stable and exciting.

AQUARIUS–SECOND DIVISION
(January 20, 29, February 2, 11)

Aquarians of the Second Division share with their astrological brethren of the First Division a deep reserve. In the case of you

Aquarius Twos, however, your reticence takes the form of shyness rather than aloofness. You are more withdrawn than independent. You don't relish the idea of needing no one. On the contrary, you do desire supportive human contact, but you are often too private a person to take advantage of it. This probably stems from your childhood years, when you strongly wanted to be on your own. You were the type of youngster who could always think of an excuse not to go on a family picnic, and I suspect you rarely brought your friends home to visit. Many of you went out into the world as early as you could; but once you were out there, making your own way, you realized how unprepared you were to meet and deal with people on a one-to-one basis. You are:

- idealistic
- sensitive
- lacking in confidence
- perceptive

You are a romantic at heart. By that, I mean that you see life in terms of ideals to be pursued, not reality to be accepted as it is. It is hard for you to understand how people in your profession can use their jobs purely as sources of profit. Whether you are a surgeon or a cook, a bus driver or a congressman, you see in your work some way to be of service and to relieve the suffering of mankind. As you grow older and find that that attitude is much too rare in our world, your idealism will face a challenge: do you abandon it and join the rat race for profit and status or do you reaffirm your separate, better path through life? I think the answer should be obvious.

We don't have much definite information concerning the Apostle Jude. Did he have a romantic streak? What else would have led him to commit his life to a heroic cause, giving up everything to carry the Master's good news to the world? Was he eager to leave his home while young and be off to strange places? Eager or not, while still in his tender years, he was roaming through Palestine with Christ. You see how marvelously your own personal characteristics are revealed in the little we know about your Apostle!

Your idealism is its own reward. In many situations, it will carry you through difficulty and embarrassment. You tend to avoid public scenes and dread being in the spotlight. But for the sake of a worthy cause, you will deliver a ringing oration at a civic meeting or speak up at work when all others remain silent in the face of injustice. Even in your high school years, you may have won the admiration of certain classmates because, despite your shyness, you stepped forward to protest inequities or to right a wrong. You may not have joined the debating society, being too self-conscious to discuss its assorted topics; but that wouldn't prevent you from jumping to your feet at a lecture to protest an insult or correct an untruth.

To some extent, your shyness is charming. When unrestrained by a realistic appraisal of your abilities, however, it can destroy all your confidence. It can make you painfully uneasy around people, especially when you are called on to contribute your views to a conversation or company discussion. That is unfortunate for anyone, but for you it is tragic. You have too much insight and foresight to be silenced by your lack of self-assurance.

Perhaps, in a peculiarly roundabout way, your idealism limits your self-confidence. Perhaps your awareness that your beliefs and values are different from those of the general community makes you feel awkward, even ashamed of being so out of step with the mass of people. There is a better way to view the situation. Think of yourself as a wrong-way lemming—the arctic rodent which, every few years, for some unknown reason migrates in vast numbers into the sea, where it perishes. It may be true that in the eyes of your neighbors, your idealism is leading you the wrong way. But it is leading you to a higher, safer course than the one taken by the other lemmings! This is one instance in which your Aquarian instincts are leading you away from water!

I advise you to become more self-reliant and proud of your accomplishments. Remember how independent you were as a youngster? Find that quality within you again. If it has weakened, make it strong by exercising it gradually, just as you would a weakened muscle. As long as you don't allow your independence to turn you into a loner, it will be a valuable asset in furthering your work and defending your ideals. Don't be so afraid to make a mistake. Your errors only prove that you are as human as the rest of us. Be prepared to take criticism, using it as a means for self-improvement rather than a crushing blow to your confidence. And then when you feel you deserve a higher grade or greater credit or a raise, you will feel free to speak up on your own behalf. You will find it is possible to be idealistic and realistic at the same time, especially when your own future is at stake.

It is a paradox that you can lack confidence when you don't lack splendid gifts: talent, creativity, the typical Aquarian inventiveness, especially an astute perception, both in the physical sense of sharp discernment and in the intellectual sense of mental acumen. With all these endowments, especially this last, you would make a fine quality control specialist in a specialized industry, like those which make parts for aircraft instruments or spacecraft. Any career involving insight and judgment, especially in dealing with abstract relationships, should suit you perfectly.

Your planetary signs indicate that your best opportunities for betterment will come in your middle years, especially if you have remained a free agent rather than having totally committed yourself to one employer. Foreign travel may well bring a radical change in your life-style, perhaps involving service as a consultant in the arts and humanities.

COLORS: Reinforce your confidence with colors that will proclaim your presence without disturbing your essentially idealistic purposes. The combination of cream and pale green is ideal. No, they aren't water shades; but they are the colors of cloud and treetop reflected in a woodland pond. And so they express your unworldly motives and ethereal ambitions.

MONEY: Expect a slow start in money matters to last through the first decade of your adult life, until you get a grip on your affairs and begin to assert yourself more forcefully. It is fine to be a behind-the-scenes operative, like Jude in his ghostwriting; but even modest individuals need and merit sufficient payment for their work.

Your determination and willingness to exert extra effort in a good cause will pay off by your middle years, and the stars of the Second Division indicate the definite possibility of grants or prizes or an inheritance that will materially improve your economic situation.

HEALTH: In this regard, there is only good news on your astrological chart. A solid constitution combines with positive attitudes toward physical fitness to make you feel fit and live long. With moderate luck in avoiding accidents, you should look forward to many years of vigor and health.

RELATIONSHIPS: It is advisable that you marry late. Let your career get off to a good start before taking on the emotional and financial commitments of a home and family. In your case, because of your shyness, it may take several years before you are confident enough to demand your share of the economic pie. If you should fall in love with someone who shares your career, however, then the chances for a happy early marriage are much better; for you will grow closer together by sharing the lean years as well as the later rich ones.

As parents, Aquarius Twos are inclined to relive their youth through their children. If this applies to you, guard against dominating your offspring. Let them find their own way, as you have found yours.

Though you can be painfully withdrawn, your stars form a potently romantic combination. Shy as you are, you will not lack lovers; and your marriage will be a passionate lifelong affair, despite its outward appearance of humdrum normalcy. No one but you, your mate, and your children will realize how powerful your love is, healing every hurt and fulfilling every dream.

AQUARIUS—THIRD DIVISION
(January 21, 30, February 3, 12)

Like Abraham Lincoln, whose division you share, you Aquarius Threes are marked for leadership. The planetary influences on your birth have predisposed you to command, either literally in a position of power or figuratively as a mover of minds. You are:

- ambitious
- driving
- intelligent
- an organizer

Many people are ambitious, but few are as fortunate as you in knowing that you can give free rein to your aspirations with every chance of actually achieving them. This trait was probably noticeable from your early years, and you might ask your parents or older relatives about it. Did you, as a child, have remarkable ambitions? While your playmates wanted to be cowboys and firemen and actresses, did you play at being a statesman, a business tycoon, a great scientist? Chances are, that was the case. And even if the course of your career hasn't run according to your youthful dreams, you haven't abandoned your ambitions.

Adult Aquarians of the Third Division often transfer their ambitions to their children. A young father and mother, supporting and loving their children full time, can't always continue their early hopes of reaching fame and fortune. But they can see to it that their sons and daughters get every opportunity to cut a path through the world. And so, as parents, you are apt to see to it that your children have extra classes, additional learning experiences, and that golden spark of your own yearning for special success.

The reason your ambition is likely to succeed is that it runs in tandem with a personal drive, through which you accept the need for hard work and prolonged effort to reach your goals. Too many people have great dreams and little callus, if you know what I mean. That is not your case. Your heroic stamina in learning, trying, experimenting, stretching for higher standards, and reaching for the stars will take you far up the ladder of success. With so much going for you, you should realize that as long as you are keenly interested in the task at hand, you will make it go well. If, on the other hand, you don't have a personal commitment to the project facing you, even your driving sense of duty will not make your performance worthy of your abilities. So choose your efforts wisely and avoid those to which you feel no sense of loyalty; for even if they promise you tremendous financial rewards, you will never be satisfied with their results.

When your work exactly coincides with your imaginative creativity, then your drive powers through it like a hot knife slips through butter. Your talents pour out like the flood of water from Aquarius' suddenly upturned water jar. Learn to regard every challenge to your abilities as another chance to loose your constructive energies. By giving your best even in situations which bore you, you will be better prepared to set the world on its heels when your ambition is fully charged.

With your intellectual gifts, that should not be difficult to do. Your primary interests are mental rather than physical. Even your leisure may involve mechanical or technical matters, whether puzzles or handicrafts or reading. You needn't be an academician to enjoy the life of the mind. On the contrary, there are front-porch and street-corner intellectuals in every town in America, whose appreciation for wisdom and innovative ideas is greater than that found on most campuses.

When you do become involved in sports, they serve as a relaxation from your daily mental stress. You favor water sports rather than rougher contests, as if the peaceful milieu of the water gives you respite from the driving ambition of your workaday world. And so you are apt to shun the intense competition of tennis or hockey, preferring diving, ice skating, or canoeing as a calming antidote to too much striving for success.

Another major talent of Aquarius Threes is organization. Sounds simple, doesn't it, as if you can take it for granted? Quite the contrary! I have a friend in Washington, D.C., who is the wife of an ambassador. Often the hostess at large parties and receptions, she one day confided to me how hopeless her efforts were in putting them together successfully. Things just did not work according to plan. I advised her to find an Aquarian of the Third Division to serve as her social secretary. From her reaction, I could see she took my advice with a grain of salt. Two months later, however, she happily telephoned to report that, out of desperation, she had followed my suggestion. Though she felt foolish in asking job applicants for their birthdates, she finally located someone who fitted the description. "The first Aquarius Three to come along got the job," she said. "And she is a godsend! Now where in the stars can you find me a good chef? Ours is quitting."

Well, that's another problem altogether. I will only point out that my friend's new employee shared Jude's trait of efficient organization. As a letter writer, he probably was one of those quiet managers of affairs who kept the traveling Gospelers informed of events elsewhere and, in today's terms, did the staff work that ensured their later success on evangelical missions.

COLORS: You have probably already anticipated my revelation that your colors are those of a leader: the whole range of purples, reminiscent of those worn by Roman emperors and royalty throughout the ages. For your gentler nature, however, I prefer a more tender comparison. In one of the many parks around Washington, D.C., a few blocks west of the White House, there is a large lily pond; and in summer, it is filled with magnificent plants whose blossoms are so large and showy that some tourists probably think they are plastic! Imagine yourself as one of those regal violet lilies, changing from pink to lavender to deepest purple with shifts in sunlight. Those hues will bring out the best in your appearance and make your home a comfortable lily pond for a very successful Aquarian.

MONEY: Although certain hasty investments are likely to cause you pain, your economic prospects are optimistic. The trend of your finances is steadily upward, thanks to your forethought and planning. That special touch for masterful organization will be both a guard against sudden loss and an aid in saving what you earn. Expect to be relatively affluent by middle age, but beware of spending money that hasn't yet come into your hands.

HEALTH: Your physical activity can be a drain on your intellectual and emotional reserves. Your body is likely to give out long before your mind, and so you may keep trying to work when you should rest and sleep. Commonsense precautions can prevent exhaustion and ensure that the quality of your work is not lessened by excessive strain. In your youth, your constitution is unusually robust; but later in life, an old injury can cause you considerable annoyance. In general, however, your life is both long and healthy, as long as you moderate your activity and appreciate the need for play as well as work.

RELATIONSHIPS: Because of your inner drive and outward display of mental powers, you possess tremendous magnetism for members of the opposite sex. Be prepared for their affectionate attempts to secure commitments from you that you may not be ready to make, especially when romantic attachments can interfere with the pursuit of your ambitions.

You have the distinct advantage in romantic relationships because you are usually able to judge a person's worth not from his or her external appearance but from hidden talents and ideals, from unspoken beliefs and quiet principles. For you, beauty is as beauty does. And if more people shared your insight, there would be far fewer heartaches in the world. You will make an excellent marriage partner, and can look forward to an idyllic home life. Just be sure your partner understands how powerful your ambition is. You don't like to wait for others to catch up with you.

AQUARIUS–FOURTH DIVISION

(January 22, 31, February 4, 13)

Life is a constant challenge to Aquarius Fours. I don't mean that it is unpleasant or burdensome. Rather, it will present you with one decision after another, many of them difficult. But like all tests, these trials will be opportunities for growth, and you would be wise to consider them chances for personal betterment rather than interruptions of an otherwise quiet life. Surmounting each challenge, you can be like the Apostle Jude, a finer person for every time you put principle before convenience. You are:

- unconventional
- strong-minded
- attracted to new ideas
- sensitive

The stars influencing your birth gave you a generous measure of the typically Aquarian trait of independence, and it surfaces in your personality as a habitual defiance of convention. Your offbeat attitudes lead to original ideas and, sometimes, to controversial actions. People consider you unpredictable because you seldom act in accordance with general notions of propriety, much less formality. Within limits, there is nothing wrong with that. Indeed, it is refreshing to come across people like you who prefer substance to form, meaning to saying, values to material acquisitions.

Because you are different, in many ways that most people cannot see, you may even have trouble explaining your motives and hopes to parents and friends. When communication has broken down over a period of years, it may be impossible to make those who love you understand why you live as you do. That is a situation as difficult as it is heartbreaking. But it needn't be that way! Just as you find unusual ways to work toward your goals, it is also your responsibility to seek unconventional means to convey your feelings, hopes, and fears to your family. When you want to do so as strongly as you want to follow your own paths through life, you will find the right words, gestures, or whatever is necessary. In fact, you are so strong-minded that the same statement holds true for most of your undertakings. When you desperately reach for something, you rarely give up the effort without grasping the prize, even if you strain your abilities in the process. Needless to say, this can put you on the high road to success if you direct your attentions toward your career.

Of course, there is no guarantee that you will do that. You may find it preferable to seek other kinds of advancement than professional and economic progress. Once again, your lack of conventionality will draw notice from the public, whether favorable or otherwise matters to you not at all. Jude was much the same way when he left his normal occupation for the unpaid, uncomfortable, and downright dangerous life of an itinerant preacher. But he remained true to his own ideas, doing the things you might be led to do in a more modern context.

For you, too, are attracted to new movements, whether they be political, intellectual, or religious. Your Aquarian independence of thought keeps you out of step with your neighbors, who may consider your beliefs silly or scandalous. You will just have to learn to live with their misunderstanding, for you are not likely to adjust your conduct to suit them. Far from it! To you, controversial matters appear black and white, clear-cut, although that is rarely how the problems of life come our way. Usually there is an ample gray area of uncertainty open to compromise, but I doubt that you see things that way.

One reason you tend to emphasize opposite points of view and to analyze issues in extreme terms is your own sensitivity to emotions. You magnify everything, good or bad, that happens to you, especially when it involves slights or hostility. That can lead you to frequent depression, which will curtail your talents and diminish your productivity in both a material and an intellectual sense. That is a needless waste of your gifts, for with a little practice you can break yourself of that indulgence. I don't mean you should be less sensitive, only that you should be more selective in unleashing your powers of emotional exchange. They are a blessing for you and can be equally beneficial to others. They act as an inner barometer to tell you of the emotional needs of those around you. What a wonderful asset that is! You would make an excellent arbiter of disputes, dispassionate and intuitive, logical and sympathetic, able to understand the unexpressed feelings of all parties.

Does that sound as if I am suggesting you have psychic powers? I am indeed, although you will have to be the sole judge of them. If you find that you are unusually attuned to what people are thinking about you, then you might contemplate the other impressions you receive from people. And if you realize that you have been communicating on levels you never before noticed, by all means exercise those rare abilities until you bring them to their fullest potential.

I caution you that your psychic gifts, as well as your other mental and spiritual powers, can be severely diminished if your Aquarian reticence leads you to withdraw from the challenges of life. Remember what I said at the beginning of this discussion: each test you will face can be a great opportunity, not only to learn, but also to teach others the true meaning of your unconventionality. No matter what roadblocks are thrown in the way of your beliefs, imitate Jude in your persistence and courage.

COLORS: Because you are both unconventional and strong-minded, you probably already use daring color schemes without the slightest regard for disparaging criticism. I admire your verve and only suggest that you also express your sensitivity through the occasional use of pastels. In fact, in your home, where you can be at peace with the world, it is advisable to surround yourself with delicate blues and grays and, most of all, light rose and pink. Those paler versions of passionate red will strike the exact balance you need between fervent commitment and gentle contemplation.

MONEY: Money is a minor factor in your life, and you make little effort to obtain or keep it. You aren't careless or indolent, but you put little value on material possessions, unlike your attitude toward your ideas and beliefs. Because you are happy to work at a wide range of jobs, you can expect to remain solvent, even fairly comfortable if you put your mind to business once in a while. There are uncertain indications in your astrological chart of a large amount of money coming into your life in your later years. If so, use it wisely, or it may leave your grasp just as abruptly as it arrived.

HEALTH: Your physical well-being is a result of your moods. When you are optimistic and eager for life, you will enjoy robust health. During your formative years, however, while you are searching for yourself and troubled about your eventual goals, you suffer bouts of infectious diseases. Once you have found your targets, once you have set your course, then you should remain fit and vigorous, as long as you avoid the threat of an accident during your thirties.

RELATIONSHIPS: Ordinarily, your shyness would keep you from making many friends; but, lucky you, that special sensitivity the stars have given you compensates for your reticence. You can sense when someone likes you and wants to know you better. More important, you can often tell when someone needs your understanding, sympathy, or aid and is reluctant to ask for it. This enables you to initiate friendships which will not only benefit you but also be a comfort and blessing to others.

Romantic attachments don't come to you frequently. You tend

to drift in and out of them, suffering little pain at their disruption. You rarely commit your deepest self, remaining, even in love, a rather private individual. In marriage, however, you make an excellent partner, usually because you have found a kindred spirit whose understanding sustains you and whose beliefs reinforce your own.

AQUARIUS–FIFTH DIVISION *(January 23, February 5, 14)*

Forceful, perceptive, independent, you Aquarians of the Fifth Division are extraordinarily endowed with powers and willingness to act for the good of mankind. Your astral influences have not given you remarkable skills to be frittered away in mere worldly success. On the contrary, every talent you see in yourself is intended for your Creator's special purposes. If you have been reading this book from its beginning, then you know that the same holds true of every person. But for you, it is emphatically applicable. Much is expected of you because so much has been given you. You are able to:

- read the intentions of others
- speak out
- stand alone
- bring peace to troubled situations

Your razor-sharp intellect cuts to the heart of an interpersonal matter like a surgeon's knife to reveal what lies beneath the words that often conceal our real thoughts. This allows you to analytically probe the minds of those with whom you deal. I don't have to tell you that this is a useful trait, in business as well as private life. You can anticipate what your colleagues will say; and in school, you often guess in advance the questions a teacher will include on your tests.

Though your intuitive understanding of others' intentions gives you all kinds of advantages, it also can cause you difficulty unless you use it sparingly and discreetly. Remember that people don't want to believe their minds are an open book to you. They resent your reading them at a glance. Some people shy away from persons with your talent, for they cherish their mental privacy and are offended by the intrusion of your acute feeling for their emotions. Respect their intellectual seclusion and never flaunt your powers of perception. There will be innumerable times when your insight will be appreciated by those who want very much to communicate with you but can't find the right words.

I needn't tell you that a lack of words has never bothered you! In fact, you are sometimes too direct and outspoken. You don't hesitate to ask awkward questions to get at the facts of a situation, nor are you reluctant to state your opinions when asked, no matter who is outraged or offended by them. It is as if, when someone tugs at the water-bearer's sleeve, you pour out a flood of truth. I admire your honesty and frankness but hope you will remember that like all strong drinks, truth takes some getting used to, at least for those who are unaccustomed to taking it straight! Seriously, be sure that when you quench others' thirst for knowledge, you don't drown them in an overabundance of your sharply spoken opinions.

Your habit of speaking your mind reminds me of Jude's conversation with Christ at the Last Supper. He asked the Lord why He had just promised to reveal Himself to the Apostles and not to the whole world. Christ's reply was equally blunt, explaining that He would show His true nature and purpose only to those who loved Him and obeyed His Father. Like Jude in another way, you stand alone when you have to, going against the prevailing sentiment of your community or colleagues. This can cause you difficulty, especially in your school years, for students tend to be intolerant toward those who won't conform to current fads. Nonetheless, your courage can get you through criticism and mockery, because you gladly forgo the approval of others to stand by your principles. That doesn't mean your lonely defense of your beliefs is either easy or pleasant. Indeed, I sense that it pains you greatly when you lose the esteem of those who disagree with you. But that is the price any free spirit must pay for independence.

You have one very special ability that is widely envied, although you take it for granted. You don't realize it, but many people marvel at the way you can calm a troubled situation. Perhaps you instinctively change turmoil into peace; perhaps you do so consciously. Whatever your intent, your mere presence on an angry scene is sufficient to restrain violent words and more violent hatred. A few words from you, spoken in your usually reasonable way, will persuade most combatants to settle down. For the few disputants who prefer continued argument and vilification, you hold in reserve an acid tongue that can further subdue them. Seldom do you lose your cool, partly because you basically like people and partly because your Aquarian reserve keeps back your passions while freeing your verbal expressiveness. I remind you of the blessing that Christ pronounced on peacemakers. Did you think he was referring only to famous diplomats who negotiate international accords? Far from it. The kind of calming and reconciling you do, day in and day out, may be more important than the treaties among statesmen even if you never win the Nobel Peace Prize.

You are fond of study and often pursue offbeat subjects. Your retentive memory, sometimes developed to a remarkable degree, has allowed you to store up immense knowledge. This enables you to deal with situations which baffle and overwhelm others. I suggest you take this talent into account in deciding upon a career, for it is far too valuable to be left for your amusement alone.

COLORS: The lighter shades of the spectrum best enhance your magnetism. The colors of the peacemaker, white and pale yellow, should be prominent in your wardrobe. If there is a particular room in your home which you use for conferences or for family discussions, fill it with those innocent hues to express your commitment to interpersonal peace and to reinforce the tranquillity you bring to others. When you are preparing to take a public stand on issues, at work or in your community, embolden your appearance to match your forceful speech. Change your white to cream and heighten your yellow to gold. Just as there is nothing timid about your frankness, so there should be nothing shy about your apparel.

MONEY: Despite the fact that you give excellent financial advice to others, you don't always follow your own best instincts in handling your personal accounts. Because you are intelligent and calm, you may be too confident that there will always be time later to concentrate on business. You cannot be frightened into suddenly saving money for a rainy day. With your astuteness, however, there should be no reason for abrupt changes in your money situation. By planning now for your later life, you will avoid an economic pinch in your middle years. I hope you take this advice as eagerly as you give counsel to others.

HEALTH: Energetic and full of vitality, you Aquarius Fives can have superb health if you work to keep yourself fit. Those of you born on the February dates of the Fifth Division may drink too much and live too extravagantly. That is a sorry waste of your vital life-force. You know already what you must do to preserve your physical well-being. I will assume that your innate good sense will lead you to take prompt corrective action.

RELATIONSHIPS: Sincere and highly idealistic in your personal dealings, you form friendships easily but tend to become too intensely involved with people. In your love life, this can lead you to sustain several passionate relationships at the same time, without attaching sufficient importance to any of them. The resulting broken hearts are rarely yours, but that doesn't lessen the folly of the situation.

You like flattery and are proud of your ability to understand people and to influence them. Partly because you can see into the hidden motives of others, you will choose your marriage partner wisely and select a spouse who will be as devoted as you. As a parent, you are slightly possessive, which is certainly preferable to the too common neglect of children afflicting our society. All in all, your relationships are sound and fruitful.

AQUARIUS—SIXTH DIVISION *(January 24, February 6, 15)*

By controlling the distractions that cross your path through life, you can focus on your formidable talents to reach your goals. There is no question about your abilities; but your astrological chart indicates a tendency to veer off your course, like an eccentric comet, attracted by momentary whims and passing fancies. Once you overcome that habit, you can follow your predetermined orbit to success. You are:

- inclined to daydream
- giving
- artistic
- personable

Your love of castles in the air obviously means that your concentration on the job at hand leaves much to be desired. Whether in your career or in school, you may miss golden opportunities for learning and advancement because your head is in the clouds of a daydream. By a quirk of your stars, you are apt to enter a profession which demands total attention to your work. This means that sooner or later, you will have to break the habit of drifting off to your fantasies. Why not take that step now and save yourself difficulties later on?

Your willingness to be helpful to others can, strangely enough, also bring you troubles. Every good thing, it seems, carries some negative effect, just as each evil brings some good. Too frequently you allow others to command your time and energies with their problems. Sacrificing your projects and studies to help them, you drain away your ambitions by diffusing your attention. I don't mean this advice to sound selfish, only prudent. Because charity begins at home, make sure your generosity doesn't disrupt your personal timetable for advancement and fulfillment. The same holds true with regard to your financial giving. Generous to a fault, you back friends in dubious investments and risky loans. Even when you lose money, you would rather write off the loss than imperil your friendships. I admire your selfless spirit, but I urge you to think first of those who are dependent on you before you allow your noble instincts to endanger their financial security.

Entirely apart from your generosity, people like and trust you, even those who never ask you for a loan. They sense your natural desire to care for others. The fact that Aquarians usually have a striking, noble physical appearance doesn't harm your popularity either! But what is more important is the fact that you are frequently as beautiful spiritually as you are handsome physically. Persons of taste and feeling will care more about your internal virtues than about your pleasing countenance.

Aquarians of the Sixth Division are usually artistic. The creative spirit of the water-bearer is bold in you, and that is why you feel ill at ease when you suppress your appetite for the beautiful and expressive. If your work doesn't allow your instincts free reign, by all means pursue a creative hobby in your spare time. You will find that even a few hours during a weekend are sufficient to satisfy the artist that lives inside the salesman, housewife, banker, or waitress. If your creativity does bring you into public attention, whether as part of your career or as a sideline, you will relish the admiration it attracts. Even if you presently shun the spotlight, wait until it turns on you the first time. It will give you an even stronger motivation to accomplish more and win greater praise. That reward will matter to you more than financial recompense. Your art—whether it be painting, literature, drama, or whatever—will be a kind of gentle statement to the world, a work of love.

Under ordinary circumstances, you are indifferent to your environment, be it your home, possessions, or neighborhood. But as you begin to enjoy the fruits of success, you are apt to go to the other extreme, going into debt to keep up the front of affluence you think you are presenting to the world. In fact, your excessive spending fools no one; nor is it necessary. Your facility for making friends is sufficient of itself. There is no need to impress people with wealth, real or feigned, when you are intelligent, well informed, and eloquent in speech and writing. In a word, you are personable, a memorable individual to those who meet you briefly, a treasured companion to those who know you well. Remember that when money comes your way and you are tempted to use it for status rather than security.

COLORS: Did I say you build castles in the air? No wonder, then, that your best color is a sky blue, as sunny as your personality. I hope you won't rush out and buy a new wardrobe in that shade, for it is only one of many that convey your personal magnetism. Your passion for helping others appears to me as a streak of deep purple flashing across your aura. Especially when you are dealing with those who seek your aid, perhaps a purple scarf, tie, or sweater would express your warm charity. But don't overdo it! Who knows, if you were to wear a purple suit, you might sign away your bank account!

When you want to emphasize your artistic talents—and I fervently hope you decide to do just that—there is a certain shade of dark royal blue that will do wonders for you, putting you in a dramatically creative mood. It is the color you would imagine for the backdrop of the ballet "Swan Lake," at the moment of the swan's death. For Aquarians, it is the color of ocean water at its deepest. Indeed, it is the color of Aquarians at their greatest depth and most profound creativity.

MONEY: Once your early, unsettled years are over, you will feel a strong tide of good fortune running your way. That won't prevent you from making poor investments and, as I have already warned you, bad loans to friends. Nevertheless, you may well enjoy several incomes, both from your regular occupation and from royalties or commissions. Although you will probably work until late in life, too committed to your career to retire from it, you should provide for your old age in case unexpected circumstances change your plans.

HEALTH: You can look forward to a long and healthy life, with only some possible respiratory troubles to cause you serious difficulty. Stop smoking, now! That will make an immense difference between minor discomfort and grave illness. Young or old, you can kick the habit if you want to, and there are people in your community ready to help you do so. Other health crises, involving your heart and intestinal system, seem at the present time to be false alarms. You may eventually require surgery, but my astrological readings can't be exact on this point. My advice is to avoid even the possibility of such trouble by attending to your health today.

RELATIONSHIPS: For your spouse to be happily married to an Aquarius Six requires the realization that your fantasies may be unfaithful but you will not be. You are a good marriage partner, although your mind wanders from home to exotic and exciting adventures.

The generosity you bring to all your relationships will warm and nourish your family. Your children will be raised to take kindness for granted, and they will be better for it. When they at last discover that the world is hardly as giving and thoughtful as their happy home, they will discover how much you have given them in a spiritual sense. Their gratitude should be directed toward imitation of your virtues, not merely verbal praise for them.

Even if your financial status prevents you from bestowing expensive advantages upon your children, you can give them, free of charge, a sharing in your artistic sensitivity. They can be raised to appreciate beauty wherever it is found: in the marble halls of art galleries or the backyard gardens of urban neighborhoods; in a plush concert hall or the lyrics of antique folk songs preserved by the old folks down the street. Your children may not be Aquarians, but you can teach them to love the creative spirit wherever it blossoms and bears fruit.

AQUARIUS–SEVENTH DIVISION
(January 25, February 7, 16)

The combination of planets governing the Seventh Division of Aquarius indicates an unusual life for those born under their influence. From childhood, you feel out of place, out of step, somehow uneasy about your identity and future prospects. It is as if you are subconsciously aware that a significant change lies ahead of you which will take apart the pieces of your life and rearrange them in a better, more dynamic pattern. The key to your eventual happiness lies in whether you accept that change and adapt to its demands on your talents or shrink from the challenge of the future. You are:

- inclined toward religion
- a student of the mind
- looking for a cause
- idealistic

When I say that you have a religious bent, I don't mean that you spend all your time in church. Indeed, because you are as independent as most Aquarians, you may dislike formal worship and the dogmas and rituals of organized denominations. But you do have a constant sense of an all-powerful God, caring for His people on this earth. Even if you prefer to worship Him in long walks in the forest, rather than by attending Sunday morning services, you feel His presence in all aspects of your life.

Because of your perception of the world and man as the inexpressibly beautiful handiworks of the Creator, you are especially interested in the interaction between the physical world and the spiritual, between the body and the mind, between earthly phenomena and the occult. This interest can take many forms. If you consider it odd or eccentric, you can suppress your own best instincts and do nothing with them. On the other hand, if you recognize that your fascination with the mind and its powers is a hint of your inborn instincts, then you can develop and direct great gifts of intuition and sensitivity. To be precise, the study of mental telepathy, ESP, and related abilities can lead you to an awareness of your own participation in rare experiences of the mind.

Of course, there is more than one approach to the extremely intricate mysteries of the mind. Philosophers have argued over its powers for three thousand years. Psychologists have claimed a monopoly of information about it for only a century; and although much of the public looks to them for answers, it may be that their scientific analyses, by ignoring the human spirit, are asking all the wrong questions. Be that as it may, you needn't feel compelled to pursue any single discipline in your search for information and, what is more important, for understanding. I suspect that you will move from the physical sciences to theology to mysticism, always focusing upon human thought processes as the point at which divine potential meets and mingles with material being.

You could even be led into the field of psychotherapy, whether as a highly trained expert or a volunteer aide. Your perceptive intuition would be uniquely useful in dealing with emotionally disturbed individuals. Even those who have largely shut out reality can sense your concern for them. Don't be surprised if such unfortunate persons confide in you and become dependent upon your care for them. I do not recommend, however, that you become an amateur psychiatrist; too many persons try to stretch a little jargon until it creates a great deal of trouble. The human mind can sometimes be as fragile as it usually is hardy, and I know you wouldn't want to be responsible for damage done to it. Because so many Aquarius Sevens have special aptitude for work in that field, however, I would encourage you to seek training in it and to earn a professional status.

In fact, any work involving the suffering or the needy would suit you; for, like Jude before he met Christ, you are looking for a cause. You need to dedicate your energies to some higher goal than just making a living, for you are a crusader at heart. If you find that your job doesn't satisfy your desire for humanitarian service, by all means arrange an outlet for your feelings during your spare time, perhaps through local charity work or civic activities. Otherwise, you will feel frustrated even as you move up the ladder of success, although you may not understand the reason for your dissatisfaction with all the good things of the world.

When you want to be, you are hard-working and selfless. Money means little to you, but the satisfaction of a job well done means everything. When your work does not bring you that feeling of fulfillment, then you are not one of the most conscientious employees, by any means. This makes it all the more important for you to combine your idealism with the realistic necessity of making a living. Remember that pursuit of your ideals doesn't have to take you to strange places in search of mighty deeds. The noblest idealism is that which tackles everyday problems in your own backyard. But when you encounter strange new circumstances, perhaps through a radical shift in careers or by meeting a remarkable set of new friends, be ready to seize the moment by making the most of those opportunities for growth and personal change. Your stars tell you to be bold, and I advise you to heed them.

COLORS: Probably because of your spiritual emphasis, the best colors for your magnetism are light, bright shades of pastels. You are concerned with abstractions—truth, beauty, peace, ideals—and therefore find a certain harmony in the pale blue of heaven and the cool gray of light filtered through a thin sheet of ice, perhaps taken from the frozen top of the water-bearer's jar. Nonetheless, you are not totally unworldly. Seeking a cause worthy of your passionate devotion, you must have a place in your wardrobe and in your home's décor for touches of scarlet and crimson. And when you venture forth to do battle with various social and moral evils, wear the blazing red evidence of your fiery zeal.

MONEY: If you ever find yourself with large sums of money on your hands, get a business manager to handle them, for you are not attuned to financial problems or opportunities. That pleasant situation—a surplus of funds—may arise in your middle age as a sizable amount of cash comes your way without your seeking it. One further word of caution: because you tend to neglect financial matters, you may also overlook the qualifications, both professional and ethical, of the person you selected to attend to your investments. A healthy measure of prudence is indicated here.

HEALTH: During your early years, you may need the attention of various specialists, whether they be ophthalmologists, dermatologists, or allergists. You can probably outgrow the need for their supervision by scrupulous regard for your physical condition. As a general rule, the health of those around you will affect your own, usually in a detrimental sense. You are sensitive to contagious illness and certain drugs. Avoid medicines not prescribed for you and, like all healthy Aquarians, drink plenty of water.

RELATIONSHIPS: Although you act from the best motives in romantic affairs, it is quite possible that you will have several close sexual relationships with persons who will never know there is anyone else who matters in your life. It is as if you sustain those attachments out of loyalty and affection, even when it would be to your personal advantage and peace of mind to break off with all but your current love. I will leave it to your Aquarian sense of justice either to avoid this dilemma altogether or to handle it with compassion and fairness should it arise.

In your choice of friends, you will be especially fortunate, having many faithful allies by your side in good times and bad. Your parents and other kin will be closer to you than is ordinarily the case, and their enduring affection will comfort you when your ideals seem threatened and your causes seem lost. In this regard, many a rich man has been poor by comparison to you.

AQUARIUS–EIGHTH DIVISION
(January 26, February 8, 17)

Your astrological chart is marked by force, not in the sense of violence but of power, of zeal, of courage and daring. You Aquarians of the Eighth Division are determined, aggressive personalities. Driven by a dynamic taste for advancement, guided by an energetic intelligence, you are:

- forceful
- competitive
- marked for travel
- a peacemaker

There are mighty forces going for you throughout life and also, I regret to say, equally powerful counterforces holding you back. For every step you take toward your goals, someone or something will get in the way. At times, you may think that all the world is uphill, at least as far as you are concerned. And yet, you are not at all like the tragic character of ancient Greek myth, Sisyphus, who was condemned forever to roll an immense stone up a hill. Each time he neared the top, the boulder fell back down again. Your boulders, that is, your accomplishments and triumphs, remain on the pinnacle of success. Despite opposition, you make headway. Strong-minded, determined, slightly ruthless with those who do not themselves play gently, you will have success pushed upon you even before you decide to seek it. At an early age, you will probably be overwhelmed with opportunities, each one of them involving tremendous effort on your part, but each one all the more tempting to you because of that very challenge.

With your first victories will come your earliest realization that some people in this world just can't stand the good fortune of others. Some of your peers, whether in school or at work, will become jealous of your talents and will initiate opposition to you, perhaps by mocking your deeds, perhaps by defaming your reputation. I fear you must develop a periscope vision, looking around you for possible assaults on your integrity and honor. Rather sneaky opposition to your ambitions can come from sources you least expect. That is the price which you of the Eighth Division, and all successful people, must pay for stepping out ahead of your associates.

Although you can't possibly be happy at the prospect of recurring roadblocks on your path through life, you don't let it upset you either. For you are a born competitor. Your work is twice as enjoyable when you are racing a rival. Your leisure activities also center around competition, whether vigorous in athletics or solemnly intense, as in chess and other games of wit. Because you learned early that life is a challenge, you tend to see contests everywhere, even in those situations which are more conducive to cooperation and mutual assistance.

That attitude can help you in the business world, and I don't doubt that you will excel in your profession, no matter what it is. But as most work grows more and more complex, it also becomes fragmented, with each person doing one set task in coordination with other workers. Your competitive nature can lead you to unconsciously disrupt such arrangements. For example, you would want your assembly line to go faster than any other in the factory. You would want your patrol in a military unit to reach the objective ahead of the others. If you are a one-man circus act, that's fine. But if you are part of a team of trapeze artists, what then? Who will be hurt if you fail to stay in time with your colleagues? That is an extreme example, but its lesson applies to all facets of life.

There are astral indications that some Aquarius Eights will be given assignments to go out of the country for purposes of work rather than relaxation. Even in your travel, it seems, you are not a tourist but a competitor on the run, thrusting ahead of your rivals. For some people this can bring ulcers, or even eventual physical collapse. When you are at your best, such things don't faze you because you have tied your ambition to noble goals. There is more than one way to be a peacemaker, and your techniques may be subtler than most. Perhaps you have the knack for getting enemies to bury their hatred for mutual profit. Perhaps your competitiveness channels antagonisms into constructive contests. Whatever your work abroad, you will be following the pattern set by your Apostle many centuries ago.

Carrying out his instructions, either from Christ or from the Apostolic council in Jerusalem or from Peter, Jude went to the kingdom of Edessa, where there was an epidemic afflicting the inhabitants. He cured people, perhaps even raised the dead as his Master had empowered him to do. In all his benevolent activities, he was preaching to the people about Christ. He was a missionary for his beliefs and, in the best sense, a traveling salesman for a new way of life.

You, too, can expect to go on a mission of healing. One of your stars suggests that your travel will relate to your ability as a peacemaker, whether in the political sense or otherwise. If you are not involved in diplomatic work, you may find yourself acting as mediator in domestic or business disputes. In any case, remember the example of your Apostle and be true to your calling, especially when you must compete, step by struggling step, against those determined red boots.

COLORS: As a peacemaker, you probably feel comfortable with lighter shades of blue, especially the shade of wild cornflowers growing along a country road, competing rather successfully to thrive in beauty amid all the weeds of life. But the calm of benevolent blues cannot fully express your forcefulness. When you must focus your intensity, whether intellectually or in social relations, I suggest you use sapphire with emerald green. Those colors are as unequivocal as your own commitment to success. There is no mistaking their presence, no avoiding their brilliance. In both respects, they are perfect symbols of your personality.

MONEY: Making money is no problem for you. It is a natural skill, a habitual penchant. You can expect to earn more than you need, and your major financial risks will arise from litigation inspired by your rivals. Be doubly sure of the reliability and loyalty of your financial advisers, especially before you embark on any new dealings involving land. Believe it or not, you will be vulnerable to betrayal.

HEALTH: You appear to be more fit than you actually are. You tend to overeat, drink excessively, and smoke too much. Then when illness does strike, you fall down like a structurally weakened building. To sustain your competitive drive, you must attend to your health by resting more, by slowing your pace a little, and by minimizing tension in your job and home.

RELATIONSHIPS: Although your marriage will be a good one, you can anticipate domestic problems involving your children if you spend too much time away from them in your travel and work. Especially during their formative years, be willing to sacrifice personal success to help them with their homework and take them to the park. Slight as these efforts may seem, one day they will be your treasured memories.

In romance, you may be as uncertain and rambling as a mountain brook. Not all Aquarian love is as deep as the ocean or as forceful as a geyser. Before I run out of water metaphors, let me advise you to use your special talent as a peacemaker to calm stormy seas in your relationships, to wash away disputes from your friendships, and to flood your home with affection.

AQUARIUS—NINTH DIVISION
(January 27, February 9, 18)

An Aquarian of the Ninth Division can look forward to a positive, promising, but extraordinarily busy life. Your dominant personality traits are both powerful and benevolent, which is good, because you'll need them to cope with the crowded agenda that the future holds. Your stars promise an active and fulfilling involvement in:

• your home		• energy
• your community	all sparked by your:	• cheerfulness
• your career		• resourcefulness

Where do I begin? It is difficult to pin you down, because from the moment your feet touch the floor in the morning, you are up and at 'em, ready to go. You are the original perpetual motion machine, much to the amazement of your colleagues. Fellow students during your school years can't comprehend your attention to study, nor do those with whom you work understand why you forgo coffee breaks to stick with a project until its completion. I suspect that this trait appeared early in your childhood, when you were the most active infant in your neighborhood, probably wandering away from home more than once in search of new mischief to get into.

This characteristic can now take you wherever you want to go. Applied to your career, it leads you to great heights. Turned to your own amusement and enjoyment, it can give you a great time, to be paid for later by great regret. In a way, your stars have made you a constantly running engine, but only you can choose the direction in which it will speed.

Unlike many exceptionally energetic persons, Aquarius Nines don't allow their hurrying to cloud their disposition. Rarely are you gruff or inconsiderate, despite your rush to do more. The sunshine of your cheerfulness demonstrates to the world that it is possible to be an achiever and a pleasant companion at the same time. So many aspiring young executives need to learn that lesson from you.

You already know that the best teaching is good example, and so I don't have to encourage you to shine your warming optimism on those accustomed to looking on the dark side of life. Show them how you direct your energies toward improving unsatisfactory situations, instead of merely complaining about things. Create a supportive atmosphere for them, showing them that their accomplishments do make a difference. In short, because your Aquarian water jug is filled with happy thoughts and zest for living, slosh it around, spill it out, pour it over the world. You will find that, just like the food pots of the poor widow who fed the prophet Elijah, your water jar of sunshine will never be emptied.

In your resourcefulness, you manifest a prominent trait of the Apostle Jude. For many centuries, he has been called the Apostle of the Impossible, to whom some pray as a last resort. He is sometimes called the patron saint of hopeless causes, on the assumption that his intercession with the Lord can bring aid even to the most desperate situations. In much the same way, your Aquarian talents will be sought out by people for whom all other alternatives have failed. You are considered the persistent doer, the one who keeps trying when everyone else has quit and gone home. More often than not, your unrelenting efforts do turn up some progress, some betterment. No wonder you sometimes feel besieged by people in need, all wanting you to set things straight for them.

That is one of the negative aspects of your positive abilities. The tendency of many people to exploit your resourcefulness and tap your energy for their own purposes is something you must learn to live with. In fact, so great are your emotional reserves that you may not even notice that other people are making demands upon them. If you do sense that your abilities are being stunted and your self-fulfillment thwarted by the constant distractions of requests for help, learn to distinguish between those needing a hand and those handing you a line. That's a blunt way to put it, but you need the warning.

Just as your Apostle had more than one name, so too, like Jude-Thaddaeus-Lebbaeus, you lead a triple life. It might be more appropriate to call it a three-ring circus! In every field of activity, you exert authority, leadership, initiative, and your customary cheerful influence. At home, you are the quiet head of the household, whether as mother or father. The children come to you with their tales of woe and skinned knees. Even when your partner is making the decisions in public, you are indirectly calling the shots through your gently persuasive explanation of the way you see things. In your career, much the same situation appears. Although you are not the nominal boss, your decisions and recommendations are usually accepted, and for the very good reason that they prove practical and profitable.

Finally, in your community, you exert an unruffled authority, not through a formal office but through an unofficial position as a responsible and respected civic spokesman. Indeed, if your neighbors had their way, they would probably force upon you an even more active role, perhaps running for office; for they see in your resourcefulness the answer to many of their local problems. Be prepared for them to make you their rallying point for various social improvements and cooperative activities.

In all three rings of your energetic circus, your perceptive ability in dealing with people is crucial. It is based on sound reasoning powers that not only direct your own actions but also make your advice to others unusually sound. You function best on a large scale, painting the pictures of your joy on a broad canvas, so to speak. The bigger the job, the better you master it. My advice to you Aquarius Nines is never to turn down any assignment. If you can't do it, then no one can!

COLORS: You have an inner sun that brightens the lives of those around you. Let it shine out in your use of color by filling your home, as well as your clothes closet, with all shades of the rainbow except the very dark ones and black. Perhaps because your dynamism is so universal and your enthusiasm unlimited, your magnetism is flattered by almost any color you use. But for your best moments, when you reach a major goal or are celebrating with a special person, remember that you are like the brilliantly flashing vermilion goldfish, swimming where Aquarius meets Pisces. You are red and scarlet, darting among violet water plants. So combine those colors into a gorgeous expression of marvelous you.

MONEY: Your generosity may cause you economic difficulty in your early years, but don't let it bother you. Even though you sometimes live beyond your means, there are no signs of serious money problems in your astral chart. If riches come your way in later life, your bequests to charity will again affirm the principles by which you have always lived.

HEALTH: Although you seldom think about it, you are blessed with a strong constitution. Though you may take it for granted in your youth, your health will need attention after your middle years. You can't run forever on sheer enthusiasm. Regular checkups will preserve your vigor far longer than most people hope to stay active, but only if you are careful with regard to chest ailments.

RELATIONSHIPS: Always openhanded and generous of heart, no wonder you will always have a warm welcome among your friends. There are few people, even among the grouchiest in this world, who can resist responding to your good-natured personality.

Marriage will be a most rewarding experience for you, giving you the bonus of exceptionally astute children, of whom you should be proud. Like Jude, whose grandsons were leaders of the Christian community in Palestine around the end of the first century, you will have ample reason to believe that the good of your life will be carried on by the rising generation. There is no greater satisfaction on earth.

PISCES—JUDAS ISCARIOT AND MATTHIAS

(February 19–March 20)

And now the end of the Zodiac cycle! Like every ending, the sign of Pisces is also a beginning. It closes the astrological circle, returning us to the sign of Aries and to another and another turning of the heavenly wheel of destiny. So it has always been, and so it is in every particle of the universe. The falling rain returns to clouds to fall again; the growing plants must die to form new shoots; and every tragedy of mankind somehow leads to new discoveries, fresh hope, another beginning.

All who live on earth today have a special tie to the sign of Pisces, for the fragile globe on which we sail through space has been, for the last two thousand years or so, in the Age of Pisces. We are now at its cusp, its tail end, living out the last few centuries before—yes!—the dawning of the Age of Aquarius. So many millions have sung the song from the rock musical *Hair,* but so few have comprehended its meaning fully. The Aquarian Age is not yet; and despite its beneficent and affirmative characteristics, we cannot be sure that the future will really be better than humanity's dark and painful past.

It is wonderfully appropriate that our present era should also be called the Atomic Age, for that is an apt parallel to the characteristics of Pisces. We have seen how the power of nuclear fission can work wonders of energy and healing. We have witnessed as well its horrid potential for destruction. The twentieth century has brought the highest standard of living to some of us and the greatest measure of barbarism to others. Indeed, the entire Piscean Age has fitted Charles Dickens' description of the French Revolution: "It was the best of times, it was the worst of times!"

Consider the meaning of the symbol of Pisces: two fish, swimming in opposite directions. Those of you who have been reading this book from its beginning probably know their meaning. Like the twins of Gemini, they express the duality of Pisces, indicating that those born under its influence may turn their lives in radically different directions. They are free to pursue the noblest good or just the reverse. They are truly children of the Atomic Age, and their lives may cast the shadow of the deadly mushroom cloud or may light up darkened minds like a thousand suns. No wonder they find themselves at the very end of the Zodiac, for their tremendous powers are the combined forces of all the previous signs.

In this, too, you who claim the sign of the opposing Fish as your own are accurate representatives of our age. We live in a time of decision, and no one is better equipped by the stars than you to choose mankind's future course. For although you see what everyone has seen since time began, you think what no one else has ever thought. Indeed, it is no exaggeration to say that Pisceans of today have it in their power to save their troubled country from disaster and, in so doing, to save the world from cataclysmic tragedy. If you follow international events, you know how perilous our times are. But it should be an encouragement to you, and a consolation to the rest of us, that you have been given enough ability to meet any challenge and more than enough talent to come safely through any trials. You can stand triumphant on the pinnacle of human aspirations, an example and incentive to others to follow you; or you can leap blindly into the chasm of doom, taking along with you many who are dominated by your powerful personality.

The Apostle who was shown in my vision to be the embodiment of the Piscean character is Judas Iscariot. Does that surprise you? Were you wondering, chapter by chapter, how Judas fitted into my vision and, more to the point, how he could possibly fit into this book? Did you think I would overlook him or try to avoid his presence among Christ's followers and in the most thrilling visions of my life? Not at all! Like each of the other Apostles, Judas was chosen by Christ for a purpose; and if we hope to understand the reason, we must look closely at the way Judas fulfilled it.

First, let us recall the factual information about Judas available in the Scriptures. He may have been the only non-Galilean among Christ's closest followers, for his name means "man of Keriot," a town in Judea. He served as the Apostles' treasurer, and so he must have been both competent and trusted. Great decisions were left to him, as they are to all Pisceans, many of whom must make the most awesome choices for the entire human race. In order to act as financial manager, Judas probably had had previous experience in running a business. Because of his special responsibilities among the group, he was naturally concerned with money and, in all likelihood, handled it shrewdly. In St. John's Gospel, it is suggested that Judas even misappropriated some of the cash entrusted to him, although we don't know whether he used it for his own good or directed it toward political efforts against the Romans. Indeed, the latter possibility—that he was directing funds to guerrillas fighting for a just and honest government—explains much about his later conduct.

Judas was a patriot and a humanitarian. He hated the corrupt and brutal Roman rule of his country and hoped that, by restoring an independent Palestine, Christ would make Himself the Emperor of Rome and, in so doing, would reform and purify the government of the entire world. He wanted his Master to clean up a corrupt political system and restore decency to a debased society. He failed to comprehend that Christ's kingdom would not be a worldly one, that He would change the hearts of men rather than their form of government. No, Judas must have been desperate for social reform to act as he eventually did.

Did Judas wish any harm to come to Christ? If so, then why was he aghast when he heard that Christ had been condemned? And why did he contemptuously return to Christ's enemies the money they had paid him to identify his Master? Why was Judas so despondent that, probably not fully cognizant of his actions, he rushed to his death? Those are not the actions of a rogue or traitor, but of a determined individual who misunderstood Christ's mission.

I don't believe that Judas wanted to harm Christ. Judas didn't seek Christ's doom, he hungered for His triumph! He believed that by creating a face-to-face confrontation between his powerful, miracle-working Master and the Romans, he would be helpfully instrumental in provoking a showdown, which Christ would surely win. Judas was impatient with talk about the kingdom of Heaven and acted to establish his Lord's kingdom on earth. He tried to force Christ's hand, expecting that the same power which had only recently raised Lazarus from the dead and healed the afflicted and blind could also raise Palestine from its humiliation under foreign rule and restore his people's lost power.

That explains why Judas was horrified when he learned that Christ was condemned to death. He had expected Him to call down Heaven's rage upon Pontius Pilate, the Roman soldiery, and their Jewish collaborators like Herod. He must have been frantic with horror, anguish, and rage. His plans had backfired! Instead of becoming king of a resurgent Palestine, his Teacher was helpless and disgraced. Put yourself in his place, and you will understand how Judas would have lost control of his thoughts and taken his fatal actions.

Of course, Christ knew what was in Judas's mind. Indeed, He must have chosen him with that foreknowledge. Jesus knew that the tragic mistakes of Judas were necessary in the Divine Plan for mankind's redemption. That is a difficult idea to accept; and yet, it brings with it a wonderful understanding of God's plan for each of us. It teaches us that even when we lose our way for a while, our paths are charted by the same Power that sent us on our journey through life in the first place.

Over fifteen hundred years ago, St. Augustine of Hippo, the great preacher and theologian of North Africa, called the first sin of Adam a "happy fall" because it would eventually be redeemed by Christ. In the same way, we might consider the horrible mistake made by Judas a fortunate occurrence; it was the necessary first step toward Christ's passion, death, and Resurrection. It was, in fact, the first step toward our own salvation.

With that in mind, you may feel differently about having Judas as the Apostle of Pisces. How accurately he demonstrated its characteristics! Rising to exalted prominence, he was faced with the gravest decisions of all the Apostles. Like the nuclear scientist of today, he held in his hands a power so great it can hardly be comprehended. You, too, may find yourself propelled toward scintillating heights and discover that your deeds can move mountains and your words can make truth thunder. The way you use that power will determine not only your own fate but perhaps also that of mankind. Pisceans face the crucial choice between material and spiritual greatness, just as Judas was torn between Christ's talk of a heavenly kingdom of the poor and his own ideas of political reform and civil rule. Is today's world in the Age of Pisces choosing more wisely than Judas did? Look closely at this earth of ours, and at your own life, too, before answering.

You needn't answer to me, but to yourself. For it is up to Pisceans to fulfill Judas's dream, to clean up the corruption that seems to be everywhere in this world. It is your special role in life to change society for the better, to end injustice and oppression. But learn from Judas's mistake. Your Piscean methods today must be based on spiritual force, not political violence. That was Judas's sad realization when he hurled the thirty pieces of silver into the temple. *It was a symbolic gesture by which he renounced his former plans to change the world by physical power—it just can't be done!* At long last he recognized what you already know: that Christ's entire life showed us how to change the world by work and love. That, in all its simplicity, is the mission of Pisces—then, now, and always. And when you accept it, you will learn the fundamental truth of life: that wisdom is only an uncommon degree of common sense!

Needless to say, Pisceans are like their fellow men and women from other segments of the Zodiac in one vital respect: some of them use their terrific powers for good, while others wear red boots. Under every star sign there are heroes and villains, sages and fools; but you who are children of the twin fish frequently go to extremes. Like the little girl in the nursery rhyme, when you are good, you are very, very good; but when you are bad, you are . . . well, what do you expect when you wear red boots!

What happens when Pisceans fail to accept the mission assigned them by the Creator? Recall what happened after the death of Judas. His colleagues assembled together and selected someone to take his place. The thirteenth Apostle was Matthias. He had long been a follower of Christ, and must have been an exceptionally worthy individual to be so honored by Peter and the others. Meditate on this: the sign of Pisces is twin Fish, moving toward different goals. And when the original Piscean Apostle lost his true direction, his replacement took over his role as your model. And that is why Pisceans of today have two Apostles representing them, Judas and Matthias, to match the two fish that symbolize the end of the Zodiac.

To some degree, all of us alternate between positive and negative poles, but Pisceans present a more complex pattern. Many of them adopt values and behavior early in life and adhere to them forever thereafter. Like the indomitable salmon, swimming upstream past waterfalls and predators, they single-mindedly pursue their original goals, for better or worse. Others are equally emphatic in their beliefs and equally determined in their objectives, but they shift between negative and positive traits. On one day, they may be dynamic powers for peace, and on another, may upset the applecart. The most admirable and most disturbing qualities are curiously intermingled in the Piscean nature, and the result is highly unpredictable. That is why you Pisceans of today rightly feel that you can be almost anything.

When your positive characteristics are ascendant, you can succeed in almost any task. You are especially suited to work involving foreign countries, travel, and shipment of goods abroad. You are often blessed with a gift for languages, even if you have never studied them; and your remarkable understanding of people allows you to learn quickly local customs, traditions, and beliefs. Little wonder, then, that many of you become translators, explorers, and anthropologists.

When your negative side is ruling your behavior, however, the same gifts can make you rootless, unable to settle down, adrift in a world where you never feel at home. Inattentive and indecisive, you can be easy prey for con artists with get-rich-quick schemes and are tempted into projects that bring more pain than profit.

Pisceans are noted for their sense of loyalty to friends. You would never consciously bring harm to those who depend upon you. Was Judas an exception to this rule? No! Wanting so much for his Master to rule in glory, he was driven to distraction when he realized the consequences of his mistake. You, too, may sometimes act as if your judgment were better than the wishes of those you love, and so you may try to force upon them, for their own good, ideas and actions they oppose. Guard against that tendency by listening more than you talk and by asking more than you order. That advice applies to all of us.

Acting from the best of motives, you must be aware that your confidence can sometimes mislead you. I admit that your mind is facile and keen, your observations acute, your intuition sensitive, and your compassion forceful; but I must warn you that occasionally, your enthusiasm will overrule all those assets. The danger arises when you make important decisions on your own, shunning advice and resenting contradiction. As long as you remain open to suggestions, however, you can avoid the disappointment of broken dreams.

Some Pisceans learn this the hard way, by seeing their plans miscarry. They thereafter swing—or should I say, swim—to the other extreme, refusing to take a stand or proclaim an idea until they have sought a dozen opinions of it. This is a slower way to reach your goals, but a surer one in the long run. It is especially advisable to exercise that prudence when the interests of those you love are involved. Your mental and emotional powers are so strong that they need some element of discipline to direct their impact.

It isn't surprising that the duality of Pisces affects your romantic relationships, whether you are single or married. If you emphasize its positive aspects by becoming unpredictably affectionate, you can be a wonderful mate and outstanding parent. If you allow your dualism to run in negative channels, just the reverse will be true. Piscean men born on the February dates of their sign are susceptible, though not preordained, to casual affairs. But they have within their personality the ability to avoid potentially destructive liaisons. If they aren't carried away with their own Piscean charms, they needn't bring sorrow to themselves or those they love.

Some Pisceans must guard against the twin dangers of alcoholic drink and addictive drugs. Because you are such powerful individuals, your lives may well be dramatic and exciting. Charging from day to day, delighting in your intellectual and psychological challenges, you run the risk of too much stress and too little reflection. That is a volatile combination for anyone, but especially for you. It can throw your mind into disarray and erode your noblest resolves. Remember that your Piscean power is not a cap gun, to be aimed carelessly, without fear of its force. On the contrary, you must consider your inner resources to be spiritual dynamite. Even when you use them in the best of causes, they mustn't be put under strain.

Piscean intelligence is that rare variety which is as astute with people as with ideas. That is why a thoughtful Pisces can be the most marvelous person in the world. My husband is a Pisces. He is my life's partner, my colleague, and my friend. The best wish I can make for all of you is that everyone could have my good fortune in being superbly happy with Pisces at its best. And at its best, Pisces is superb. Not to flatter you, but for the sake of your own self-fulfillment, you must be told how magnificent your future can be once you decide to make it so. You can be not the sharks and barracudas of this world but the gentle dolphins, guiding storm-tossed voyagers across the sea of life to safe harbors.

To put aside the fish imagery of Pisces, I will say plainly that you should be among life's healers, whether figuratively or literally. By bringing health—physical, mental, or moral—perhaps to millions, you Pisceans can set the world on the road to spiritual as well as material greatness. For when you are open to the Creator's words, then you know the road to peace leads not through diplomatic conference halls but through clinics and operating rooms, in fact, through all the places where Pisceans conduct their everyday activities.

And where, may I ask, do you work? In a classroom or a kitchen? Then let them be chambers of peace. In a skyscraper or factory or the Congress? Then let those edifices be palaces of peace and monuments to brotherhood. It may sound impossible, but if anyone can do it, you Pisceans can!

I'm not the only one who has good reason to appreciate Piscean traits of mind and spirit. Children of the twin Fish have blessed this world in many ways, and all of us are indebted to them for spiritual as well as material enrichment. Four American Presidents have had Piscean birthdays: George Washington (February 22), Andrew Jackson (March 15), James Madison (March 16), and Grover Cleveland (March 18). Among contemporary political leaders, both Senator Edward Kennedy (February 22) and Senator James Buckley (March 9) are Pisceans, though they differ markedly in personalities and policies.

I have always loved the paintings of Winslow Homer (February 24) and Pierre Renoir (February 25); Michelangelo, the mightiest Piscean genius, was born on March 6. Two artists who used words instead of oils were Henry Wadsworth Longfellow and John Steinbeck, both born on February 27.

If you relish music, you owe a debt to Chopin (February 22), Handel (February 23), Ravel (March 7), and Rimsky-Korsakov (March 18). For music of a different kind, we are all indebted to Pisceans like Lawrence Welk (March 11), Glenn Miller (March 1), and Harry James (March 15). Perhaps you have no formal training in music and couldn't even play a simple tune on a piano keyboard. You may have neglected your special Piscean harmony with the music of the heavenly spheres, or perhaps you never had the opportunity to develop that sensitivity to sound which reflects the even deeper emotional sensitivities of Pisceans. This doesn't hinder your appreciation of the beautiful, however; for you are apt to be an avid record buyer and concertgoer. From my own experience, I can testify to the native musical genius of your sign; my husband is an amateur composer, and many of his works are of professional quality.

Inquisitive Pisceans have included Alexander Graham Bell (March 3), inventor of the telephone; Luther Burbank (March 7), noted botanist and horticulturist, and Amerigo Vespucci (March 18), the explorer and map maker whose name was given to half the world.

Two modern Popes, Leo XIII and Pius XII, have shared a March 2 birthdate. Quite a different kind of religious leader, the Victorian missionary and explorer Dr. David Livingstone, was born on March 19.

Disparate as all these individuals have been, they have had in common the trait of all successful Pisceans: a determination to excel. To some extent, each of them has known the same surging idealism, the same passion for achievement, that energized Judas and made him yearn to see Christ rule in glory. Whether it took the form of religious commitment, political action, scientific experiment, or artistic creativity, their Piscean power could not be stifled or subdued. What was true of them was equally true of Judas and Matthias, though it produced different results in different personalities.

The same holds true for you Pisceans of today. Standing at the crossroads of fate, endowed with strengths and talents unsurpassed in the Zodiac, you hold the future in your hands. You can form it with your words, shape it with your beliefs, and make it live with your ideals. May you always have the zeal of Judas, the perseverance of Matthias, and the peace that comes to those who do their best. Now let us review the nine divisions within your astral sign.

PISCES—FIRST DIVISION *(February 19, 28, March 1, 10, 19)*

Great changes lie ahead for you Pisceans of the First Division, and you should welcome them. The combination of planetary influences governing your birth indicate that 1978 will be your key year, bringing you experiences which will lead to an entirely new lifestyle. Even if you are hesitant about making serious adjustments in your life, you will find yourself moving into new patterns which will last for twenty-four years; and if you make the most of the opportunities coming your way, they will be happy years indeed!

No matter what your age now, my vibrations tell me that the imminent reordering of your life is sure to occur and may involve traveling, through which you will find yourself living on a higher economic level than you now do. Obviously, the specific changes will vary from person to person within the First Division. You will not all face the same problems and find the same blessings. Nonetheless, you should all be prepared for the role of leadership or authority that is reserved for your special talents. You are:

- psychic and intuitive
- either patient or well able to become so
- compassionate
- adaptable

Most of you are probably not yet aware of your psychic gifts, for it is just like you to need someone to convince you of your powers. You think you have "lucky hunches," but much more than fortune is involved. In fact, your perception borders on the uncanny. That is why you solve problems so easily, often finding lost objects without great effort. Especially in personal relations, you see a little more than others. You sense a person's pain or joy or anger even when it isn't expressed; and because you assume that everyone shares your keen insight, you don't recognize how rare your sensitivities really are.

Let me offer a suggestion. It would be a good idea for you to keep a diary for recording the events and conversations in which your special gifts of perception have played a role. For example, if you meet a friend and sense that something unusual is about to happen in his or her life, jot it down. If you feel uneasy in your dealings with someone, make a note of it. The reason for this record is that you will face skeptics and maligners, who will not believe that you, or anyone for that matter, have precognition of extrasensory insights. Believe me, I speak of this from personal experience. It isn't a happy precaution to have to take, but it will help you cope with those few people whose egos require criticism of others.

A Pisces One is apt to be a headstrong, impetuous youth, as frisky as a colt in summer. As you mature, however, a growing sense of your own worth will make you less inclined toward showing off and more at peace with yourself. Especially if you explore your psychic gifts to see inside your personality, you will find therein a wondrous patience. That word means more than being able to put up with a late bus or a long line at the grocery store. It means a will to endure, an ability to take life's troubles as they come without losing hope and cheer. When you are at your best, your patience flowers into a mystical recognition of the Divine Plan in all things; and so you will delight in all things, even those which bring you pain or disappointment.

Your patience with your own troubles will develop along with a compassion toward the more serious troubles of other people. Indeed, those two characteristics are intimately related; for the less you think about your own setbacks, the more you concentrate on helping the truly unfortunate and needy. Those who know you are well aware of this trait, even if you yourself are not. They know personally your deep concern for the suffering and love you for it. It is pertinent to recall here that Judas was chosen to handle the Apostles' distribution of alms to the poor. A Pisces One is happiest in that role.

Because you put your own comforts last for any worthwhile cause, you are an adaptable individual. Your versatility enables you to work in uncomfortable surroundings, to deal with unpleasant people, even to perform successfully those tasks that bore or depress you. You already know the secret of your ability to fit in. It doesn't come automatically, but rather is the result of a psychological disposition that welcomes hardships for the sake of a noble goal. If your work should ever be solely related to purposes for which you have no respect, you would then find yourself unable to adapt to your co-workers. As long as you know your efforts are directed toward a good end, however, you can be sunshine personified to those around you.

By telling you that you are adaptable, I don't mean to imply that you should take whatever comes your way. On the contrary, I urge you to be on the lookout for opportunities by which to better your place in society. You stand on the threshold of great things. When the chance appears for a radical change in your circumstances, take it! Use your flexibility to adjust to transitions, both emotionally and socially, as you move up the ladder of success.

COLORS: Your psychic vibrations are attuned to shades of blue and gray, especially the darker ones. It is difficult for color to convey your personality, which is simultaneously cool and compassionate, restrained and potentially forceful. If you wrap yourself in midnight blues, you will exaggerate your control and underestimate your exuberance. Two colors will, however, strike the balance you need. Let a pale yellow, like sunlight breaking through a morning mist, express your psychic insight, which breaks through secrets to reveal the truth of human hearts. Let a vivid sapphire, almost gaudy in its boldness, inform the world that underneath your external composure, there is a vibrant Piscean love of people. Of course, no matter what the shade of your attire or surroundings, you adapt to them as you do to everything else!

MONEY: I predict a significant change in your life in 1978. Expect it to involve your economic situation. Your business horizon will expand abruptly; and even though sudden affluence will bring many investment opportunities, check them all carefully or your loss of wealth will be as sudden as your acquisition of it. Though you may have problems caused by a reluctance to play second fiddle in financial dealings, the year 1978 can be just the beginning of your good fortune.

HEALTH: A strong constitution and great vitality sustain your eagerness for work and active play, but you must nonetheless guard against overwork. It sneaks up on a Pisces One, especially when you are overly confident of your powers. Pace yourself steadily, so that you can enjoy to the fullest those twenty-four years of opportunity that lie ahead of you.

RELATIONSHIPS: It would be better for you to marry, or in some cases, remarry, late in life rather than early. If you are unattached, I suggest you wait until 1978 before settling down. First make your adjustments in your new life-style, and then take on extra responsibilities only when you have become accustomed to the changes in yourself.

Your natural compassion and warmth cause others to respond to you with equal sincerity. In addition to your friendships, you will always have people near you who seek, if not material aid, at least your solace and advice. That can be a blessing for you, as well as for them, if your insight reveals to you how their tribulations are a reflection of God's plan for all the world. Your role in it, of course, is to heal their hurts and comfort their wounded spirits.

Your spirit, on the other hand, should not be wounded; for I see one major romance in your life which will endure as a source of ever greater joy. Cherish that relationship, and you will be one of the most fortunate of all Pisceans.

PISCES—SECOND DIVISION
(February 20, 29, March 2, 11, 20)

Artistic and lively, you Pisceans of the Second Division should prepare from your youth for a career which allows free rein to an expressive and path-breaking spirit. Don't hem yourself in prematurely; for even if economic circumstances hold you back, even if you can't take for granted the best educational and social opportunities, you do have:

- an active imagination
- exceptional self-expression
- short interest spans
- sensitivity

There is no end to the interests in your life. In school, you tend to take more courses than you can handle because you want to try a little of everything. You probably don't have one hobby, but a dozen of them; and your social calendar often looks like a thorough list of your community's activities. This broadness in taste keeps you happy; but it can also be a negative factor, diluting your abilities by spreading them too thin. It can stall your pursuit of career success and, time and again, detain your best ideas in favor of an untried notion.

It is necessary to train yourself, even late in life, to stick with what you are doing. This is always important, but it becomes vital if you intend to fulfill your artistic potential. No accomplishments in the arts are possible without discipline. When you hear of an artist or writer whose work just spills across the canvas or typing paper, the chances are that that individual's success will be limited. Great performances on stage are the result of hundreds of rehearsals. One supreme moment at the keyboard comes after a thousand hours of practice. So if you hope to be a professional in your area of the arts, channel all your energy into it and ration the time you spend in other pursuits.

That will take time, and in your youth, it is especially vital that you learn discipline. For until you are out of your teen-age years, you usually have the attention span of a kitten. It's a lovable trait, but an exasperating one. I recall driving through Washington one day and stopping at an intersection by a park where two small boys were playing a rough version of baseball. The batter seemed disinterested, dallying around the plate and watching the passing traffic. His pitcher insisted that he either play ball or forfeit the game. That's the same attitude others may have toward you when your flighty interests take you from one project to another.

This same problem can be turned into a strength. Your fertile imagination tempts you down interesting side roads of life, where few others ever go. Because your need for self-expression can't be stifled, you will find ways to create beauty and to let the world know you are here, even if you can't make up your mind what may be the best way to go about it. I suggest you purchase a daily schedule book, one large enough to hold the details of your numerous activities. Then, a few days in advance, chart out your plans, allotting so much time for each of your priority items. This will be a great help to you in completing your work and reaching your goals, step by step. If any of your children is a Pisces Two, be sure he or she has such a schedule; it will prove a great aid in learning discipline and mental order.

Is it possible to be intellectually orderly and at the same time wildly imaginative? I think so. And you of the Second Division can be the proof of that if you try. Your imagination can actually startle those who are used to a timid conformity of thought, for you peer into unseen worlds and trace the possibilities of the unexpected. Judas was like that. In his private musings, he convinced himself that Jesus was soon to be Emperor of Rome. His imagination, in fact, ran away with him. While you restrain yours, be sure that you don't tie your soaring mind down too tightly. Especially with children, the gift of fancy and make-believe shouldn't be diminished by impositions of harsh reality.

Sensitivity is one of your greatest gifts, but it brings with it tremendous responsibilities, as you have already discovered. You perceive the moods and wishes of those around you. You read their sorrows and their fears. You know when a colleague is unhappy, when your child is worried, when your lover is holding something back from you. You are an emotional seismograph. Instead of recording earth tremors, you react to psychological vibrations, and that makes it difficult for you to shut out the problems and cares of other people. Indeed, that very fact should alert you to the reason for your sensitivity. Just as a music box isn't intended to be kept closed, so your reception of others' feelings wasn't meant to be turned off. Yes, it can be a bother to offer sympathy and encouragement, but that is your role, your mission, your finest purpose. And in doing so, you will find your own troubles receding into memory. The reward for your sensitivity, you see, is a personal peace which grows each time you share it.

Your Piscean receptivity toward beauty isn't limited to man-made art. The handiwork of the Divine Architect of the Universe draws you outdoors. Music delights you, whether it comes from a symphony orchestra or a ragtag band of feathered minstrels in your backyard bushes. Discord, on the other hand, will depress you, whether it involves angry people or the violation of nature by pollution and litter. You discern the relationship between man's evil to man and mankind's mistreatment of our common environment. Let it be your Piscean determination to act positively in defense of all beauty, both that which is exhibited in galleries and that which grows exultant in God's garden.

COLORS: Responding so well to color, you should use it to bring out your stellar quality. By that I mean both your astrological nature and your ability to be a star, in the popular sense of the word. You are not down-to-earth, so there is no reason to tie yourself down with earthly shades. Try instead a dove gray, verging into blue, like the sky when it is trying to become morning. And for your most expressive moments, especially when you are performing either on stage or in life's perpetual drama, flaunt your lively spirit with the colors of fresh life, especially the pale but promising greens of new growth in the spring. When you are decorating your home, remember to use the colors of a Piscean environment: the mingled blue and green and gray of a sunken grotto, through which the twin fish of your sign can sport to their delight.

MONEY: Money matters are not your strongest suit because you lack not only all interest in finance but also the determination to make your way to wealth. To you, money is a means to sustain life and support your family. It is not an obsession, indeed, not even a concern. I suggest, however, that you learn to save and to invest. For only when you have a comfortable economic base can you afford to pursue your interests without worrying about day-to-day costs.

HEALTH: Any mental or emotional discord will threaten you with physical illness. You are finely attuned to feelings and moods. Consequently, when those around you are tense, you may actually "catch" their nervousness and develop a headache or an upset stomach. Prolonged unhappiness can drive a Pisces Two to seek escape in alcohol, with bad results. To avoid all these ills, be positive! Your personality can overcome rancor and subdue malice. Above all, realize that some people refuse to be happy, and relish their grievances. Leave them to their world and return to your own.

RELATIONSHIPS: Seeking a refuge from life's storms, you will tend to seek persons with hardier emotions than your own. It seems advisable for you to live alone sometime in your youth, toughening yourself for life and learning to make your own decisions. Then when you do marry, your spouse will be a partner to you rather than a protector. If you marry for the right reasons, rather than mere expediency, your home life will be splendid and your children protected by their loving Piscean parent.

PISCES—THIRD DIVISION *(February 21, March 3, 12)*

When the stars illuminated the hour of your birth, day or night, they must have been dazzling. They marked out for you an easy path through life in any endeavor you choose. Fireball that you are, from your youth to old age you remain:

- ambitious
- dynamic and determined
- confident
- wide-ranging

I am delighted to tell you that your ambition is not the ruthless kind which we all too often see these days. From my vantage point in Washington, D.C., I note the many newcomers to government who bring with them an uncontrolled desire for personal advancement. That sometimes leads them to put success above principle and new conquests above old friends. As fate would have it, they usually don't make it to the top; their frustrations catch up with them and reveal their true characters. You can be relieved to know that you are not among them.

The ambition of a Pisces Three is based on vast reservoirs of mental and physical energy. Seeking to use your powers for constructive purposes, you advance yourself by advancing worthy causes.

Whether you are running for office or building a housing development, teaching a class or planting trees along the roadway, your work excels because your purpose excels. Your exuberance gives shape to your endeavors and will bring you attention whether or not you seek it out.

Now, that's the kind of ambition appropriate for a dynamic leader! And you are a steadfast one at that! I wonder if you have ever learned to take it easy. In childhood, you must have given your parents constant trials in controlling your energy. St. Paul reminds us that in adulthood, we put away the things of a child; but don't you put away your vitality! Just learn to channel it where it is most needed. Considering the state the world is in, you can start almost anyplace and find more than enough to keep you busy.

Too often we observe dynamic individuals who fritter away their talent by running from one project to another like a child set loose in a toy store. That is not your problem, for you have never learned to give up an effort that means something to you. Determined to see through what you begin, you are both a superb employee and an excellent employer; in both cases, your persistence is contagious. One Pisces Three in an office is enough to improve the productivity of the entire staff. Like those who know you, I admire you for that and only suggest that you learn to take credit for your hard work.

Partnerships generally work out for you, whether they are in business or relate to neighborhood ventures. Perhaps you are part of a homemakers' club whose members share the supervision of children on an alternating basis. Perhaps you and fellow students are engaged in joint projects in science lab. Whatever the situation, your participation is apt to snowball until you are functioning as the informal leader of the group. Unafraid of assuming responsibility and knowing how to delegate it, you sum up the very definition of executive talent.

Your confidence inspires those who work with you. Remember that your Apostle, Judas, was probably a highly successful businessman before joining Christ's followers. And as the treasurer for the Apostles, he must have been noted for his confidence in dealing with both strangers and enemies. I suspect his own awareness of his abilities impressed the other Apostles and led them to put their finances in his hands. In other words, his confidence in himself fostered their confidence in him. The same can happen to you, so be prepared to accept the leadership that others ask you to exercise.

Do you know how to discern truly confident persons? They give compliments! They are so self-assured that they can applaud the efforts of others, even their rivals. That is impossible for a braggart or a phony. Because a Pisces Three is secure in the awareness of his or her personal worth, your confidence generates kind remarks and encouragement instead of demanding attention for yourself. This allows you to be generous and relaxed in all your dealings.

One of the grandest assets on your balance sheet is your wide-ranging vision. Receptive to all stimuli, your mind has never been limited in its appetite. Even when you daydream, there are no boundaries to your fancies, no fences around the castles you build in the air. Because you have already had a taste of success, whether in business or school or athletics, you cannot be surprised to learn that your achievements are limited only by your desires. That is, you can do what you want. You belong in the forefront of industry, mining, transport, real estate, education. As a photographer, doctor, or writer, your Piscean genius is equally adept. Idealistic and free from serious prejudices, you will bring to your work an inward sense of purpose which is the best guarantee of success.

Learn to trust your hunches, for they are usually right. I'm not speaking of gambling luck; that isn't the proper preserve of Piscean insight. Rather, in your judgments of people and circumstances, reflect on your extra sense, that intuition which is a gift from God.

COLORS: The vibrations of the Third Division indicate shades quite different from those of the preceding divisions. There is nothing of the sea in your palette, unless it be the colors of a tropical coral reef. Red and rose, deep pink and purple, these suit your dynamic nature. Indeed, any color that seems to spark with fire will express the electricity of your high-voltage intellect. For your public occasions and whenever you seek excitement, use that emphatic scarlet of the sun when it first rises on the eastern horizon on a hazy morning. For your private times, and whenever you wish to subdue your energy, surround yourself with the lavender pink of the redbud blossoms; for those bold flowers grace the stems of what is also called the Judas tree!

MONEY: You will undoubtedly make money. With your talents, you can hardly help it! But be wary of exploiters who will try to use your name to promote their schemes. Don't be overly trusting of financial advisers, especially if they are not personal acquaintances. By exercising prudence now, you will keep sufficiently large sums of money to be able to make large donations to charity later; for that will eventually bring you your greatest satisfaction.

HEALTH: Ordinarily, I would advise someone as active as you to slow down before your frenzy impairs your health. But in your case, activity can be a cure-all. Your health is most vigorous when you are busy and tends to weaken during periods of idleness. For your family's sake, however, be sure you keep business out of your vacations. Your mate and children must not be made to live your hectic schedule. Remember that your children learn from you in many ways, and they may try to match your speed through life without having sufficient stamina to take it. Be sure that you relax with them. Also, guard against the accidents which always threaten people in a hurry. It is good for you, and all Pisceans, to recall that a careless fish ends up on an angler's hook.

RELATIONSHIPS: Your intuition about people and events lets you size up strangers within minutes, as long as you keep your wits about you. As I have already mentioned, your financial enthusiasm may mislead you about your advisers. In social relationships, however, when you are at ease, you are rarely mistaken in analyzing people. This is always a great blessing, but especially so in matters of romance; and your choice of a partner is bound to be astute and perceptive. You cannot be misled by charm or promises. Women of the Third Division are almost mind readers in this regard, and their husbands are chosen carefully. The result is marital bliss. All you have to do is be honest with yourself about whatever you see in the one you love.

Because your ambition hurts no one, your friends will always respect and admire your talents. Unlike many successful people, you will not have made a long list of enemies by your behavior, and so you can have the best of both worlds—popularity and prominence. Rely on your family to be your refuge and comfort during the one or two occasions of personal grief that will come your way.

PISCES—FOURTH DIVISION *(February 22, March 4, 13)*

Once upon a time, people were wary of Pisceans of the Fourth Division. You are inclined to seem eccentric, out of step, sometimes in a world apart. Moreover, there is a likelihood that you possess psychic powers; and in the past, that alone would have been enough to brand you as a witch or wizard. Today, things are different, at least to some degree. Society is more tolerant of individuals who stand apart from the crowd, and a large percentage of the populace understands the reality of psychic phenomena. So the same unusual abilities that once would have brought persecution upon you can today win the respect even of scientists, many of whom are themselves investigating the unexplored powers of the mind. You are:

- different
- intuitive
- unambitious
- reserved

I realize that "different" is a vague word, but so is your prominent characteristic of being unconventionally set apart from your fellows. Your fine mind just refuses to fit into the commonplace mold. The way you display this trait will vary from person to person, but it will invariably have something to do with thought, values, and the expression of rare intellectual insight.

Many Pisces Fours become aware of their mental powers at an early age and sense that they are somehow different from their playmates and the rest of their family. This can be an unnerving experience; for a youngster, even a teen-ager, craves to belong, to fit in, to be like everybody else. That is true even among a generation which preaches self-expression; you have only to visit your local high school to see how conformist their nonconformity can be. You may even have been ashamed of your mental abilities, retiring bashfully from social gatherings, as if your special gift were a character defect to be suppressed. This has probably kept you from being gregarious, and the fact that you have been a voracious reader from the time you first were able to put letters together has still further limited your social contacts. The resentment of other children toward your intelligence and your rather adult intellectual concerns made you retreat from them and find company in books and meditation. In fact, you may well have most enjoyed playing alone, talking to a host of imaginary companions and shaping your own world out of stories you had read.

The same habits continue into adulthood. Few of you develop your powers fully, for that old embarrassment about them still lingers. From time to time, when you do or say something that may reveal your secret potential to others, you explain away your remarkable condition and restrict your interaction with the people involved. This can disrupt your most rewarding relationships; and, to put this bluntly, it is foolish for you to behave that way. A covered candle soon goes out! Don't let your psychic gifts wither away from lack of attention. Explore them, exercise them, expand them, and when the occasion is appropriate, share them with those who are dear to you. You will be surprised at their favorable reaction; and, at long last, you will feel free to be yourself completely, without regard to possible sanction from the uninformed and prejudiced.

In much the same way as you hide your mental powers, you also suppress your capacity for leadership. Unlike your astrological kin of the Second Division, you are unambitious to a fault. For someone whose work is usually magnificent, you are peculiarly reticent about accepting authority and supervision over others. Perhaps as you develop more confidence by the appreciation of your mind's tremendous treasures, you will also find yourself ready to accept the positions of responsibility that are rightly yours. I hope so, for otherwise you will waste priceless Piscean talent which the world sorely needs.

You tend to be careful with money. Indeed, one of the few things which can rouse you to anger is waste. In our world of diminishing resources, your conserving instincts are irreplaceable, and you should use your innate leadership to convince others to stop frittering away the limited bounty of this good earth. Like Judas, you would make a good financial manager; your clients could rest secure in your tightfisted handling of their money, which would be soundly invested and prudently spent.

A Pisces Four is no hermit, but neither are you a social lion. Emotionally reserved, you show your heart of hearts to few people, avoid crowds, and follow your own narrow path through life. If others want to join you in that confined walkway, they must accept your standards of personal privacy. Once you learn to accept yourself as a richly talented, though unusual, person, your new confidence will make you less retiring and more willing to interact with larger numbers of people. I don't expect you ever to be a Pisces-about-town; that would contradict your astral personality. But I do hope you will learn to be freer in sharing your special blessings with others, for your psychic sensitivity can be a healing and nurturing force for a wounded world.

COLORS: The colors to suit your personal magnetism should be obvious to you if you have been reading this book chapter by chapter. They are the shades of mental activity, of abstraction, of the intellectual life. All yellows, from daffodil to ocher, announce the mind's radiating power, which, like golden sunlight, illumines dark spirits and starts fresh things developing. All shades of gray, especially those with a touch of blue, reflect your commitment to the life of the mind. When you want to express your deepest self to a very special someone, a combination of those colors—lemon and light blue, perhaps—will be your most sincere calling card. On the other hand, when you want to bolster your social courage and exert your neglected leadership, heighten your vibrations by intensifying your colors through a raucous gold and exuberant sapphire blue.

MONEY: You are certainly not a spendthrift! You may not have a single credit card or charge account, and only rarely splurge on a night on the town. You are likely to inherit money and property during your middle years, and I needn't advise you to avoid speculation with your new wealth. You will treat it as carefully as you used to handle your childhood allowance. Good for you!

HEALTH: At the risk of being considered fastidious and finicky, you usually take exceptional care of your health, often through specialized diets, organic foods, and vegetarianism. Even more important is an easy tempo of living. I see no serious problems for you in the way of illness as long as you stick to your guns and refuse to accept the life-styles of those who destroy their fitness through overindulgence. Do remember, however, to take occasional breaks from your reading to exercise and enjoy the unwritten poetry of growing plants and starry skies.

RELATIONSHIPS: As a reclusive thinker, you make few friends. In fact, because so many people fail your strict standards for fellowship, you prefer few acquaintances. Your fear of being hurt through mockery or misunderstanding may lie behind your selectivity in companions. In any case, as long as your small circle of intimates shares your interests and respects your intellectual concerns, your friends will make up in depth what is lacking in numbers.

If you are very lucky, you will meet someone early in life who will understand you and accept your delicate personality as God's work of art. Otherwise, you had better wait until later in life to marry; a wedding to someone who wants to make you over into a party person will be the first step on the road to disaster. Take your time to make sure your partner is prepared to treasure you for what you are, not for what you might become.

PISCES—FIFTH DIVISION *(February 23, March 5, 14)*

Time and again, I tell people that their future is in their own hands; that is true, to an extraordinary degree, of a Pisces Five. Few persons ever have your total freedom of choice between the most positive and, sad to say, the most negative traits of your sign. Throughout life, you walk a razor's edge between greatness and failure. Awesome as your responsibilities are, they needn't intimidate or frighten you as long as you understand how great your powers are and how vital your role is in human affairs. On the positive side, you have been given remarkable gifts with which to improve the world, including:

- exceptional intellect
- adaptability
- ingenuity and inventiveness
- superb judgment for speculation

Those assets are plain enough without my elaborating upon them. You share the intellectual powers of your astral kin in the Fourth Division of Pisces, the versatility and flexibility of a Pisces One, and the shrewd handling of money which characterizes your sign as a whole. Moreover, you add to those components a dash of ingenuity, which makes your use of them totally unpredictable and rather enchanting.

Am I flattering you? Not at all, for life seems cut and tailored to the satisfaction of a Pisces Five. There is no limit to your career choices, though I advise you to find a position which challenges your mental powers. Otherwise, you will feel uneasy and unfulfilled, even if your work brings you great profit. A Pisces Five housewife must explore ways to be constructive and creative outside her home, for her inventive genius will be insufficiently challenged if kept confined within her kitchen and garden.

As we all do, you, too, have negative traits. They are the result of your failure to develop your strong points. If you neglect your intellectual gifts, if you let your spark of ingenuity flicker out, then you should be prepared for:

- indecision

- boredom
- self-indulgence
- restlessness

These negative characteristics can be brought to the surface through some disappointment or setback in an effort which means a lot to you. This can occur at any stage in your life. Perhaps you fail to reach an important goal; perhaps someone you love rejects you; perhaps your security is abruptly threatened by events beyond your control. If, at that crucial juncture, you decide that everything is against you and that further effort is futile, then your negative side will rear its unpleasant head and dominate your life. That need never happen—not to you of the Fifth Division, nor to any of us. All we must do is take an honest look at ourselves. If we identify in our daily behavior any advance warnings of our negative traits, we can root them out as seedlings, before they become flourishing weeds that choke and smother our fruitful spirits.

If you find in your own life evidence of a disconcerting restlessness, you would do well to meditate regularly, both morning and evening if you have the time. You must turn your search for excitement inward, for therein lies its true source. Only there will you find what you are seeking. What you are looking for is yourself. Discovering how you fit into the cosmic pattern, through which this world develops in its Creator's plan, will be more enriching to you than all the treasure you may accumulate through the exercise of your formidable talents in business and social relations.

If, on the other hand, you don't discern any of those negative signs in your customary conduct, then you are well on your way to becoming one of the greatest Pisceans; for the Fifth Division of your sign produces human powerhouses in a world short of energy! When you have mastered all your negative inclinations, you will find that your astute judgment is sharper than ever. It is as if your burning insight is focused into a laserlike beam that penetrates into the heart of things and reveals their inner truth. That is why you may be sought after by organizations, both charitable and business, for your financial advice. Indeed, it is fair to say that our governmental accounts would be in much better shape if they were handled exclusively by Pisceans of the Fifth Division!

Judas may have been a Pisces Five. Throughout his life, he seemed to make all the right choices, giving up his comfortable life as a merchant to become an itinerant preacher in Christ's austere band. Loved and trusted by his fellows, he displayed the positive traits of his division at their best. But he must have neglected to guard against their negative counterparts; when a crisis came, he upset all his years of success with one profoundly misguided error. That is why I urge you not to take your worldly triumphs for granted. Even at the peak of your career watch out for those little warnings of habits that could ruin everything you are building up with such skill.

COLORS: To emphasize your positive side, use light colors in your clothing and home furnishings. Pastels will lift your spirits and remind you of the airy potential of your mind. If I had to choose a single color for you, I would pick pale rose, like streaks of a melting sunset on an evening sea. There is nothing drab about your Piscean powers: you aren't just another silver-gray ocean fish. Your Zodiac creatures are elegantly marked denizens of tropical waters; so splashes of pink and rose will convey your rich personality while brightening your attitude toward life's little annoyances.

MONEY: You are usually a genius at handling money for others; but when you are dealing with your own resources, they slip through your hands. When your positive traits are dominant, you are overly generous and can be exploited by greedy sharpsters. In your negative phases, you are downright wasteful, which is a remarkable reversal of the ordinary Piscean pattern. By exercising your inherent self-control, you can remain solvent, brilliantly handle the finances of clients and corporations, while arranging for a colleague to do the same for your own budget. That way, you will have the best of everything.

HEALTH: Your major weakness is nervousness. Knowing you can do better and be more than you are, you ceaselessly strive for perfection, which isn't to be found in this world. Nonetheless, you can get upset, even sick, over your shortcomings. Remember how Judas was driven to extreme and desperate actions by his fixation on making the world perfect under Christ's rule. Learn a lesson from his failure: take things slowly, do all you can, and leave the perfecting of mankind to its Creator. Then feel those headaches and backaches disappear.

RELATIONSHIPS: Talented as you are, you mustn't expect everyone to equal you. Try not to criticize others for not meeting your standards. What you intend as helpful advice may appear to them as nagging. Even though you find apologies painful, learn to give them when due. Use that adaptability of yours to fit into social situations where you ordinarily would not venture. Having so much to give the world, you shouldn't restrict the number of beneficiaries of your gifted personality.

Romance is a bright area of your star chart. Expect several happy and enriching relationships with members of the opposite sex who want to spoil you with pampering and attention. Use those fortunate encounters to bring as much joy to your beloved as you receive from being treasured by those who appreciate your Piscean worth.

PISCES–SIXTH DIVISION *(February 24, March 6, 15)*

In a rare combination of astral characteristics, you of the Sixth Division were born to be both artistic and businesslike. Some people would think those two traits contradictory, but that isn't the case. It is possible to cherish beauty and be a keen entrepreneur at the same time. Indeed, many of the greatest collectors of art this world has known were also involved, on a daily basis, in keeping business records and making practical investments.

Your drawback is that you may not recognize your artistic talents until late in life. Your career will keep you so occupied that, unless you set aside a few inviolate hours each week, the press of business will keep you from your creative endeavors. That would be a waste, not only to your personal fulfillment, but also to the world, which needs the beauty you can give it. Of course, it would be equally unfortunate if you were to pursue your artistic bent to the exclusion of your managerial and organizational talents. Man thrives on beauty as a dessert, not as a main course. The blunt fact is that our museums and galleries, our concert halls and great libraries, don't run on love of wisdom and zest for intellectual delights. Behind the paintings and operas and symphonies there are generous people, often nameless to the public, who sustain those treasures from their hard-earned wealth. Ironically, some people who fancy themselves lovers of culture might consider those benefactors of the arts to be grubby money-makers. So be it! And we all should bless them for it!

In your personality are combined delicately balanced influences that make you:

- artistic
- emotional
- gregarious
- openhanded

And with all that exuberance, you may be leading the most conservative workaday life, for true artistic sensitivity thrives best where there are order and discipline. No matter what your age or your status in life, when you finally realize your creative abilities, you can find time to fulfill them. If you are a busy executive, inform your staff—promptly—that hereafter you will not be available to callers on weekends. If you are an even busier housewife and mother, surprise your children with the news that you are going to join them in their play. While they do their drawing and coloring and finger painting, set up your own easel or practice your favorite musical instrument or write those little pieces of verse that come to you when you are doing the laundry. Have a daily family play session with your young ones. Let them know that you enjoy the time as much as they do. Not only will you be enriching yourself with those moments of artistic ease, you will also be giving your children the priceless gift of your sensitivity.

Not all of us have the financial wherewithal to collect works of art, but that shouldn't stop you from pursuing your avocation. Your local library has a store of great books that can bring to you and your family the greatest treasures of man's creativity. Your love of beauty may even take the form of a passion for gardening, and that is another activity in which your children and spouse can join you. In doing so, they will all learn what you already know: that the beautification of the world makes more beautiful those who are engaged in it.

Your emotions are easily triggered, especially the more benevolent ones. Softhearted to a fault, you too quickly become involved in another's misfortunes. Your generosity toward charities and emergency relief funds allows your idealism to shine through your life in ways you may later find embarrassing. It isn't possible to hide the heart you wear on your sleeve; and even when your giving disrupts your life, it enriches you in the long run.

Because you fall in love easily, you may marry more than once.

Let your innate idealism guide you away from frivolous affairs, lest your emotions undermine your better judgment.

Loving company, you naturally like to entertain. Consequently, it is worth your while to investigate careers in hotel management, the restaurant business, or the catering profession. Because you are drawn to the glamorous life as a fish is drawn to a bright light at night, you may try to emulate the celebrities whose elegance and style delight you. Be careful that your efforts to match their life-style don't bring you financial distress. Every piper must eventually be paid. And many a fish has found that bright lights are used by fishermen to lure the unsuspecting into nets. So treat yourself to a little luxury from time to time, but keep it within your budget.

Not only do you enjoy comfort in your surroundings, but you also are free with money to help others secure luxuries. That is foolish. Your astral signs indicate that you were meant to bring beauty into the lives of others, but that doesn't mean you should pay for frills and playthings. Beauty isn't tied to cold cash. If you want to enrich a loved one, go on a joint trip to the museum. When your children clamor for their own color TV, give them instead worthwhile magazine subscriptions. And if your mate thinks that expensive possessions indicate high status, teach him or her by your own example that there is nothing as rich as the contemplation of wisdom in the form of great art.

COLORS: Express your artistry in the striking use of color, especially all shades of blue; for that friendly and innocent color sums up perfectly your outlook on life. Avoid bright and startling hues, which would only upset your tender emotions. Indeed, on occasions when you face appeals to your generosity, it is vital that you restrain your impulses by calm and dignified clothing. If you should wear a scarlet dress or a crimson sportcoat to a charity auction, you might come home with the entire bill of goods! Especially in romantic situations, you will benefit from cool and serene blues in your dress and surroundings, and their soothing influence may help to save you from later heartbreak.

MONEY: I see money coming to you from unexpected sources. Even apart from those windfalls, you can expect to do modestly well, as long as you remember that your generosity exceeds your prudence. In short, you would not serve in Judas's role as financial manager for a group; your good intentions would dispense more cash than was coming in to you. Even if you are still in school, it isn't too early to consider means by which your retirement can be economically secure. Some thought now will save much worry later.

HEALTH: During your youth, your constitution is splendidly robust and you enjoy boisterously good health. Later on, your active career and busy home life will strain even your hardiness. If you engage in a pattern of excessive excitement and stress, expect trouble ahead. Begin today to protect yourself through dietary restraint and proper rest.

RELATIONSHIPS: Once you learn to deal with those hangers-on who regard you as a meal ticket, you will find many faithful friends who appreciate you for your talents rather than your pocketbook. Indeed, when acquaintances get a glimpse of your artistic spirit, you will be much in demand as a guest, a colleague at social functions, and a teacher in various civic betterment efforts.

Your emotional sensitivity can lead you to fall in love so often that you can hardly resist one romantic fling after another. Recognize that habit for what it is: a substitute for enduring affection. The true thing will be yours for the taking as long as you are ready to give it first. Marriage holds some difficulties for you, probably involving your in-laws, although even serious marital problems can be overcome if you put into your home life the same zest you apply to your social activities.

PISCES—SEVENTH DIVISION *(February 25, March 7, 16)*

A Pisces Seven has the same duality of nature that characterizes all children of the two Fish, but in you Sevens there is an off-planetary influence that enables you to exhibit both sides of your personality at the same time. It is as though you could run hot and cold simultaneously. For example, you have:

- high ideals and ambitions
- a tendency to involve yourself in shady dealings
- leadership ability, often obscured by your shunning the spotlight
- a personal privacy

Your values are important to you, more so than profit and fame. Your ambition isn't merely for personal gain but for the vindication of your beliefs. Your advancement in the community and your career seems to be a triumph for your ideals and your way of life. And so your relationships can become a grand morality play, as you interpret events according to the success or failure of your grand design. Your motivating hope is that once you become sufficiently powerful, you can improve life for others.

That is a noble and admirable goal, and I hope you reach it. But in the process, there is a danger you may not recognize. Without renouncing your high-minded ideals, you may at times be ready to take part in adventures and schemes that most people would consider unethical, even immoral. You may be so disconcerted with the evil and suffering you see in the world that you are willing to use any means to alleviate them. When you are thinking along those lines, remember the thoughts that occurred to Judas when he let his best intentions run away with his more prudent judgment.

There is a hard lesson you must learn. Very few people in this world intentionally create horrendous evil. Most of mankind wishes good most of the time. When great tragedy is unleashed, it is usually the result not of deliberate wickedness but of good intentions gone astray. An example is the First World War. None of its participants expected their actions to result in such a catastrophe, but all of them must be held responsible for helping to provoke it. What does that have to do with you? Ask yourself what would happen if everyone dared to enforce his or her lofty ideals through any means whatsoever. We would live in anarchy. That is why you must learn tolerance and restraint. Keep your principles high, but make your defense of them every bit as exalted as your beliefs. Don't demean a heroic purpose with unworthy tactics.

Your dualism is nicely displayed in your leadership, for it functions like one of those marvelous geysers in Yellowstone Park. When you turn it on, it is forceful and awesome; but when you shut it off, it is hard to believe it was ever there. The root of the problem is that you exert command only around your subordinates, not in the presence of higher authorities. You can run a home to perfection, make an assembly line function at top speed, inspire students to learn in your classes. But when your superiors are around to inspect your work and assign credit, you hide your sterling qualities from them. Shying away from your just rewards, you can be passed over for promotions and raises.

You are being unfair to yourself. It is time to realize that by accepting credit for your work, you advance the ideals you are desperate to serve. If you learn to assume leadership publicly and to expand the horizons of your influence, you will find it unnecessary to engage in shady conduct in a good cause. You will have legal, ethical opportunities to improve the world. So assert yourself; and when command is offered you, take it!

You of the Seventh Division are not loners, but you often act as if you were. Though you enjoy social gatherings, you despise small talk and prefer to eat alone rather than engage in meaningless chitchat. Rather than listen to trivia, you keep to yourself. When it is time for serious communication, you are forceful, even eloquent. Is it any wonder that you are a mystery to those around you? They may even assume, entirely incorrectly, that you disdain or resent them.

Don't run that risk. Make an effort to express your interest in people, even if you don't join them in their frivolity. After all, you may profit from even minimal contact more than you realize. In the casual exchange of ideas, many a great notion has been born, many a priceless gem of wisdom uncovered. It is possible to be perfectly serious about your vital principles without being perfectly solemn about your every word. There is no greater antidote to depression than a sense of humor, so open up your exalted ideas to a little cheer, indeed, even a little nonsense.

Your varied interests probably include an attraction to the supernatural. The arts are a source of peace and pleasure to you; for whether or not you know it, you have latent talents in creative expression. In fact, drama or music or writing would be fine outlets for your burning idealism. You will never know how much mightier is the pen than the sword until you pick up the former and wield it in defense of your beliefs. Remember that what Judas did not accomplish by his course of drastic action other Apostles did perform by writing and speaking with their native eloquence. It was not military might that toppled Roman paganism. It was words, vibrant words expressive of a living faith. To speak those words and teach them to others is the highest calling of a Pisces Seven.

COLORS: The correct use of color is important for you. Having so much to offer the world, you must magnify your good intentions and avoid anything that would deflect them into counterproductive channels. Your vibrations are generous and well meaning. To keep them innocent and harmless, though forceful in a good cause, your wardrobe and home décor should emphasize white and cream, like the shade of freshly churned milk. And to break the monotony of ivory and eggshell, splash yourself with emerald, as brilliant as your idealism, as mysterious as your privacy, as deep and dark as the watery green of a woodland pool.

MONEY: If money meant much to you, you could easily earn more of it. You probably have patentable ideas and could be a talented writer if you worked at it. The creative eye of a fashion designer is yours, as is the feel for environmental beauty that characterizes a gardener, a landscaper, or an architect. Whatever your profession, you must pay more attention to your bank balance, not to secure luxuries but to provide for your later years.

HEALTH: You are usually in good shape, but nervous tension can erode your natural vigor. You may find yourself nearing collapse, purely from too much exertion. The cure for your ills is travel, even when you think you don't need it. The prevention of illness is always better than its cure, so be generous to yourself with vacations and pleasure trips. You owe it to your family to stay well.

RELATIONSHIPS: In general, you will have a reputation as the "cold fish" of the sign of Pisces. That is an undeserved rebuke. You can be warm and loving when you are willing to expose your emotions and take a chance with someone special. Let your softer side be more visible. You will be surprised and delighted to discover how many people will respond to your idealistic approach to life.

Your marriage partner should be found through common interests rather than in social meandering. Your joint efforts, whether in politics or religion or intellectual pursuits, will lead to a mutual realization of how good you are for each other. That is always the best ground for a successful marriage.

Because the members of your family have the best opportunities to know you well, they will respond to your hidden virtues and remain faithful to your example. When you see in your children the same lively commitment to principle which energizes your life, you will understand at last the true meaning of success.

PISCES–EIGHTH DIVISION *(February 26, March 8, 17)*

Problems tend to weigh down the broad shoulders of a Pisces Eight; but you can, and will, carry them off to your appointed goals.

It is an appropriate blessing that you have a noble spirit because many times during your eventful life you will feel that you are bearing all the burdens of the world. And you will be right! You are:

- dutiful and loyal
- unable to quit
- susceptible to slander

Your sense of duty is profound, and it will carry you through numerous occasions when a less devoted individual would give up and go home. When the stars passed out our shares of faithfulness, you received a double helping. Although this applies especially to your family, it extends to institutions you are associated with as well. Your high school and college, your employer, your community have all benefited from your dutiful allegiance. In giving of your time and money, you have enriched them beyond your comprehension. For even when you are unable to make generous bequests, the very example of your loyalty inspires others to do as much as you have.

It is to people that you are especially devoted, and I suspect that your life will be changed by your assumption of responsibility for a close relative who needs either your care or your financial support. This may happen as early as your teen-age years, and I would be dishonest with you if I didn't say that it will bring you problems. It is likely that your commitments to dependent loved ones will burden you, even when you deny that you are being held back from your objectives. Expect repeated trials of your perseverance, for sometimes you may be tempted to throw in the towel and renounce the obligations you have assumed. I doubt that you will do so, however; your appreciation of duty overrides all other considerations.

Whatever the reasons, you will sooner or later feel that your talents are being stifled and your growth as an individual is being choked. It may be a lack of money that is preventing the realization of your potential, and this could cause you to grow sullen and bitter over your fate. Only rarely does this happen, however, for even in poverty, your loyalty thrives. Indeed, it may take a dose of real hardship to bring out the best in your faithfulness. And when that happens, you will discover reserves of fortitude which will soon drastically rearrange your life.

I see for all of you in the Eighth Division a radical change for the better in your early thirties. As long as you haven't stopped dreaming by then, your dreams will suddenly be within reach. If your grandest hopes haven't been smothered by adversity, you will find them coming true before your startled eyes. Even though you may have missed out on several glittering job opportunities and may have had to forgo many of life's pleasures, the good that is bound to come your way will make you forget all your previous disappointments.

That is the pattern of your stars: the greater the trial, the greater the reward for coming through it. The longer your fulfillment is postponed, the more complete will be the eventual triumph of your talents. It is true that duty is its own reward; but in your case, it will bring benefits you never expected during those years when you gave up much for the sake of others.

The fish most appropriate to represent the Eighth Division of Pisces is the indefatigable salmon, fighting its way upstream past every obstacle man and Nature can present to its progress. It is an understatement to say that you are no quitter. Tenacious as a bulldog, determined as a migratory swan to reach your goals, protective of those you love as a mother bear is with her cubs, you don't know the meaning of surrender. That is a great asset, and I admire you for it. But be sure you don't forget the meaning of compromise. In fact, when your golden chance appears sometime after your thirtieth birthday, it may well involve a series of compromises, none of which will impair your loyalties.

It is a peculiar characteristic of your division that your noble qualities sometimes provoke entirely unjustified rumors about you. If you give up a splendid career opportunity to help those who need your presence at home, some people will say you are afraid of competing in the rough-and-tumble world. If you stay with one employer out of loyalty, some shortsighted critics will consider you foolish for not selling your work to the highest bidder, without regard for personal ties. If you react vehemently to what is said against you, then, and only then, will you be damaged by it. It is best to ignore foolish slanders and refuse them the dignity of a reply.

In a way, this characteristic was shared by Judas. For centuries, his motives in leading the Jewish leaders to Christ have been the subject of misunderstanding and distortion. Many people think that that shrewd businessman would have betrayed his Master for a mere thirty pieces of silver. Why, that was the sum due to a man if one of his slaves died while working for him! If Judas had wanted to turn in his Lord for cash, he could have obtained a huge sum. If you are still doubtful about this matter, I urge you to reread the introduction to this chapter. There you will see how Judas, and many another Piscean, has suffered from the misrepresentation of his motives and character.

Because you can expect more than your share of downs on the roller coaster of life, I want to reassure you that the ride is worthwhile. A Pisces Eight inspires others to live by duty rather than expediency. You can have an impact on people whom you do not even know but who have occasion to witness your determination and faithfulness to ideals and people. In those moments when you consider yourself powerless, you are exerting tremendous influence through the force of your example. Think about these things when the going gets rough, and you will see the future straighten out smoothly before you.

COLORS: Because you face a hard time now and then, it is especially important that you know how to use color to lift and sustain your spirits. Avoid dark shades as a general rule, because they do nothing to enliven your environment. In fact, the best expression of your faithfulness and commitment to the service of others is a pure white. That is the emblem of devotion, of selflessness, of dedication. Male or female, you should make ample use of it in your attire; for it is the most dignified and emphatic summation of all your noble qualities. It must be accented, of course; and I suggest you let your emotions, quiet and restrained as they are, speak to the world through muted hues of mauve and lilac and lavender. Those are as delicate as your spirit, as appealing as your kindness. And yet, there is something ageless about them, something of endurance and final triumph. How apt they are for you!

MONEY: Money is not your goal. You have already learned to live without it. It will come to you in your middle years, as you have the chance to realize your lifelong ambitions. But you are likely to have sizable expenses then too, and so the overall effect will be only a little improvement. Look ahead to that eventuality by taking financial precautions now.

HEALTH: Your attitudes determine your health. When your burdens depress you, your overall fitness declines. By staying busy and cheerful, you won't have time for ailments, and will be blessed with the hardy constitution you need to carry your burdens. I do see an injury coming your way before your fortieth birthday if you aren't careful in your travels. Caution and common sense can prevent it.

RELATIONSHIPS: You will always be a family standby, forever on call to those who need you. When there is trouble, you will be expected to share in it. That is the role assigned you by the stars, but it isn't a negative one. Your reward is the love and trust of your family, the respect of close friends, and the personal contentment that comes from knowing you have done your best.

In romance, you must avoid casual affairs; they will bring you only grief. Marriage is a good thing for you. Your prospects for a happy home life are excellent, whether you wed early or late in life. The only exception to this rule occurs if you select a mate while in a fit of depression, for then your best instincts are ignored. So choose slowly and in good spirits if you want a spouse who will return your devotion and treasure your love.

PISCES—NINTH DIVISION *(February 27, March 9, 18)*

You are the unique midnight of the stars, Pisceans of the Ninth Division. You stand at the ultimate segment of the Zodiac before it begins its cycle of destiny anew. In you the duality of your sign is shown clearly. You are both end and beginning, both night's darkness and dawn's light. Just as your Apostle was the essence of midnight in his misguided actions concerning Christ, so, too, his actions brought on the dawn of the Christian era. Without his deeds, there could have been no expurgation of mankind's sins through the death of the Redeemer. You, too, promise a new dawn, but it is up to you to transform the promise into reality. Formidable as that task is, your astral characteristics are more than a match for it. You are:

- cheerful and optimistic
- competitive
- forward-looking
- magnetic

To you, the world is a fundamentally good place, whose defects can be remedied with enough effort. To you, a half-empty glass is really half full. To you, all bad things can be reformed and all good things made better. I wish there were more of you! Complaints are not your business, but compliments are. I do believe that in the midst of a tornado, you would observe that the crops could use the needed rain! Seriously, your cheerfulness is not a matter of giddy wishfulness. Your habit of looking on the brighter side of events bespeaks an internal attitude of hope and trust in God. That is at the root of your seemingly unrealistic optimism; for you know that in the long run, the Creator's world does make its way through tragedies and cataclysms. Even if the present looks glum, your faith in the future is based on your understanding of the past.

Jovial as your spirits are, you nonetheless live in a fiercely competitive world and relish the contest each day offers you. The roadblocks in your way are like so many intriguing puzzles to test your ingenuity. In fact, a project in school or in your profession which offers no challenge will bore you and fail to bring out your best work. That is why it is vital for you to settle into a career that promises constant testing, especially in head-to-head competition with rivals. Even in your relaxation, you prefer those sports and games which have a winner and a loser, and usually you are on the triumphant side.

Because you enter into competitive relationships with good spirits and a friendly combativeness, your victories will not alienate your opponents. There is one notable exception to this rule, however, and you should learn it right now. Never fight back at the personal level. When your professional competitors provoke you into litigation, you are bound to come out second-best. Even in winning court suits, you will lose in terms of your health and peace of mind. Let your rivals stew in their own broth of trickery or deceit. Never get in with them!

There will be occasional conflicts in your life, no matter how much you try to avoid them. In those situations, a simple maxim should govern your behavior. Look ahead. That sounds easy, but try it sometime when you are tempted to nurse a grudge or even an old score. It isn't as easy as it seems. The results, however, are well worth the effort. Things will fall into place for you once you set your sights ahead and ignore past unpleasantness.

The personal magnetism of a Pisces Nine makes friends readily, especially among those in high places. It is your confidence which impels you upward, and those who have already reached the top recognize in you a natural peer, their potential equal. Don't be surprised when they welcome you as one of them; you still have stardust on your shoulders from being showered with astral talents.

As we have seen repeatedly throughout this book, every asset brings with it a parallel liability. In this case, your confidence and magnetism can be excessive. Those whom you most wish to impress favorably are the kind of people who are least tolerant of boorishness or boastfulness. Keep a close eye on your colleagues and your superiors, so that your driving personality doesn't run over them. Remember that as you progress upward toward your goals, your continued success will require less brute effort and more tactfulness, subtlety, and charm. Adjust your speech, dress, and attitudes accordingly.

COLORS: Just as there is nothing shy about your personality traits, so, too, there should be nothing meek about your dress and home furnishings, although the colors I recommend should accentuate rather than envelop your foremost characteristics. The entire spectrum of reds works wonders for you because your impact upon people is as vivid as a sunburst. Your cheer is like a rose in winter; and so on gloomy days amidst bad news, brighten your own spirits and those of your colleagues with a touch of crimson or scarlet.

Notice I recommend a touch, not a dousing, of red. This is especially important as your abilities push you higher into positions of authority. You must learn by experience that a fiery red tie is more impressive than a suit of the same shade, that a brilliant piece of coral jewelry expresses your interior fire better than a coat of that color. If all the fish in the sea of Pisces were magnificently colored in cerise and vermilion, none of them would stand out. So, too, if all your appearances are flashes of red, none of them will be memorable.

MONEY: Achievement is the reward you want, and money is only a side benefit. No matter, for your work will probably bring you financial security by middle age, whether you plan things that way or not. Do avoid wasteful extravagance in your youth, looking ahead in money matters as well as in personal relationships.

HEALTH: You should reach your forties without facing serious illness other than minor injuries from accidents, but the hectic pace of your life will then begin to catch up with you. Diseases of the internal organs are a possible threat unless you learn restraint in diet and regularity in exercise. By turning your entire life over to the competitive struggle for success, you will shorten your days. My advice is to settle for a little less achievement and much more time to enjoy the wonders of God's earth.

RELATIONSHIPS: Needless to say, your magnetism has made you the center of attention of a wide circle of disparate friends all your life. The only hostility you face is that which comes your way from business rivals who can't accept your honest triumphs. As I have already said, don't let those tiffs degenerate into court litigation.

In affairs of the heart, your powerful personality will attract many persons into fleeting liaisons. Try to keep your vitality and charm under restraint, for you don't realize the impression you can make on sensitive members of the opposite sex. What you intend as a casual expression of affection may be interpreted by them as a commitment of spirit. Adjust your behavior accordingly. When you do marry, your relationship will be mutually satisfying, even if your first union ends in divorce. In that case, you and your spouse will probably part amicably and remain friends, though no longer lovers.

All in all, the future is pleasant and bright for a Pisces Nine. And that is a good note on which to end our day-by-day analysis of the Zodiac cycle. There is so much more to say. There are lessons to be learned, principles to be affirmed, warnings to be repeated and made stronger. And so, whether you are a Pisces or any of the other astrological characters, I close this chapter with urgent advice: read on! For the wisdom in the stars, read on! For the best that you can be, the greatest you can hope, the deepest you can love, read on!

A WORD TO THE WORLD

Readers of my previous books know that I never leave them without offering forecasts of the future. And so, even though this book is not intended to be a collection of predictions, before we close our discussion I do want to cast an inquiring glance toward the future to see what may be in store for all of us, no matter what our star signs. I want to look not at our separate, individual futures but at the world's. What awaits this globe and its inhabitants, spinning through space, hurtling into the dawning Age of Aquarius?

In my travels around America and overseas, so many people, worried yet hopeful, ask me, "When will the world get back to normal? When will things get back on the right track?" What they want to know, of course, is when the world will enjoy peace, prosperity, order, respect for individual rights, and a universal acknowledgment of the moral law of the cosmos. In other words, when will we be able to live quiet, safe lives without the commonplace wars and man's brutality to man that are unleashed on every continent?

Unfortunately, peace, quiet, prosperity and respect have not been normal for mankind. When we look back over history, beyond the overly optimistic confines of the twentieth century, we discover that the record of humanity's presence on earth has been one long cry of grief. Normalcy has meant anguish, oppression, and terror. It has not involved orderly government through a dignified political process but, rather, violence, riot, and tyranny. Especially in this Bicentennial season, Americans should gratefully realize that for most of the human race, normalcy has not been the learned Jefferson, the prudent Washington, the canny Franklin, the humane George Mason, father of the Bill of Rights. No, it has been Genghis Khan and Attila, Hitler and Stalin, Mao and Napoleon. Normalcy has been rule by the ruthless, suffering by the innocent, and, for a few, the ever faithful confidence in God's eternal governance of all things.

Do those last words surprise you? Do they seem out of place among the somber things I was discussing? On the contrary, our faith should burn brightest when we are most distressed, just as a glowing ember flares up when stirred or blown upon. That is why, as the world continues in its old ways, disappointing the hopes of dreamers and the plans of society's greatest thinkers, we should feel our faith resurgent within us, preparing us for whatever may occur.

And so, glowing with that special light of faith, let us look now at what will happen in the near and distant future. Being forewarned of it, we will find within our spiritual and intellectual resources not just solutions to our problems but, even more important, the meaning of this remarkable experience called life.

Do you remember how, only a few years ago, learned scholars spoke of the world of tomorrow: gleaming cities run by nuclear energy, jet-powered cars, machines to do man's every bidding? How a few years have changed our perspective! We have discovered that there are limits to man's ability to change the earth, to exploit its resources, and to adapt to an electronic civilization. In short, we have learned that like animals and plants, we, too, are living creatures who must harmonize with the natural environment.

Perhaps the greatest folly of the last three decades was the assumption that because we could work wonders with our machines, we could also work wonders with ourselves. Because we could put rockets on the moon with pinpoint precision, we could also program the thoughts and wills and emotions of human beings with the same accuracy. We spoke of social problems—racial conflict, international discord, family troubles—as if the people involved were only so many malfunctioning parts in a complex mechanism. We learned, to our dismay, that it is easier to touch down on the planets than to touch the hearts of our fellow humans.

Now the era of the machine is drawing to an end. Oh, we will still use our electrical contraptions and invent new and more complicated ones, like hovercraft that will sail through our streets on a clean cushion of air. We will still computerize everything worth counting (and much that is not), and many homes will have direct telephone connection to their city's computer data bank. But we will no longer treat people like machines. Most important, we will consider ourselves in a radically new way, not as interchangeable elements in the large factory we call society, but as absolutely unique snowflakes which, even as they fall to earth and perish, contribute, each of them, a special beauty and life-giving water to the thirsty earth. What an appropriate thought for the Age of Aquarius, the kindly water-bearer!

It is this realistic yet irrepressibly optimistic interpretation of life that I want to share with my readers. And so, keeping in mind that cautiously hopeful view of the human condition, let us see what the future, near and far, holds for us.

Anyone who is familiar with my work already knows that because I believe it is my solemn responsibility to relay faithfully my own glimpses of what is to be, I do not equivocate about them. In other words, I do not pull my punches. When persons are in danger, it is no favor to them to minimize it. When good fortune awaits them, it is only honest to say so frankly and so to share their joy in advance. That is why I prefer to discuss the future clearly and directly, in simple language, making it neither prettier nor more perilous than it actually will be.

If some of my forecasts are unpleasant, I beg my readers to remember that the highest compliment I can pay them is to tell them only the truth, sure that each of them has been given the spiritual fortitude to master whatever challenges come his or her way.

That brings to mind one of my recently fulfilled predictions. Late in 1974, I included in my year's end forecast the warning that when Aleksandr Solzhenitsyn, a great writer and a greater champion of liberty, visited America he would tell us things which many would not want to hear. His popularity would be diminished in some quarters because he would speak harsh truths, which some Americans would not want to face.

He did just that. He startled people, in and out of our government, with his blunt insistence that America's détente with the Soviet Union is a charade, that it profits only Communist tyranny and works against the survival of the free world. He was right, of course; and those of us who had all along shared his feelings cheered his open declaration of them in Washington, D.C. We knew he did not intend to offend Americans but to awaken them, to alert them and arouse them for their own good.

So, too, is it my intention not to offend a single soul but to sensitize my readers to the possibilities of the future, so that they may take advantage of all its good things and be prepared for its more ominous aspects. With that understood, let us turn to tomorrow's roster of world events.

A decade ago, I startled many people by predicting that the United States would soon have a President and Vice-President who were not elected by the people. Some political experts may not have agreed with me at that time. But now, with President Ford and Vice-President Rockefeller in office, for both of whom I have the greatest respect and admiration, my forecast has become a reality. I sense that it will occur again! The American voters will find, sooner than they imagine, that their Chief Executive has been chosen not by them but for them by other people.

The international order of the future will be far different, not only from its present shape but also from what today's statesmen think it will become. Their expectations will prove sadly erroneous. A world government, maintaining peace among all peoples, will not be established. Indeed, there will be even less cooperation among nations than exists at present. Many international organizations, which have brought together even hostile countries to combat epidemics, exchange scientific information, and distribute food to the hungry, will be disrupted by growing antagonism among their member states. The United States will learn to be more selective about joining those groups. This country will cooperate with a few of them and ignore the rest, for their leadership will be controlled by forces inimical to our way of life.

Here at home, before this century is over, there will be an attempt by the Government of the United States to seize all large businesses in the country. Either the Congress or the President will declare that all companies employing more than a few workers are the property of the nation. Our country will teeter on the brink of dictatorship. But at this time, I do not sense that this drastic change will be actually put into effect. Whether it will be halted by the Higher Power which guides the destinies of men, women, and nations I do not yet know. But the outcome of that crisis will determine the shape of the American economy and the quality of American life in the twenty-first century.

The future world will be an unequal one. Despite current trends, it is shortsighted to think that all nations will become more alike. They will grow farther apart economically, for instance. Most of them will never become as industrialized as the United States, Western Europe, the Soviet Union, or Japan. Most of mankind will continue to live in agricultural societies. They will work the land, harvest their crops, and hope for the best from the weather. Of course, they will have better medical facilities and more schools. Television and movies will be everywhere, for they are like the dust in a sandstorm that enters even the most tightly sealed container. But there will not be skyscrapers in every corner of the world, or superhighways, or jetports. Those will be luxuries for a few rich nations, while most of the world continues on in its traditional pattern of living.

In underdeveloped countries, the Atomic Age will hardly intrude upon the daily life of average folk. In fact, I see an old means of transport serving as the lifeline for most of the world. Those poor countries that are investing in railroad systems will find that they have purchased not just a means of locomotion but also a stable system of communication, of social cohesion, and internal development. For most of the earth, the iron horse will be the main line to a better world, far into the twenty-first century.

Transportation and communication on the sea and in the air will present a less admirable situation, for international rivalries will keep the oceans boiling and the sky throbbing with the threat of conflict. I sense that decisions already made within the Kremlin will lead to Soviet domination of the world's sea lanes; and by the time the United States realizes its naval weakness, it will be too late to reverse the power balance from the Caribbean to the Mediterranean, from the Persian Gulf to the Bering Sea.

That will be all the greater a misfortune, because even in the Space Age, the role of sea power will become more and more important to America. For more than two hundred years, when the American people looked abroad, they instinctively turned toward Europe and the Middle East. From there came most of our ancestors. Our religious beliefs are rooted there, and those lands have been the basis of our political alliances of this century. In the future, although our ties with them will remain, far stronger ones will be developed with the Pacific world. From Korea and Japan in the north, through the southern archipelagoes to New Zealand and Australia, America will establish close new bonds, both commercial and political. The dream of Atlantic Union, for which Franklin Roosevelt and Winston Churchill so fondly hoped, will be replaced with a Pacific Union, as Americans realize that they are as much a people of the Orient as of the Occident.

In fact, in a broader sense, the European Age is drawing to a close. For five hundred years, the current of world history has run, by and large, in a European channel. All the peoples of the earth have been dominated by the decisions, the values, the events in Europe. That relatively small portion of the globe has exerted a disproportionate influence upon the fate of people everywhere, but the day is soon coming when Europe will seem a backwater, culturally and economically stagnant. Its traditional role as the intellectual pacesetter in human affairs will be reversed, and it will grow increasingly dependent upon ideas from the rest of the world.

Europe's cultural decline will be closely linked to its political fall. The forces of disintegration may actually lead to the dissolution of more than one ancient state and the creation of smaller countries, Medieval principalities reborn in our own time. Can that process of social and political decay be halted? Yes, it can be; but the chances that it will be done are not good. That is because a nation's weakness does not stem from any temporary troubles: not from bad crops or poor sales or natural disasters, not even from wars and terrorism. A once strong nation becomes weak only when it loses its spiritual values, when its people allow prosperity and comfort to seduce them from their traditional virtues, when they substitute material possessions for heroic achievements. That is the affliction which has befallen most of Europe and which will, in time, reduce that once glorious continent to a diminutive status within the family of man. If those same symptoms seem to apply equally to America, then perhaps, as we celebrate our country's two-hundredth birthday, we should look closely at our own way of life and what it is doing to us.

Unlike Europe, South America is entering a period of tranquillity. Governments there will be more stable than they have lately been. I sense the beginning of expansive economic development in the Latin world, as its explosive political tensions are held in check by forceful and frequently dictatorial regimes. The focus of that constructive energy will be Brazil, whose national flag portrays a constellation of the starry heavens. This astral symbolism sums up that country's future: brilliant and exalted. Her creative people, combining the genius of every continent, will soon startle the world with their economic productivity and cultural expression.

And what will be the terrific force behind the Brazilian resurgence? Solar power, hydroelectric energy from great dams on her interior rivers, the development of the lush and lovely forests of Amazonia. All that and more. Most important, Brazil is still in spirit the land of the Holy Cross, or Santa Cruz, as she was first named by her earliest explorers. As long as the Brazilian people have faith that their national destiny is guided by a Heavenly Power, they will be able to chart their course to the stars.

A different kind of chart dominates the future of Asia, for the map of that continent will be redrawn before this century ends. The conglomeration of peoples, languages, religions, and cultures which the British jammed together in the nineteenth century and called India will come undone. That long-suffering land, a place of immense cultural treasure and ancient wisdom, will again be broken into many small states. This cannot occur without violence; and in the process, the great powers, including the United States, will become involved in the partitioning of the Indian subcontinent.

Farther to the east, the economic marvel that is the new Japan will begin to crumble. Within this century, Westerners have considered the land of Nippon to be many things: a formidable foe, a showplace of democracy, a storehouse of industrious talent. But in meditating upon those venerable islands, I see none of those things. Rather, I sense that Japan is a tightly coiled spring inside a very delicate clockwork. Unlike aggressive nations, which channel their tensions outward against their neighbors, Japan will turn inward under the pressure of economic disorder and will require stronger governmental authority than the Japanese people will be willing to accept.

In the Soviet Union, on the other hand, there will be no question as to what the people will accept. I do not see any relaxation of the iron rule of the Presidium. Indeed, contrary to the expectations of many overly optimistic officials in the State Department, the Soviet government will become even more repressive than it now is. Chairman Brezhnev's heirs in power (for he will not remain in office long) will confront a religious resurgence in their officially atheistic land. And their response to the revival of traditional beliefs will be the same harsh treatment that made an international celebrity of Solzhenitsyn and still assaults those who speak out against it.

A far worse assault will occur in Central Asia, probably before this decade ends. As I have sensed in the past, so now I repeat this dire forecast: border disputes between the Soviet Union and Red China will escalate into a major war, and the prize will be control of the Eurasian heartland. Although the United States will not become directly involved in the fighting, this country will be faced with crucial decisions relating to the war's effects upon Eastern Europe and the Middle East.

That brings us to an especially crucial area, the cockpit of the last quarter century. In my meditations upon the Middle East, I see opposing winds blowing at the same time, as sometimes happens in Washington, D.C., when unusual air currents around the Washington Monument cause the flags on one side to wave to the right while those on the other side fly to the left.

Both the winds of war and the winds of peace will blow through the Middle East, and the conflicts there will involve more than the tragic struggle between Arabs and Israelis. Those who are now allies in that region will turn upon one another in senseless disputes, quarreling over resources instead of developing their rich, untouched potential. In time, after needless sorrows, the peoples of the ancient lands from Morocco to the Persian Gulf will at last discover their destiny. For in my mind's eye, I have seen the desert turning lush and green, as if oases were springing up across the Sahara and into the Arabian peninsula.

That is a symbolic manifestation of the transformation of wasteland into productive farms and pastures. It promises a change from poverty to plenty, from disease to health, from ignorance to learning. And it *shall* happen.

The deserts of the Middle East will bloom like the rose, just as was promised long ago in Scripture. The entire Middle East and all of its peoples are on the unseen brink of a cultural and economic renaissance. Their future resurgence in spiritual and material accomplishment will be to the next century what the Italian Renaissance was to Europe some five hundred years ago.

Asia, too, will be the birthplace of several dramatic advances in agriculture, beginning with a great increase in the world's food supply. Ocean water will be made fresh for thirsty fields. Beneath the starving heartland of Asia there runs a mighty river, a subsurface Ganges. In my meditations, I can see its life-giving waters coursing under the parched earth, far below the feet of hungry millions. It will be brought up to the daylight and will transform the desolate plains of Central Asia into a flourishing garden.

When the seas are turned into fabulously rich fish-farms, as they soon will be, we will discover, lurking deep down in the mid-Pacific, fantastic creatures, gigantic in size and countless in number. Giant squid! These denizens out of science fiction stories will not terrorize the world. On the contrary, they will feed it! Rich in protein, squid steaks will become an inexpensive and very healthy food source.

And so shall the world move along its appointed course, outlined by the Creator long before the cosmos settled and condensed into solar systems. Will mankind endure long enough to appreciate the direction in which the Creator has sent us moving these billions of years? I am sure we will. Even the worst we can do to our poor planet cannot alter our common destination, our predestined reunion with the Creator of all worlds.

I do not think that we will do our worst. A full-scale nuclear conflict will be avoided, but that does not mean mankind will live in peace. The recent lessons of Southeast Asia should have taught us differently. The perils of atomic power are nothing when compared to a far greater danger, a far deeper threat; and that is the capacity for evil lurking within the human spirit when it has not been touched by the love of God.

Consider this startling fact: in the thirty years since 1945, not a single atomic or nuclear weapon has been employed against humanity. And yet, in that period, tens of millions have been killed by their neighbors. In religious as well as political wars, in tribal conflicts as well as superpower clashes, in primitive lands and in modern societies, the record of suffering continues as it has since time immemorial. We can destroy one another with spears and arrows and rocks as well as with multiple-warhead missiles. That is the stark, unlovely fact which our diplomats avoid. That is the embarrassing reality which few of us are willing to admit.

Thus, even without nuclear explosions, we can expect the tragedy of war to be with us still. Despite all the pledges exchanged by statesmen, it will linger on. For the evil that causes it is not found in the strategic plans of generals or the schemes of politicians. It is located within the recesses of the human heart, where each of us keeps hidden away the secret belief that we are in some way better than our fellow pilgrims in this journey through life.

And so it is not enough to tell my readers to come out of their bomb shelters, to put away their civil defense manuals and walk without fear in a world without violence. We must go to the root of the problem. We must tell the world to put away the notion that there is any peace, freedom, or safety without the acceptance of God's will in our own life. Many of my readers can remember the old League of Nations, and all of us today are familiar with its successor, the United Nations. Neither body lived up to its tremendous expectations. No man-made council will ever accomplish the pacific dream for which those international organizations were created. For the peace that man most needs, the peace for which all the earth is thirsting, is not merely the absence of war. It is more than that. It is, as the Buddhist scriptures would express it, *"shantih,"* the inner peace which surpasses our mere human understanding.

That personal tranquillity originates not in international agreements but in our personal life-style and private values. It is reflected in the way we live our daily routine, the way we treat strangers and friends, the way we devote even our humdrum work to the Creator's purposes. That is why it is now fitting for us to turn our vision from a world view to a smaller scope, to examine the little things of life in the years and decades to come.

Although the future will be an age of science, it will be a far different kind of investigation from today's test-tube studies. Its greatest breakthroughs will occur not in laboratories but in the human mind. Science itself will become spiritualized. We will put aside the silly notion that there must be a wall of separation between the investigation of material phenomena and the life of faith. At long last, researchers will comprehend the mystical significance of the lives of men and women like Albert Schweitzer and Mother Theresa, whose missions of healing were motivated by the deepest spiritual commitments. They will allow the light of the spirit to illumine dark recesses of learning. They will reach a new appreciation of faith-healing and of the mind's power to discover unknown data through meditation.

This spiritualized science will bridge the present gap between those who work for man's physical welfare and those who attend to his moral salvation. Soon, a person's health will be understood to mean the total condition of his body and soul. That knowledge, as new as the next century and as old as Hippocrates and Galen, will initiate tremendous advances in both scientific research and religious thought.

Although tomorrow's new cities will be magnificent, that has been true of all freshly built cities since humans first gathered together in villages. Remember that the great metropolitan centers of antiquity—Thebes and Karnak, Babylon and Tyre and Jerusalem—were, each in their own time, marvels of the very latest design and innovation. So, too, it will be in the future. Urban areas of the next century will be shaped like gigantic wheels, with government facilities at their center, towering residential buildings along their spokes, and industrial development along their outer rims. The areas between the spokes will be left free and green, often covered over in translucent material for all-season parks so that even among the soaring towers, children will have easy access to grassy knolls, streams, and little forests. Today's most renowned city planners seem to have forgotten what every youngster knows: that no city is complete without sparrows and squirrels!

Our urban specialists have overlooked another simple fact: that only a small percentage of earth's population will be able to live in the bright new cities of their dreams. Most people will inhabit quite different communities. Indeed, surprising as it would be to most of today's experts on metropolitan affairs, an increasingly large number of the American people will not live in cities at all. They will return to the farms. The best agricultural land will become as valuable as urban property.

The farms of the future will grow the same crops to which we are now accustomed, but many of them will mature in a matter of weeks instead of months. This will allow several harvests within a single year and thereby ensure ample food for the hungry. Not only will there be more food, but also better use will be made of it. We will come to understand that different foods are uniquely suited to different personalities. With an individually programmed diet, the human body will consume less food and yet enjoy better nutrition from it.

A very different use will be made of certain plants which are sensitive, beyond the limits of human perception, to climatic changes and imminent earth tremors. They will be grown as indicators of conditions in the air and deep in the earth, and will keep man in closer touch with the world about him.

The American people will not become jet-setting nomads, ever on the move. They will, in fact, travel less than at present. Indeed, many houses purchased this year as temporary residences will turn out to be permanent homes for their new occupants, and will be handed over to children and grandchildren, just as family homesteads were in days gone by.

Jobs, too, will be handed down from parents to children, much as in colonial America. Young people will learn their work by watching their elders. This will apply not just to the arts and crafts but also to learned professions. Many young lawyers, nurses, and teachers of the future will learn their skills as apprentices to their parents.

In the future of religion, in America and around the world, I sense a return to the private and personal aspects of belief, as opposed to their social application. I do not mean to suggest that those who love God will stop loving their fellow men. Rather, many religious leaders will realize what they are now forgetting: that no one can change the world who has not already changed his own life. And so there will be a much greater emphasis upon individual devotions, including meditations. On this point, the faiths of the East and of the West will come together to explore their common traditions of mysticism. We will discover that the human mind can approach its Creator much more closely than most mortals have ever dreamed.

Along with this emphasis upon the inner life of the soul, there will be a return to more formal and ancient liturgies. The very churches which have recently abandoned elaborate rituals and rich ornamentation in favor of casual simplicity will discover that the human spirit yearns to express the mysteries of life through grandeur and splendor and beauty. And so I would advise clergymen who have stored away their candles and incense and vestments to keep them handy. For in the near future, a younger generation will demand the return of the venerable traditions they represent.

In the communities of tomorrow, sports fans and music lovers will congregate, as they now do, in huge stadiums and auditoriums to watch their favorite performers and to cheer their hometown teams. But I sense a countercurrent running in opposition to their concentrated attention. People will again become participants, as opposed to spectators. Instead of supporting one large symphony, a city will have dozens of neighborhood groups, less professional than a great orchestral assemblage, but giving lovers of music an opportunity to take part in the creation of beauty. In the same way, few armchair athletes will be content to watch sporting events. Instead, they will insist upon playing, even if that means a town will have a thousand amateur teams rather than one pennant-winning club.

To the amazement of the entertainment industry, much the same thing will happen in show business. Vaudeville will return! It will not be quite like the wonderful old shows of the early twentieth century, but it will generate the same grand excitement, the same thrilling discovery of new talent. Instead of paying gigantic sums to superstars, the public will discover that in their own communities, there is neglected talent in folk singers, actors, poets, and comedians. Audiences will turn away from entertainers who are out of touch with their tastes. They will patronize local family entertainments, many of them outdoors in the parks and on the streets. Of course, this will undermine the present financial structure of the entertainment world. The salaries of star performers will plummet. But the overall quality and diversity of American culture will be improved by the Space Age resurgence of Vaudeville.

Television also will be localized, as the major networks encounter more and more competition from specialized broadcasters, many of whom will reach only small areas of the country but will serve them much better than do today's media giants. Television will be a means of neighborhood communication, with special channels in large cities to provide constant reports on local sales, traffic conditions, community affairs, school events, and even lost pets!

Of course, television will play an ever larger role in education, in some instances entirely replacing personal instruction. But that will be a relatively minor change compared to other alterations in schooling. Formal education as we have known it will virtually disappear in many places. Especially in the United States, many parents will teach their children at home. Needless to say, this will disrupt present educational institutions. But over the long run, this transformation of education will allow little minds to learn more and faster. Even more important, it will liberate the spirit of youth to search for a better world and to redefine the future on its own terms.

There will still be schools, and in them, students will have access to computers and other learning machines. Youngsters with learning problems will there receive special computerized assistance to bring out their hidden inborn talents. Although daily attendance will not be absolutely required, tomorrow's schools will be such lively and exciting places that students will eagerly attend.

As education moves out of the schools, as learning becomes everybody's business rather than the special preserve of professional teachers, the students of the future will become more diverse, like a field of wildflowers in which the different blossoms are of infinite variety yet retain their distinct identities. That is why, despite the pressures for conformity, society in the future will be composed of people who are even less alike than we are today. We will all be freer to march to different drummers. That, of course, is how it should be.

The children of the future, like youngsters in all eras, will be both good and bad, noble and unworthy, displaying the best and worst in human nature. Many of them will be unwanted by their families, in rich as well as poor lands. They will be turned out of their homes at early ages and will gather together in juvenile communities, living beyond the control of their parents and the law. Youth gangs will ravage society, preying especially upon the elderly and the weak.

On the other hand, the growth of psychic awareness, fostered through the churches, will enable many parents to give their children, while they are still toddlers, a now undreamed of power to appreciate life and to understand other people. The children of the future will rediscover mankind's lost sensitivity to all of nature; and as those youngsters grow into adulthood, they will carry with them the ability to reshape society through psychic force. They will be walking examples of transforming love.

Just as there will always be a youthfulness in the human race, so, too, will there always be aging, no matter how much medical science tries to avoid it. Indeed, the next century will see whole cities populated by the elderly, as senior citizens come together to find peace and dignity in one another's company. They will discover that they need not be dependent upon the young: that senior physicians, dentists, and nurses can provide health services, that senior policemen and firemen can keep their community safe, and that senior public officials often have greater wisdom than do young candidates for office.

In fact, age will be much more respected in the future than it is now. Instead of stressing "youthful images," as they have lately done, politicians, as well as business executives, will emphasize their maturity and experience. They will be proud of their white hair and long years of labor. That is as it should be. This is one lesson the West is about to learn from the Orient: that a wise society treasures its oldest ornaments.

In all walks of life, retirement will be an optional decision. Many people will continue working long past the age of sixty-five. We will at last abandon the silly notion that elderly bricklayers, surgeons, electricians, and salesmen should be sent out to pasture just when they have accumulated their greatest skills. Their talents will be needed in the future, and the whole of society will be enriched by the gifts they have to offer.

The elderly themselves will benefit most by this change. Gerontologists will find, almost accidentally, that the end of forced retirement will greatly lengthen the life span of the aged. The longer they work, the healthier they will stay; for work is merely love in action!

And what will be the dress of the future? Space helmets and flying suits? Underwater goggles and wet-suits? Animal skins and bear's teeth necklaces? All of those, just as they are now used to a limited extent. In fact, contrary to the expectations of science fiction writers, most of us will wear what we now wear, with very little change in overall styling. The apparel of men and women will not become more similar, despite passing fads in that direction. It will, however, become more practical, much like the clothing our ancestors wore. For cold weather, capes will be universal. In sophisticated cities and farming communities alike, men and women will wrap themselves in heavy cloaks against the tooth of winter. Similarly, warm weather will find us wearing light and billowing attire, even on formal occasions. Sandals and slippers will be more common than shoes.

There will be no universal language in the future, not English or Chinese or a combination of tongues. On the contrary, there will be a gradual breakdown in English and other widely spoken languages. There was a time, before the age of Shakespeare, when English was fragmented into regional dialects, with different vocabularies and pronunciations. Although we will not return to quite that much confusion, the kind of English spoken in North America will diverge from that used in Britain, in Africa, and in parts of Asia. A century hence, only a specialist in linguistics will be able to understand the many varieties of English spoken at an international gathering.

The art of the future will be far different from what many readers expect. It will not be paintings without meaning, sculpture without form, and mechanical devices. On the contrary, there will be a resurgence of careful artistic craftsmanship, and it will restore the unity between the high culture of the intelligentsia and the popular culture of mid-Americans.

That may seem impossible after the drastic changes in the world of art during the twentieth century. But artistic revolutions always reflect profound changes in the human spirit. Accordingly, the radically different shape of future art will be a key to an immense shift in attitude that awaits our civilization.

Have you ever wondered why talented men and women have devoted their genius to artistic expression of the senseless, the confused, or the ugly? The reason is that art portrays the artist's conception of reality. A painter who believes there is no order or meaning in life, no Creator in Heaven and no dignity in man, naturally paints canvases without order or meaning or dignity. He dribbles and splashes his paints, hacks at his marble, re-creating in them only the formless chaos that dominates his mind. Sad to say, that has been the self-destructive spirit of art in this century.

The tide is turning, however. I foresee a new generation of artists and performers and musicians, in whom the best traditions of our culture will be reborn. Because they will reestablish their own belief in the guidance of Heaven and the purpose of life on earth, their paintings and sculptures and symphonies will be governed by order and full of meaning.

This does not mean, however, that the high culture of the next century will return to Victorian styles, aristocratic and detailed. The art of the future will draw upon all cultures and all eras of human expression. The austere and mystical traditions of Medieval art—flat and shadowless but vibrant with a spirit of the great masters—will combine with the ascetic beauty of Oriental art, in which little is said but much is implied. The styles of ancient Egypt will be revived through grandly monumental sculpture and hauntingly mysterious murals like the tomb paintings of the pharaohs. The chastely intricate art of the Islamic world will teach the West anew the value of discipline and design. Even the glories of the Renaissance—the masterworks of Titian and Rubens, of Michelangelo and Raphael and Rembrandt—will be rivaled by as yet unborn artists who will rediscover what many contemporary artists have never learned: that all great art must stem from a belief in the greatness of man as part of God's creation.

In fact, greatness of any sort can come only from that belief. What a sobering fact! It reminds us that all the progress, all the learning and building and healing previewed in these predictions, depends less upon what we do than upon what we believe. Armed with that assurance, we can face whatever comes our way. Remember what I said at the outset of this discussion: that for most of man's history, normalcy has been a most unhappy state of affairs? But through it all, humanity has achieved heights of wisdom, of beauty, of love.

That, too, is part of normalcy, even when it is marred by disaster, natural or provoked by man. Is it important that I sense the likelihood of an international depression toward the end of this decade? Or that the splashdown of a comet striking the Atlantic Ocean a few years thereafter will create a tidal wave and flooding in low-lying areas? Or that the immense tail of an erratic comet, coming close to the earth in the 1990's, will affect the earth's axial balance and lead to dramatic changes in the earth's weather and geography? Yes, all those phenomena matter greatly, but of far greater import is our reaction to them. If we see in them reminders of our human vulnerability and of God's providence in all things, then even the tremors of the earth will work to His glory.

The damage done by a storm or earthquake can, after all, be soon repaired. It is the damage wrought by human initiative that most grievously defaces life on this planet. And what is the root of that evil? Why, with endless opportunities for joy, do so many of God's children pass through life unhappy? You who have read this book from its beginning already know the answer to those questions. Whenever we are out of touch with our true identities, when we are out of tune in the Creator's cosmic symphony, then our days fill with troubles and the world sinks under its grief. But when, on the other hand, we comprehend the role assigned to us in God's plan, when we accept our responsibilities and develop our talents, then we walk in an eternal springtime and others are blessed in meeting us.

All of the frustration and anger that afflicts mankind is caused by the refusal of proud and headstrong people to accept their appointed place in the universal pattern of life. And all the greatness to which mankind aspires is reached by our humble willingness to use our individual talents for the good of all. A splendid example of that has been a man to whom the whole world looks as a symbol of freedom, of genius, and of faith: Aleksandr Solzhenitsyn. I have already mentioned my previous prediction concerning his visit to America, and now I sense that his future will be more powerful and dramatic than even he suspects. He will become an international force for religious renewal. Single-handedly he will fire the minds of millions to return to their belief in God.

What gave him greatness? Noble birth? Wealth? Powerful friends in high places? None of those things! For years, he toiled with his hands at the lowliest work, a prisoner of men who could not hope to understand the glory of his faith or the might of his ideals. What he did, he did well, even in bondage. True to himself, he has become a voice of truth for hundreds of millions who are not permitted to speak. *Because he triumphed in the little things of his common hours, he was given a magnificent mission and triumphed in his entire life. That fact, more than any other, is the ultimate lesson of this book.*

Americans especially should take those words to heart. The national festival in which we are now engaged, the celebration of our country's two-hundredth anniversary, is a memorial to thousands of men and women who, during "the times that try men's souls," displayed the moral commitment, the spiritual daring of Aleksandr Solzhenitsyn. In so doing, they gave to the world an enduring example of what can be accomplished when common people aspire to uncommon deeds.

Let us, then, be mindful of them as each of us sets out to make our mark upon the world. Let us know that the work we do, great or minor, contributes to a better world.

That brings us back to my purpose in writing this book: to share with each of you the wonderful assurance that was given me concerning God's loving direction of our lives. I hope these chapters have brought you a new appreciation of the wonderfully complex yet startlingly simple lessons of astrology, especially the way it can aid us in comprehending ourselves and in serving our Creator.

The Gospels begin with the Star of Bethlehem, shining down on a newborn baby; and they conclude with the Apostles, filled with their revolutionary faith, looking up to Heaven after their ascended

Lord. We have begun this book with the stars. Let us now end it by following the example of those Apostles who have become our astrological representatives. Let us, too, look up to Heaven, sure that in the will of the Lord is all our happiness, all our fulfillment, and all our future blessings.

A SPECIAL NOTE TO THE CLERGY

Because I frequently receive suggestions, questions, and—yes, at times—criticism from clergymen concerning my work, it seems appropriate that I should close this book with a special consideration of them. Its subject matter is, after all, very close to their essential concern: the universal struggle between good and evil, the contest within each one of us between God's will and the power of dreadful "red boots." And so, I would like to take this opportunity to reflect with my readers upon what we have learned from this book and to discuss quite frankly with clergymen just how its lessons might pertain to their work and to their calling, the noblest calling of all on this earth.

There are bound to be varying reactions to this book from clergymen. Some may ignore it altogether, considering it beyond the scope of their customary reading. Others, especially those who read these pages in careless haste, may disapprove of them, thinking them somehow inappropriate, perhaps even erroneous. But most clergymen, I am convinced, will take the time to understand what this book tries to do. I am confident they will come to share my hope that it will catch the interest of those who have been tempted to wander from their faith in search of the modern religions of science, the occult, and blind destiny.

Those who keep their minds locked against the relevance of ancient truths to today's world, those whose vision stops at the limits of yesterday, should at least be aware of what this book does *not* do. It does not set aside Scripture or replace it with anything else. It does not pretend that Divine Revelation can be augmented with contemporary additions of secular wisdom. Nor does it approve of any substitute for faith, any excuse for evil, any belief in magic or superstition. On the contrary, these pages again and again have reminded readers of their responsibility for their own actions, their duty to explore their abilities, to develop their divinely given talents, and to turn them to the service of our Creator.

To those who object to any part of this book, I express my respect for your disagreement. I realize that astrology is a complex system of learning and that some people, hitherto uninformed of its intricacies, are taken aback when exposed to its depth and subtlety. I recognize, too, that some will protest any linking of religion and astrology, as if the two must be kept utterly separate.

I emphatically disagree. That, after all, was what some unthinking people tried to do with science and religion. They insisted that there was a wall between the two fields, and that scientific truth must be suppressed if it threatened to touch upon Scripture. In time, we came to see that a true faith affirms and accepts all truth, even that which is discovered in laboratories, and that the validity of Scripture does not depend on its detailed agreement with every fact of astronomy, geology, and physics.

Now it is time to come to the same realization with regard to astrology. We must see that it helpfully supports our faith, never taking its place but aiding us to live it more fully. Recall how in the introduction to this book, I explained that astrology can help us to know God, the Author of creation, but that only Christ can effect our union with God. That is a crucial distinction. It shows that astrology is only a means, not an end in itself. It furnishes us with tools, but the kind of life we build with them is up to each one of us.

I do not claim that astrological knowledge will of itself make people better, just as physical health and material comforts do not by themselves improve our spirituality. But all those good things, if we use them correctly, can benefit our souls as well as our bodies. They can free us from fear and worry and pain, and can thereby direct our energies toward the fulfillment of God's plan for us. So can astrology.

The Bible speaks often in parables, and so might we here. There are times in our lives when we are like a fruit tree in fall and winter. We all have our brown periods, when times are hard and we feel crushed to earth. But what follows the fruit tree's many months of wintry desolation? A splendid show of blossoms in spring, and even later, a rich harvest that is its reward for endurance! So it is with us when we remain loyal to our tasks and suffer through harsh, unlovely times. Astrology, by giving us a better understanding of our own potential, helps us to endure until we, too, reach the summer of our fruition. It enables us to bring our resources to bear on crucial problems in both our own lives and in the lives of those who need our help.

And there are plenty of problems! Let us be frank about the challenge we face. Some social scientists call our present age the post-Christian era. They mean that the time has ended when religion shaped Western civilization and spread its beneficent and humanizing influence throughout the world. They mean that belief itself is no longer valid, that everything is relative, that all that matters is selfish pleasure and personal comfort. They mean, in short, that after two thousand years, the paganism of ancient Greece and Rome is resurgent and triumphant in the modern world.

They may be partially right. For in our own country, in Europe, and elsewhere, there is profound uncertainty over the future of religion and the way it is presented by some clergymen. But it is not God's message that is at fault. It is the values and attitudes of modern man that are faulty.

Even in the most advanced countries, millions have reverted to groundless worship of the stars. Like the ancient Babylonians, searching for a religion to sustain them, they have turned to astrology without God. They wear signs of the Zodiac without knowing their full meaning. They use the terminology of astrology without understanding that its truth must interact with the much greater truth of revealed religion.

These errors cannot be ignored. They will not go away. They must be honestly addressed. We must realize that the current popularity of astrology is not a threat to religion but an opportunity, a chance to show searching minds how they can combine all the world's wisdom into one coherent, living faith in our Creator.

The old Age of Reason is drawing to a close. That Western Enlightenment, which began five hundred years ago in the Renaissance, stressed man's powers rather than God's will. It claimed that all the world could be understood by man and brought under his dominion. But now it is all ending. Our science has backfired in our faces. It has ruined the dreams it was intended to sustain. It has destroyed as much as it has built. It has broken as many hearts and bodies as it has healed.

We have learned the hard way that although man's tremendous mental powers can master the wonders of nuclear energy, they cannot work the greatest wonder: the release of spiritual energy from the human soul. All over the world, especially within Western cultures, people young and old are seeking, pondering, experimenting, looking within themselves and out across the universe, wondering if anything can get this fractured, splintered world back together again.

Yes, something can; but it is not astrology. That is only a means, one of many ways to approach the only unifying, healing, ennobling force in today's world: the divine love which can live within each of us. That is the miraculous power we need, and it is generated by the dynamo of faith. Unlike man-made miracles of our technetronic age, unlike our autos and televisions and weapons systems, the love of God has no negative consequences. It does not pollute, does not wear out, does not destroy or disappoint. It perfects the natural and nurtures it. It is, indeed, the ultimate environment for mankind.

And how is astrology related to that love? Just as any single element of wisdom is related to this all-encompassing truth of the universe: that God cares for each human being and has endowed us with powers and talents necessary for a life of peace and plenty, if only we will use them constructively. Thus, astrology fits into God's plan for mankind by helping us understand both our talents and our shortcomings. Being better informed about ourselves, appreciating our strengths and aware of our weaknesses, we will be much better equipped to turn everything we are to the service of the Lord.

Each human being is like an essential instrument in the cosmic symphony. Without each person's unique contribution, the music is incomplete, lacking, imperfect. When a clergyman looks out over his congregation, what does he see? Many instruments, including some silent, some untuned, devoid of the jubilant melodies they were meant to play. What a waste for even one to be out of harmony! Let us provide new ways to get those instruments back into tune and back into the orchestra, so that, whether we are piccolo or cymbal, tuba or harp, we all can sound our best in the chorus of daily life.

Let us show the world that the good news of Christ's coming is as applicable today as it was two thousand years ago. Our speech and dress and machines have changed, but the human heart continues as ever, full of good and evil, searching for hidden answers to unformulated questions. It is therefore prudent for clergymen to address this world in the language it understands. They should show doubters that faith alone can make sense out of both modern and ancient wisdom, both laboratory science and the study of the stars.

As the Beatles once sang, "Let it be"! Let the philosophers of old and the scientists of tomorrow all acknowledge that their words are only different paths toward the same goal. Let the wisdom of the Orient and the machines of the West join together to effect that spiritual unity of mankind which is the Creator's wish for all of us. Let the abstract treatises of theologians and the heartfelt alleluias of ten thousand little Gospel churches join in one shout of joy, recognizing that all of mankind's praises are equal expressions of our delight in God's good earth.

And finally, let the lessons of the stars shine their own enlightenment upon earth's troubled darkness. Let astrology reverently serve the purposes of the Creator of the heavens. And let those who read this book, whether clergymen or common folk like the rest of us, understand that there is no truth that does not lead to the Maker of Truth, no insight that does not reveal His presence, and no future that is not in His hand.

That, as I said at the onset of this book, is the way it must be: yesterday, today, and forever.